d States, in Order to form a more perfect Union, establish Justice,
the general Welfare, and secure the Blessings of Liberty to ourselves
ed States of America.

Congress of the United States, which shall consist of a Senate and House

chosen every second Year by the People of the several States, and the Elector shall
Branch of the State Legislature.

e Age of twenty five Years, and been seven Years a Citizen of the United States,
be chosen.

States which may be included within this Union, according to their respective
rs, including those bound to Service for a Term of Years, and excluding Indians
ade within three Years after the first Meeting of the Congress of the United States,
Law direct. The Number of Representatives shall not exceed one for every
til such enumeration shall be made, the State of New Hampshire shall be
Plantations one, Connecticut five, New York six, New Jersey four, Pennsylvania
Carolina five, and Georgia three.

cutive Authority thereof shall issue Writs of Election to fill such Vacancies.
; and shall have the sole Power of Impeachment.

from each State, chosen by the Legislature thereof, for six Years; and each

lection, they shall be divided as equally as may be into three Classes. The Seats
ear, of the second Class at the Expiration of the fourth Year, and of the third
nd Year; and if Vacancies happen by Resignation, or otherwise, during the
pointments until the next Meeting of the Legislature, which shall then fill

hirty Years, and been nine Years a Citizen of the United States, and who shall

shall have no Vote, unless they be equally divided.
, in the Absence of the Vice President, or when he shall exercise the Office of

The Illustrated History of

THE SUPREME COURT
OF
THE UNITED STATES

The Illustrated History of

THE SUPREME COURT OF THE UNITED STATES

Robert Shnayerson

Harry N. Abrams, Inc., Publishers, New York
In Association With
The Supreme Court Historical Society

Editorial Consultant to the Supreme Court Historical
Society: Burnett Anderson

Photography: Lee Troell Anderson

Editor:
Adele Westbrook

Designers:
Samuel N. Antupit and Melissa Feldman

Photo Research:
Eric Himmel, Gail A. Galloway, and
Marguerite Glass-Englehart

Library of Congress Cataloging-in-Publication Data

Shnayerson, Robert.
     The illustrated history of the Supreme Court of the
United States.

     Bibliography: p.
     Includes index.
     1. United States.   Supreme Court—History.
I. Title.
KF8742.S52   1986   347.73′26′09   86–1225
ISBN 0-8109-1644-4   347.3073509
          © 1986 by the Supreme Court Historical Society

Published in 1986 by Harry N. Abrams, Incorporated,
New York
Times Mirror Books

Printed and bound in the United States of America

JACKET FRONT COVER:
Pediment, Main Entrance (West Facade), The Supreme Court Building, Washington, D.C. Carved marble group by Robert Aitken, representing Liberty Enthroned guarded by Order and Authority. On either side are groups of three figures depicting Council and Research. On the architrave beneath is incised "Equal Justice Under Law."

JACKET BACK COVER:
The Supreme Court Building at Night (West Facade). Designed by architect Cass Gilbert. Completed in October 1935. Bronze Doors 17 x 9½′ designed by sculptor John Donnelly, Jr., in collaboration with Cass Gilbert. Each valve or half-door weighs 3,000 pounds. An electronic device rolls each valve into its adjoining wall. The low relief panels depict famous episodes in the evolution of justice.

JACKET SPINE:
The Seal of the Supreme Court of the United States. Solitary star below the American eagle distinguishes the Court's Seal. Justices ordered the emblem at their third meeting on February 3, 1790. Its designers adapted the Great Seal of the United States, adding the star to symbolize the Constitution's grant of judicial power to "one Supreme Court." The Clerk of the Court affixes the Seal to official papers—judgments, mandates, and writs.

END PAPERS:
Front. Page one of the Constitution of the United States of America, signed September 17, 1787, and ratified in 1788.
Back. The Bill of Rights began as a joint resolution proposing twelve amendments to the Constitution, which were submitted to the states for approval in 1789. Articles three through twelve were ratified in 1791 and became the first ten amendments, popularly known as the Bill of Rights.

TABLE OF CONTENTS

The main entrance to the Supreme Court Building is on the west, facing the United States Capitol.

The bronze doors depict historic scenes in the development of the law.

On the left side of the main steps is a seated marble figure, the Contemplation of Justice, by sculptor James Earle Fraser.

On the right side of the steps is another marble figure, the Guardian or Authority of Law, by the same sculptor.

The main corridor is known as the Great Hall. At each side, rows of monolithic marble columns rise to a coffered ceiling. Busts of former Chief Justices line the side walls. The frieze is decorated with medallion profiles of lawgivers and heraldic devices.

The Courtroom measures 82 feet by 91 feet, and is 44 feet in height. Its 24 columns are Old Convent Quarry Siena marble from Liguria, Italy; its walls are Ivory Vein marble from Alicante, Spain, and its floor borders are Italian and African marble.

The raised Bench, behind which the Justices sit during sessions, and other furniture in this room are made of mahogany. The Bench was altered from a straight-line to a "winged" or half-hexagon shape in 1972, providing sight and sound advantages over the original design. The Chief Justice is seated in the center with the Associate Justices to his right and left in order of seniority.

Side view of the Courtroom, showing the recording equipment used during all sessions of the Court.

Alcove behind the Bench where copies of all United States Reports are kept for use by the Justices when the Court is in session. To the right is the drapery division through which the Chief Justice and the two most senior Justices enter the Courtroom.

The Robing Room with oak doors open. The Justices' robes can be seen within.

The Robing Room with oak doors closed. There is a brass name plate on each door.

Chambers of the Chief Justice

Chambers of three Associate Justices: A

B

C

The Justices' Conference Room. Twice a week during the regular term, the Justices meet here to decide cases and also to determine which cases to review. The portrait hanging above the black marble mantel is of Chief Justice John Marshall.

11

The East Conference Room. Pilastered and paneled in oak with hand-carved capitals, this room and the West Conference Room are illuminated by two crystal chandeliers and by natural light from large bronze-framed windows opening onto inner courtyards. The portrait over the mantelpiece by Rembrandt Peale is of Chief Justice John Marshall. The other portraits shown are of Chief Justice Roger Brooke Taney, Chief Justice Salmon Portland Chase, and Chief Justice Morrison Remick Waite.

The West Conference Room. This room is architecturally identical to the East Conference Room with the exception of the pattern and color of the ceiling. The portrait above the mantel is of Chief Justice Charles Evans Hughes. The other portraits are of Chief Justice Harlan Fiske Stone, Chief Justice Fred M. Vinson, and Chief Justice Earl Warren.

Both of these Conference Rooms are for the general use of committees or individuals associated with various functions of the Court.

The East Conference Room. Preparations completed for a gala Dinner Party.

The East Conference Room. Set for a working session of the Judicial Conference of the United States.

In each of the four quarters of the building is an inner courtyard ornamented by a central fountain.

Interior of an elevator.

Bronze elevator doors.

Architectural splendor of one of the two marble staircases looking down toward the main floor.

Wide-angle view of the John Marshall Dining Room. Portraits of William Marbury and President James Madison are displayed above the sideboard. The mahogany Regency table is from England

The John Marshall Dining Room. Beneath the portraits of William Marbury and President James Madison are a Hepplewhite mahogany sideboard, c. 1810–20, two Hepplewhite mahogany knife boxes, c. 1870–80, and two Hepplewhite mahogany chairs, c. 1795.

The Justices' Dining Room. The table, sideboard, and drop leaf table are Sheraton mahogany, c. 1800–10. The chairs are Sheraton mahogany, c. 1795. The Sèvres gilt bronze mounted three-piece garniture, c. 1840, is painted in pastel colors. Above the drop leaf table is a portrait of Associate Justice Philip Barbour. In the corner of the room is a musical grandfather clock made of mahogany, c. 1806. In the anteroom can be seen a Chippendale mahogany block front secretary, c. 1760–70.

The Office of the Reporter of Decisions.

The Office of the Counsel.

The Justices' Reading Room.

The Library. Paneled, pilastered, handcarved oak is the predominant feature of the Main Reading Room. The reference collection of the Library includes 250,000 lawbooks, records, and journals.

Data Base Equipment room adjacent to the Main Reading Room of the Library.

The Gymnasium.

Rising five stories are two self-supporting, elliptical staircases made of marble and bronze—one on either side of the center of the building. Few others are known to exist. The Paris Opera, the Vatican, and the Minnesota State Capitol are among those with similar structures.

Antique cabinet in Curator's Office holds old law books once owned by Chief Justice John Marshall, and other books and memorabilia relating to the Court's history.

File Room—Office of the Clerk. The Clerk maintains copies of all pleadings in current cases as well as correspondence files for five prior terms. After five years, files are transferred to the National Archives.

Public Information Office.

The Cafeteria.

The Law Clerks' Dining Room.

The Ladies' Dining Room. Sheraton mahogany table (1790) and sofa (1800). English grandfather clock (1765). Oriental rug (Kerman-Shah).

The Police Room.

The Court's Documentary History Project. Researching private and public collections in preparation for a multi-volume publication of a "Documentary History of the Supreme Court of the United States, 1789–1800."

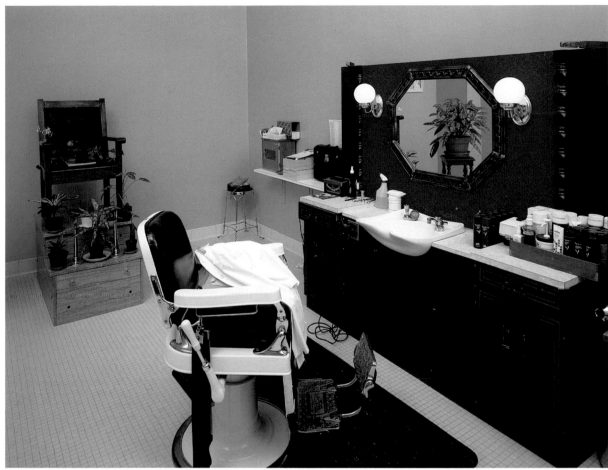

The Barber Shop.

The Seamstress's Room.

The Computer Room. The opinions of the Court, preliminary prints, slip opinions, bound volumes, and the journal of the Court are now produced by this system.

25

The John Marshall Statue and the Exhibit Area. The bronze statue of the robed Chief Justice was cast in the Nelli foundry in Rome. It is signed on the right lower side: *W.W. Story Roma 1883*. (William Wetmore Story, sculptor, was the son of Justice Joseph Story who served on the Court with Chief Justice John Marshall.)

Introduction

LIBERTY AND LEGITIMACY: THE COURT'S ROLE IN AMERICAN LIFE

At precisely ten o'clock, more than fifty solemn mornings a year, the Marshal's wooden gavel punctuates the buzzing conversation in the vast courtroom, bringing several hundred spectators and lawyers to attention. "The Honorable, the Chief Justice, and the Associate Justices of the Supreme Court of the United States," the Marshal intones; and simultaneously, with unexpected suddenness, the nine black-robed figures materialize behind the bench. They appear in trios, and as they quickly take their seats along the angled bench, the Marshal calls for silence with his familiar measured chant:

"Oyez! Oyez! Oyez!

"All persons having business before the honorable, the Supreme Court of the United States, are admonished to draw near and give their attention, for the Court is now sitting. God save the United States and this honorable Court."

Here is the apex of a coequal branch of the American government that consists of a mere nine Justices with a total staff of some 315 people working in a single building. The yearly budget of the entire judicial system is less than one percent of the entire federal budget. Yet the Supreme Court has the power to invalidate laws enacted by Congress and to rule illegal the actions of a President.

Moreover, the losers in these cases, including Presidents, accept the Court's decisions. Most Americans simply assume the moral as well as the legal authority of the Supreme Court. Indeed, public support is the taproot of Supreme Court power. The Court has virtually no other means of enforcing its orders.

As the final interpreter of the world's oldest written constitution, the Supreme Court has become a sort of political gyroscope. Writing in 1954, the late Justice Robert H. Jackson put it this way:

> In a society in which rapid changes tend to upset all equilibrium, the Court, without exceeding its own limited powers, must strive to maintain the great system of balances upon which our free government is based. Whether these balances and checks are essential to liberty elsewhere in the world is beside the point; they are indispensable to the society we know. Chief of these balances are: first, between the Executive and Congress; second, between the central government and the States; third, between state and state; fourth, between authority, be it state or national, and the liberty of the citizen, or between the rule of the majority and the rights of the individual.

The gyroscope is hardly flawless. The Court was responsible for issuing the *Dred Scott* decision of 1857, which helped to ignite the Union's most centrifugal explosion, the Civil War. Yet the fact remains that without the Constitution as secular scripture, without the Supreme Court to expound it, America would not have become the singular nation we know—fifty quasi-sovereign states united in harmony not only as a tariff-free common market, but as the world's oldest, most stable federal republic.

Liberty needs protection, and ineluctably it must come from a government strong enough to provide it. The Framers of the American Constitution sought, above all, to safeguard liberty by creating an effective national government; one whose powers are limited, yet sufficient to hold the Union together and make it work.

The American version of limited government assumes the sovereignty of the people: law is said to express their will. Thus no individual, however rich or powerful, can put himself above the law, above the people's will. In terms of practical justice, of course, the system requires a complex balancing of rival interests. On the one hand, it must guarantee that majority rule shall prevail; on the other hand, it must guarantee equal rights for all individuals, preventing the many from oppressing the few.

It is crucial to the American system that millions of people continue to perceive the government as being theirs—not as some remote force beyond their control but as the instrument of majority will, reflecting the most recent election in which they have presumably cast their ballots. It is equally crucial to the system that majority government be checked in any tendency to downgrade the rights of minority groups and powerless individuals.

The Supreme Court has unique opportunities to reaffirm the American principle that government ultimately belongs to the people, not the other way around. Given the Court's ultimate reliance upon public acceptance of its powers, it is particularly important for the people to try to understand how the institution functions. Simply put, the Supreme Court is fascinating—irresistibly so. Hence this book: an effort to explain how the world's most famous judicial body works from day to day; to trace its origins and evolution; and to explore its possible future in the centuries to come.

FIRST IMPRESSIONS

The Supreme Court of the United States, Washington, D.C. Photo: Lee Troell Anderson

Austere, gleaming white in all weather, it stands watch on Capitol Hill, a national monument to the virtues of clarity, integrity, and fairness. As Washington edifices go, the marble-columned building on First Street is relatively small, but its name alone, *Supreme Court of the United States*, evokes memories of historic decisions and judicial giants. It perches atop thirty-six steps, rising from a spacious white plaza, and its imposing design—equal parts of Roman majesty, Victorian sobriety, and American neoclassicism—gives it a severity that may intimidate as much as inspire the visitor seeing it for the first time.

Here is the nation's final arbiter between assertions of power and the limitations on power derived from a written constitution. Here the nine Justices independently assess each of the 5,000 or more detailed petitions for hearing that arrive each year—a relentless caseload which has been rising by well over fifty percent each decade.

Starting their annual "term" on the first Monday in October, the Justices spend the next nine months alternating between two-week "sittings" (open sessions) during which lawyers argue cases before them in the courtroom; and "recesses" during which the Justices toil away at the complex process of producing written Court decisions. Throughout the term, they hold regularly-scheduled conferences. In these private sessions, the Justices reject the vast majority of all those petitions imploring the Court's attention; they accept and fully review only especially significant cases, most of them requiring the Court's interpretation of either the Constitution or the meaning of specific federal statutes.

It is no easier for nine Justices to agree on precisely which cases should be reviewed, however, than it may be for them to agree on a majority decision for every case. It frequently takes them weeks, even months, to resolve their divergent views in the most difficult cases. Decisions are issued each week as they are completed, and generally half of the term's cases have been decided and published by May, when all oral arguments end until the new term begins in October. Then comes the June blizzard of opinions, lasting until late June or early July, when the annual term ends and lawyers all over the country can study the Court's answers to a variety of questions:

. . . Does Nebraska have the legal power to regulate the use of well water after it flows across the state line into Colorado?

. . . Can the federal writ of habeas corpus be used in child custody cases?

. . . Are black civil rights workers liable to white merchants for business losses attributed to a black boycott?

. . . Can Rhode Island subsidize the salaries of teachers of non-religious subjects in church schools?

. . . Can New York force a landlord to permit a cable television company to use his building as a transmission station?

. . . Can a state-supported women's nursing school bar qualified male applicants solely on the basis of their gender?

. . . Can Florida impose the death penalty on an accomplice who was not physically present during a murder?

. . . Can a President of the United States be sued for damages resulting from his admitted violation of a subordinate's constitutional rights?

In all these cases, the Court's answer was "No," the frequent response of a national referee. The Court exudes authority; it is a serious place. From the two massive bronze front doors weighing six and one-half tons apiece, to the ornate courtroom with its coffered ceiling forty-four feet high, the whole building is a cathedral of law—hushed, dignified, full of long marble halls lined with portraits of former Justices. Inside the 218-seat courtroom, bailiffs suppress the audience's least sign of partisan "favor or disfavor," and any writing, sketching, taping, photographing, or whispering.

Yet the passion for decorum seems entirely fitting here. Most visitors anticipate nothing less. Some are surprised that the Justices speak plain English, but seem to be quite ungodlike figures, as ready to console a nervous lawyer as to needle

a contentious one, and not at all above punning with intent to lighten tedium.

Watching the rapt, respectful faces of the spectators—invariably a striking gallery of America's ethnic diversity—one realizes anew how much people expect from the Supreme Court of the United States. Somehow the place casts a spell that brings forth in lawyers and visitors alike a rare sense of belonging to something substantial and appropriate. In this building, even cynics fall silent when yet another earnest tour guide points out the Justices' direct view from the bench—the sculptured frieze over the main door, high above that sea of attentive visitors' faces, where a winged figure representing Justice, flanked by Truth and Wisdom, confounds the Powers of Evil (Corruption, Slander, Deceit, Despotic Power) and vindicates the Powers of Good (Virtue, Charity. Peace, Harmony, Security).

To share that view from the bench, to be a Supreme Court Justice, is rather akin to playing an allegorical role oneself. Despite all the angry words that may be hurled at the Justices for their decisions on combustible issues, the Court has accumulated so much moral capital over the years that the great majority of Americans sees little reason to question the Court's ideal self-image. It resembles a living frieze: nine serene oracles—wise, humane, dedicated—settling historic arguments, correcting injustices, and introducing ever more reason into American life.

Most of the above is borne out by the Court's 200-year history of generally superior performance and personal conduct. Nominated by the President, Supreme Court Justices must be confirmed by the Senate, which has turned down some twenty percent of the 139 nominees since 1789. Under Article III of the Constitution, the Justices (and all other Federal judges) hold their offices for life "during good Behaviour." Under Article II they may be removed by "Impeachment for, and Conviction of, Treason, Bribery, or other high Crimes and Misdemeanors." Of the Court's 102 Justices thus far, only one has been impeached (but not convicted); one other resigned in the face of that possibility.

But the Court's rectitude tends to blur its reality. What most people think the Justices do, and what they actually do are quite different matters. The Supreme Court is a marvel of paradoxes. Its

Sculptured frieze in the Courtroom. Photos: Lee Troell Anderson

first members were relatively powerless, yet they succeeded in making the Court epitomize the rule of law. The Court has never stood for long against the country's majority opinions, yet it is capable of inspiring Americans to temper their most cherished biases. At times it is prone to expediency, yet it frequently emerges as the voice of the national conscience.

On duty, the Justices customarily display the august demeanor suitable to paragons of impartiality. But only in their formal group photographs are they unfailingly solemn. Off-duty, most of them come across as the cordial best, the unstuffy brightest. In the cafeteria, the man at the next table is as likely to be an off-bench Justice chatting with his law clerks as he is to be a tourist from Holland or a leading lawyer from Atlanta, and if you run into a distinguished white-haired man moving purposefully about the halls, he may very well be the Chief Justice.

Or consider the Court's famous tradition of secrecy: no other government agency, not even the Central Intelligence Agency, outdoes the Supreme Court in protecting the confidentiality of its decisions until they are published. In a city where the President's private remarks one evening may appear in the next morning's headlines, the Supreme Court is so leak-proof that no outsider has the slightest idea of how or when the Justices will decide any of the cases before them. This virtually eliminates the chance that speculators, for example, could profit from advance knowledge of a Court decision in a business or tax case. Paradoxically though, no government agency is more willing to explain the rationale behind its decisions. Apart from the Justices' inner-sanctum debates, which are entirely private, all Court business is completely on the record. The briefs and oral argument in all pending cases are open to public scrutiny. The rhetoric of written opinions is aimed at principled persuasion, not mere fiat. Split decisions often include vigorous dissents that show the world how the Justices disagreed and—of even greater importance—why.

The central paradox of the Supreme Court is that its power depends heavily upon the Justices who comprise a majority at any given moment, and especially upon whether their most controversial decisions will be sufficiently accepted to overcome the Court's lack of a specific enforcement arm. In a sense, the Court's institutional priority is to cope with an ambiguous mandate and with the fact that Congress has the power of the purse and other means to affect the authority and work of the Courts by legislative action. The Court has thus far survived all congressionally-imposed changes in its structure and jurisdiction, or threats of them, but not without acquiring a few psychological scars, some of them beneficial, some less so. One forgets that the nation's highest judicial authority was not born that way, nor was its future status inevitable. Its position of trust had to be earned by the Court itself through a series of brilliant decisions that made the Justices the indispensable element in the interpretation of our written constitution.

Another paradox is that everyone wants the Justices to examine the legality of government actions, using the Constitution as an instrument of deliverance, but no one wants the Court to become "political," a fate deemed repugnant to its tradition of impartiality. Indeed, the Court possesses no political authority whatever—at least not officially. Yet it cannot avoid, nor would many Justices wish to avoid, numerous public issues that in some ways are clearly political. If it failed to act in this sphere, it would eventually become irrelevant.

Accordingly, the Court deals with political issues and the Justices do their best to cultivate an aura of political neutrality. Should they take sides, no side would respect their opinions, and public respect is essential to the maintenance of the Court's authority. But if the Justices strive to be above reproach, they are hardly above politics in the best sense of the word. Many were politically active before donning their robes; many were nominated in accordance with a President's political assessment of the tone of their possible opinions, and in consideration of his need to leaven the Court's decisions with the views of the people who elected him. Indeed, the ability of politically sensitive Justices to analyze the country's political climate is often crucial to the breadth, timing, and impact of the Court's decisions. That famous aphorism, "The Supreme Court follows the election returns" (coined by a cartoonist in 1901), should be considered disparaging only when the Justices ignore the broader meaning of those returns.

People who expect the Supreme Court to be strictly "nonpolitical" are misinformed. The Court is "political" if only because it is the apex of a coequal branch of government, charged with a significant portion of the governing process. As is true of the other branches, it is steeped in public policy issues.

But the Supreme Court is also a very odd political institution: it is compelled by a key principle of the Constitution—the separation of powers—to conduct itself as a court rather than as a legislature or an executive agency. The Framers were convinced that a systematic diffusion of authority throughout a government would deter any part of it from becoming omnipotent. By defining separate powers for the legislature, the executive, and the judiciary, the Constitution was intended not only to prevent the three branches from encroaching upon one another, but also to encourage each branch to become fully responsible for its own territory, thus energizing the whole government and making it more efficient.

The principle of separate powers is the constitutional cement that holds together an otherwise potentially fragile governmental system. And the Supreme Court is mainly responsible for keeping the principle alive.

At the least, this means that the Supreme Court remains first and foremost a court—an institution that waits for business instead of seeking it. Unlike Presidents or Congressmen, the Justices cannot initiate new laws and policies, much less carry them out. They must work entirely within an established legal framework, limited to resolving specific disputes that litigants bring before them.

Even the kinds of cases the Supreme Court can handle are strictly limited by law and custom.

Limited jurisdiction is characteristic of all federal courts, as opposed to state courts, which are presumed to have jurisdiction over any case that comes before them—until persuaded otherwise.

Yet the Supreme Court is hardly running short of cases. The Justices await business atop a federal judicial system that divides the United States into thirteen judicial circuits, each covering three or more states (the District of Columbia is one circuit). The front line of the system consists of ninety-four district courts that hear all federal cases at the trial level, except for those referred to one of the specialty courts, the United States Tax Court, the Customs Court, or the Court of Claims.

Each state has at least one federal district court; large states have as many as four, and each district may have as many as twenty-five judges hearing individual cases. Above these trial courts are middle-level United States Courts of Appeal, one for each judicial circuit. They handle appeals from district courts in their circuits, together with appeals from the Tax Court and from certain federal administrative agencies. Supreme in their circuits, the federal appellate courts are usually the last stop for federal litigants, unless different circuit courts issue conflicting decisions, in which case the Supreme Court may be called upon to maintain uniform interpretations of federal laws.

The number of cases filed in United States Courts of Appeal is rising so fast (by an estimated eighty percent between 1975 and 1983) that an ever larger spillover is boosting the Supreme Court's own filings to record levels. Some 5,144 cases were appealed to the high court in 1980, for example, compared with 2,360 in 1960. Explanations for this phenomenon vary. Some experts attribute it to a steady growth in federal statutes, especially those involving welfare benefits and business regulation, which in turn raise legal issues concerning equal access and fair treatment. Other experts point to the fact that Congress authorized the appointment of additional federal judges in 1979 and 1980—a view much like the argument that more highways create more traffic.

Chief Justice Charles Evans Hughes meeting with judges of the Federal Circuit Courts at the Capitol, October 1, 1930. The Judicial Conference had been established by William Howard Taft. Underwood & Underwood/Bettmann Archive, New York

Whatever the reasons for the upsurge in federal litigation, the response of the Supreme Court suggests yet another paradox. On the one hand, the Justices have extremely broad discretionary powers in rejecting cases. On the other hand, they have been accepting more and more cases for argument.

The Court's objective is to focus on the truly significant cases. As the Justices of the mid-1980s saw it, that standard obliged them to issue well over 150 major rulings a year.

Ultimately, it comes down to "The Rule of Four": the reality that since 1925 the Court has been empowered to deny review in most of the cases brought to its attention—unless four of the nine Justices agree that a particular case warrants the full Court's consideration.

As a result, the Justices' first concern is not deciding cases, but deciding which cases to decide.

2

POWER & PROCESS:
THE COURT AT WORK

The Courtroom in the Supreme Court Building, Washington, D.C. Photo: Lee Troell Anderson

THE RIGHT TO REVIEW

The Court at the apex of what Alexander Hamilton called the federal government's "least dangerous branch" eventually became the world's most powerful tribunal by virtue of "judicial review"—the Supreme Court's singular power to decide whether governmental actions are in violation of constitutionally-guaranteed liberties or principles. The power of the courts to declare a legislative or executive act unconstitutional is an American invention, still virtually unique to this country. In Britain, by contrast, Parliament is supreme and the courts must uphold its acts.

In his *Federalist* essays urging the Constitution's ratification, Hamilton openly espoused judicial review, stressing the "complete independence" of life-tenured federal judges and their special duty to "invalidate all acts contrary to the manifest tenor of the Constitution." Without impartial courts to maintain constitutional limits on official power, he wrote, "all the reservations of particular rights or privileges would amount to nothing." Fifteen years later, Chief Justice Marshall adopted Hamilton's reasoning in his landmark *Marbury* opinion. Marshall there struck down an act of Congress for the first time.

In the typical constitutional case, there is a clash between individual liberty and government power, the latter presumptively representing majority will in a democracy. Thus an individual may claim that some official action violated his right to behave or speak in a way guaranteed inviolate by the Constitution. The government may claim that in a particular instance, private rights must give way to public necessity. Such clashes are inherent in the American constitutional system, notably in the Bill of Rights, which removed specific freedoms (religion, speech, press, property, etc.) from government control or majority caprice. But no right can be absolute, if only because one man's liberty can infringe upon that of another. Courts must therefore find limits, exceptions, balances, and accommodations. Although some Justices have insisted on a literal reading of certain constitutional guarantees, ranging from property rights to free expression, the Court as a whole has been more flexible, partly in response to changing national moods.

Writing in 1963, Justice William J. Brennan, Jr. explained that fully one-half of the Supreme Court's business differed from that of any other court in the world. "The central quality of this half of the docket," he said, "is that the real contest in any case is not so much between the actual parties to it." The real contest involves the individual's relationship with government in America, or the separation of powers in the triadic federal government, or the boundaries between national and state sovereignty. One need only recall Alexis de Tocqueville's observation:

"Scarcely any political question arises in the United States that is not resolved, sooner or later, into a judicial question."

"Nearly every significant decision of the Supreme Court has to do with power," wrote Attorney General Robert H. Jackson in 1941. "The ultimate function of the Supreme Court is nothing less than the arbitration between fundamental and ever-present rival forces or trends in our organized society." And Jackson, himself about to become a Justice, added: "Conflicts which have divided the Justices always mirror a conflict which pervades society. In fact, it may be said that the Supreme Court conference chamber is the forum where each fundamental cause has its most determined and understanding championship."

The Supreme Court can only hear cases over which it has jurisdiction. Article III of the Constitution grants the Supreme Court "original" or trial jurisdiction in very few situations—notably disputes between states, which typically involve boundaries or water rights and seldom burden the Court with more than three or four cases a year. In all other cases, Article III says, the Court "shall have appellate Jurisdiction, both as to law and Fact, with such Exceptions, and under such Regulations as the Congress shall make."

Over the long run Congress has generally bolstered the Court, partly by expanding its jurisdiction, but mainly by giving it more and more discretion to review only those cases it considers truly important. This Court prerogative was firmly established by the Judiciary Act of 1925, the so-called "Judges Bill" drafted largely by the Court itself under the leadership of Chief Justice Taft. His premise was that the intermediate federal appellate courts should be the last word for nearly all federal litigants, freeing the Supreme Court to focus on constitutional issues except when the Court itself grants review. To achieve this, the Court's non-original cases were divided into two classes depending upon the nature of the dispute. So-called "appeals of right" must be reviewed, whereas review in "certiorari" cases is left to the Justices' discretion. The Court's jurisdiction is mandated by the Constitution and by the statute permitting it to reject any "cert petition" that fails to attract a four-Justice vote in favor of granting review. Ever since the 1925 act, the Justices have urged Congress to limit further

appeals of right and make discretionary writs of certiorari the nearly exclusive avenue to Supreme Court review. Technically, only appeals of right are "appeals"—the certiorari cases are petitions for review. But the word "appeal" is generally used for cases brought to the Supreme Court by either route.

Mandatory appeals are limited mainly to aspects of comity in the federal union. For example, the Supreme Court is obliged to grant review of any federal court ruling that a state law is unconstitutional. Also directly appealable to the Justices are decisions by top state courts that declare a federal law unconstitutional or uphold a state law against a federal constitutional challenge. Both federal and state interests are thus protected.

A significant "threshold" curb on federal judicial power is the fact that Article III authorizes federal courts to deal only with "cases" and "controversies." These words limit the Court's agenda to actual disputes between real adversaries with specified interests at stake. The Court must shun abstract issues and hypothetical situations. Thus it is not to render advisory opinions, even if the President himself seeks the Justices' counsel, as George Washington did in 1793, when the Court first adopted the no-advice rule.

To possess a bona fide federal "case," the plaintiff must show that he is injured or benefited by some provision of the law, and the Court must be able and willing to remedy the situation. The need for a real-life contest is fundamental to the judicial method of resolving controversies. If a state law punished "seditious speech," for example, a judge must not determine whether or not it infringed the First Amendment right of free speech except by examining actual words from an actual speaker accused of violating the statute under particular circumstances. Such specific facts plus adversarial argument provide the concreteness needed to make abstract principles come alive. Accordingly, the Court rejects friendly suits between collusive parties, and even the most obvious test case requires a plaintiff who will suffer real consequences if he or she loses.

The most important corollary of the "case" requirement is that a challenger must have "standing to sue," meaning a stake in the outcome of the case. Many of the Court's important rulings on "standing" have involved taxpayer

The Justices' Conference Room, taken during a lunch break. Photo: Lee Troell Anderson

suits, the most famous being *Frothingham* v. *Mellon* (1923). Mrs. Frothingham, a Massachusetts matron, alleged that her federal taxes supported federal spending for child care, an effort she disapproved. Had she been allowed to pursue her claim, the government might have ground to a halt. Every federal taxpayer in the nation would have been entitled to challenge every dime of federal spending. The Court prudently held that as a federal taxpayer her interest was too small and remote to challenge spending authorized by Congress, and further that it was not a "justiciable issue," meaning one the Court was equipped to resolve.

Among other rules of "justiciability," the Court will not take a "moot" case in which the dispute is dormant. Conversely, the Court will not review cases that lack "ripeness," meaning that the issues have not reached a stage which, in the opinion of the Justices, qualifies them for review by the highest court. Nor will the Court normally

review a "political question," which it says the Constitution implicitly assigns to the political branches, and which, in any case, is beyond the Court's remedial powers. Most notably, the Justices accord the President carte blanche over foreign relations. In dealing with other countries, the President is "the sole organ of the federal government," according to a key 1936 ruling, and his authority is "plenary and exclusive" in virtually all respects save the power to declare war (*United States* v. *Curtis-Wright Export Co.*).

A summary of the Court's "rules of restraint" was set forth by Justice Louis D. Brandeis in the 1936 case of *Ashwander* v. *Tennessee Valley Authority*. Citing numerous precedents, Brandeis wrote that the Court:

. . ."Will not pass upon the constitutionality of legislation in a friendly, non-adversary proceeding . . .

. . ."Will not anticipate a question of constitutional law in advance of the necessity of deciding it . . .

. . ."Will not formulate a rule of constitutional law broader than is required by the precise facts to which it is applied . . .

. . ."Will not pass upon a constitutional question . . . if there is also some other ground upon which the case may be disposed of . . .

. . ."Will not pass upon the validity of a statute upon complaint of one who fails to show that he is injured by its operation . . . [or] at the instance of one who has availed himself of its benefit . . ."

. . .Will not declare even a dubious act of Congress unconstitutional without first ascertaining "whether a construction of the statute is fairly possible by which the question may be avoided."

Hallowed as these canons are, they are subject to varying applications, if only because the Court has nine autonomous members. The question of whether a particular litigant has standing, for example, might produce nine different answers. Thus the Court's normal abstemiousness has served it extremely well, keeping it from reaching out for cases that might well strain the judicial process.

ADVERSARIES AND ADVOCATES

Between the Roosevelt and Reagan Administrations, private legal groups defending or asserting minority rights achieved notable successes in their appeals to the Supreme Court, among them the American Civil Liberties Union, Jehovah's Witnesses, and the NAACP Legal Defense Fund. More recently, the Court has frequently upheld federal and state prosecutors seeking reversal of lower-court decisions involving police procedures and the rights of criminal defendants. Beyond the immediate case, many of these actions have been aimed at legitimizing police methods deemed essential to combating modern crime, especially the drug traffic, and in the process to narrow, if not repeal, some of the Warren Court's criminal-law decisions.

Term after term, the Court's most prominent litigant is the United States, represented by the Solicitor General, the third-ranking official in the

A portrait of Chief Justice *John Marshall* (c. 1828) by John Martin hangs above the mantel in the Conference Room. The small carriage clock on the mantel belonged to Oliver Wendell Holmes. Photo: Lee Troell Anderson

Charles Annos. *John Tucker*. 1791. Oil on canvas, 29⁷/₁₆ × 24¹/₂″. John Tucker was the first Clerk of the Supreme Court, serving from 1790 to 1791. Collection of the Supreme Court of the United States, Washington, D.C. Photo: Lee Troell Anderson

Early Supreme Court cases were named after the Clerk of the Court, who recorded and published them. *4 Wheat. (U.S. 1819) 518*, is better known to posterity as the Dartmouth College Case (*Dartmouth College* v. *Woodward*). This entry from the notebooks of Clerk Henry Wheaton records the beginning of Daniel Webster's plea for the plaintiff, March 10, 1818. Taking notes rapidly in Court, Wheaton recorded Webster's legal argument, leaving out the famous rhetorical flourishes. Wheaton Papers, The Pierpont Morgan Library, New York

Department of Justice. Free of administrative chores, the Solicitor General (Britons might call him Barrister General) is a full-time appellate lawyer charged with selecting and then arguing only those cases the federal government seeks to resolve in the Supreme Court. The Solicitor General's office traditionally is renowned for professionalism. On the average, he and his staff participate in roughly half of the Court's entire docket and perhaps two-thirds of all argued cases. By acquiring great expertise and by selecting only significant federal cases from a vast list of possibles, the Solicitor General assists the Court and accordingly enjoys its special confidence. Indeed, a Federal government appeal is at least six times more likely to get a Court hearing than appeals from any other litigant. Given this experience, a Solicitor General may well have a Court future. The office has thus far produced four Justices—Taft, Reed, Jackson, and Marshall.

DECIDING WHAT TO DECIDE

At nine-thirty nearly every Friday morning, a buzzer summons the Justices to an all-day meeting in the Conference Room, a large antechamber between the Chief Justice's two offices. With its crystal chandelier, high coffered ceiling and white oak paneling, the room evokes the heyday of colonial elegance. The room is lined with *United States Reports*—volume after volume of Supreme Court decisions bound in beige, black, and scarlet—and over the marble fireplace hangs a huge portrait of John Marshall, the great Chief Justice, his shrewd eyes permanently challenging his successors.

The purpose of the Friday Conference, longest of two such meetings per week, is to select new cases for Court review and to vote on the cases already argued during the week. As the Court's prime time for deciding what to decide, the Fri-

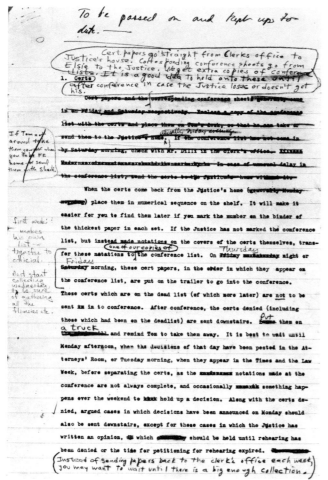

Typed memorandum detailing the duties of law clerks, prepared by Justice Felix Frankfurter, inscribed in his hand: "To be passed on and kept up to date." Frankfurther Papers, Harvard Law Library, Cambridge

Among Justice John Marshall Harlan's papers was a clipping from an unknown newspaper of an article called "How the Justices Study," dating from a time when each Justice worked at home. The reporter was particularly impressed by Justice Harlan's method of working on two desks, one for work in progress and one for corrections on finished work. Harlan Papers, University of Louisville Library

day Conference effectively begins rather than ends the Justices' typical in-session week, and it is arguably the most important stage in the entire Supreme Court process. Apart from procedural matters, Conferences remain a closed book. Historians rarely if ever see the participants' notes, the custom being for most Justices to destroy their Conference papers or otherwise restrict access to them.

After ritually shaking hands at the door, a symbol of harmony begun in the 1880s, the Justices take their regular places at a long table in front of the fireplace, beneath Marshall's gaze. The Chief Justice sits at the east end of the table, the senior Associate Justice facing him at the west end. The seating order clockwise from Chief Justice Burger's left today consists of Justices Powell, Rehnquist, Stevens, and O'Connor along one side of the table, with (senior) Justice Brennan at the end, followed by Justices White, Blackmun, and Marshall along the other side. Nobody else is

allowed in the room—no clerks, no pages, no secretaries—a security measure going back to 1907 when a decision was either leaked or guessed at before the Justices announced it.

With a short break for coffee at eleven o'clock and another for lunch, the Justices confer for about seven hours, frequently referring to books and papers in carts parked behind their chairs. Should they need anything else from outside the room, the junior Justice is required to deal with the matter, whether documents or messages, as the case may be, and otherwise to guard the door at all times. "For five years," Justice Tom C. Clark fondly recalled, "I was the highest paid doorkeeper in the world."

Of each week's batch of 100 or more new petitions, two-thirds never make it to the Justices' Conferences. Incoming cases are pre-screened by the Chief Justice and law clerks, enabling him to place the important ones on the "Discuss List" that serves as the Conference agenda. All other

Nine sets of the Conference List of *in forma pauperis* petitions ready for delivery to the Justices. Photo: Lee Troell Anderson

Twenty-one color coded briefs from one case heard by the Supreme Court in 1980. In the center of the circle, tied with red string, are the lower court pleadings. Photo: Lee Troell Anderson

cases are rejected without discussion, although any case can be placed on the Discuss List at the request of a single Justice.

As a matter of fact, each Justice is individually responsible for each case. Justices can truly say, as Justice Brandeis did, "We do our own work." Today the petitions pile up rapidly (even following the Justices to their summer vacation hideaways). Since 1972, several Justices have joined a "cert pool" in which their clerks work together to screen petitions and provide the Justices with group memorandums.

By Conference time, all the Justices have taken a preliminary look at every item on the Discuss List, usually permitting fairly quick disposition.

The procedure calls for the Chief Justice to work down the Discuss List, presenting the facts of each case and summarizing his own views. The other Court members then briefly comment on the case, beginning with the senior Associate Justice and continuing in order of seniority. Their positions for or against granting review generally emerge in the course of the discussion. Chief Justice Burger records everything in a notebook perched on a vertical wooden stand he designed for that purpose, and individual Justices may make their own informal tallies of the voting.

When any case receives four or more votes in favor of granting review, it is normally transferred to the Oral Argument List. Those which

An application for admission to the Bar of the Supreme Court, 1929. The Court has kept all such applications on file, from 1925 to the present. Photo: Lee Troell Anderson

A lawyer's eye view of the bench. Crank to the right adjusts height of podium. Lights indicate time remaining for argument. Photo: Lee Troell Anderson

The Marshal, seated to the left of the bench, facing the courtroom, keeps track of the time taken by oral argument. The wooden box in the center contains two digital clocks, one for petitioner and one for respondent. Immediately to the left is the Chief Justice's signal box for extension of time granted to arguing lawyers, and to the left of that is the box that signals time remaining on the podium. Photo: Lee Troell Anderson

receive only four votes, however, may be relisted for a second look. If a case fails to receive four votes, any Justice can request that it be rediscussed at another Conference. Also, any Justice can be recorded in the Court's published Orders as having dissented from a decision to deny a hearing. Another possibility is that the Court may grant review but also summarily reverse or affirm a lower-court decision at the same Conference. This is said to occur only when the decision below is so clear that the high court's ruling is inevitable. Ordinarily, the Court does not reverse decisions without oral arguments, which generally take place about four months after the vote to grant review.

Only about half a dozen of the cases on the Discuss List survive the Conference. One official guide to this winnowing process is Supreme Court Rule 17 entitled "Considerations governing review on certiorari." The rule suggests that the Supreme Court will step in whenever federal appellate courts or top state courts issue conflicting opinions on the same subject. Another criterion for selecting a case is, simply, "importance," as when four or more Justices consider a lower-court decision so wrong that reversing it would serve important judicial concerns. The record shows that eighty percent of the Court's decisions have been reversals.

After his 1981 retirement, Justice Potter Stewart was asked by an interviewer to define a Justice's objectives, as he saw them. His answer:

The Supreme Court, unlike others, is a passive court. It reacts to what's brought before it, rather than acting on its own. Its duty is to react to every single petition it receives. So it's the first duty of each Justice to decide each case according to his best understanding of the Constitution and the law. He must be objective and detached. But in addition to a sense of history and precedent, he must remain aware of the Court's great tradition of simplicity—the idea expressed by Brandeis that "Here we do our own work." And another great tradition to bear in mind is the Court's accessibility—the fact that any poor wretch can send us a handwritten note and get attention. These are precious qualities: If the Court ever loses

Card issued to each lawyer appearing before the Supreme Court. Collection of the Supreme Court of the United States, Washington, D.C.

simplicity and accessibility, it will be a dying institution.

A Justice's second most important duty is to persuade other Justices in order to produce a consensus for a coherent, orderly Court decision. In effect, it's an advocacy job and the other Justices are the jury. This is not easy. The issues before the Supreme Court are normally close, difficult, extremely hard to call, and by definition you're nearly always dealing with claims from contentious or unpopular people, many of them criminals.

The persuasion process takes place mainly at the Conference. Some Justices are more interested in persuading their brethren than others. Douglas never tried; if others agreed with him, he was almost embarrassed. Black, on the other hand, who is usually perceived as Douglas's twin, was quite the opposite. A very powerful advocate.

The Conference is conducted in an orderly and systematic way, but there's nothing inhibited about it. I'm a smoker and I went off in a corner periodically to smoke. Frankfurter, who was still on the Court when I arrived, often performed dramatically at the Conference, striding to the bookshelves to pull open Volumes of *United States Reports* for citations supporting his argument. Bill Douglas used to devastate Frankfurter in Conferences. After one of Felix's orations,

Bill was likely to say, "Felix, I came here this morning absolutely certain I would vote in favor of your position. Now you've talked me out of it . . . ."

THEATER OF THE LAW

When the Conference orders a case placed on the Oral Argument List, lawyers for both sides produce formal briefs for the Justices' perusal no later than thirty days before the courtroom hearing. Written to rule book specifications, briefs arguing the merits are limited to fifty printed pages—blue binding for petitioners, red for respondents. In a major case, the reading package for each Justice may include not only these briefs but the parties' yellow-bound replies to one another, green-bound amicus curiae briefs from interested organizations, a gray-bound brief from the Solicitor General, and various tan-bound appendices. The advocate's hope is to compose a peerless brief and then prepare and present an oral presentation that further sharpens the argument.

Modern Court hearings are very different from the nineteenth-century spectaculars featuring charismatic counsel such as Daniel Webster or Henry Clay. Then the Court's oral arguments often continued for days. Legend has it that one case was even reargued for the benefit of a tardy dowager whom the Justices wished to please. But today's Court dramas, although no less gripping, are necessarily brief. Relentlessly mounting caseloads have truncated the time available for oral arguments. Only by limiting each side to thirty minutes can the Court squeeze in twelve one-hour arguments per week and still have time for writing opinions. These oral argument sessions occur three days a week (Monday, Tuesday, and Wednesday) during fourteen weeks interspersed from October through April, making an average of 168 argued cases per term.

With only a brief chance to state one's case, a lawyer has good reason to watch a number of oral arguments before attempting his own. The Justices may interrupt as frequently as they wish. Their questions, often extremely difficult, must be answered immediately and impressively. The Court's view was described once by Justice William J. Brennan, Jr. "Oral advocacy is the abso-lute indispensable ingredient of appellate advocacy," he said. "Often my whole notion of what a case is about crystallizes at oral argument. This happens even though I read the briefs before . . ."

MEMBERS OF THE JURY

For a lawyer, nothing matches the Supreme Court ordeal, the ultimate summation before the world's most rarefied jury. But if the last-chance aspect makes lawyers apprehensive, they are not alone. Most Justices find it humbling. "We are not final because we are infallible," Robert Jackson acknowledged. "We are infallible only because we are final."

Charles Evans Hughes, then governor of New York, made a classic comment on the subject. "We are under a Constitution," remarked the future Chief Justice. "But the Constitution is what the Justices say it is."

Although the Constitution does not require Justices to be lawyers, the obvious prerequisite is superb legal achievement. The vast majority of Justices have been politically active before their Court service, and most of them were personally acquainted with the President who nominated them. Of the fifteen Chief Justices since 1790, ten had previously been outstanding politicians at the level of governor, cabinet member, or even President (Taft).

Since the Court averages one vacancy every twenty-two months, nearly every President has a chance to nominate at least one Justice for approval by a majority of those voting in the Senate. In making his selections, the President has considerable help from the Attorney General, the American Bar Association, special interest groups, and even sitting Justices, especially Chief Justices. Since most Presidents have a strong interest in avoiding the embarrassment of a Senate defeat, they try to select distinguished candidates who will be a credit to them. Recent Justices have thus tended to be chosen at a later, career-capping age than their predecessors were.

Free as they may be from pressures, Justices do bear the weight of accountability—to the assessments of their peers, and to the judgment of history. They work extremely hard, sometimes to the point of exhaustion. Service on the Supreme

Justice Joseph McKenna, who served on the Court from 1898 to 1925, seems to symbolize the nineteenth century in this 1925 photograph for which he sat with his successor on the bench, Justice Harlan Fiske Stone. Justice Stone was Associate Justice from 1925 until 1941 and then Chief Justice until 1946. Underwood & Underwood/Bettmann Archive, New York

THE CREATION OF CONSENSUS

In its decision in the case of *Erie Railroad Company* v. *Tompkins* (1938), the Supreme Court overturned a doctrine of liability law established by *Swift* v. *Tyson* (1842). Justice Louis Brandeis delivered the opinion of the Court. These are some of his papers regarding the case, from the Brandeis Papers, Harvard Law Library, Cambridge.

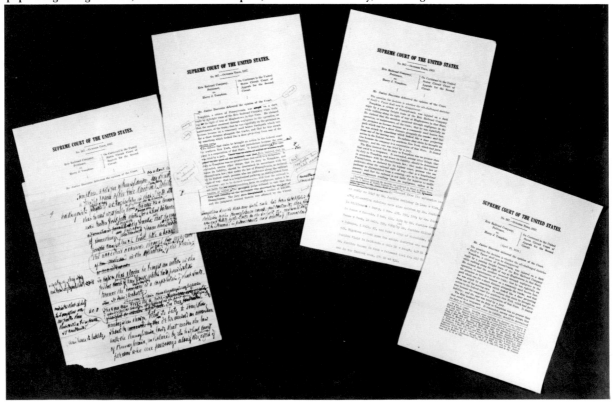

Three drafts (among several in the papers) and the final version in printed form. Justice Brandeis began with a handwritten draft of the opinion, which he then had printed by the Clerk. Footnotes with full citations of cases were prepared, probably by his clerks, and added. *(Continued on page 48.)*

Charles Evans Hughes, a New Yorker educated in Ivy League schools and a powerful force in the Republican party, serving in both elective and appointive positions, was the quintessential Supreme Court Justice. Here, representing the two strands of his career, are his gold pocket watch, given him by the classes of 1887 and 1888 of the Columbia College School of Law where he held a teaching fellowship after graduating in 1884, and his walking stick, given him by the Kalamazoo Michigan Republican Club, purportedly made from a rail split by Abraham Lincoln. Photo: Lee Troell Anderson

Court more often than not has a salutary effect upon its members, because it appeals to an appointee's best instincts and provides him or her with years of intellectual challenge and the opportunity for growth.

Of the 102 Justices thus far, forty-eight died in office. Another forty-five resigned, mainly for reasons of age and infirmity. Today it is possible for a Justice to retire voluntarily with full pay at sixty-five, after serving fifteen years, or at age seventy, whichever comes first.

THE CREATION OF CONSENSUS

With each week's oral arguments fresh in their minds, the Justices discuss those cases at their Conferences on Wednesday afternoon and all day Friday. The purpose is to forge a majority vote, the larger the better, permitting a strong Court opinion with minimal separate opinions. The resulting search for majorities of five or more Justices is a blend of both competition and accommodation, making the Court a singularly collegial body, with touches of a corporate board room, a legislature, and a jury.

As chairman of this process, the Chief Justice has special opportunities to influence the outcome. Although a Chief Justice's vote is not weightier than any other, managing the Conference agenda may allow authentic leadership. Whether his style is predominantly social, intellectual, or political, a magnetic Chief Justice unifies the Court, making it more effective. Most important, the Chief Justice has reason to vote with any emerging majority, even if he doesn't wholly agree with it. When in the majority, the Chief Justice has the key role of deciding which Justice is to write the court opinion. If the Chief Justice is in the minority, the senior Associate Justice voting with the majority designates the writer. These assignments are made after the Conference vote.

In more important cases, the Chief Justice is likely to bargain hard for a unanimous Court and then to stress unity by writing the Court's opinion.

A Court decision is never final and never

Supreme Court of the United States
Washington, D.C.

CHAMBERS OF
JUSTICE HARLAN F. STONE
1929 TWENTY-FOURTH STREET, N.W.

March 25, 1938.

Dear Justice Brandeis:

Since our conversation about your opinion in Erie Railroad v. Tompkins, I have obtained from your clerk my copy of the opinion and have examined it in the light of Justice Reed's concurring opinion, which has just come in.

In view of the long history of our support of Swift v. Tyson, I realize the force of the constitutional aspects of the case as an impelling reason for overruling Swift v. Tyson, and the long line of cases which have followed it. Nevertheless, I think it is important that we should not discuss the constitutional question unless we definitely conclude that without it we would not overrule the precedents of one hundred years. I therefore suggest that the second sentence on page 7 of your opinion be reframed as follows:

"If only a question of statutory construction were involved we would not be prepared to abandon a doctrine so widely applied throughout nearly a century. But the unconstitutionality of the course pursued has now been made clear and compels us to do so."

If you would prefer not to make the change, or find it inconvenient to make it, I will concur with a sentence making plain my position that I come to the constitutional question only because otherwise I should, as Mr. Justice Holmes said, leave Swift v. Tyson undisturbed, but without allowing it to spread the assumed dominion into new fields.

Will you ask your clerk to let me know your preference over the telephone?

Yours faithfully,

Stone

Supreme Court of the United States
Washington, D.C.

March 22, 1938

My dear Justice Brandeis:

Your requiem over Swift v. Tyson is one of your best—and that is saying much. While I am not always in agreement with the opinions delivered by my Alabama predecesors, Mr. Justice McKinley and Mr. Justice Campbell, I am personally very happy that their dissents mentioned in your Note 1, will now be in accord with "the law of the land." I hope that sometime hereafter this Court may deliver another opinion in harmony with the spirit and purport of the dissents of Mr. Justice McKinley and Mr. Justice Campbell, respectively, in the cases of Bank of Augusta v. Earle, 13 Peters 519, 597 to 606, and Dodge v. Woolsey 18 Howard 331, 362, 380.

I hesitate to make a suggestion in connection with your decision and personally hope that not a word will be changed relating to the last repose of Swift v. Tyson. I hope that there may be no misunderstanding as to the application to this particular case which might bring about an unintentional injury to the injured litigant. On Page 2 of the opinion in the first paragraph, and on Page 8 in the fourth paragraph the issue is stated as limited to the single question as to whether injury sustained on a "longitudinal pathway" relieves the railroad from liability under Pennsylvania law. The respondent rather forcefully insisted on Pages 26 and 27 of his brief that the Falchetti case was not applicable to the facts involved in this particular case because it was "uncontested in the case at bar that plaintiff was at the intersection of a diagonal and a longitudinal pathway when he was struck." [Page 27]. I am wondering if you would feel justified in inserting something to show this fact on Page 2 where you say, "Tompkins denied that any such rule had been established by the decisions of the Pennsylvania courts." If it could be shown that this Court realized there was a further controversy as to the applicability of the Falchetti rule, I believe that it would prevent anyone from reaching the conclusion that this Court was attempting to foreclose any further consideration of Pennsylvania law as to the facts in this case.

With kind regards, I am

Sincerely,

Hugo L. Black
HUGO L. BLACK

Mr. Justice Brandeis,
Washington, D. C.

Meanwhile, various drafts had been circulating among the Justices. In two letters preserved in Justice Brandeis's files, Justices Harlan Fiske Stone and Hugo Black requested changes in the opinion.

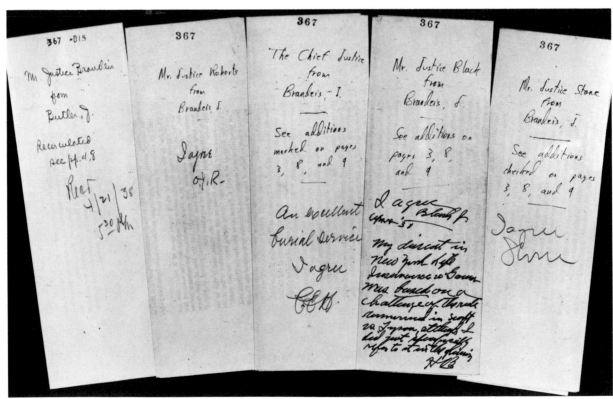

The Justices endorsed the final opinion, and returned it to Justice Brandeis. Chief Justice Charles Evans Hughes wrote on his, "An excellent burial service [for *Swift* v. *Tyson*]."

announced until five or more Justices approve the written opinion, or agree with the decision but choose to write their own opinions. To hold this majority, the designated writer must please not only himself, but also the majority members, so that more than one draft is inevitable. Indeed, seven or eight drafts are common, and perfectionists have been known to produce twenty or more for a single case. Each draft is secretly printed, circulated, discussed, marked up with marginal notes ("Please join me"), and criticized among the Justices, sometimes over a super-private phone line connecting their chambers. The writer is thus under steady pressure to amend the opinion or see it weakened by a rash of concurring or dissenting opinions. The worst outcome for a Justice is to lose a majority and wind up in the minority.

The bargaining that goes into Court decisions suggests that Justices' votes do not necessarily represent their personal feelings, one reason why ideological labels are so misleading. Although the Court *is* its members, the drive for public consensus may subordinate private wishes, making the institution more than its members. Fortunately, the Court values dissent, one of its most fruitful if confusing traditions. The Court's finest political essays frequently have come from its great dissenters, among them Brandeis, Cardozo, Harlan, and Holmes. Justice Holmes wrote 173 dissents; fewer than twenty shaped future reversals, but American literature would surely be poorer without those commentaries. The first Justice Harlan produced an astonishing 380 dissents and did help to change the future, most notably by his lone stand against the separate-but-equal doctrine of *Plessy* v. *Ferguson* (1896). Chief Justice Hughes, seldom a dissenter himself, offered a memorable defense of the practice. "Dissent in a court of last resort," he wrote, "is an appeal to the brooding spirit of law, to the intelligence of a future day, when a later decision may possibly correct the error into which the dissenting judge believes the court to have been betrayed."

By permitting change and continuity, flexibility and permanence, the Court has mastered self-correction, survived political attacks, and kept American law in step with the country's development. Writing in 1932, Justice Brandeis summarized the Court's basic method: "*Stare decisis* is

usually the wise policy, because in most matters it is more important that the applicable rule of law be settled than that it be settled right. . . . But in cases involving the Federal Constitution, where correction through legislation is practically impossible, this Court has often overridden its earlier decisions. The Court bows to the lessons of experience and the force of better reasoning, recognizing that the process of trial and error, so fruitful in the physical sciences, is appropriate also in the judicial function."

THE BOTTOM LINE

What happens after a Supreme Court decision? As to *litigants*, the Court typically "remands" a case to the lower court for "further proceedings consistent with this opinion." In remanded criminal cases, the defendant is often reconvicted in a new trial. As to promulgating legal *rules or policies*, the Court's main reason for deciding cases, the next step is for lower courts to apply the Court's decisions in all similar cases. By and large, they do just that. The rule of law continues in America.

The Court does have direct impact in certain areas—far more on the states, for example, than on national policies. As Justice Holmes put it: "I do not think the United States would come to an end if we [the Court] lost our power to declare an Act of Congress void. I do think the union would be imperiled if we could not make that declaration as to the laws of the several states. For one in my place sees how often a local policy prevails with those who are not trained to national views and how often action is taken that embodies what the Commerce Clause was meant to end." By 1978 the Court had invalidated 1,007 state laws and local ordinances. In turn, many such decisions required other states to repeal similar laws. Equally significant if less quantifiable were all the cases in which the Court *upheld* challenged laws and policies. As the final arbiter of the constitutionality of state actions, the Court has most assuredly extended its writ across the nation.

3

THE NEED FOR A CONSTITUTION

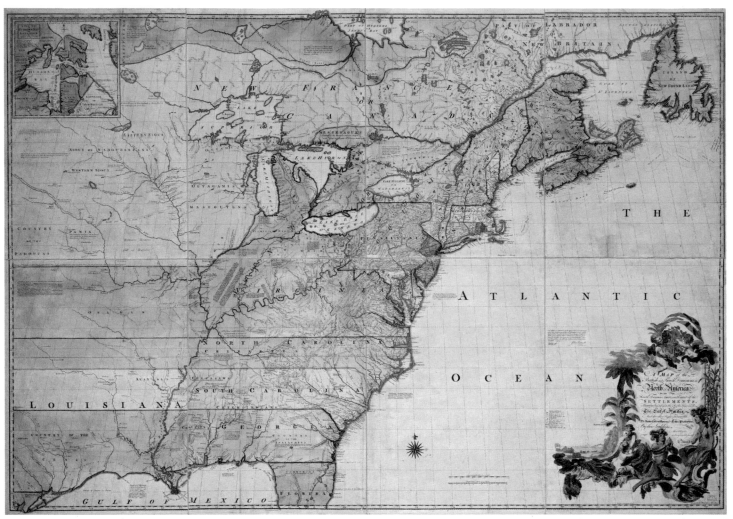

This 1755 hand-colored map by James Mitchell, titled *A Map of the British and French Dominions in North America with the Roads, Distances, Limits, and Extent of the Settlements,* was consulted during 1783 Treaty of Paris negotiations, which set the western boundary of the United States at the Mississippi River. Strains between small states with no room to expand and large states with seemingly limitless land temporarily deadlocked the Constitutional Convention in 1787. Litigation over ownership of the western lands continued well into the nineteenth century. Geography and Map Division, Library of Congress, Washington, D.C.

The mutual antipathies and clashing interests of the Americans, their differences of governments, habitudes, and manners, indicate that they will have no centre of union and no common interest. They can never be united into one compact empire under any species of government whatever. . . .

—Josiah Tucker, Dean of Gloucester, 1787.

The population was miniscule compared to the enormity of the country. America was overpowering—endless forests teeming with wild animals; distances so daunting that any long journey was an ordeal. Such was land travel in the 1780s that a trip by stagecoach from Boston to New York took eight days, and mail sent to Georgia by ship from England arrived much faster than mail sent overland from New England.

Profoundly suspicious of centralized authority, the states themselves had stunted the growth of Congress back in 1776 when John Dickinson of Pennsylvania (later of Delaware) proposed a document entitled "Articles of Confederation and Perpetual Union" as the first framework of national government. Article II of the final draft came out with a wing-clipping clause: "Each state retains its sovereignty, freedom, and independence, and every power, jurisdiction, and right, which is not by this confederation expressly

The Articles of Confederation. Photograph by Jonathan Wallen. National Archives, Washington, D.C.

delegated to the United States, in Congress assembled."

The result was a feeble central government. The Articles of Confederation lacked any provision for a chief executive to carry out the few national laws that Congress managed to enact. There was no national judicial system to settle disputes between citizens of different states. The only national institution was the one-chamber Congress, which could not pass laws or ratify treaties without the consent of nine states out of thirteen, a majority difficult to obtain.

Congress had no power to levy taxes and the states ignored its appeals for money. It could not enforce treaties, leaving foreign countries dubi-

ous about America's word. Indeed, Congress lacked power to do anything not *explicitly* authorized by the Articles of Confederation. Nor could the Articles be changed without unanimous approval by all thirteen states. When Congress desperately tried to give itself taxing power, it was stymied by a single negative vote from Rhode Island.

All this worsened the new country's precarious financial condition. A severe depression from 1783 to 1788, aggravated by rival currencies and runaway public debts, triggered numerous commercial disputes between the states that Congress was powerless to resolve.

Eventually, interstate commerce deteriorated

Five-shilling note issued by Massachusetts, 1782, designed by Paul Revere. National Museum of American History, Washington, D.C.

A N.W. View of the State House in Philadelphia taken 1778. Engraving by J. Trenchard after Charles Willson Peale from the *Columbian Magazine.* The Metropolitan Museum of Art, New York. Bequest of Charles Allen Munn, 1924

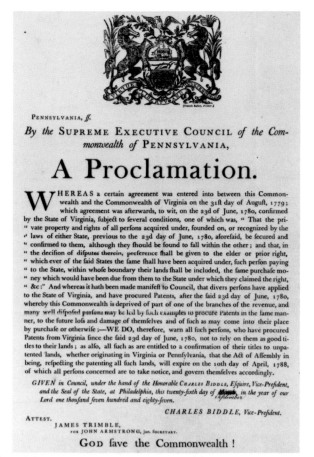

Proclamation of the Supreme Executive Council of the Commonwealth of Pennsylvania, Philadelphia, September 26, 1787, warning that certain land patents issued by Virginia will not be respected by Pennsylvania. Independence National Historical Park Collection, Philadelphia

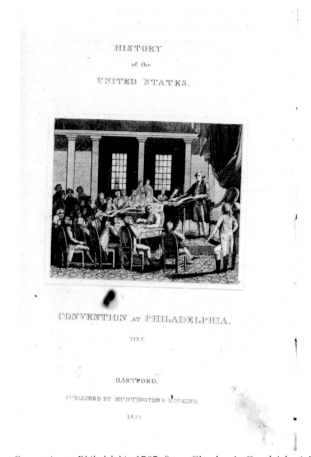

Convention at Philadelphia 1787, from Charles A. Goodrich, *A History of the United States of America*, 1823. Rare Book and Special Collections Division, Library of Congress, Washington, D.C.

to the point that influential Americans agreed on the urgent need to reform the Articles or replace the American Confederation with a more effective national government. Ultimately, a brilliant array of such leaders—among them Alexander Hamilton, James Madison, Benjamin Franklin, and George Washington—convened in Philadelphia during the summer of 1787 and in less than 100 working days achieved the seemingly impossible feat of writing a strong new Constitution for a reborn United States.

After intense debate in each state, exemplified by Hamilton's and Madison's classic endorsement, *The Federalist Papers*, the proposed Constitution survived a bitter ratification struggle and became effective on September 13, 1788. One of the keys to ratification was an agreement by the Constitution's proponents, called the Federalists, to amplify the document with a later Bill of Rights, the first ten amendments, designed to protect individual liberties from potential abuses by the federal government.

Ratified in 1791, these significant additions included a safeguard for states' rights, the Tenth Amendment, which seemingly paralleled the Articles of Confederation in limiting federal powers. A difference of one word, however, made a huge difference in the future of American government.

Under the Articles of Confederation, the states retained all powers not "expressly" delegated to the national government. Reaffirming that idea, the Tenth Amendment forbade the national government to act without specific authorization from the Constitution. The states, for their part, were permitted to do anything *not* forbidden by the Constitution. But the Tenth Amendment used subtly different language: "The powers not delegated to the United States by the Constitution, nor prohibited by it to the States, are reserved to the States respectively, or to the people."

By omitting the word "expressly," the Tenth Amendment discarded a key qualification of the

A Display of the United States of America. Engraving by Amos Doolittle, 1788. Federalists firmly identified the well-being of the nation with the person of Washington. The John Carter Brown Library, Brown University, Providence, Rhode Island

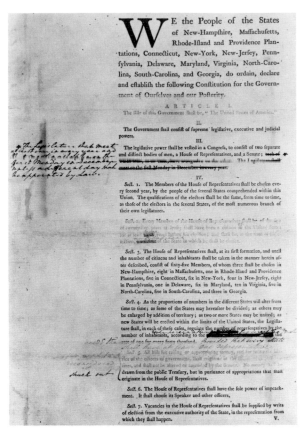

A page of Washington's copy of the first printed draft of the Constitution, dated August 6, 1787, and annotated by Washington and others. National Archives, Washington, D.C.

powers granted to the federal government. In time, it permitted Congress and the President to exercise *implied* federal powers, meaning the authority to take whatever steps were necessary and proper in carrying out their written constitutional duties. Whether those steps were legitimate, however, was not a matter left to Congress and the President to decide for themselves. The federal system required an umpire, the Supreme Court.

In a 1789 speech proposing the amendments that became the Bill of Rights, Congressman James Madison argued that the future of those hard-won safeguards would be largely in the hands of the federal courts. "Independent tribunals of justice will consider themselves in a peculiar manner the guardians of these rights," Madison told Congress. "They [the courts] will be an impenetrable bulwark against every assumption of power in the Legislative or Executive; they will naturally be led to resist every encroachment upon rights expressly stipulated for in the Constitution by the declaration of rights."

Article III of the Constitution defined the third branch of government—an independent federal judiciary consisting of a Supreme Court and "such inferior Courts as the Congress may from time to time ordain and establish." Federal judges would be insulated from interference by lifetime tenure and irreducible salaries. The need for these protections was underscored by the breadth of the national judiciary's responsibilities. Article III empowered federal judges to resolve what then seemed a huge variety of cases that obviously required national rather than state adjudication—everything from admiralty cases to interstate land disputes.

Even so, the federal courts were not authorized to exercise all this potential jurisdiction as they saw fit. Congress alone could expand or contract both the size of the federal judiciary and the scope of its jurisdiction. The only federal court that Congress could not abolish on any given day was the Supreme Court itself, and even that Court's exact role was left so unclear as to invite conflicting theories concerning its functioning for years to come.

. . . . Justice is the end of government. It is the end of civil society. It ever has been and ever will be pursued, until it be obtained, or until liberty be lost in the pursuit. In a society under the forms of which the stronger factions can readily unite and oppress the weaker, anarchy may as truly be said to reign as in a state of nature, where the weaker individual is not secured against the violence of the stronger: and as, in the latter state, even the stronger individuals are prompted, by the uncertainty of their condition, to submit to a government which may protect the weak as well as themselves; so, in the former state, will the more powerful factions or parties be gradually induced, by a like motive, to wish for a government which will protect all parties, the weaker as well as the more powerful. It can be little doubted that if the State of Rhode Island was separated from the Confederacy and left to itself, the insecurity of rights under the popular form of government within such narrow limits would be displayed by such reiterated oppressions of factious majorities that some power altogether independent of the people would soon be called for by the voice of the very factions whose misrule had proved the necessity of it. In the extended republic of the United States, and among the great variety of interests, parties, and sects which it embraces a coalition of the majority of the whole society could seldom take place on any other principles than those of justice and the general good; whilst there being thus less danger to a minor from the will of the major party, there must be less pretext, also, to provide for the security of the former, by introducing into the government a will not dependent on the latter, or, in other words, a will independent of the society itself. It is no less certain than it is important, notwithstanding the contrary opinions which have been entertained, that the larger the society, provided it lie within a practicable sphere, the more duly capable it will be of self government. And happily for the *republican cause*, the practicable sphere may be carried to a very great extent, by a judicious modification and mixture of the *federal principle*.

PUBLIUS (James Madison)
The Federalist No. 51
February 6, 1788

The Framers hesitated to displace state courts except at the highest levels of national or constitutional judgment. Yet the Framers did, in fact, repeatedly allude to the same kind of restraining role for the federal courts that Chief Justice John Marshall eventually asserted for them. Madison's notes from the 1787 Constitutional Convention make it clear that, despite individual differences, the delegates took it for granted that "the courts" would pass on the constitutional validity of laws and governmental actions.

The Philadelphia plan was a marvel of reciprocal restraints aimed at preventing abuses of power and providing America with a government of laws, not of men. The plan's great organizing principle, the separation of powers, merely began with the division of government into three equal branches with different functions. In fact, the powers of all the branches were so commingled that each one had significant braking power on the other two. As Louis H. Pollak, former dean of the Yale Law School, summed up in *The Constitution and the Supreme Court*:

Pursuant to the constitutional plan, Congress can make laws; but a President, whose salary is inviolable during his term, can veto them; Congress can, in its turn, pass laws over the President's veto, but the ultimate impact of any laws enacted depends, *first*, upon the vigor with which the President enforces the laws, and, *second*, on the interpretations put upon them by the judges—men appointed by the President, with the Senate's assent, but thereafter holding office for life. On the other hand, the President has to reckon with Congress's power to withhold needed appropriations—and he also has to reckon with Congress's correlative power to inquire into the way in which sums appropriated to the executive department are actually utilized. Similarly, the judges are not unaware of Congress's latent power to contract their jurisdiction. And both the executive and the judiciary are potential targets of the congressional power of impeachment.

4

THE WEAKEST BRANCH

An excerpt from James Madison's *Notes on the Debates in the Federal Convention*, Monday, September 17, 1787. This was the day for signing the Constitution. Edmund Randolph is here recorded as saying, "that in refusing to sign the Constitution, he took a step which might be the most awful of his life, but it was dictated by conscience, and it was not possible for him to hesitate, much less, to change." James Madison Papers, Library of Congress, Washington, D.C.

After F.J. Fisher. *Edmund Randolph*. Oil on canvas, 30 × 25″. Randolph was Attorney General of Virginia (1776–86), Governor of Virginia (1786–88), and the first Attorney General of the United States (1789–94). Virginia State Library, Richmond

In Philadelphia during that famous summer of 1787, the Framers took for granted the concept of an independent judiciary comprising a third branch of government (already the case in six states). But they avoided organizational detail. Most of their debates about the courts arose in a larger context: the great issue of how to enforce the Constitution, especially in Congress and the state legislatures. This would require checks and balances between the three branches of the federal government and the thirteen states.

Madison's notes suggest that the Framers were virtually unanimous in hoping the Supreme Court would become a powerful countervailing force, strong enough to combat abuses of power from that most feared quarter, the legislature. Those favoring a high federal court called it essential to maintaining the separation of powers, shaping national common law, championing individual rights, curbing a despotic Congress, etc. Yet the Court's proponents portrayed the federal judiciary as being harmless, or what Hamilton in *The Federalist* Number Seventy-Eight later called "beyond comparison the weakest department of power," since it would command neither arms nor money.

Thus Article III does not mention the concept of judicial review. Still, it does inform us that "the judicial power of the United States" shall extend to all cases and controversies "arising under this Constitution."

To check Congress, for example, James Wilson proposed that "the supreme national judiciary should be associated with the executive in the revisionary power." This was defeated by a vote of four states to three on the ground that it would

Jean-Pierre-Henri Elouis. *James Wilson*. c. 1795. Watercolor on ivory, 2⁵/₈ × 2¹/₁₆″. National Museum of American Art, Smithsonian Institution, Washington, D.C. Museum Purchase, Catherine Walden Myer Fund

Ralph Earl. *Roger Sherman*. c. 1775. Oil on canvas, 64⁵/₈ × 49⁵/₈″. Yale University Art Gallery, New Haven. Gift of Roger Sherman White

mingle the judiciary and the executive, defeating the purpose of the separation of powers, to say nothing of giving the Supreme Court a "double-negative" that could expose it to popular resentment and endanger its independence.

Some weeks later, Madison moved "that all acts before they become laws should be submitted both to the executive and supreme judiciary departments, that if either of these should object, two-thirds of each house should be necessary to overrule the objections and give the acts the force of law." In other words, the Supreme Court would have had veto power over legislation, similar to the President's veto power. James Wilson warmly supported Madison's proposal, arguing its utility in blocking a voracious Congress from "swallowing up all the other powers." But the motion was voted down, eight states to three, largely because the delegates, in Roger Sherman's words, "disapproved of judges meddling in politics and parties."

The Philadelphia debates confirm the Framers' unwritten assumption that federal judges would inevitably review acts of Congress for con-

John Trumbull. *Alexander Hamilton*. c. 1792, Philadelphia (?). Oil on canvas, 30¹/₄ × 24¹/₈″. National Gallery of Art, Washington. Gift of the Avalon Foundation, 1952

. . . . The complete independence of the courts of justice is peculiarly essential in a limited Constitution. By a limited Constitution I understand one which contains certain specified exceptions to the legislative authority; such, for instance, that it shall pass no bills of attainder, no *ex-post-facto* laws, and the like. Limitations of this kind can be preserved in practice no other way than through the medium of the courts of justice, whose duty it must be to declare all acts contrary to the manifest tenor of the Constitution void. Without this, all the reservations of particular rights or privileges would amount to nothing.

Some perplexity respecting the right of the courts to pronounce legislative acts void, because contrary to the constitution, has arisen from an imagination that the doctrine would imply a superiority of the judiciary to the legislative power. It is urged that the authority which can declare the acts of another void, must necessarily be superior to the one whose acts may be declared void. As this doctrine is of great importance in all the American constitutions, a brief discussion of the grounds on which it rests cannot be unacceptable. . . .

. . . . It is far more rational to suppose, that the courts were designed to be an intermediate body between the people and the legislature, in order, among other things, to keep the latter within the limits assigned to their authority. The interpretation of the laws is the proper and peculiar province of the courts. A constitution is, in fact, and must be regarded by the judges, as a fundamental law. It therefore belongs to them to ascertain its meaning, as well as the meaning of any particular act proceeding from the legislative body. If there should happen to be an irreconcilable variance between the two, that which has the superior obligation and validity ought, of course, to be preferred; or, in other words, the Constitution ought to be preferred to the statute, the intention of the people to the intention of their agents. . . .

PUBLIUS (Alexander Hamilton)
The Federalist No. 78
May 28, 1788

stitutional conformity. As further evidence we have Hamilton's post-Philadelphia analysis in *The Federalist* Number Seventy-Eight, confidently spelling out the necessity of judicial supervision in the constitutional design. To summarize Hamilton (as John Marshall was later wont to do):

. . . Interpretation of the Constitution, the nation's fundamental law, is best left to the courts.

. . . Any law or act contrary to the Constitution is null and void.

. . . Congress must not be the sole judge of its own actions (as per the Separation of Powers). Courts are thus required for determining whether acts of Congress are within constitutional bounds.

. . . A fully independent judiciary is essential to ensure that judges can issue rulings of unconstitutionality without fear of retaliation.

Madison himself was so concerned about run-

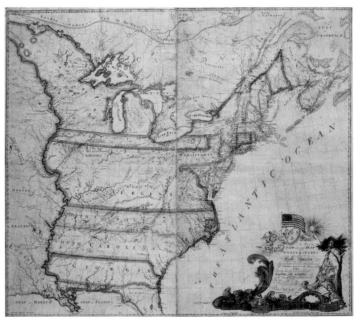

Abel Buell's *A New and correct Map of the United States of North America Layd down from the latest Observations and best Authority agreeable to the Peace of 1783*, published in 1784, was the first known map to display the American flag. Such maps were used, largely unsuccessfully, in litigation in state courts arising out of conflicting land claims during the Confederation period. The New Jersey Historical Society, Newark

Charles Willson Peale. *James Madison* (from life). c. 1792, Philadelphia. Oil on canvas, 23¼ × 19″. Thomas Gilcrease Institute of American History and Art, Tulsa, Oklahoma

away state legislatures that he kept urging the Framers to give Congress "a negative in all cases whatsoever, on the legislative acts of the states, as the king of Great Britain heretofore had."

Given the uncertainty of ratification, even ardent nationalists agreed that it would be best to leave the problem of invalid state laws to state courts and let them cope with their own legislatures. To that wishful thinking, Madison naturally responded that state judges would be highly vulnerable to political pressure, such as being sacked for decisions irksome to lawmakers, as in the cautionary Rhode Island case of *Trevett* v. *Weeden*. His point was well taken and contributed to Article III's eventual safeguards for federal judges. Even so, the Convention decisively rejected Madison's proposed congressional "negative" by a vote of seven states to three, doubtless because its political flaws eclipsed its merits.

We owe the Supremacy Clause to Luther Martin. A Maryland lawyer opposed to strong central government, Martin abhorred the proposed Constitution for its looming contraction of states' rights. Yet he was moved to suggest the words that suddenly connected its parts, sending power surging throughout. Martin composed the crucial sentence (Article VI) that made the Constitution and all federal laws and treaties "the supreme law of the land," binding "upon the Judges in every State."

After C.W. Peale. *Luther Martin.* Oil on canvas, 25¹/₈ × 20¹/₂". Maryland Historical Society, Baltimore

The Framers had provided only for a Supreme Court in Article III, leaving all further details of lower courts entirely to the discretion of Congress. In 1789 the First Congress provided those details in the First Judiciary Act. By amplifying Article III, this statute created the federal court system, a giant step in national development.

The Judiciary Act of 1789 was drafted by two Framers then serving as United States Senators—William Paterson of New Jersey (named an Associate Justice in 1793), and Oliver Ellsworth, a Connecticut lawyer who later became the nation's second Chief Justice. Their handiwork left the vast majority of American legal cases to the state courts. But the nature of federalism required a judicial back-up, a parallel court system committed to reinforcing the rule of law, the sovereignty of the Constitution, and the dual citizenship of Americans.

In Philadelphia, many delegates had disputed the need for federal courts below the Supreme Court; they stressed the expense, and argued in favor of deciding all cases in state courts, with appeal only to the national high court. A compromise left the final choice to Congress. And in the First Judiciary Act, Congress created not one but two sets of lower federal courts, together with the specific composition of the Supreme Court itself.

At the primary level, the law established thirteen federal district courts, one for each state. Next, the country was divided into three federal judicial circuits (East, Middle, West), each with its own court. At the final level, Congress authorized a six-man Supreme Court (a Chief Justice and five Associate Justices) to meet at the national capital twice a year, with one session beginning on the first Monday in February and the other on the first Monday in August.

The circuit courts were given no judges of their own. Instead, each circuit court had three part-time members—a district judge and two Supreme Court Justices assigned to "circuit rid-

James Sharples. *William Paterson.* c. 1749. Pastel, 7¼ × 10″. Collection of the Supreme Court of the United States, Washington, D.C.

A Bill to Establish the Judicial Courts of the United States. 1789. The New York Public Library. Astor, Lenox and Tilden Foundations. Rare Book Division

ing" in addition to their high-court duties. Circuit courts met twice a year at each district court in their circuits. In practice, this required eight or nine sessions a year in several different states, forcing the Supreme Court Justices to spend inordinate periods of time on the road.

The jurisdiction conferred on the various federal courts by the First Judiciary Act was a barometer of national concerns at the time. Shipping was then the country's leading business, for example, so the new courts were to forge uniform maritime law in the process of settling admiralty cases that typically arose outside a state's borders, and often involved other nations as well. The district courts thus began as courts of original jurisdiction that handled admiralty and maritime cases, plus some federal crimes and a few other limited matters.

The circuit courts had both original and appellate jurisdiction. In the first category were diversity suits between citizens of different states, most criminal cases, and major disputes involving the

United States as a party. In addition, circuit courts heard appeals from the district courts in civil cases where the amount in controversy exceeded fifty dollars, and in admiralty cases where the amount exceeded $300.

Article III had given the Supreme Court original (and irrevocable) jurisdiction in two

Archibald Robertson (attr.) *View of New York from the Jupiter.* 1794. Watercolor, 24 × 30½″. Two French naval vessels lie in the harbor. Maritime law, as it related to domestic and foreign shipping, was of pressing importance to the new nation. Museum of the City of New York

kinds of disputes—those between states and those involving ambassadors, ministers, and consuls. But the Constitution empowered Congress to regulate the court's appellate jurisdiction, and the initial rules were strict. The Court could hear appeals from the federal circuit courts in civil cases, but only where the amount in dispute was greater than $2,000; it could also review state court decisions, but only those raising one kind of federal question.

Not until 1875 were lower federal courts allowed to hear all federal questions, a power exercised previously only by state courts. Not until 1891 was the Supreme Court itself allowed to review federal criminal cases.

As a matter of fact, the First Judiciary Act harbored several powerful devices that eventually made the new courts significant indeed. For one, it introduced a radically new legal tactic—the removal of cases from state courts to federal courts. Where claims exceeded $500, this privilege was open to certain litigants who might get fairer treatment in a federal court—aliens, for example. Another noteworthy provision in the 1789 law was the innocent-appearing clause in Section 13, purportedly authorizing the Supreme Court to issue writs of mandamus to public officials, such as the Secretary of State.

The most significant feature of the First Judiciary Act was its Section 25, which implemented the Supremacy Clause with a device that eventually (some twenty-seven years later) made federal law paramount over state action. Specifically, Section 25 empowered the Supreme Court to

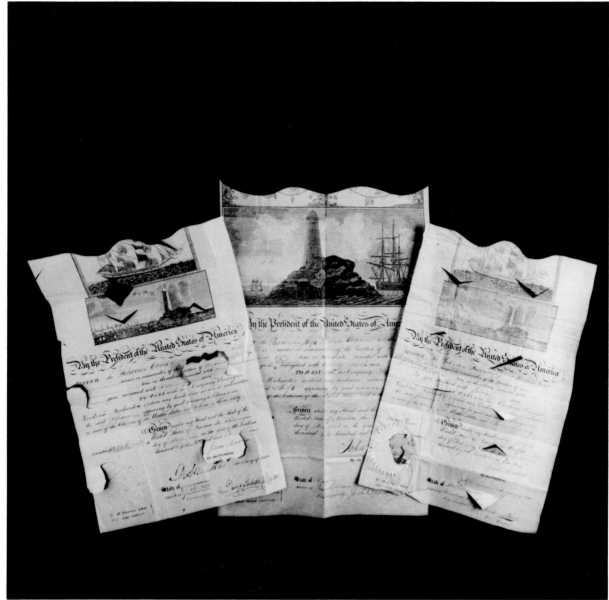

"Sea Letters," issued by the United States to American sea captains traveling in the Mediterranean. A treaty of 1795 with the Dey of Algiers made these documents valid passports guaranteeing protection against Barbary Pirates. Photograph by Jonathan Wallen. National Archives, Washington, D.C.

reverse or affirm state court decisions in which the state judges had rejected claims that a state law violated the Constitution or federal laws or treaties. As a result, the Supreme Court could now employ its appellate jurisdiction to check errant state courts and slowly impose constitutional order throughout the Union.

Section 25 was the target of incessant attack by states-righters, especially after 1810, when the Supreme Court increasingly struck down state laws, declaring them unconstitutional. In the immensely significant case of *Martin* v. *Hunter's Lessee* (1816), the Court decisively upheld Section 25 against a powerful challenge.

Congress has strengthened Section 25 at least twice since 1789, a record that tends to reinforce the value of the Court's self-restraint. The importance of this great power was summarized by Justice Holmes in the early 1900s. "I do not think the United States would come to an end if we [the Court] lost our power to declare an Act of Congress void," he wrote. "I do think the Union would be imperiled if we could not make that declaration as to the laws of the several states."

5

JUSTICES ON PROBATION

Representation of the FEDERAL CHARIOT, from *Bickerstaff's Boston Almanack, or, The Federal Calendar*, Boston, 1788. Men representing the thirteen states pull the "Federal Chariot," driven by Washington and Franklin. The end of the journey is ratification. American Antiquarian Society, Worcester

President Washington did his best to launch the Court with the strong impetus of his own prestige. After signing the First Judiciary Act on September 24, 1789, he submitted the names of six Supreme Court nominees to the Senate in a manner that produced confirmation in two days. He had chosen with care. All six Justices were veterans of either the drafting or the ratification of the Constitution, and some had participated in both.

James Wilson, one of Madison's main allies in Philadelphia, had led the ratification fight in Pennsylvania and was generally considered the young nation's leading constitutional scholar. John Rutledge of South Carolina had chaired the Committee on Detail; he was credited with writing the Supremacy Clause into the document when it was suggested by Luther Martin. John Jay had shone as the Confederation's equivalent of a foreign minister, helped write *The Federalist Papers*, and starred in the New York State ratifying convention. At forty-three, he was the first Chief Justice.

Jay was Washington's good friend and frequent advisor. In a letter enclosing the New

Yorker's commission, Washington expressed "singular pleasure" that a lawyer-diplomat so widely respected would now head "the department which must be considered the keystone of our political fabric." The President's warm words, the new Chief Justice responded, "will never cease to excite my best endeavour."

At the Court's first session in New York City's Royal Exchange Building on February 1, 1790, only three members were present, making less than a quorum. They promptly adjourned.

The next day, a quorum was obtained with the arrival of Justice John Blair (another Framer), together with his fellow Virginian, Edmund Randolph, now the country's first Attorney General. The occasion drew crowds of curious lawyers as well as laymen to the temporary courthouse at the foot of Manhattan's Broad Street, and the city's newspapers faithfully reported the Justices' actions, such as the admission of attorneys to Supreme Court practice and the important appointment of the Court's first Clerk—John Tucker of Massachusetts. The Justices commanded interest if not power: those first press reports were reprinted throughout the country.

John Trumbull. *Chief Justice John Jay.* Begun c. 1783; completed c. 1804–1808. Oil on canvas, 50³/₈ × 40¹/₂″. National Portrait Gallery, Washington, D.C.

Elias Boudinot, engraving after Thomas Sully. Boudinot was the first attorney admitted to the bar of the Supreme Court, on February 5, 1790. He served in the Continental Congress as a representative from New Jersey during the Revolution, and was its President in 1782. He later became the first President of the American Bible Society. Collection of the Supreme Court of the United States, Washington, D.C.

Several days later, the Court reached its fullest strength when Justice James Iredell arrived from North Carolina, replacing Washington's first choice, Robert Hanson Harrison, who had died en route to New York. Iredell was selected by Washington in recognition of his hard work for ratification in North Carolina. That state was also underrepresented in the Federalist administration. At thirty-eight, Iredell was the Court's youngest member and the last to join it, since John Rutledge (irked at being a mere Justice rather than Chief) could never bring himself to attend any of the sessions.

With virtually no cases to decide, the Court's first term was mainly ceremonial and ended after nine days. The second term, in August of 1790, lasted only two days. In 1791 and 1792, having moved to the national capital in Philadelphia, where the nation's highest court shared quarters with the mayor's court, the Justices failed to decide any cases. Before the Court moved again, to Washington, Philadelphia's yellow fever epidemics had forced the Justices to cancel three years' worth of August terms.

Throughout that first decade, nearly all signifi-cant federal cases were decided not in the Supreme Court but in the circuit courts below, and often without any precedents to light the way. While this caused some feelings of unease, there was pressure to keep the high court docket lean. For one thing, purists questioned the propriety of Supreme Court Justices serving on circuit courts in cases later reviewed by the high court. In those years, even their relatively important decisions were vitiated by the delivery of opinions seriatim, one for each Justice for each case. Instead of speaking with a single clear voice of final authority, the Justices risked sounding like a debating society.

The Court's major burden was circuit riding. As exponents of the Constitution, the Justices performed a nationalizing service. Charges to juries were especially useful for implanting legal values in local minds. Here, for example, is Jay charging a federal grand jury in New York on April 4, 1790:

> Let it be remembered that civil liberty consists not in a right to every man to do just what he pleases; but it consists in an equal

Letter from President Washington, to the Justices of the Supreme Court, April 3, 1790, on the commencement of the first Circuits. Washington Papers, Library of Congress, Washington, D.C.

Above: Supreme Court Chamber in Independence Hall, Philadelphia, where the Supreme Court sat in 1791. Library of Congress, Washington, D.C. Below: Supreme Court Chamber in Old City Hall, Philadelphia, where the Supreme Court sat from late 1791 to 1800. Library of Congress, Washington, D.C.

right to all the citizens to have, enjoy, and do, in peace, security and without molestation, whatever the equal and constitutional laws of the country admit to be consistent with the public good.

As early as 1792, however, weary of holding twenty-seven circuit court sessions a year in thirteen states, plus those of the Supreme Court itself, the Justices wrote to George Washington seeking relief "in strong and explicit terms." The President conveyed their complaints to Congress. The lawmakers were not moved. In a Senate speech in 1810, for example, Pennsylvania Democrat Truman Lacock insisted that Justices allowed to linger in the capital would become "completely cloistered within the City of Washington, and their decisions, instead of emanating from enlarged and liberalized minds, would assume a severe and local character." Even heads as wise and gray as theirs might be turned by the "dazzling splendors of the palace and the drawing room" and the "flattery and soothing attention of a designing Executive."

Circuit riding forced the typical Justice to spend far more time in the saddle or in a coach than on the bench. The average per Justice was about one thousand miles a year, and riders of the ever growing Southern circuit were known to clock ten thousand miles, using steamboats as well as horsepower. All this squandered judicial energy, to say nothing of exposing the Justices to bad weather, poor food, and disease. At least two Justices resigned from the Jay Court because of travel-related disabilities; the rigors of circuit-riding shortened the tempers of others, and doubtless their lives as well.

Historians tend to slight the Jay years, implying that the Supreme Court's true birth awaited John Marshall. But Marshall's majestic assertions of judicial power had their roots in the Court's early years. Many grew out of a series of shrewd insights and quiet moves by which the Jay Court provided opportunities that Marshall later seized. In various cases of the Jay era, writes Robert G. McCloskey, author of *The American Supreme Court*, "the Justices quite evidently assumed in their opinions that they *could* set unconstitutional state or federal laws aside, but

66

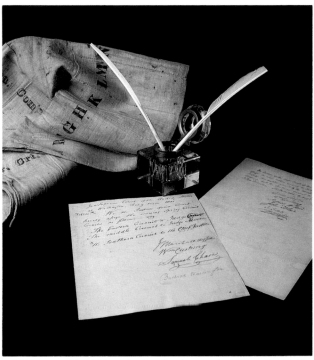

Allotment Orders dated August 11, 1792, and February 10, 1801, assigning Justices to their Circuits. Collection of the Supreme Court of the United States, Washington, D.C. Photo: Lee Troell Anderson

An American stagecoach, from Isaac Wald's *Travels through the States of North America, and the Provinces of Upper and Lower Canada, during the years 1795, 1796, and 1797*. Wald traveled to Philadelphia by stage with a Justice of the Supreme Court and several southern lawyers. The Justice was either Justice Chase or Justice Iredell, and John Marshall was among the lawyers. The New York Public Library. Astor, Lenox and Tilden Foundations

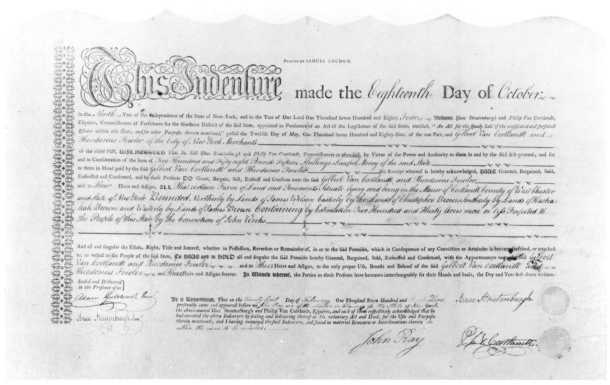

Conveyance from the Commissioners of Forfeitures, New York, October 18, 1784, deeding two hundred and thirty acres in The Bronx, "forfeited to the People of this State by the Conviction of John Wicks," to Gilbert Van Cortlandt and Theodosius Fowler. Litigation over American obligations to Tories and British citizens after the Revolution dragged on for years, giving rise to two important cases decided by the pre-Marshall Court, *Chisholm* v. *Georgia* and *Ware* v. *Hylton*. The New York Public Library. Astor, Lenox and Tilden Foundations. Vanderbilt Papers

they elected in these circumstances not to do so. This approach had the double advantage of disarming critics concerned with the outcome of the immediate cause and at the same time adding a brick or two to the edifice of precedent on which the judicial future would depend."

Jay firmly believed that the Court's authority depended on its ability to stand clear of the other branches of government and develop its own identity. In 1793, for example, President Washington sought the Court's advice on the legal complexities arising from his struggle to keep America neutral in the Anglo-French war sweeping Europe. Jay bluntly urged the President to "get that advice from the heads of the departments, that is the cabinet members."

The Supreme Court itself would not furnish even presidents with advisory opinions about foreign policy or any other matter. The high court, Jay insisted, must never depart from its constitutional function as a strictly judicial body. Jay saw clearly that the Court's perceived independence was essential to public belief in its impartiality. And that belief was the Court's strength: it had no other.

The early Justices made progress in carving out the Court's boundaries with respect to Congress as well as to the President. Although John Marshall decisively stated the Court's power to review acts of Congress in 1803 (*Marbury* v. *Madison*), the fact is that John Jay's Court had already done the same thing twelve years earlier (first *Hayburn* case). The difference was that Jay was presiding at the time (April 1791) not over the Supreme Court but rather over the circuit court in New York City. At issue was an act of Congress requiring Justices on circuit to settle pension claims of disabled war veterans. Jay and his two colleagues held that the Constitution empowered Congress to assign the courts only to "properly judicial" duties. Since the pension chore subjected judges to supervision by the executive and review by the legislature, they ruled the act unconstitutional as a violation of the separation of powers.

A year later, the *Hayburn* case came before the Supreme Court itself, but Congress by then had "provided in another way" for aiding veterans, so the high court did not rule. The circuit precedent thus stood intact, a trail blaze waiting for

Marshall a decade later.

While sitting on circuit courts, Jay and other Supreme Court Justices upheld federal supremacy over *state* laws as early as 1791. In Connecticut, for example, a state law permitted American creditors to add interest to prewar debts owed them by British subjects. The federal judges struck down that law as a violation of the peace treaty with England. In a Rhode Island case in 1792, they voided a state law immunizing a debtor from arrest and attachment of his property; they called the law an unconstitutional impairment of the obligation of contracts.

But one attempted giant step forward by the Supreme Court itself proved to be an instructive setback. Article III extended federal judicial power to controversies "between a state and citizens of another state." During the ratification debates, Anti-Federalists warned that this meant any state could be sued in federal court by citizens of other states—a prospect unthinkable to defenders of state sovereignty.

Federalists such as Hamilton and Madison had scoffed at that notion, citing the doctrine of sovereign immunity from suit ("the king can do no wrong"). Even then, sovereign immunity was questionable, since the original meaning could have been the reverse—i.e., "the king has no right to do wrong." But the Federalists argued further that the order of words in Article III ("between a state and citizens of another state") referred only to disputes in which the state was plaintiff, and the clause therefore confirmed state immunity. At the Virginia ratifying convention, for example, John Marshall called it "not rational to suppose that the sovereign power should be dragged before a court. The intent is to enable states to recover claims [against] individuals residing in other states."

In fact, the Anti-Federalist reading of Article III was accurate—or so ruled the Supreme Court in *Chisholm* v. *Georgia* (1793), when it upheld the right of a South Carolinian to sue Georgia for the recovery of debt.

Early in the Revolution, a Tory merchant named Captain Robert Farquhar had sold $170,000 worth of goods to the state of Georgia. He never collected: Georgia refused to pay, having by law erased all Tory claims and, in effect, expropriated the goods Farquhar had sold. Years later, after his death in England, Georgia

Entry in the Minutes of the Supreme Court, February 22, 1796. The only business concluded on that day was the admission of Alexander Hamilton to the Bar of the Court. Collection of the Supreme Court of the United States, Washington, D.C.

still refused to pay, even though his executor, Alexander Chisholm, argued that the law in question had been enacted after the sale and should not be retroactive.

Chisholm lived in South Carolina. To get his due from Georgia, he brought an original suit against that state in the Supreme Court, assuming that Article III permitted him to do so. His private suit, under then standard procedure, was handled by Attorney General Edmund Randolph, who particularly wanted the Supreme Court to enforce any judgment it might render against the defendant state.

Georgia refused to appear in her own defense, but sent a written "remonstrance and protestation" invoking sovereign immunity and denying the Court's jurisdiction. After hearing Randolph's argument, the Court entered a default judgment against Georgia and took up the issue of jurisdiction.

Each of the five Justices present for the argument (Thomas Johnson was absent and soon to resign) filed a separate opinion, but the four upholding Alexander Chisholm generally concluded that Georgia's reading of Article III was inconsistent with the Constitution's primary values of federal supremacy and individual liberty. Justice Wilson attacked sovereign immunity. In a federal Union founded by popular consent for the benefit of all, he said, a state government had no right to renege on its obligations by hiding

John Trumbull. *Justice John Rutledge.* 1791. Oil on wood, 3³/₄ × 3 ¹/₈″. Yale University Art Gallery, New Haven

behind state sovereignty. Allowing it to do so would subvert the Constitution's guarantees, notably the ban on impairment of contracts. "As to the purposes of the Union," Wilson wrote, "Georgia is not a sovereign state."

In much the same vein, Chief Justice Jay saw Article III as the vehicle for carrying out the Preamble's second great purpose (to "establish justice"). To illustrate the anomalies of sovereign immunity, Jay noted that Georgia itself was currently suing two South Carolinians in the Supreme Court, while opposing the correlative right. "The citizens of Georgia are content with a right of suing citizens of other states; but are not content that citizens of other states should have a right to sue them."

Jay was sure that if the Constitution permitted a state to sue other states—that is, all the people of one state to sue all the people of another—"it plainly follows that suability and state sovereignty are not incompatible." As to the notion that Article III's language confined federal jurisdiction to cases where the state was plaintiff, Jay found it "inconceivable" that the Framers would "convey that meaning in words so incompetent."

Justice Iredell alone dissented, arguing that the Court's powers under the Constitution were only potential and could not be implemented without specific congressional authority. He found no language in the First Judiciary Act covering Chisholm's case. He was quite certain no such authority had ever or would ever attach to "a compulsive suit against a state for the recovery of money." By limiting his dictum to suits in assumpsit (an action to recover damages from a breach of contract or promise), Iredell perhaps implied that states might be sued on other grounds.

Except for Iredell, who must have been keenly aware of popular feelings in his own state of North Carolina, the Justices were apparently unanimous in regarding their joint rejection of sovereign immunity as a defense of constitutional liberty. In the abstract, they were right.

Chisholm outraged Georgia. Indeed, the legislature there immediately passed a bill declaring that anyone who enforced the Supreme Court's decision would be "guilty of felony and shall suffer death, without benefit of clergy, by hanging." The bill did not become law. But Georgia's reaction was hardly an isolated one.

All the states were stunned by the implications of *Chisholm* v. *Georgia*. For one thing, the Supreme Court had as much as said that Union did not permit Georgia or any other state to take its sovereignty for granted.

But the real source of the public outcry was not the Court's distaste for the dogma of sovereign immunity. It was a grassroots fear of the probable result: soaring taxes. The decision left every state ripe for plucking by long evaded creditors. Tories could now sue the states to recover properties sequestered during the Revolution; speculators could cash in on state obligations bought in wartime for a few cents on the dollar. *Chisholm* v. *Georgia* could very well have driven every state's finances into the federal courts, forcing the states to satisfy all those creditors by sharply raising taxes.

With dazzling speed, Georgia mobilized the other states to join in overriding the Court by devising the Eleventh Amendment to the Constitution. No state, it says, can be sued in federal court by the citizens of another state or a friendly country. For those who felt that complete sovereign immunity is antithetical to constitutional liberty, the Eleventh Amendment was at least preferable to other possibilities. In New York, for example, there was a proposal to forbid "any suit to be brought against any state in any manner whatever." The Eleventh Amendment in fact blocked only two kinds of plaintiffs from suing states. Federal courts retained jurisdiction over suits brought by states against other states, by the United States, and by citizens against their own states.

Even so, the Eleventh Amendment was a blow to the Court's prestige. The nation's highest court had found itself at odds with higher authority—a popular consensus flatly rejecting its decision. Future Justices would be overridden twice again in this fashion: by the Thirteenth Amendment (abolishing slavery) and the Sixteenth (authorizing income taxes). There has been no recurrence since 1913.

Yet the early Justices bounced back from *Chisholm* in the important case of *Ware* v. *Hylton* (1796), another example of legal fallout from the Revolution's financial disorders. At issue was whether the Supremacy Clause required states to concede the supremacy of federal treaties over conflicting state laws.

In common with other states, Virginia had enacted a law that encouraged debtors to ignore their British creditors and instead satisfy their obligations by direct payments to the state in cheap paper money. But the 1783 peace treaty forbade either country to impede the other's citizens in recovering debts from its own citizens. The stakes were high: Virginians alone owed Britons some two million dollars.

Starting in 1791, British creditors pursued Virginia debtors in federal courts for five years before *Ware* v. *Hylton* finally reached the Supreme Court, where the debtors' counsel turned out to be John Marshall. In his only Supreme Court argument, Marshall assailed "those who wish to impair the sovereignty of Virginia." But the Justices were not moved. In a unanimous decision, the Court upheld the British creditors in an opinion by Justice Samuel Chase that, according to the late, renowned constitutional scholar, Edward S. Corwin, "remains to this day the most impressive assertion of the supremacy of national treaties over state laws."

Fortunately, the blow *Ware* v. *Hylton* dealt to

Ralph Earl. *Oliver Ellsworth and His Wife.* 1792. Oil on canvas, 76 × 85″. Painted four years before Ellsworth became the third Chief Justice of the United States Supreme Court. He and his wife, Abigail Wolcott, are shown seated in the library of their house, Elmwood, in Windsor, Connecticut. In his left hand, Ellsworth holds the Constitution. Wadsworth Atheneum, Hartford

state sovereignty did not provoke anything like the rage that had been ignited by *Chisholm* v. *Georgia.* And yet, the Court's role remained hazy.

For example, Chief Justice Jay found circuit riding "intolerable" and, beginning in 1794, managed to be absent from the Court entirely by serving as Ambassador to Britain as well as Chief Justice. He next ran successfully for the governorship of New York and resigned from the Supreme Court.

At that point, John Rutledge reappeared on the scene as Acting Chief Justice. He had resigned from the Court in 1791, lured away by what he considered the more important post of chief justice of South Carolina. Now the high court seemed to be worth Rutledge's attention, and he importuned President Washington for a recess appointment as John Jay's successor. But Rutledge lasted only for the length of the August 1795 term. The Senate rejected his nomination in December 1795.

Washington next turned to Justice William Cushing; he declined elevation. The President's third choice was Senator Oliver Ellsworth, a wealthy Connecticut lawyer noted for his organizing skills. The Senate was unable to reject one of its own, especially not the principal author of the First Judiciary Act, and Ellsworth was con-

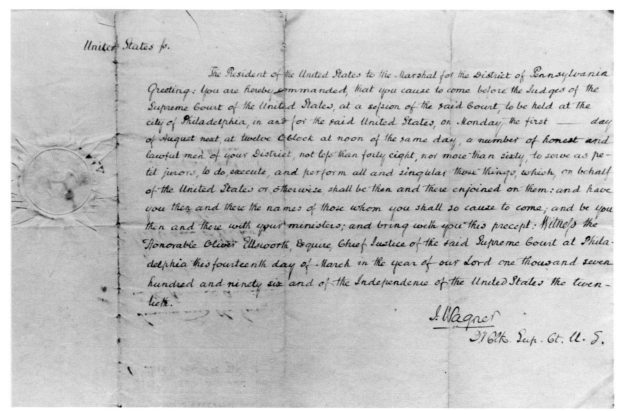

Venire Facias, 1796. Collection of the Supreme Court of the United States, Washington, D.C.

firmed a day after his nomination.

Ellsworth gave every sign of becoming a distinguished Chief Justice. But in 1799, only three years after his appointment, President John Adams borrowed the Chief's negotiating skills and sent him to Paris in an effort to prevent war between France and the United States. The mission destroyed Ellsworth's health. When he resigned from the Court even before returning home, Adams looked backward and nominated John Jay for a second tour as Chief Justice. Jay struck Adams as the country's "best security . . . against the increasing dissolution of morals," and the Senate rapidly confirmed him.

But Jay, whom Adams had neglected to consult beforehand, declined this second appointment. The Supreme Court had no chance to survive as a coequal branch of the national government, he said. In a harshly candid letter, Jay told Adams why he had resigned five years earlier:

> I left the bench perfectly convinced that under a system so defective it [the court] could not obtain the energy, weight, and dignity which was essential to its affording due

support to the national government; nor acquire the public confidence and respect which, as the last resort of the justice of the nation, it should possess.

Jay's rebuff came in December 1800, just after Adams had been defeated for reelection to a second term. The nation had wearied of the old guard Federalists, headed by Adams, and chosen a new party, Thomas Jefferson's Democratic-Republicans. This shift of power had important consequences for the judiciary.

In the 1800 campaign, the strongly nationalist views of federal judges appointed by two Federalist presidents had become a bitter partisan issue. Much controversy arose from the hated Sedition Act, passed by a Federalist Congress in 1798 for the unabashed purpose of punishing critics of the Adams administration. The law made it a crime to publish or even utter "false, scandalous and malicious" criticism of high government officials.

Federalist judges enforced the law with gusto. Even Supreme Court Justices were involved. In their circuit-riding role, they presided over the trials of outspoken Republicans, including Con-

Cinque-tetes, or the Paris Monster. In an engraving of 1798, a monster representing the French Directory demands money from the three American envoys. The Henry E. Huntington Library and Art Gallery, San Marino, California

An ACT in addition to the act entitled An Act for the punishment of certain crimes against the United States, November 13, 1797. The Sedition Act. National Archives, Washington, D.C.

gressmen and newspaper editors. Justice Samuel Chase personally lobbied for the Sedition Act and then proceeded to try alleged seditionists as if he were prosecutor rather than judge. Chase imposed the law's harshest sentences; after convicting Massachusetts editor David Brown under the act for criticizing President Adams, for example, Chase sent him to jail for eighteen months.

In the trial of John Fries, a Pennsylvanian whose strenuous support of Jefferson resulted in his being accused of treason, Justice Chase accepted only jurors who flatly declared their prejudice against the defendant. Chase informed Fries, who had no lawyer, that anything he said could be held against him, "but if you say anything to your justification, it is not evidence." When, predictably, Fries was convicted, Chase sentenced him to death. Fries survived only because President Adams rejected his cabinet's advice and set aside the sentence.

6

THE TESTING OF JOHN MARSHALL

Gabriel Fevret de Saint-Memin. *John Marshall.* 1808. Pencil and chalk on colored paper, 20½ × 15½". Duke University Museum of Art, Durham, North Carolina

In January 1801, John Adams was a lame-duck President and the House had not yet resolved the tie in electoral votes between his victorious Republican rivals, Thomas Jefferson and Aaron Burr. Seizing this opportunity, Adams nominated a new Chief Justice—his secretary of state, John Marshall, then forty-five. Confirmed by the Senate on January 27, 1801, Marshall would devote the rest of his life—thirty-four years—to making the Supreme Court everything John Jay doubted it could ever become.

In February 1801, the House broke the Burr-Jefferson electoral deadlock, naming Jefferson as the nation's third president. Before he took office on March 4, however, the outgoing Federalists made other moves designed to brake the incoming Republicans.

One was the Judiciary Act of 1801, passed by Congress a few days before Jefferson's selection. The law eliminated circuit riding (the most recent victim of which had been Justice Iredell, whose death at forty-eight was attributed largely to the effects of riding circuit more than 2,000 miles a year). The same law created six new circuit courts, to be manned by sixteen new federal judges and numerous government lawyers, clerks, marshals, etc. The entire federal judiciary then numbered only nineteen judges, and the growing country surely needed sixteen more.

But the law also reduced the number of Supreme Court Justices from six to five, guaranteeing that when the next vacancy occurred, President Jefferson could not fill it. Adams thus confirmed Jefferson's lament that despite his victory, the federal judiciary would "remain a strong fortress in possession of the enemy."

Another last-minute law enabled Adams to appoint forty-two Federalist loyalists to five-year terms as justices of the peace for the sparsely populated District of Columbia. By midnight

Textile banner celebrating Thomas Jefferson's election in 1801. National Museum of American History, Smithsonian Institution, Washington, D.C.

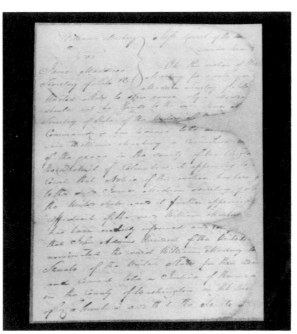

Show-cause order filed by William Marbury, and served on James Madison. December, 1801. Damaged in the Capitol fire of 1898. Photograph by Jonathan Wallen. National Archives, Washington, D.C.

March 3rd—the end of the Adams administration—the commissions for all these appointees had been signed and sealed. But most appointees never received the actual documents. The man responsible for delivering them—Secretary of State John Marshall (now also Chief Justice)—considered the commissions legally in effect, whether or not they were literally in the appointees' hands.

When President Jefferson discovered all this, he immediately ordered Marshall's successor, James Madison, to impound the undelivered commissions and consign them to one of the pigeonholes for which the State Department even then was famous. It was this situation that brought the famous case of *Marbury* v. *Madison* before the Supreme Court.

In December 1801, William Marbury and four other Adams appointees sought the justice-of-the-peace commissions they had never received. Marbury, forty-one, was a prosperous land-owner and future Georgetown bank president. With his co-plaintiffs, he filed an original suit in the Supreme Court asking the Justices to issue a writ of mandamus—a direct order—commanding Secretary of State Madison to deliver the commissions.

Under common law, such writs required officials to perform their statutory duties. The Constitution itself had not empowered the Supreme

Court to issue writs of mandamus, but Congress had corrected that lack. According to the First Judiciary Act (Section 13), the Court had original jurisdiction over mandamus cases. Chief Justice Marshall duly assumed jurisdiction and ordered Secretary Madison to show cause during the Court's next term (June 1802), why the writs should not be issued.

Madison ignored Marshall's order. The State Department refused to let the plaintiffs even see their signed commissions. The documents may have actually been destroyed months before.

As President Jefferson saw it, the Court planned to use the Marbury case as a weapon against his administration. Thus in March 1802, after much heated debate, Congress repealed the Judiciary Act of 1801 and passed a new law that abolished the circuit courts, sent the Justices back to riding circuit, and put the Supreme Court on a new schedule of one annual term, beginning in February.

By no coincidence, the effect of passing the Judiciary Repeal Act *after* February 1802 was to eliminate the Court's June term and to postpone the arguments in *Marbury* v. *Madison*—indeed, to close down the Supreme Court for fourteen months between December 1801 and the start of the February term in 1803.

When the reconvened Court finally began examining *Marbury* witnesses on February 10,

1803, four Justices were present—Marshall, Chase, Paterson, and Bushrod Washington (the late President's nephew). The two absentees were either ill or traveling. By today's standards, given his personal involvement in the case, Marshall should have disqualified himself, but that would have left the Court without a quorum. Moreover, the footdragging tactics of the administration witnesses had a tonic effect upon the Chief Justice. He plunged ahead, presiding with scrupulous fairness.

The lawyer for the plaintiffs was Charles Lee, former Attorney General under both Adams and Washington. Lee set out to prove, first, that Adams and Marshall had properly completed the commissions; and second, that the Court was empowered to order James Madison to deliver them. Lee called three government employees, including Attorney General Levi Lincoln, all of whom professed ignorance of the commissions in question.

But Lee then produced affidavits from a State Department clerk and from James Marshall, stating that the commissions had in fact been signed and sealed. James said he knew all this because he had been on hand that night to help his brother, the Secretary of State/Chief Justice. As James told it, he had actually carried off some of the disputed commissions in his pocket, intending to deliver them to the appointees, but he had run out of time and so returned the papers to the State Department. In his closing argument, Charles Lee stressed both the Court's mandamus authority under Section 13 of the First Judiciary Act, and the need to defend judicial independence—a principle far more important to the plaintiffs, he said, than mere "emoluments or the dignity of office."

The administration refused to participate any further. No government lawyer appeared to argue or sum up the other side of the case.

Marshall had abandoned seriatim opinions in favor of consensual decisions, announced by one Justice (usually himself) representing the Court as a whole. But never before had the new procedure so amplified the Court's voice as on February 24, 1803, when Marshall read the Court's exhaustive decision in *Marbury* v. *Madison*. Marshall first strongly upheld the plaintiffs' legal right to their commissions and reprimanded Secretary Madison (meaning Jefferson) for with-holding them "in plain violation of national law."

When a cabinet officer fails to do his duty, Marshall said, a mandamus is the proper remedy. For the Court to issue one did not mean the Justices wished to pry into the Cabinet's secrets or investigate its performance. That notion was "absurd and excessive." The Court disclaimed "all pretensions" to any jurisdiction over "questions political in their nature." But while the Executive's dominion over political questions is invulnerable to judicial invasion, the Court is responsible for protecting individual rights. And where it finds such rights being violated by a cabinet officer, it must compel remedial action.

Marbury was fully entitled to a writ of mandamus, Marshall said, and the First Judiciary Act (Section 13) had empowered the Court to issue such writs to "persons holding office under the authority of the United States." Unhappily, Marshall added, Section 13 itself was unconstitutional. In short, the Court was powerless to issue a writ of mandamus in this case because Congress had wrongly authorized it to do so in the first place!

The Court could issue these writs only in cases that came before it on *appeal* from lower courts. Because the Marbury case had *originated* in the Supreme Court, he said, it was governed by different rules. The Constitution grants the Supreme Court original jurisdiction "in all cases affecting ambassadors, other public ministers and consuls, and those in which a state shall be a party." This case involved none of the above: William Marbury was in the right, but he had chosen the wrong court in which to seek redress.

For the first time, the Supreme Court had flatly declared an act of Congress unconstitutional, a precedent embedding the doctrine of judicial review in American law.

More than half a century would pass before the Court again overturned a national law. (Since then, the power has been used repeatedly.) But the true significance of *Marbury* became apparent much sooner. With Marshall's broad ruling as a stepping-stone, the Court began moving very slowly toward the day when it would rule a *state* law unconstitutional.

John Marshall had come a long way from the log cabin where he was born in 1755 near Germantown on the Virginia frontier. He was blessed

Silhouettes of Chief Justice John Marshall and his wife, Mary Willis Ambler, by J. Guenther, 1929. The former is after an 1808 portrait by Gabriel Fevret de Saint-Memin in the Duke University Museum of Art at Durham; the latter after a miniature by Thomas Marshall in the Marshall House at Richmond. Collection of the Supreme Court of the United States, Washington, D.C.

with strong parents. His mother, daughter of a Scottish clergyman, raised fifteen children, of whom Marshall was the first. His father, descended from Welsh immigrants, worked for George Washington as an assistant surveyor and pursued learning wherever he could find it. Although the elder Marshall's education was "very limited," according to his son, he nonetheless became a member of the Virginia House of Burgesses and introduced John as best he could to English literature and Blackstone's *Commentaries*. Apart from his father's efforts, Marshall had only two years of formal schooling, one under a clergyman, the other under a live-in tutor.

At twenty-one, John Marshall was already a veteran of the Revolutionary War. He had joined the Culpepper Minute Men and fought at the siege of Norfolk, then seen action at Brandywine, Monmouth, and Stony Point as a lieutenant in the third Virginia regiment. During the dismal winter at Valley Forge, his athletic feats helped to cheer the members of Washington's frozen army. He was nicknamed "Silver Heels" for his prowess at footracing and other games. He left the army as a twenty-four-year-old captain.

Unlike his father and later his own sons, who kept moving westward, Marshall turned east to find his future. His frontier stretched back to the headwaters of national power. The practice of

law seemed to point the way. America was run by lawyers, and a young man aspiring to join their ranks at that time needed talent more than credentials.

Marshall's entire formal legal training spanned six weeks of lectures at the College of William and Mary. True, the lecturer was the renowned George Wythe, America's first law professor, Jefferson's legal mentor, and one of the first American judges (in 1782) to endorse judicial review—the doctrine that Marshall would ultimately turn into a mighty judicial dynamo.

Licensed to practice in 1780, only six months after the lectures, he began penniless and with only rudimentary legal knowledge.

As a green young Richmond lawyer, Marshall was so poor that his complete law library consisted of his notes from reading a borrowed copy of Francis Bacon's *Abridgement* of English law. He learned law by trial and error, and the pressure to succeed against stiff competition was apparently a good teacher. Slowly, case by case, he began to build a thriving practice as a specialist in defending Virginians against their prewar British creditors. As the most popular cause around, it was a natural conduit to politics.

Within three years of attending Wythe's lectures, Marshall had been elected to the Virginia state legislature and married Mary Willis

The Great Hall of the John Marshall House, Richmond, Virginia. An 1834 portrait of John Marshall by William James Hubard hangs over the fireplace. The breakfront was a gift to the Marshalls in 1790; it contains porcelain acquired by Marshall in France. Photograph by Rob Dementi.

Ambler, daughter of the Virginia state treasurer. Marshall was known for positively doting on "Dearest Polly," whose fragile state of health required his unremitting care. (Polly eventually had ten children, six of whom survived.)

By 1789, Marshall had figured prominently in Virginia's constitutional convention and was considered one of the state's leading Federalists. President Washington, a family friend, wanted to appoint him United States Attorney for Virginia, but Marshall gracefully declined. In fact, he began to establish a pattern of refusing higher and higher office, including United States Attorney General in 1795, Supreme Court Justice in 1798, and Secretary of War in 1800.

Even so, Marshall was intensely loyal to his friends, among them John Adams, and in 1800 the President persuaded him to become Secretary of State. That fall, when the voters rejected the Federalists, the Chief Justiceship could not have been further from Marshall's mind. But suddenly Oliver Ellsworth resigned, John Jay refused the job, and President Adams turned to Marshall, saying, "I believe I must nominate you." Recounting the incident later, Marshall wrote, "I had never before heard myself named for the office, and had never even thought of it."

Marbury enraged President Jefferson; he saw judicial review as tantamount to giving Federalist judges veto power over the Republican administration. A week after the decision, the Marshall Court responded with a disarming surprise. At issue in *Stuart* v. *Laird* was the right of the Republican Congress to repeal the Judiciary Act of 1801 and send Supreme Court Justices back to circuit riding. Instead of using their right of judicial review to overturn the Repeal Act of 1802, the Justices upheld the law as a perfectly legitimate exercise of congressional power, even though all of them dreaded their return to the circuit. Speaking for the Court, Justice Paterson affirmed the constitutional authority of Congress "to establish from time to time, such inferior tribunals as they may think proper; and to transfer a cause from one tribunal to another."

This little sidestep, a case of Marshallian wisdom, helped deter a new Republican tactic, the use of impeachment to try to oust the five Federalist Justices—Marshall, Chase, Cushing,

Benjamin Henry Latrobe. *View of the City of Richmond from the South side of the James River.* 1798. Watercolor, pencil, pen and ink, 7 × 10¼″. The capitol, designed by Thomas Jefferson, dominates the view. On a hill in the distance, to the left, can be seen the house once owned by Associate Justice Bushrod Washington. Maryland Historical Society, Baltimore

Paterson, and Bushrod Washington. The Court's attackers began with Chase, a maverick whose partisan politicking had made him particularly vulnerable. In voting to impeach him on March 12, 1804, the House supported eight charges against Chase, including his conduct during the Fries treason trial and his anti-Republican tirade before a federal grand jury in May 1803.

When the Senate trial finally began a year later, in February 1805, Vice President Burr presided with studied impartiality, greatly irritating President Jefferson, who had openly pressured the Senators for conviction. In the end the impeachment managers could not mobilize the required two-thirds of the Senate to convict Chase on a single one of the House's eight articles of impeachment. The Justice was acquitted on March 1, 1805, partly because, by upholding the Repeal Act of 1802, the Court had dampened the anti-judicial fervor of many Senators. As a result, the Court had survived its first and only such political assault, creating a major deterrent against partisan attacks in the future.

In a special message to Congress in February

1807, President Jefferson ordered Aaron Burr arrested on sight and proclaimed him guilty of treason "beyond question." The charge derived from the former vice president's alleged scheme to carve a separate nation out of the Western territories. John Marshall's unavoidable role in the Burr case inevitably deepened Jefferson's hostility toward the Supreme Court.

When two of Burr's arrested associates petitioned the Court for a writ of habeas corpus, challenging their detention by federal officials, the Jefferson-controlled Senate passed a bill suspending habeas corpus. But the House refused to go along, whereupon the Court, affirming its power to issue writs of habeas corpus, ordered the suspects released on the ground that the government lacked sufficient evidence to convict them of treason. Jefferson viewed this ruling *(Ex parte Bollman)* as yet another affront to his presidential authority; Federalists cheered it as a blow for civil liberties.

In Richmond, on March 30, 1807, Burr himself was brought before John Marshall, acting in his capacity as Circuit Justice. Marshall found sufficient evidence to hold Burr only on a misde-

79

Chief Justice John Marshall on the Circuit, holding forth in a tavern. The Chief Justice's clothing is in its characteristic disarray. Note that while Marshall is wearing old-fashioned knee breeches, his interlocutors are in trousers. It was considered a great blow for democracy when Chief Justice Marshall's successor, Roger B. Taney, appeared at his swearing in wearing trousers. Library of Congress, Washington, D.C.

meanor charge—violating the neutrality law by planning an expedition against Mexico. Over Jefferson's opposition, Marshall also freed Burr on bail. Moreover, he granted Burr's own motion for a subpoena *duces tecum* (under penalty you shall bring with you), ordering the President himself to appear in court bearing evidence seized by federal agents. Jefferson rejected the subpoena, as Burr had expected, so that no jury ever saw the material—which conceivably might have been incriminating.

In rebuffing the subpoena (and a similar one later), Jefferson did not simply remain silent. He explained his position, a form of acknowledgment better than none. A President must not obey a judicial order to appear in court with unedited state papers, he said. Compliance would endanger executive independence, which the President is duty-bound to uphold.

Marshall had carefully ruled that while the documents must be produced, they would first be used only for his private assessment of their relevance to Burr's case. But Jefferson was willing to provide Marshall only with expurgated papers, and without a personal appearance. No

presidential papers were used in the trial. Although the confrontation thus evaporated, Marshall had managed to establish the precedent (to be cited 167 years later in *United States* v. *Richard M. Nixon*) that even a President cannot totally ignore a court order to produce criminal evidence in his possession.

But Jefferson was hardly through with Burr. On June 24, 1807, Burr was indicted for treason, as well as for the previously-mentioned misdemeanor, by a grand jury consisting of two Federalists and fourteen Jeffersonians. During the subsequent treason trial, which lasted from August 17th to September 3rd, Jefferson was so avid for conviction that he might as well have been the prosecutor. To entice Burr's alleged accomplices to testify against him, for example, the President blatantly offered them everything from blanket pardons to lifetime jobs.

Marshall made every effort to shield the defendant from a runaway conviction. For a President to accuse a political enemy of treason was, after all, a matter of concern to a free country. Burr was clearly a plotter: did that make him a traitor?

Citing English common law, the government

John Wesley Jarvis. *Justice Samuel Chase*. 1811. Oil on canvas, 28¼ × 23″. National Portrait Gallery, Smithsonian Institution, Washington, D.C.

John Vanderlyn. *Aaron Burr.* 1802. Oil on canvas, 22¼ × 16½″. The New-York Historical Society

argued that mere contemplation of treason is the same as participating in it. But such a standard had hardly satisfied the American Framers, who declared in Article III (Section 3) of the Constitution: "Treason against the United States shall consist only in levying War against them, or in adhering to their Enemies, giving them aid and comfort. No Person shall be convicted of Treason unless on the Testimony of two Witnesses to the same overt Act, or on Confession in open Court."

The government's case against Burr was decidedly thin. His main co-plotter, General James Wilkinson, appeared for the prosecution but impressed the jury unfavorably. Burr's lawyers showed that another government witness had been paid for his testimony.

In his charge to the jury, Marshall defined treason so narrowly that Burr's conviction on the available evidence was virtually impossible. Treason required an overt act—actually "levying war" against the United States, or actively aiding and comforting the country's enemies. Moreover, each overt act must be specified in the indictment and then corroborated by two independent witnesses. Lacking such proof, Marshall declared,

the accused should be acquitted. With those instructions, Burr's jury needed only twenty-five minutes to do just that. Soon after, Burr was also found not guilty on the misdemeanor charge of planning an attack on Mexico.

Jefferson was appalled by Burr's escape from the law's clutches. To make it easier to remove federal judges, he proposed a constitutional amendment ending lifetime tenure in favor of fixed terms, and permitting the President himself to remove judges with the consent of two-thirds of each house of Congress. But the proposal went nowhere—nor did a later bill aimed at broadening the law of treason.

Meanwhile, the Court continued its unavailing search for a decent home. By 1808, the Justices' ground-floor room under the Capitol had fallen into such a state of disrepair that they moved into the House of Representatives' former library. Those quarters proved so cold that a year later they switched their winter session to the warmer premises of Long's Tavern, scene of the first Inaugural Ball, on a site now occupied by the Library of Congress.

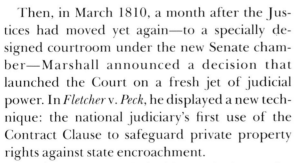

Subpoena issued by Chief Justice Marshall against Aaron Burr, March 30, 1807. Virginia State Library, Richmond

Charles Willson Peale. *General James Wilkinson.* 1797. Oil on canvas, 24 × 20″. Independence National Historical Park Collection, Philadelphia

Then, in March 1810, a month after the Justices had moved yet again—to a specially designed courtroom under the new Senate chamber—Marshall announced a decision that launched the Court on a fresh jet of judicial power. In *Fletcher* v. *Peck,* he displayed a new technique: the national judiciary's first use of the Contract Clause to safeguard private property rights against state encroachment.

In 1795 the Georgia legislature had passed a law authorizing the sale of thirty-five million acres of the state's potentially richest farmland—most of what is now Alabama and Mississippi. The fortunate recipients of this immense grant were assorted speculators who called themselves the Yazoo Land Company. They paid the state $500,000, or considerably less than two cents per acre (a miniscule fraction of the land's value), and then immediately unloaded large tracts on equally avaricious Northerners for whatever the market would bear. Some land went for ten cents per acre, still a bonanza for buyers and sellers alike.

It turned out that the Yazoo speculators had secured their grant by bribing every single mem-

ber of the Georgia legislature, except one, to sell the state land at giveaway prices. This revelation inflamed the voters of Georgia. An entirely new legislature was elected and it quickly rescinded the Yazoo grants. The state repossessed the land and refused to surrender title to any of it.

Weary of waiting, the buyers sought title by suing the sellers in Georgia. They lost: the state courts upheld the legislative revocation of the land grants. So the buyers turned to the federal courts and their case finally reached the Supreme Court, where it was pleaded by a Massachusetts lawyer named Joseph Story, who was destined (two years later at the age of thirty-two) to become the youngest Supreme Court Justice in history. Story argued that the buyers' titles remained valid because the rescinding act was unconstitutional—a violation of Article I (Section 10), which forbids any state to pass any law "impairing the Obligation of Contracts."

Georgia's lawyers argued that the Contract Clause obviously applied to contracts between private individuals, not to grants from states to individuals. And whatever it was, it had been obtained by fraud in contempt of the public

Photograph of East Capitol Street and 1st Street, taken from the Capitol by J.F. Jarvis, showing Carroll Row in the right foreground. Long's Tavern, where the Court held winter sessions in 1808, was in the building on the left in Carroll Row. The site is now occupied by the Library of Congress. Library of Congress, Washington, D.C.

interest; it was worthless, and Georgia had every right to repudiate it.

John Marshall, speaking for a unanimous Court, upheld Story's clients, ruling that the original land grant was a valid contract and, therefore, the buyers' titles were sound. But Marshall did not explicitly declare the rescinding act unconstitutional. The Contract Clause had not yet been sufficiently expounded for him to rely on that ground alone.

Upholding Georgia's right to repeal the grant, he said, would empower any legislature to remove anyone's vested property rights for any reason it saw fit. And that the Court would not permit. A legislature could still repeal its predecessors' laws, but it could not erase the obligations incurred by those laws. "When, then, a law is in its nature a contract, when absolute rights have vested under that contract, a repeal of the law cannot devest [sic] those rights."

Fletcher v. *Peck* not only unlimbered the Contract Clause for future exercise; it was the first Supreme Court decision to strike down a state law as unconstitutional.

The way was now clear for the Marshall Court to begin a quarter-century of extraordinary constitutional creativity, vastly strengthening the Union and slowly turning the hard-won right of judicial independence into the hallmark of a Supreme Court truly supreme.

The publication of Guillaume Delisle's 1718 map, *Carte de la Louisiane et du Cours du Mississipi*, coincided with the beginning of land fever in the Mississippi Valley, inspired by the dealings of the notorious French financier John Law. Here, "Yasous" (Yazoo) can be found northeast of Natchez. Private Collection

7

MARSHALL'S AMERICA: GREAT POWERS FOR GREAT TASKS

After the British burned the Capitol in 1814, allegedly using Supreme Court documents as kindling, the Justices spent four terms in makeshift quarters, including the future Bell Tavern.

For the first time, the Court began turning abstract nouns—Supremacy Clause, Contract Clause, Necessary and Proper Clause, Commerce Clause—into active verbs commanding the states to look outward and recognize their common interest in building a peaceful Union and a prosperous economy.

In Marshall's mind, there was a distinction between "political questions," which the Court must avoid, and those issues it must confront.

In the forbidden category were all matters that the Constitution assigned to the sole discretion of the "political" (elective) branches. In *Marbury*, for example, Marshall had disavowed any judicial interest in the President's job performance; in *Fletcher*, he refused to void an otherwise sound law solely on the ground that its makers were bribed to pass it. The Court's restraint in such matters was pragmatic as well as constitutional. Political questions were those impervious to judicial solution.

In the Court's apparent weakness—its insulation from the political process—lay its strength.

From the first day of its inaugural session, the Supreme Court had been empowered to review state court decisions. Congress had so provided in the Judiciary Act of 1789. Under Section 25, the Supreme Court could review cases in which state judges had rejected claims that state actions violated the Constitution, or federal laws, or treaties. The losing party in such a case could petition the Supreme Court for a "writ of error." If the Justices agreed that the state court had erred, they could issue an order overturning its decision and whatever state law was involved.

The threshold issue in *Martin* v. *Hunter's Lessee* (1816) was not the legitimacy of Section 25 but something more mundane—the legal ownership of 300,000 acres of Virginia land. The original owner was Britain's Lord Fairfax, who had died in 1781, leaving the land to his nephew, Denny Martin. But Martin was an English citizen: Virginia not only declared that aliens had no right to inherit land within its borders; it also confiscated the Fairfax estate during the Revolution and parceled it out to others, notably one David Hunter, who then began a seemingly endless legal battle to evict Denny Martin.

Almost thirty years passed before the British heirs finally lost in the Virginia courts and appealed to the Supreme Court. By then, Martin's claim rested on the strong grounds that both the Treaty of Paris (1783) and Jay's Treaty (1795) guaranteed British subjects the right to own American land; and that federal treaties now overrode conflicting state laws, as the Supreme

Court had ruled in *Ware* v. *Hylton* (1796).

The Virginia Court of Appeals, the state's top court, had upheld the Hunter claim. So, in 1813, the British heirs asked the Supreme Court to review the state ruling on a writ of error authorized by Section 25. Marshall disqualified himself, apparently because his brother had bought part of the disputed land, as Marshall himself may have. The consequent vote in this decision was only three to one, with Justice William Johnson dissenting and two others, including Marshall, not taking part. Speaking for the Court, Justice Joseph Story firmly upheld Denny Martin's title to the land claimed by David Hunter, and ordered the Virginia court to follow suit.

The presiding judge of the Virginia court was Spencer Roane, a zealous states'-righter. Dismayed by the effect of Story's ruling on Virginia's inheritance laws, Judge Roane's state court declared Section 25 unconstitutional, at least in Virginia, and proclaimed the preeminence of state courts in divining the meaning of the Constitution—a massive rejection of national supremacy that bounced *Martin* v. *Hunter's Lessee* right back to the Supreme Court.

Only three weeks later, on March 20, 1816, Justice Story spoke again for the Court (Marshall having once more disqualified himself) and delivered a sweeping affirmation of Section 25's constitutional validity.

Story's *Martin* opinion demolished the notion that the Supreme Court's writ in constitutional matters was limited to the federal courts. And his reasoning provided the strategy that Marshall would perfect in the great cases just ahead.

The people, Story said, had clearly delegated their "supreme authority" via the Constitution to the national government as the most effective instrument of their needs. They held the Supreme Court responsible for construing national power broadly while supervising all lower courts (state tribunals included) to make sure that all judges safeguarded property rights against unconstitutional state actions. Doubts about the Supreme Court's jurisdiction under Section 25 were misguided, Story maintained. The people had empowered the Court to act as final arbiter in all constitutional cases, no matter in which court they originated. "It is *the case*, then, and not *the Court*, that gives the jurisdiction," Story ruled.

Justice Joseph Story. Collection of the Supreme Court of the United States, Washington, D.C.

In 1821, Marshall turned a minor criminal case (*Cohens* v. *Virginia*) into a major podium for delivering what his biographer, Albert Beveridge, calls "an immortal Nationalist address." The case arose when a Virginia court found two partners named Cohen guilty of violating the state's anti-lottery law by selling District of Columbia lottery tickets in the city of Norfolk. The defendants claimed immunity from prosecution because Congress had authorized the lottery and federal law overrode state law. But the state barred them from appealing their conviction. Judge Roane's court, Virginia's highest, ignored their "federal question." As a result, the Cohens appealed directly to the Supreme Court by writ of error under Section 25.

The vital question in *Cohens* v. *Virginia* was whether the Supreme Court could issue a writ of error to a state court below the state's highest court. If it could not do so, then any state could ignore the Supreme Court—and vastly weaken the Supremacy Clause—by simply forbidding constitutional appeals to the highest court in its own judicial system.

In his opinion for a unanimous Court, Marshall invoked a higher vision: "For most important purposes," the United States "form . . . a single nation," and in many fundamental respects, "the American people are one." Then, expanding upon Story's basic points in *Martin* v.

Charles Burton. *View of the Capitol.* 1824. Watercolor and pencil, 15⅝ × 24⅜″. The Metropolitan Museum of Art, New York. Purchase, Joseph Pulitzer Bequest

Samuel F. B. Morse. *The Old House of Representatives.* 1822. Oil on canvas, 7′2½″ x 10′10¾″. Members of the House gather for an evening session. The Justices of the Supreme Court are on the dais on the far side of the chamber. The Corcoran Gallery of Art, Washington, D.C.

Old Supreme Court Chamber in the Capitol. The Court met in this chamber intermittently from February 1810, until December 1860. Restored 1975. Photo: Lee Troell Anderson

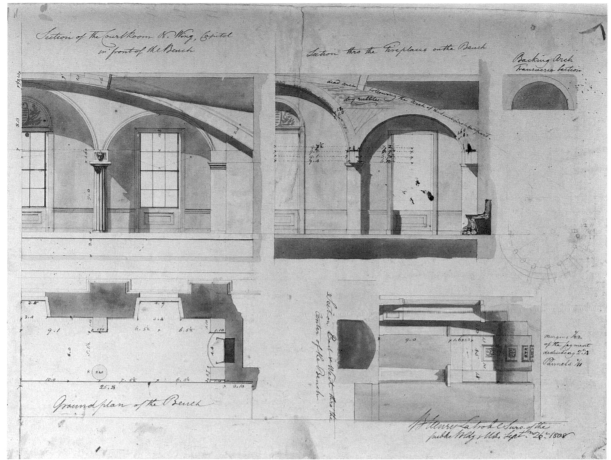

Benjamin Latrobe. *Section of the Court Room N. Wing, Capitol in front of the Bench.* September 26, 1808. Watercolor. Office of the Architect of the Capitol, Washington, D.C.

Baroness Anne-Marguerite-Henrietta Hyde de Neuville. *The Corner of F Street, Washington, D.C.* 1817. Watercolor, 7 × 11¼". The New York Public Library. Astor, Lenox and Tilden Foundations. I. N. Phelps Stokes Collection

Brown's Indian Queen Hotel, Washington City. Justices of the Marshall Court boarded at Brown's Hotel in the 1820s, around the time this lithograph was printed. When the Justices decided to move in 1831, Chief Justice Marshall wrote to Justice Story, "We have, like most unquiet men discontented with things as they are, discarded accommodations which are reasonably convenient without providing a substitute." Library of Congress, Washington, D.C.

Hunter's Lessee, the Chief Justice defended the right of appeal as being essential to federal sovereignty and stressed the Court's duty to remain completely accessible. As stewards of the Supremacy Clause, key to the Union, the Justices must allow nothing to stand between them and all cases arising under the Constitution.

The Eleventh Amendment, he ruled, bars individual suits against states *only* if the individual "commences" the suit. If the state itself takes the initiative by prosecuting an individual, that person can then appeal and thus bring the state before the Supreme Court. The Cohens were not plaintiffs suing a state, but appellants seeking review of their lower court convictions; and because their case raised important constitutional issues, they had every right to appeal to the Supreme Court and the Justices had every right to hear their appeal.

None of this actually benefited the Cohens. The Chief Justice, in fact, agreed with Virginia that the federal statute authorizing a lottery had no validity outside the District of Columbia, so the Cohens remained duly convicted under Virginia law. But the importance of *Cohens* v. *Virginia* to the nation's constitutional development can hardly be exaggerated. *Marbury* v. *Madison* was a landmark: it affirmed the Court's power of judicial review over the actions of the federal government. But *Cohens* was equally significant: it reaffirmed the indivisibility of the nation and upheld federal supremacy as the organizing principle of the United States.

By 1819, the federally chartered Bank of the United States, the nation's largest corporation, had become widely unpopular. The Bank was notorious for harsh foreclosures. But just when it hit bottom in public esteem, Marshall upheld the Bank's long debated legality in *McCulloch* v. *Maryland*, which historian Robert G. McCloskey called "by almost any reckoning the greatest decision John Marshall ever handed down—the one most important to the future of America, most influential in the Court's own doctrinal history, and most revealing of Marshall's unique talent for stately argument."

At issue in *McCulloch* were two questions: 1) Is Congress empowered to create a national bank, even though the Constitution does not specify any such power? 2) Can a state tax a national bank, when the effect (indeed, purpose) of the tax is to force the bank out of business?

Article I, Section 8, granted Congress seventeen specific powers, none of which mentioned national corporations such as banks. But the eighteenth and final clause of Section 8 granted Congress the general power "to make all laws which shall be necessary and proper" for carrying out "all other powers" vested in the national government. Did the so-called Necessary and Proper Clause give Congress "implied powers" *not* specified in the Constitution?

The question held profound implications. An affirmative answer could pose the specter of a runaway national government free of constitutional restraints. A negative answer could render the American government unable to deal effectively with national problems. The "elastic clause" had provoked intense debate ever since that summer of 1787 in Philadelphia. In a certain sense, the history of the United States had been the history of that debate—the perpetual argument between those who welcomed a strong national government and those who resisted it.

Back in December 1790, Alexander Hamilton had proposed that Congress charter a national bank for storing government funds, collecting taxes, and issuing sound currency. The first Secretary of the Treasury characteristically designed the first Bank of the United States as both a boon to the specie-starved populace and a windfall for a few private investors, who would purchase eighty percent of the stock, control the board of directors, and reap huge dividends from the free use of government deposits belonging to all the people.

President Washington hesitated to sign the enabling act passed by Congress. He found nothing in the Constitution that licensed Congress to enter the banking business. As usual when in doubt, he asked his two most astute cabinet members for written advice. Since Jefferson and Hamilton were enemies, they outdid themselves in clarifying the issues. According to Secretary of State Jefferson, the phrase "necessary and proper" limits Congress to passing only laws that are *indispensable* in carrying out a specified power. A federal bank might be a convenience, say in collecting taxes, but it is not indispensable (necessary) and thus is not constitutional. If the Necessary and Proper Clause were so construed as to

Bank of the United States, in Third Street, Philadelphia. Colored line engraving by William Russell Birch, 1798–99. This was the first Bank of the United States. New York Public Library. Astor, Lenox and Tilden Foundations. Print Division

authorize the Bank, wrote Jefferson, the clause "would swallow up all the delegated powers and reduce the whole to one power." That, said Jefferson, was precisely why the Framers intended "necessary" to encompass only "those means without which the grant of power would be nugatory."

Hamilton replied with a forceful statement of "implied powers," summarized by the following excerpt:

> This general principle is inherent in the very definition of government, and essential to every step of the progress to be made by that of the United States; namely, that every power vested in the government is, in its nature, sovereign, and includes, by force of the term, a right to employ all the means requisite and fairly applicable to the attainment of the ends of such power and which are not precluded by restrictions and exceptions specified in the Constitution, or not immoral, or not contrary to the essential ends of political society.

According to Hamilton, the criterion for determining a law's constitutionality is:

> . . . the end to which the measure relates as a means. If the end be clearly comprehended

within any of the specified powers, and if the measure have an obvious relation to that end, and is not forbidden by any particular provision of the Constitution, it may safely be deemed to come within the compass of the national authority. . . .

Accepting Hamilton's counsel, Washington signed the bill. The first Bank of the United States was a success from that moment. When the stock went on sale at a total price of ten million dollars, private investors snapped up their eight-million-dollar controlling share in two hours. As to the government's share, Hamilton made light of the embarrassment that the Treasury did not then possess two million dollars. He bought the stock with spurious drafts drawn on Dutch banks, then immediately borrowed two million dollars from the new Bank. He returned this cash on the same day and retrieved the spurious drafts. In their place, he gave the Bank unsecured government notes to be repaid over the next ten years.

The Bank flourished until its charter expired in 1811. Even the anti-bank Republicans missed it. So, in 1816, President Madison put ideology aside and launched the second Bank of the United States, which was capitalized at thirty-five million dollars and designed mainly to force the country's overextended state banks to cease their outpouring of paper money and resume payments in specie.

Unhappily, the second Bank rapidly foundered. Some of those who ran its eighteen branches were corrupt; most branches were mismanaged, and all were widely depicted as sinister tools of Eastern monopolists bent on ruining state banks while bilking honest farmers, widows, and orphans. That caricature was not unjust. For example, no Bank shareholder was entitled to more than thirty votes, however large his holdings, yet one director regularly cast 1,172 votes. Having bought that many shares, he simply registered each in a different name and appointed himself proxy for all. By law, the Bank's total outstanding loans were never to exceed a sum twice the size of its specie reserves; by 1818, its loans had ballooned to more than ten times its reserves, just when the country was about to plunge into a depression.

At the Baltimore branch, cashier James W. McCulloch was caught lending himself the depositors' money. He and three confederates, including the branch president, had embezzled more than one-and-a-quarter million dollars, a huge sum at the time.

In May 1818, a year before his peculations were proven, McCulloch represented the Bank in a collision with the state. Maryland ordered the Bank to pay a new $15,000 annual state tax for the privilege of buying state-approved paper on which the Bank thenceforth was to issue its notes. Noncompliance would bring a massive fine and close the Bank's doors. McCulloch refused to pay. The tax applied only to the Bank of the United States branch in Baltimore which Maryland yearned to banish from its soil, leaving state-chartered banks in sole command.

Five other states in the Bank-phobic South and West were using the same ploy with even stiffer taxes ranging up to $60,000 a year in Kentucky. The Bank called the state tax unconstitutional; the state called the Bank unconstitutional. Having lost in all Maryland courts, the Bank appealed to the Supreme Court by writ of error under Section 25.

When the Court heard *McCulloch* in February 1819, the issues were considered so significant that six advocates were permitted to argue the case for nine days. The Justices were beginning their first term back in the rebuilt Senate ground-floor courtroom.

The attention of the Justices was abruptly captured by the Bank's legal cast, starring Daniel Webster, always a magnet for lady spectators who appeared to be bewitched by his constitutional rhetoric. But even Webster was upstaged that week by his colleague William Pinkney, a young Baltimore lawyer who overwhelmed the Court with his eloquence on the Bank's behalf. Pinkney made it relatively easy for John Marshall to issue the Court's decision in record time—a mere three days after the argument had ended.

Marshall's *McCulloch* opinion is based upon two premises. First, the Constitution derives its legitimacy from the whole people, not from the states, and the people are sovereign. Second, a constitution necessarily speaks in great outlines, shunning "the prolixity of a legal code," so that it can always be "adapted to the various crises of human affairs." To make proper use of this flexibility, "we must never forget that it is a *constitution* we are expounding."

In this vein, Marshall acknowledges that the Constitution authorizes a national government strictly limited to its enumerated powers, none of which literally entitles Congress to start a bank or create corporations. But though the government is limited, he says, the people made it supreme over the states "within its sphere of action." However few its powers, it must be sovereign in each. Such responsibility requires matching authority. To equip the government for the "various crises" ahead, its limited powers must be construed as broadly as the Constitution permits.

According to Marshall, nothing in the Constitution requires it to be read so literally that each enumerated power must be confined to the precise words on the page. Nothing in the Constitution forbids a reading that reflects the overall spirit of the document—a reading that sanctions, for example, the reality of enumerated powers giving rise to implied powers. As Marshall puts it, "Even the Tenth Amendment, which was framed for the purpose of quieting the excessive jealousies which had been excited, omits the word 'expressly,' and declares that the powers 'not delegated to the United States, nor prohibited to the states, are reserved to the states or the people,' thus leaving the question whether the particular power which may become the subject of contest has been delegated to the one government, or

Charles Bird King. *William Pinkney.* c. 1815. Oil on canvas, 43³/₄ × 33⁹/₁₆″. Maryland Historical Society, Baltimore

prohibited to the other, to depend on a fair construction of the whole instrument."

Marshall then went on to apply these principles to the question of whether Congress can incorporate a bank. Since the people have entrusted Congress with "ample powers" (to tax, regulate commerce, declare war, etc.), he says, Congress surely must be "entrusted with ample means for their execution." Accordingly, Marshall finds the missing authority for the bank in the clause (Article I, Section 8) empowering Congress to make all laws "necessary and proper" for executing all the enumerated powers. He rejects Jefferson's dictum that "necessary" means "indispensable." As urged, he interprets "necessary and proper" generously to mean "appropriate" and "plainly adapted." In a memorable passage, he sums up:

Let the end be legitimate, let it be within the scope of the constitution, and all means which are appropriate, which are plainly adapted to that end, which are not prohibited, but consist with the letter and spirit of the constitution, are constitutional.

Finally, Marshall swiftly invalidates the Maryland tax. Since "the power to tax involves the power to destroy," upholding the tax would empower that state (and, of course, all states) to defeat the necessary supremacy of the national government. The tax must therefore fall because of its "plain repugnance" to the constitutional scheme ordained by the people.

McCulloch is the classic statement of national authority. Unlike most previous Marshall Court decisions, which reined in the power of Congress or the states, *McCulloch* not only restrained the states but also unleashed Congress by judicially approving broad construction of delegated fed-

91

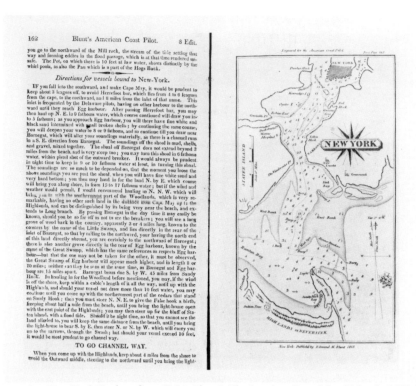

Chart and printed directions for entering New York Harbor, from E. M. Blunt's *The American Coast Pilot,* 18th ed., 1815. Reference books such as Blunt's, which began to appear around the turn of the century, combined directions for navigating the American coast with advice and instructions regarding clearing customs, local maritime laws, and keeping accounts. Their readers clearly did not make a distinction between commerce and navigation. The New York Public Library. Astor, Lenox and Tilden Foundations

eral powers, and especially of the Necessary and Proper Clause. The constitutional liberation of the federal government, now subject to often intense debate but then crucial to national survival, can be traced back to March 7, 1819, the day Marshall spoke for a unanimous Court in *McCulloch* v. *Maryland*.

In a sense the Marshall Court was far ahead of Congress in *McCulloch*, just as it also proved to be in Marshall's third great decision, *Gibbons* v. *Ogden* (1824), the Court's first interpretation of the Commerce Clause. In these cases Marshall's construction vastly enhanced the national government's power to make laws broadly regulating national affairs, particularly in the area of the economy. But for quite some time that power was rarely exercised. Except during the Civil War emergency, the nineteenth-century Congress undertook very little positive lawmaking. Not until the late 1880s did the headlong growth of American capitalism spawn problems so clearly beyond the competence of individual states that Congress began to attempt national solutions.

During the Marshall era, then, the states continued to make nearly all the laws affecting commerce. At the same time, such laws were increasingly challenged in the Supreme Court as infringements upon the national powers enunciated by the Court but largely unexercised by Congress. Thus, by default, the Justices became arbiters of national economic policy throughout the nineteenth century. And because the national policies were more potential than actual, the Justices tended to set national policies on the basis of their individual concepts of social and economic wisdom. Under John Marshall, the result was a liberation of American business from parochial state restrictions and the consequent growth of a free-trade national common market.

Gibbons v. *Ogden*, the explosive steamboat case, has been called "the emancipation proclamation of American commerce." The dispute vividly recalled the commercial anarchy that had inspired the Constitution in the first place—and from which many businesses still needed emancipation thirty years later.

In 1798, New York's powerful Chancellor, Robert R. Livingston, had persuaded the New

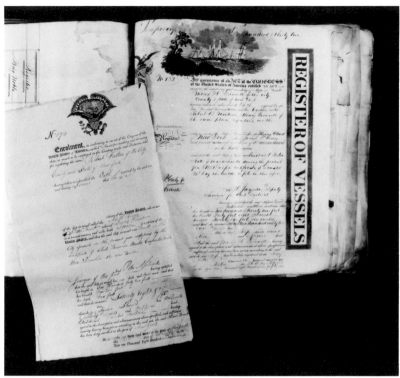

Certificate of Enrolment for Robert Fulton's *North River Steamboat* (known as *Clermont*), and Certificate of Registry for Donald McKay's clipper, *Flying Cloud*. Photograph by Jonathan Wallen. National Archives, Washington, D.C.

York legislature to grant him an exclusive privilege to run steamboats in state waters, including the Hudson River and New York Harbor. Joining forces with Robert Fulton, the steamboat promoter, Livingston established a monopoly so successful that in 1811 the partners extracted from Louisiana a similar exclusive right to all steamshipping in the waterways of New Orleans. The two thus controlled shipping at both of the nation's largest ports, fed by the nation's two biggest rivers.

New York enforced the Livingston-Fulton monopoly. The Hudson River became a battleground between licensed New Yorkers and unlicensed New Jerseyans. The former were legally empowered to confiscate the latter's vessels. Each state arrested the other's crews when caught on the wrong side of the river. Rival crews raided one another's docks, causing waterfront riots.

New Jersey finally closed its own waters to New York steamboats. Connecticut and Ohio followed suit, while five other states created their own steamship monopolies. As the chaos worsened, the states were impelled toward what Attorney General William Wirt called "almost . . . the eve of war."

The steamboat case grew out of a conflict between two partners turned competitors. One was Aaron Ogden, a former governor of New Jersey. The other was Thomas Gibbons, a wealthy Georgia lawyer then living in New Jersey.

In 1815 Ogden bought a license from the Livingston-Fulton monopoly to run a steam ferry between New York City and Elizabethtown, New Jersey. Gibbons held a federal permit to operate his own two steamboats under the Coastal Licensing Act of 1793. The original idea was for Gibbons's boats to pick up Ogden's passengers in Elizabethtown and ferry them on to New Brunswick, or vice versa, thus limiting Gibbons to New Jersey waters and Ogden to New York.

Even this irked the monopolists, who claimed that Gibbons, by picking up Ogden's passengers, was effectively operating in New York waters—for which he had no license. Gibbons countered that his national coasting license gave him every right to navigate between two ports in New Jersey. But the monopolists had an old friend in

Asher B. Durand. *Aaron Ogden*. 1833. Oil on canvas, 30 × 25″. The New-York Historical Society

Anonymous. *Thomas Gibbons*. Pastel, 19 × 25″. Collection William L. Hopkins, Jr.

court. New York Chancellor James Kent, shamelessly claiming jurisdiction right up to the New Jersey shore, banned Gibbons from steaming between Elizabethtown and New Brunswick, while leaving Ogden's route intact.

That doomed the partnership. Gibbons now recruited a ruthless captain—the already infamous Cornelius Vanderbilt. They ran the Gibbons boats into New York, stealing Ogden's passengers in defiance of his monopoly rights. New York courts duly enjoined Gibbons.

Gibbons now became obsessed with forcing Ogden into the Supreme Court. To maneuver the case up the legal slopes, Gibbons spent much of his fortune hiring the country's best lawyers, including Daniel Webster and Attorney General William Wirt. He even provided in his will for a $40,000 fund to keep the case going should he die before it ended.

His lawyers earned their hefty fees. Carving a

then novel theory out of very thin precedents, they argued that Gibbons should be allowed to continue ferrying in New York because his federal license took precedence over the state-granted monopoly. The 1793 Coastal Licensing Act, they asserted, derived from Article I, Section 8, empowering Congress to "regulate Commerce with foreign Nations, and among the several States, and with the Indian tribes." As they saw it, the state monopoly was unconstitutional and never should have been granted because navigation is interstate commerce—a field that only Congress is authorized to regulate.

First docketed in 1820, *Gibbons* v. *Ogden* was not argued until February 1824, when the Court allotted opposing counsel four days to address these questions: 1) Did the Commerce Clause empower Congress to regulate navigation, and if so, was that power exclusive? 2) What power to regulate commerce was left to the states?

Daniel Webster delivered the answers for Gibbons. The New York monopoly law, he said, had created navigational chaos inimical to "the general intercourse of the community." Whether or not the law conflicted with an act of Congress was irrelevant. The state had no right to regulate navigation in the first place. In Webster's bold view, the power of Congress to regulate all forms of commerce, including navigation, was "complete and entire."

Thomas Adis Emmet, the distinguished New York lawyer representing Ogden, extolled his state's wisdom in creating the monopoly. Singlehandedly, New York had nurtured the advent of the steamboat: "She has brought into noonday splendor, an invaluable improvement to the intercourse and consequent happiness of man." New York had benefited "the whole civilized world . . . from Archangel to Calcutta."

As to the constitutional dispute, Ogden's lawyers urged a narrow reading of the Commerce Clause. They declared it applicable only to "transportation and sale of commodities," excluding navigation, a field they deemed entirely reserved for state regulation. The Constitution neither specifies that Congress has power over navigation, nor prohibits the states from exercising such power. Ogden's lawyers thus argued that under the Tenth Amendment, navigation is a power "reserved to the States, respectively, or to the people."

Speaking for the Court on March 2, 1824, Chief Justice Marshall took Webster's basic points and rendered them into constitutional commands both politic for the time and permanent for the nation. First, Marshall defined commerce as being far more than buying and selling. "It is intercourse," he ruled. It encompasses every kind of commercial intercourse between nations, and "all America understands" that commerce includes navigation, a field that particularly concerned the authors of the Commerce Clause, navigation then being the new nation's principal form of commerce.

Second, Marshall interpreted the phrase "among the several states" to mean that the federal commerce power reaches all "commerce which concerns more than one state." Interstate commerce does not halt at state boundaries, he said, but passes through states, so that transactions between any two points, near or far, remain subject to congressional regulation as long as they start in one state and finish in another, or involve trade with foreign countries.

Once a subject is found to be in interstate commerce or foreign trade, Marshall held, the power of Congress to regulate it is "complete in itself, may be exercised to its ultimate extent, and acknowledges no limitations other than are prescribed in the Constitution."

Where did this leave the states? Webster had argued that Congress had exclusive power over commerce, precluding the states from undertaking *any* kind of commercial regulation. That argument had "great force," Marshall remarked, and "the Court is not satisfied that it has been refuted." Indeed, Justice William Johnson, an alleged Republican, supported Webster's nationalistic formulation in the Court's only separate opinion. But Marshall prudently avoided a possible states' rights backlash. Leaving the exclusivity issue to another day, he simply noted that the states retained full power within their borders to regulate "their own purely internal affairs, whether of trading or police" (the Court's first allusion to state "police power").

In fact, Marshall doomed the New York monopoly on the now familiar basis of the Supremacy Clause, sidestepping the issue of whether the Commerce Clause alone would suffice. Where state laws purported to regulate fields already covered by federal laws, Marshall ruled, the Supremacy Clause obliged the states to give way to congressional enactments. Thus the federal Coastal Licensing Act superseded the New York steamboat monopoly law. With his federal permit, Gibbons could trade in any American port; all he needed was a seaworthy vessel, whether it was "wafted . . . by the winds" or "propelled by the agency of fire." The federal law covered all coasters in interstate commerce. In regulating commerce, Marshall declared, "the laws of Congress . . . do not look to the principle by which vessels are moved."

Gibbons v. *Ogden* was the only Marshall opinion that won instant popularity. By destroying the hated New York monopoly, this decision opened interstate navigation to any small operator able to raise the few thousand dollars required to build or buy a small steamboat. The resulting competition produced cheap, efficient ferry service throughout the country, a boost for all kinds of businesses and their customers. What Marshall had actually done, though, was something more profound, if not yet visible. He had given the word "commerce" a meaning so broad that in the near future the Justices would apply their own laissez-faire standards to foil state business regulations; and in the distant future Congress would apply the Commerce Clause to everything from air travel, to television transmission, to racial discrimination.

Chief Justice Marshall's deftness in expanding the federal commerce power while avoiding the stumbling block of state power kept his critics guessing. In 1827, for example, the Marshall Court held in *Brown* v. *Maryland* that states could not tax imported goods as long as they remained unopened in their original packages. Yet in the 1829 case of *Willson* v. *Blackbird Creek*, a gain for the states, the Justices held that states could exercise their police power over aspects of interstate

commerce that Congress had not seen fit to regulate. In fact, the Supreme Court did not begin to make clear distinctions between federal and state commercial regulatory powers until the mid-1850s, years after Marshall's death. By that time, Marshall's seminal *Gibbons* decision had gone far toward achieving a consensus that properly-regulated commerce was among the few bonds that might prevent the United States from dissolving.

Marshall's key decisions—*Marbury, Cohens, McCulloch, Gibbons*—guaranteed his place in the American pantheon. But other opinions were less enduring, and not all his dreams came true. For example, Marshall viewed contracts as pillars of liberty and hence urged the broadest possible reading of the Contract Clause (Article I, Section 10), which forbids states to pass any law "impairing the Obligation of Contracts." Marshall's opinion in *Fletcher* v. *Peck* (1810) sounded the first if uncertain trumpet in his campaign to foil state actions harmful to property holders. His next advance nine years later was far more aggressive. In *Dartmouth College* v. *Woodward* (1819), he made a leap to the postulate that contracts are truly inviolable.

The *Dartmouth* case remains famous largely because of Daniel Webster's tearful peroration in his alma mater's behalf ("It is, sir, a small college, and yet *there are those who love it*."). At issue was whether the New Hampshire legislature could revoke Dartmouth's charter, pack the board of trustees, and convert the private college into a state university. The prime mover behind all this was Dartmouth's deposed president who wanted his job back, but his rights or wrongs became irrelevant. Webster, probably the greatest thespian ever to appear before the members of the Supreme Court, represented the beleaguered trustees and earned every penny of his thousand-dollar fee with a choked-voice performance that mesmerized the Justices and caused the Chief himself to reach for his handkerchief.

In his opinion for the Court, Marshall held that New Hampshire's attempt to annex Dartmouth was unconstitutional under the Contract Clause. He said the college charter remained as binding in 1819 as it had been in 1769 when the Dartmouth founders received it from King George III. In succeeding the Crown by virtue of the Revolution, the state of New Hampshire had inherited all royal contractual obligations, and lacking any showing that the trustees had abused their powers, the state must honor the charter.

The Framers almost certainly designed the Contract Clause to protect the private property rights of individuals; the Dartmouth trustees suing the state had no such rights at stake. Even so, Marshall ruled that a charter is a contract, a state is bound by its contracts, and New Hampshire must leave Dartmouth alone.

The consensus was that Marshall's *Dartmouth* opinion had immunized every state-chartered corporation from state regulation. Once a company was past the chartering stage and actually doing business, optimists declared, *Dartmouth* would prevent any state interference. But that hope soon died. The states swiftly insisted that all new corporate charters include a clause empowering the legislature to amend them at any time.

Only two weeks after his *Dartmouth* opinion, Marshall applied the Contract Clause to a situation more obviously congruent with the Framers' intent. In *Sturges* v. *Crowninshield*, he invalidated a New York bankruptcy law on the ground that it freed debtors from obligations contracted *before* the law was passed. This decision assured lenders that the rules for lending money would be unchanged when it came time to collect.

But in his decision, which barred states from retroactive meddling with contracts, Marshall hinted that the Contract Clause also barred prospective interference—in other words, *any* state impairment. That millennium was not to be attained. Eight years later, over his bitter dissent (his only dissent in thirty-four years on the bench), Marshall's colleagues outvoted him, four to three, and ruled that a state bankruptcy law is constitutional when it frees debtors from obligations contracted *after* the law is passed.

That 1827 decision (*Ogden* v. *Saunders*) greatly disappointed Marshall, not only because it was the first (and last) time he failed to command a majority for his view, but also because it aborted his theory that contractual obligations derive from natural law and cannot be impaired by the whims of transient legislators. Once the political majority makes it possible for debtors to be forgiven their debts, Marshall believed, then the Contract Clause is no longer a reliable guarantee.

But insolvency laws cannot be divorced from changing economic conditions, the Court major-

Francis Alexander. *Daniel Webster.* 1835. Oil on canvas, 30 × 25″. Hood Museum, Dartmouth College, Hanover, New Hampshire. Gift of George Shattuck

ity held, and the Contract Clause is satisfied if a contract is maintained according to the law of the time and the place where it was drawn up.

The Court suffered a collision with prevailing public opinion during Andrew Jackson's first term, when frontier values dominated national politics and the President saw no reason to put judicial interpretations of the Constitution ahead of his own. The Court's clash with Jacksonian Democracy arose from Georgia's harsh treatment of the Cherokee Indians living on their own lands within that state. Jackson, an old Indian fighter, had a low opinion of Indians, as did most white men of the day, and he openly approved the state's actions.

Americans then considered it humane to "remove" Indians from the path of western settlement (the alternative being slaughter). Jackson himself insisted that "this unhappy race" be fairly paid for leaving their native grounds and that the government should finance their resettlement on distant lands not yet coveted by white Americans. Most tribes submitted; some resorted to armed resistance, but to no avail. The Cherokees of Georgia made an ingenious

New York and Environs, from Williamsburgh. Shipping in New York Harbor increased dramatically after *Gibbons* v. *Ogden.* Cornelius Vanderbilt prospered. The steamboat in the center of this hand-colored lithograph by E. W. Foreman and E. Brown, Jr., published in 1848 is the *C. Vanderbilt.* The New York Public Library. Astor, Lenox and Tilden Foundations. Eno Collection

attempt to retain their lands, however, by adopting white customs. They began farming, created a written language, drafted a constitution, and established a "nation" in northwestern Georgia.

Georgians found this galling, and the state refused to recognize another state within its borders. Beginning in 1828, Georgia passed various drastic laws dissolving the Cherokee Nation and imposing stringent controls on its inhabitants. One 1830 law required white missionaries living among the Cherokees to obtain state licenses and sign a state loyalty oath.

The Cherokees finally made a valiant attempt—acting as an independent nation—to file an original suit in the Supreme Court requesting the white man's highest tribunal to order Georgia to stop enforcing its anti-Cherokee laws. The state not only refused to appear in the case but precipitously executed a Cherokee named Corn Tassel, who had separately appealed his state murder conviction to the Supreme Court. The state knew the Court intended to review Corn Tassel's claim that he should have been tried under Cherokee law; he was dead before the Justices had a chance to do so.

The Court declined to rule on the Cherokees' suit against Georgia, holding that it lacked jurisdiction because the Cherokees were not a foreign state. Whatever the wrongs at stake, Chief Justice Marshall wrote in *Cherokee Nation* v. *Georgia* (1831), "This is not the tribunal which can redress the past or prevent the future."

Soon Marshall had another chance to deal with Georgia. Two white missionaries working the Indian territory—Samuel Worcester and Elizur Butler—had refused to procure state licenses to do God's work. In its zeal to control the Cherokees, the state sentenced these presumed subversives to four years at hard labor. They appealed to the Supreme Court by writ of error, and once again Georgia refused to appear in its own defense.

The Justices absorbed this insult; and two

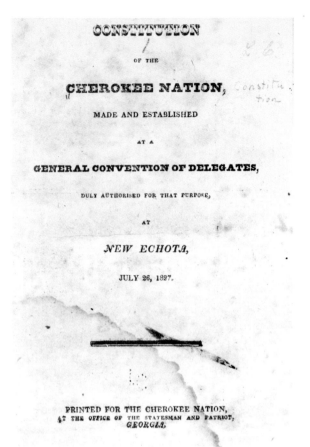

Constitution of the Cherokee Nation, New Echota, Georgia, 1827. Library of Congress, Washington, D.C.

weeks later, on March 3, 1832, Marshall spoke for the Court in *Worcester* v. *Georgia*. Because the federal government had exclusive jurisdiction over Indians, he ruled, Georgia had no power to pass any laws affecting the Cherokees. Because the missionaries had been convicted under such invalid laws, he added, their convictions were reversed and they should be released. The Court refrained from saying they *must* be released, however, leaving the case in limbo and the missionaries locked up for an entire year until the Court's next term in 1833.

The Court had good reason to move slowly. Georgians were incensed about the *Worcester* decision, which the state continued to ignore, and the whole country seemed to approve of this defiance. President Jackson himself supposedly said, "John Marshall has made his decision; now let him enforce it."

These legendary words were almost certainly put in Jackson's mouth by the imaginative New York newspaperman, Horace Greeley, some thirty years after Jackson allegedly uttered them.

Left: George Catlin. *The Virginia Constitutional Convention.* Richmond, 1830. Oil on wood, 24^1/$_2$ × 36^1/$_2$". In 1829, Virginia held a convention to rewrite the Virginia Constitution, an occasion that united James Madison, James Monroe, and Chief Justice John Marshall—each was past seventy—in the great task at which the Founders excelled, that of Constitution-making. Monroe is seated on the dais, while Madison takes the floor. Chief Justice Marshall is seated ninth in the front row, counter-clockwise from the lower right. Virginia Historical Society, Richmond

Samuel Austin Worcester. By permission of the Houghton Library, Harvard University

Still, they sound precisely like something Jackson would have said, had he thought of it, and the fact remains that the President happily shirked his constitutional duty to help the Court enforce *Worcester*. John Marshall spent most of 1832 anticipating the decline and fall of the judicial sovereignty he had worked so diligently to establish. "I yield slowly and reluctantly to the conviction that our Constitution cannot last," he wrote in a letter to Justice Story. "The Union has been prolonged thus far by miracles. I fear they cannot continue."

But yet another miracle did occur. First, Jackson's approval of Georgia's defiance had led radical South Carolinians to believe the President would support them in a bold attack on a new federal tariff law. In November 1832, South Carolina accordingly enacted a so-called Nullification Ordinance. This curio, inspired by John C. Calhoun, proclaimed the constitutional right of any state to disobey ("nullify") any federal law it considered unconstitutional. As an afterthought, South Carolinians were forbidden to challenge the ordinance in the Supreme Court.

South Carolina had totally misread President Jackson. Instead of applauding the new ordinance, the Hero of New Orleans counterattacked with such ferocity that Calhoun himself feared for his life. Jackson denounced the nullification notion as "treason," threatened personally to hang nullifiers from the nearest tree, and vowed to enforce federal law with his own army of 200,000 men. "Union men, fear not," Old Hickory cried. "*The Union will be preserved.*"

This committed Jackson to a policy of federal supremacy, and having denounced nullifiers as traitors, he could hardly continue to support Georgia's defiance of the Supreme Court in the case of the jailed missionaries. The governor soon pardoned the missionaries and they dropped their suit against the state. Even more remarkable, in 1833 Jackson persuaded Congress not to reduce the power of the federal courts but to expand it.

The Bank of the United States had flourished after *McCulloch* and had become essential to the country's economic stability, but it had made enemies. Although the Bank's charter was not due to expire until 1836, the National Republicans per-

Figurehead of Andrew Jackson, carved by Laban S. Beecher in 1834 for the frigate *U.S.S. Constitution.* Museum of the City of New York

Nullification, or A Peep at South Carolina in 1832–33. In this anonymous cartoon, England watches gleefully while "The Union Pie" begins to crumble. The New-York Historical Society

General Jackson Slaying the Many Headed Monster. The President attacks the Bank, in this popular lithograph of 1836 by H. R. Robinson. The New-York Historical Society

Rembrandt Peale. *Chief Justice John Marshall.* c. 1826. Oil on canvas, 70 × 52½″. In 1858, Peale recalled in a letter, "My portrait of Chief Justice Marshall was painted in Washington about 30 years ago, when he was in perfect and vigorous health, living on Capitol Hill and walking to and from my Painting Room on Penn. Avenue." Collection of the Supreme Court of the United States, Washington, D.C.

suaded Congress to renew it before the election of 1832 in which Jackson was running for a second term against their candidate, Henry Clay. They hoped Jackson would sign the recharter bill, but if he vetoed it, Clay would have a powerful issue in the campaign. The National Republicans were so out of touch with the country that they assumed Jackson's hostility toward the Bank would destroy his popularity.

He knew otherwise. When Congress passed the recharter bill in July 1832, Jackson vetoed it. His veto message attacking the Bank's alleged evils was widely admired and he won the fall election by a landslide—219 electoral votes to Clay's 49.

From John Marshall's viewpoint, the most pernicious aspect of Jackson's veto message was that he not only declared the Bank unconstitutional, dismissing *McCulloch* in the process, but he also declared himself the nation's constitutional arbiter, dismissing the Supreme Court as well. With

Old Hickory, words were nearly always followed by actions. In the case of the Bank, he behaved like a man possessed. "Until I can strangle this hydra of corruption," he vowed, "I will not shrink from my duty."

All during his seventies, which paralleled the Jackson era, Marshall was filled with forebodings about the Union's future and what he considered his own failure to harmonize relations between the states and the federal government. It may be no coincidence that in his last constitutional opinion, *Barron* v. *Baltimore* (1833), the Court held that the Bill of Rights was intended to curb only federal power and did not apply to state action. *Barron* set the stage for the Fourteenth Amendment, the future vehicle for applying the Bill of Rights to the states.

Marshall did not realize that he had created an institution of a scope that transcended its transient members, one capable of evoking not only their best instincts but those of the nation as well. John Adams, the man who made it all possible, sensed the immensity of Marshall's accomplishment when he said in 1826: "My gift of John Marshall to the people of the United States was the proudest act of my life. There is no act of my life on which I reflect with greater pleasure."

8

A WISE MAN'S FOLLIES: TANEY V. TANEY

Nine Justices who served on the Taney Court. Back row, from left: Associate Justices Robert Cooper Grier (1846–70), Benjamin Robbins Curtis (1851–57), John Archibald Campbell (1853–61), John McKinley (1838–52). Front row, from left: Associate Justices Levi Woodbury (1845–51), Philip Pendleton Barbour (1836–41), Chief Justice Roger Brooke Taney (1836–64), Associate Justices Peter Vivian Daniel (1842–60), Samuel Nelson (1845–72). Collection of the Supreme Court of the United States, Washington, D.C.

When John Marshall died on July 6, 1835, leaving the Center Chair vacant for the first time in thirty-four years, the Liberty Bell was tolled in mourning. It promptly cracked, as if confirming the worst Whig fears that Democrat Andrew Jackson would appoint a successor hostile to everything Marshall stood for. The man Whigs dreaded most was former Treasury Secretary Roger B. Taney (pronounced "Tawney"), a Jackson ally best known for having virtually destroyed the Bank of the United States by withdrawing all its government deposits and transferring the money to state banks. To his critics, Taney seemed likely to demolish the Supreme Court as ruthlessly as he had the Bank.

With customary verve, President Jackson duly nominated Taney as Marshall's successor. The Senate debated Taney's alleged shortcomings for three long months before reluctantly confirming the new Chief Justice in March 1836.

In fact, Roger Brooke Taney was a first-rate lawyer who soon became one of the Court's finest Chief Justices. He was also destined to become one of the Court's most tragic figures.

Born in Maryland in 1777, Taney, at thirty, was a rising Frederick attorney and Federalist leader described by one contemporary as "a tall, gaunt fellow, as lean as a Potomac herring, and as shrewd as the shrewdest."

In Maryland during the war of 1812, Taney was elected to the State Senate, where he specialized in banking and learned early about a scandalous fraud at the Baltimore branch of the Bank of the United States. Although he had previously supported the Bank and opposed the prohibitive state tax that led to *McCulloch* v. *Maryland* (1819), Taney was appalled by the fraud and began to turn against "The Monster," as Jackson called the Bank.

As a prosperous Baltimore lawyer, Taney

jumped on the Jackson bandwagon in 1824 and became the general's state campaign chairman, a move that helped make him state attorney general in 1826. In 1831, Jackson summoned him to Washington to serve as Attorney General and presidential confidant. Historians differ as to whether Taney wrote all or part of Jackson's Bank veto message, but no one doubts his responsibility for stripping the Bank.

When the Taney Court issued its first decisions in early 1837, the press was filled with predictions of doom, and there was no question that profound changes were in the making. The new Chief Justice even wore ordinary trousers under his robes instead of the customary formal knee breeches. The most drastic change, of course, was in the composition of the Court itself. Of the seven Justices who began the term (Congress soon added two more), five were Jackson appointees and only Justice Story remained as the last voice of uncompromising Marshallian nationalism. As anxious Whigs pondered the Taney Court's first three opinions, moreover, it was generally assumed that the Marshall Court would have decided every one of them differently.

Little did anyone then suspect that the first twenty years of Chief Justice Taney's leadership would turn out to be a vital period of judicial moderation. Instead of damaging John Marshall's work, the Jacksonian Justices did their best to defend, improve, and expand the Court's influence in American life.

The Taney Court's most important 1837 case raised a fascinating question: Do public rights ever take precedence over private property rights? The political balance in America had clearly shifted away from the Federalist/Whig concern with property rights and toward the Jacksonian stress on public power to meet public needs. In a period of explosive growth, Americans everywhere began to demand new bridges, roads, canals, schools. But in meeting these needs, the states invariably collided with entrenched property rights protected by the Supreme Court's Marshallian rigor concerning the sanctity of contracts.

In the famous case of *Charles River Bridge* v. *Warren Bridge*, Chief Justice Taney dealt with the Contract Clause in a way that adapted it to new conditions.

ROGER B. TANEY

Chief Justice Roger Brooke Taney. Collection of the Supreme Court of the United States, Washington, D.C.

The case involved an old charter granted by the Massachusetts legislature in 1785 to the Charles River Bridge Company, a group of Boston investors headed by the ever enterprising John Hancock. They received exclusive rights to build and collect tolls from a new bridge over the Charles River between Boston and Charlestown, replacing a ferry long operated by Harvard College. To make up for its lost ferry income, Harvard was to receive a fixed annuity ($666.66 per year) for seventy years. When the Boston environs began to fill with new businesses and people, the bridge became extremely profitable, and prudent Harvard bought Charles River Bridge Company stock, which increased six-fold in value.

By the late 1820s, Boston commuters were tired of paying to get in and out of the city; most people viewed the bridge monopoly as a symbol of Whig/Harvard privilege, and Democratic politicians happily supported growing demands for a second *free* bridge across the Charles. Feelings

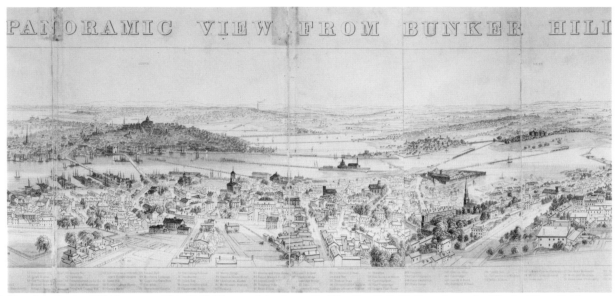

A Panoramic View from Bunker Hill Monument. This 1848 lithograph by James Smillie after R. P. Mallory shows the Charles River Bridge and the Warren Bridge side by side (on the left). Boston Athenaeum

ran so high that Massachusetts even produced a Free Bridge Party. In 1828 the legislature chartered a second company to build the toll-free Warren Bridge (named for the hero of Bunker Hill). The new bridge was designed to parallel the Charles River Bridge at a distance of only 260 feet.

The bridge monopolists, having by now collected almost a million dollars in tolls, were outraged at the prospect of losing their entire market to the rival Warren Bridge. They went to court seeking an injunction against the construction of the Warren Bridge. By violating their charter rights, they argued, the state had violated the Contract Clause forbidding states to impair the obligation of contracts.

The state's top court split evenly on the issue, so the case went to the Supreme Court, where it was first argued in 1831 before the Marshall Justices, most of whom were presumed sympathetic to the Charles River Bridge Company and its counsel, Daniel Webster of *Dartmouth* fame. Repeatedly held over because of various deaths and illnesses among the Justices, including the death of Marshall, the bridge case was stalled for six years and had to be reargued in January 1837. By then, the toll-free Warren Bridge had long since put the Charles River Bridge out of business. But the issues were too important to ignore. For one thing, the outcome would heavily influence potential investors in the country's embryo railroads, which hesitated to expand until the courts had clarified the extent of existing charter rights.

Moreover, Chief Justice Taney correctly perceived the core issue: the social role of corporations chartered to perform public services. As Attorney General four years before, Taney had resolved his own position on public-service corporations (known today as public utilities) when he was asked his opinion as to whether the New Jersey legislature could issue a railroad charter that specifically exempted the railroad from competition. In his written opinion, Taney said the legislature had exceeded its powers. It could not permanently commit the people to something potentially adverse to their interests. He further declared that public-service corporations had special obligations. Their charters, he wrote, can "never be considered as having been granted for the exclusive benefit of the corporators. Certain privileges are given to them, in order to obtain a public convenience; and the interest of the public must, I presume, always be regarded as the main object of every charter for a toll-bridge or a turnpike road."

Taney now proceeded to put that formulation to work. Speaking for a sharply divided (four-to-three) Supreme Court, he ruled against the Charles River Bridge Company in a judicious opinion that accommodated both old contract rules and new public needs. The state, of course, must adhere to the original bridge charter, he said, but it needn't yield beyond the charter's explicit terms, none of which limited the state's power to sponsor competing bridges for public use. Nor could such a limitation be assumed to lurk somewhere in the document.

"In grants by the public," Taney wrote, "nothing passes by implication." He attributed this rule to no less an authority than John Marshall, who in 1830 had rejected a Rhode Island bank's ingenious claim that its charter implied an immunity from state taxes.

Taney applied Marshall's rule for construing the taxing power to what might be called "the bridging power," meaning the state's vital interest in providing for adequate public transportation. According to Taney, "The object and the end of all government is to promote the happiness and prosperity of the community by which it is established, and it can never be assumed that the government intended to diminish its power of accomplishing the end for which it was created." The Charles River Bridge Company simply had no basis for assuming that Massachusetts had licensed a private monopoly to exact bridge tolls without competition for seventy years. "While the rights of private property are sacredly guarded," wrote Taney, "we must not forget that the community also have rights, and that the happiness and well being of every citizen depends on their faithful preservation."

Justice Story filed a bitter dissent in the bridge case, asserting that the majority had practically "overturned . . . one great provision of the Constitution." In a letter to his wife, he fumed, "A grosser case of injustice . . . never existed."

Marshall had defined federalism almost entirely in terms of national supremacy; the Taney Court offered an alternative called "dual federalism." It did so because Marshall's approach seemed flawed by the reluctance of Congress to exercise national supremacy in many areas. Distracted as it was by sectional issues—especially slavery—Congress had neglected myriad problems besetting the states as a result of America's phenomenal growth through immigration and naturalization. Ironically, the supremacy of Congress's unexercised powers had in turn inhibited state action and threatened to block *any* governmental response. Accordingly, the Taney Court began to refine Marshall's precedents in order to distinguish constitutional powers still reserved to the states.

Movement toward that goal became apparent with those very first decisions of 1837. At issue in *City of New York* v. *Miln*, for example, was the validity of a state law requiring all ships entering New York harbor to report to the mayor every passenger's age, birthplace, previous residence, and occupation. George Miln, owner of a ship named *Emily*, refused to comply. After losing in the state courts, he appealed to the Supreme Court on the ground that the state law was an unconstitutional invasion of the federal government's power to regulate foreign commerce and navigation.

The law certainly impinged on foreign commerce, and Justice Story was quick to argue in conference that it should be overturned because, pursuant to *Gibbons* v. *Ogden*, Congress had preempted that field. Justice Smith Thompson, on the other hand, argued that a state law regulating commerce was valid as long as it did not conflict with any federal law. But neither of these extremes won the day. Neither one would have served the purpose of avoiding the inflammatory question of whether the federal commerce power was exclusive.

Instead, the Court majority found a way around this prickly issue. It upheld the New York law as a valid exercise of the state's "police power" rather than an invalid regulation of commerce. Indeed, the purpose of the law was to ease the impact of immigration on the state's port city by excluding paupers from the public rolls. The law was concerned with welfare costs, not commerce per se.

So began the advent of state "police power," a constitutional convenience enabling states to cope with social and economic problems to which the national government was paying scant heed. The police power derived from the Tenth Amendment, that repository of unspecified powers reserved to the states and to the people. Even Marshall regretters could not fault the deft use in *Miln* of the police power—avoiding the commerce quandary. Marshall himself had been the first to acknowledge the power's existence (in *Gibbons* v. *Ogden*) and had later actually invoked it to permit a state to dam a navigable river. Thus sanctioned, Chief Justice Taney had stressed in his own *Charles River Bridge* opinion the need to protect the states' "power over their own internal police and improvement, which is so necessary to

J. Gear. *Half Past Eight O'Clock, The Cook Enrag'd at the Steerage Passengers Being Late with their Breakfast on Board the Ship Acasta, Dec. 1824.* Watercolor. Travelers to America might be simply unruly, as in this sketch, or worse: carriers of contagious diseases, or escaped criminals. States claimed the right to police their ports, which gave rise to *City of New York* v. *Miln.* Chicago Historical Society

their well being and prosperity."

For nearly fourteen years after *Miln*, the Taney Court fought a losing battle to leave unanswered the great question Marshall had so assiduously avoided. Could the states, in fact, directly regulate any commerce at all?

The answer lay somewhere at the bottom of conflicting interpretations. In the *License Cases* (1847), the Court upheld the right of states to require licenses for the sale of all intoxicating liquors within their borders. Although imported liquors were included, the licensing was ruled a valid exercise of state police power. The decision itself was a minor classic of judicial incoherence. While no Justice dissented from the result, none could agree on the reasoning, so that six Justices wrote nine opinions, and the states were left unencumbered by anything resembling a logically consistent Court decision.

In the *Passenger Cases* (1849), on the other hand, the Court voted five to four to strike down state laws that levied head taxes on alien passengers arriving in United States ports. The tax revenues were intended to support immigrant paupers. To the four dissenters, including Chief Justice Taney, this was a valid exercise of state police power, aimed at controlling disease and poverty, and consistent with the Court's decisions in *Miln* and the *License Cases.* To the five majority Justices, headed by former United States Postmaster-General John McLean, the state passenger taxes conflicted with the federal commerce power, even though Congress had passed no laws on the matter. The *Passenger Cases* had to be argued three times before five Justices could reach a consensus of sorts; and even then, the Court was so fissured that all nine Justices wrote separate opinions. Reading them aloud took seven hours.

All this confusion was dispelled in early 1852 when the Court finally faced the question that had caused so much disagreement. An old state law required ships using the Philadelphia harbor to employ local pilots or else pay a fine earmarked for the care of disabled pilots and their families. In the case of *Cooley* v. *Pennsylvania Board of Wardens*, a shipmaster named Aaron B.

108

Fitz Hugh Lane. *New York Harbor*. 1850. Oil on canvas, 36 × 60″. A steam tug pilots a schooner into port. The Museum of Fine Arts, Boston

Certificate of the Society for the Relief of Distressed and Decayed Pilots. Pilots constituted a powerful interest in an economy that depended heavily on maritime commerce. Benevolent organizations in Philadelphia, such as the one for which Samuel Seymour engraved this handsome certificate after a design by Thomas Birch, c. 1810, succeeded in obtaining the revenue from a tax on shipping for retired pilots. This tax was challenged in *Cooley* v. *Pennsylvania Board of Wardens*. The Library Company of Philadelphia

Cooley refused to obey the pilotage law on the ground that the state had no right to regulate commercial navigation. The law was unconstitutional, he argued, because it conflicted with the federal government's exclusive power under the Commerce Clause. Thus free of police power concerns, the Court faced the issue: Could the state regulate pilotage in the absence of any evident Congressional interest in the subject?

By a solid majority of seven to two, the Court upheld the state law in a decision written by junior Justice Benjamin R. Curtis, a Boston lawyer of forty-one whom the Senate had confirmed barely a month before. Justice Curtis, a product of Justice Story's law teaching at Harvard, had been appointed by Whig President Millard Fillmore to a Court dominated by Southern Democrats, but his intelligence and gift for conciliation enabled him to forge a compromise between the Marshall concern for the national interest and the Taney preoccupation with state interest.

The compromise upheld federal regulatory power while safeguarding local freedom of action. It was called "selective exclusiveness," and it meant that while Congress had exclusive power

Tyrants Prostrate Liberty Triumphant. An 1844 lithograph by J. Baillie, attacking the government of Rhode Island. The events surrounding the Dorr Rebellion eventually culminated in the case of *Luther* v. *Borden.* Rhode Island Historical Society, Providence

to regulate commerce that was national in nature and required uniform rules, the states retained authority over any local commerce that Congress chose not to regulate. The *"Cooley* Rule," as the Curtis formula came to be known, did not satisfy proponents of total national power over commerce, such as Justice McLean; nor proponents of full concurrent state power, such as Chief Justice Taney. But it did resolve a dilemma by expressing the common sense of the matter, as in the pilotage case.

By 1850, when Roger Taney was seventy-three, the Supreme Court had achieved a degree of authority, derived from public respect, that made it unique in judicial history, as well as altogether singular in a country as irreverent and quarrelsome as the America of that period. Despite their philosophical differences, the Justices had worked hard at compromise under a

wise and decent Chief; and their contributions to the country's economic and legal progress had been reinforced by the popular yearning for something to admire. Most Americans considered the Taney Court refreshingly above "politics," an island of integrity in a sea of perfidy.

By 1858 all this was gone—the Court had shattered its own image and almost destroyed its influence in American life.

The Court had made the classic error of taking itself too seriously. Writing in 1835, for example, Alexis de Tocqueville declared, "The peace, prosperity, and very existence of the Union rest continually in the hands of these seven federal judges." Such praise, echoed by others for the next two decades, made perspective difficult.

To retrace the consequences, one might well examine the Court's contrasting sense of its own limitations in *Luther* v. *Borden* (1849). That case began as two simple trespass suits and ended with

110

View of Washington. Hand-colored lithograph by Edward Sachse, c. 1851. The New York Public Library. Astor, Lenox and Tilden Foundations. Prints Division

significant effects on American government. The suits were brought by a Rhode Island shoemaker and his mother, Martin Luther and Rachel Luther, against a group of state militiamen who had broken into the Luthers' house seeking a man accused of treason against the state. On being sued for damages, the militiamen claimed immunity because the Rhode Island legislature had declared martial law over the entire state, ostensibly to prevent revolution. In response, the Luthers argued that the state government itself was illegal, making the militiamen in effect outlaws—and in any event, no state government had the power to suspend civil rights.

The Luthers were the point-persons in a test case brought by a political reform group, the Rhode Island Suffrage Association, seeking to rid the state of its anti-democratic charter, a relic of colonial days that permitted a privileged minority to control the legislature and prevent most citizens from voting. The Suffragists had drafted their own People's Constitution, persuaded a majority of the state's male citizens to approve it, held elections, and set up their own state government. Not surprisingly, the incumbent or charter government declared martial law, passed a treason statute, and persuaded President John Tyler to promise vaguely that if a shooting war broke out, he would protect the charter government.

The Suffragists believed that government in America derived from the people, and that the majority is entitled to change the government when and how it sees fit. The Suffragists persisted in these ideas, which by the 1840s seemed not only foreign but also quite dangerous to the established order. They firmly believed that courts were obliged to protect political rights. Assuming that the Supreme Court would respect the wishes of Rhode Island's political majority,

111

they pinned their hopes on the constitutional command (Article IV, Section 4) that "The United States shall guarantee to every State in this Union a Republican Form of Government . . ." In ruling by force rather than representation, they argued in the Luther case, Rhode Island's charter government had violated the Guarantee Clause and should be dissolved in favor of their own, clearly republican, government.

As counsel for the incumbents, Daniel Webster insisted that the only legitimate government was the one in existence, and that it had every right to maintain itself by force of arms.

Speaking for the Court in January 1849, Chief Justice Taney coolly dismissed the matter for lack of jurisdiction and turned the Guaranty Clause into a dead letter. The Court would not attempt to unravel the "political question" of which competing group was entitled to govern Rhode Island. The Guaranty Clause applied to the admission of new states to the Union, Taney said, and once Congress was satisfied with the form of a new state government, the Guaranty Clause had no further bearing on the situation.

The Taney Court was doubtless wise to stay out of the Rhode Island situation. None of the rights at stake were *judicially* enforceable, or so it appeared to those particular judges—and indeed they had no weapon such as the Fourteenth Amendment (1868) to help them at the time. To save the Court from a predicament, they took refuge behind the Political Question doctrine.

Nine years later, the self-preserving lessons of *Luther* were swept away in the Dred Scott case, when Roger Taney and his colleagues attempted to impose a judicial solution on the politically intractable issue of whether Congress should permit slavery in Western territories that would soon become new states.

No one doubted the power of Congress (Article IV, Section 3) "to dispose of and make needful Rules and Regulations respecting the Territory or other Property belonging to the United States . . ." But whether that power encompassed slavery in the territories was a matter of great dispute. Northerners in Congress predictably took the affirmative view and history apparently supported them.

In 1787 the Confederation Congress had prohibited slavery in the Northwest Territory; and while this antedated the Constitution, the fact was that Congress had again confronted the problem in 1819 when the pro-slavery Missouri Territory applied for statehood. The Missouri Compromise of 1820 had split the difference between Maine and Missouri, leaving a Union of twelve free states and twelve slave states. Congress had also banned slavery in the remaining area of the Louisiana Purchase north of latitude thirty-six degrees, thirty minutes North, except for the new state of Missouri, which remained a pro-slavery stronghold jutting into the territories.

But the Missouri Compromise was a political arrangement, not a constitutional interpretation. Still unanswered in a legal sense were two questions: 1) Was Congress really empowered to prohibit slavery in the territories? 2) Were blacks, free or slave, citizens of the United States with full constitutional rights?

The Taney Court initially skirted the slavery issue, avoiding the contagion that was weakening the political branches of government. Back in 1842, the Court had upheld the original (1793) federal Fugitive Slave Law and declared in Justice Story's opinion (*Prigg* v. *Pennsylvania*), that *any* state laws concerning fugitive slaves were invalid because Congress had exclusive power in that area.

In 1851 the Court deliberately ignored a chance to rule on slavery in the territories. In *Strader* v. *Graham*, the question was whether runaway slaves became free when they entered free states or territories. Had the Court attempted an answer, the Justices would have plunged into the deep waters of the territorial issue. Instead, they deftly held that the fugitives in *Strader* had not changed their status by entering free-soil Ohio. What governed their status, ruled Chief Justice Taney, was the law of the state where they *now* lived. And since that state, Kentucky, considered them slaves, the Court followed suit. It dismissed the case for lack of jurisdiction and thus escaped the entire question of how the slaves had been affected by entering free Ohio.

A year later, the Missouri supreme court invoked the *Strader* rule in a case involving a St. Louis slave, Dred Scott, the plaintiff of record in a suit against his legal owner, John F.A. Sanford.

Dred Scott had ostensibly sued Sanford in order to gain his freedom. But Sanford was, in fact, a New York abolitionist who probably never met Scott and was interested in him only as a means to a greater end. What the Supreme Court eventually called *Dred Scott* v. *Sandford* [sic] was actually a test case by which the real plaintiffs sought to force the courts to deal at last with slavery in the territories.

Born about 1795, Dred Scott began his unremarkable early life as the property of a Virginia family named Blow, who moved to St. Louis in 1827, taking their slaves with them. In 1833 the Blows sold Scott to Dr. John Emerson, an army surgeon. In 1834 Dr. Emerson was posted to Rock Island, Illinois and later to Fort Snelling in the Wisconsin Territory. During his tour in these places, the doctor used Scott as a body servant. Illinois state law forbade slavery; the Missouri Compromise banned it in the Wisconsin Territory. Accordingly, Scott had spent five years on free soil by the time Dr. Emerson returned to St. Louis in 1838, taking Scott back to the slave state of Missouri.

Dr. Emerson soon died, leaving Scott to his widow, who moved to New York in the mid-1840s, delegating Scott's care to his original owners, the Blow family. In 1846 Harry Blow, a young lawyer who abhorred slavery, launched a suit in the Missouri courts seeking Dred Scott's freedom by reason of his five-year sojourn on free soil. Of course Scott's owner, Mrs. Emerson, could have freed her slave with the stroke of a pen. But Mrs. Emerson shared Blow's antislavery sentiments and so became the original defendant of record when the case began as *Scott, a Man of Color* v. *Emerson*.

Harry Blow spent six years pushing the case upward to the Missouri supreme court; years during which the county sheriff had loose charge of Dred Scott, hiring him out for odd jobs. But the effort proved disappointing. In 1852 the Missouri court followed *Strader* v. *Graham* in ruling that Scott's status was controlled by Missouri law and he must remain a slave.

That might have been that, but suddenly the bitter clashes in the neighboring Kansas Territory stirred new interest in the status of slaves being moved to free soil, and Harry Blow revived Scott's case. It was now called *Dred Scott* v. *Sandford*, Mrs. Emerson having supposedly sold Scott

Dred Scott, 1858. Missouri Historical Society, St. Louis

to her brother, John F.A. Sanford of New York, and in 1854 the case was docketed by the federal circuit court for Missouri.

The immediate issue was not Scott's freedom but whether he was entitled to sue in a federal court. If Scott was legally a citizen of Missouri, he could proceed with a federal diversity suit between citizens of different states, the defendant being John Sanford of New York. But could a slave be a citizen? By arguing that Scott as a slave could not be a citizen of Missouri, Sanford's lawyers persuaded the circuit court to rule that it lacked jurisdiction—thus enabling Scott's lawyers to appeal directly to the Supreme Court on a writ of error. The case was first argued in February 1856, a presidential election year in which the incumbent Democrats were relying on Southern support and the newborn Republican Party was attracting antislavery Northerners.

When the Justices discussed the Scott case at conference in April, they agreed only that their disagreement must not be used to fuel the presidential fires. At the suggestion of Justice Samuel Nelson (a New York Democrat), the Court

View of St. Louis, from Lucas Place. The white-domed courthouse at right, in this hand-colored lithograph by Edward Sachse from the late 1850s, was the first venue for *Dred Scott* v. *Sandford.* The building is still in use. Chicago Historical Society

ordered the case reargued in December—conveniently after the 1856 election.

After conferring again in February 1857, seven of the nine Justices were ready to decide the Scott case on the narrow ground offered by *Strader* v. *Graham,* namely that Missouri law determined Scott's status, and the Supreme Court had no power to revise a state court's interpretation of the state's own laws. Justice Nelson was assigned to write the opinion, which would have left Scott a slave, unable to sue in federal court. It would also have defused the test case, avoiding the subsequent explosion.

But that outcome hardly satisfied Justice John McLean (Ohio Republican), a devout Methodist who was not known for disguising either his antislavery sentiments or his presidential ambitions. McLean prepared a dissent asserting that Dred Scott was a citizen, his sojourn on free soil had made him a free man, and Congress was empowered to ban slavery in the territories. McLean was joined in dissent by Justice Curtis (Massachusetts Whig), who offered historical evidence supporting Dred Scott's claim to freedom. Curtis

reported that in 1787 five states had made free blacks both citizens and voters; and that Congress had regulated slavery in the territory fourteen times. In effect, the two dissenters were summarizing the Northern consensus on slavery that ultimately entered the Constitution by way of the Civil War and the Fourteenth Amendment.

The seven majority Justices refused to let the dissents go unanswered. Each of them decided to write a separate opinion addressing the issues he considered paramount.

The Taney Court had acquired such prestige that many Americans, including most of the Justices, believed it quite capable of resolving the slavery dilemma.

The leading propounder of that illusion was Democratic President-elect Buchanan, who thought it would be splendid if he could say in his upcoming inaugural address on March 4, 1857, that the Supreme Court had a plan to end the awful tensions vexing the nation. Buchanan wrote letters to Justices John Catron (Tennessee Democrat) and Robert Grier (Pennsylvania Democrat) soliciting their advice as to whether he could safely promise America imminent judicial salvation. Duly assured, Buchanan plunged ahead with his famous inaugural bromide, asserting that slavery in the territories was "a judicial question, which legitimately belongs to the Supreme Court of the United States, before whom it is now pending and will, it is understood, be speedily and finally settled. To their decision, in common with all good citizens, I shall cheerfully submit, whatever this may be."

Two days later, on March 6, 1857, the Court issued a decision so divisive that President Buchanan must have wished he had been struck dumb on Inauguration Day. Of the nine assorted opinions, the most divisive as well as the most official was that of Chief Justice Taney (Maryland Democrat).

Taney, now a frail but fiery octogenarian, took it upon himself to deny federal jurisdiction in the Dred Scott case on what seemed to many the three most inflammatory grounds he could have devised.

First, Taney held that the Constitution ruled out citizenship for slaves or their descendants. Citing law after law, Taney recalled white America's racial attitudes before, during, and after the Revolution, finding it unarguable that the Framers shared a national consensus that even free blacks "had no rights which the white man was bound to respect; and that the Negro might justly and lawfully be reduced to slavery for his benefit." Having sketched this background (sharply questioned by Justice Curtis in *his* opinion), Taney found the same attitudes reflected in the Constitution itself. Only two provisions covered slavery. According to Taney, both "treat them [slaves] as property and make it the duty of the government to protect it."

Second, Taney held that Scott's five years on free soil had not made him free—because the soil *itself* was never free. This leap brought Taney to settling the territorial issue. According to his reasoning, slaves were property; the Fifth Amendment barred Congress from violating the property rights of slaveholders; and the Missouri Compromise's ban on slavery violated the Fifth Amendment. Ergo, the Missouri Compromise was unconstitutional—the first Act of Congress to be so declared since *Marbury* v. *Madison* in 1803.

President James Buchanan, c. 1856. National Archives, Washington, D.C.

As to Scott, his residence in the Wisconsin Territory was irrelevant. That was slave country, no matter what Congress said, and Scott had been no freer there than when he had lived in Missouri.

Finally, Taney held that Scott's status was permanently governed by the laws of Missouri (even when he had lived in the free state of Illinois), and the Supreme Court was bound by Missouri's judgment. Since Missouri considered Scott a slave, the Court could not treat him as an American citizen entitled to sue in federal courts. Moreover, Taney added, it didn't really matter whether states abolished slavery or retained it—blacks were excluded from national citizenship.

Taney's opinion was universally misread to mean that the Court had ruled blacks were inferior creatures devoid of any rights a white man need respect. Taney's use of the Bill of Rights to keep blacks enslaved struck Northerners as truly outrageous. No less galling was the Court's apparent fiat that Congress had no right to control slavery in the territories; even local choice

115

Justice John A. Campbell, who became a high-ranking official in the Confederate government, and ended the war in a Union prison. Collection of the Supreme Court of the United States, Washington, D.C.

was now questionable and certainly no road to peace. Calling the decision "the greatest crime in the judicial annals of the Republic," the Northern press spun conspiracy theories, alleging a proslavery deal between the Court and the President. "If the people obey this decision," one editorial warned, "they disobey God."

The extent of the *Dred Scott* decision's contribution to the onset of the Civil War is a matter of debate. It certainly did nothing to relieve the polarization and feelings of hopelessness that ultimately made war inevitable. But nobody questions the decision's impact on the Court itself; the damage was immediately clear. By devastating public confidence in judicial integrity, warned the *North American Review* of October 1857, the decision might "well be accounted the greatest political calamity which this country, under our forms of government, could sustain."

Many Northerners now considered the Supreme Court pro-slavery and hence unworthy of being obeyed. In *Ableman* v. *Booth* (1859), for example, a Milwaukee editor named Ableman,

jailed for helping a fugitive slave escape from federal custody, had been released by the Wisconsin supreme court, based on its finding that the federal Fugitive Slave Act was unconstitutional. The Supreme Court reversed this highly popular decision on the obvious ground of federal supremacy. Waves of angry protest then swept the North, breathing new life into the supposedly moribund theory that the Supreme Court had no right to overrule a state.

Already friendless among Northern states, the *Scott*-tarnished Supreme Court entered the Civil War as the truly weakest branch of a suddenly galvanized federal government. The Justices were generally disregarded in Washington for the duration.

In his 1860 presidential campaign, Abraham Lincoln repeatedly attacked the *Dred Scott* decision and at times seemed to be running as hard against Chief Justice Taney as against Democrat Stephen A. Douglas. In his inaugural address, the first Republican President managed to portray the Supreme Court as a danger to democracy, and he calmly asserted the chief executive's equal right to interpret the Constitution in the interests of "the whole people."

As civil war erupted, Lincoln's urgent priority was to keep Maryland and other border states from joining the Confederacy; he considered some expedients justified to foil secessionists. But Chief Justice Taney felt that a Union without the rule of law was not worth saving. As the Circuit Justice supervising Maryland's federal courts, he quickly collided with Lincoln's policies.

In Taney's hometown, Baltimore, secessionists had attacked trainloads of Union troops headed south to defend Washington. To prevent guerrilla warfare and secure the vital rail corridor, Lincoln authorized the military to suspend habeas corpus and other civil liberties that might have hampered the swift roundup of all suspected troublemakers in the area.

The Constitution permits the suspension of habeas corpus "when in Cases of Rebellion or Invasion the public Safety may require it." But it does not specify just who may do the suspending. Since the clause (Article I, Section 9) appears in a list of limitations on the powers of Congress, however, Taney naturally believed that the Framers had intended any such suspension to be carried out by Congress, and that the President's

THE POLITICAL QUADRILLE
Music by Dred Scott

The Political Quadrille, Music by Dred Scott. The famous *Dred Scott* decision had both an immediate and lasting impact on national politics. In this anonymous cartoon of 1860, almost four years after the decision was issued, Lincoln, Bell, Douglas, and Breckinridge, the candidates in the 1860 presidential election, are forced to dance to Scott's tune. Library of Congress, Washington, D.C.

unilateral action had violated their intent.

In May 1861, Taney chose to make his point in the case of one John Merryman, an alleged Confederate sympathizer arrested by Union troops in Baltimore. The military suspected—but offered no proof—that Merryman had participated in a Baltimore riot and blown up railroad bridges. Jailed at Fort McHenry, Merryman managed to petition Taney for a writ of habeas corpus challenging his detention for lack of specific charges. Taney rushed to Baltimore and issued the writ ordering the fort's commander, General George Cadwalader, to produce Merryman in federal circuit court and explain his arrest.

Merryman remained in jail, his captors explaining only that they intended to obey Lincoln's orders, not Taney's. Exasperated, Taney held the general in contempt, ordering *his* arrest. The lone federal marshal sent to remove General Cadwalader from Fort McHenry was unceremoniously ejected from the grounds.

Enraged—and apparently concerned that the military might arrest *him*—Taney next wrote an opinion, dispatched to Lincoln himself, holding that only Congress could suspend the privilege of habeas corpus, and thereby declaring the President's orders unconstitutional. If the military can usurp judicial and legislative authority, warned Taney, "the people of the United States are no longer living under a government of laws, but every citizen holds his life, liberty, and property at the will and pleasure of the army officer in whose military district he may happen to be found." Taney informed Lincoln that every person arrested by the military, unless subject to military justice, must be turned over to the civil authorities. And he urged the President forthwith to "perform his constitutional duty."

Lincoln did not even acknowledge Taney's exhortation, nor feel any political need to do so. Indeed, the Northern press excoriated Taney as, among other things, "a hoary apologist for treason."

Although Congress was initially full of doubts, especially about the fate of civil liberties, the lawmakers eventually recognized the insurrection, approved Lincoln's reactions, and soon disputed only the President's military decisions—many congressmen imagining themselves potential commanders-in-chief.

Taney's *Merryman* concerns were prophetic. Although John Merryman himself was eventually freed, Lincoln's State Department launched press censorship and a large network of spy-seeking agents, a secret police that arrested hundreds of citizens without explanation and subjected them to military trials and detention without recourse to habeas corpus. The War Department later fell prey to the security mania, arresting thousands of citizens for suspected disloyalty or resisting the draft. Many were harshly

Fort McHenry, Baltimore. This hand-colored lithograph by Edward Sachse, 1865, shows the fort as it looked during the war, when it was a prison camp run by the Union Army. Maryland Historical Society, Baltimore

punished by military courts; others were simply released after having been sufficiently cowed to impress the local populace. By war's end, the Union army was ready and eager to govern the defeated South in a similar fashion.

Taney's outspokenness was almost unique on the wartime Court, which by 1863 included four Lincoln appointees—among them, Samuel F. Miller, and the President's close friend, David Davis. The Lincoln-era Justices were under constant pressure to support the government's war measures. They found reason to deny jurisdiction in cases challenging military trials of civilians and the Legal Tender Acts. But in *The Prize Cases* (1863), involving Lincoln's Southern blockade, the Court upheld the President's power to make war without a congressional declaration. Writing for the majority, Justice Robert Grier said Lincoln had no choice but to respond when civil war suddenly erupted. "The President was bound to meet it in the shape it presented itself, without waiting for Congress to baptize it with a name."

Chief Justice Taney predictably joined the anti-administration dissenters. Of the nine participating Justices, four declared Lincoln's actions unconstitutional, meaning that the Court supported the President by a single vote. One more dissenter and all of Lincoln's wartime poli-

cies might have become legally questionable, making his leadership even more difficult.

Shrinking from any further risk, the wartime Court spent the 1864–65 term in virtual hibernation. During that judicial eclipse, Chief Justice Taney spoke for many in lamenting that the Supreme Court would never be "restored to the authority and rank which the Constitution intended to confer on it."

When Taney died in October 1864 at the age of eighty-seven, his eulogists were drowned out by his detractors. But time's healing hand reveals a very different Taney—the political blind man of *Dred Scott*, of course, but also the superb judicial architect of dual federalism. He was the gallant heretic who seriously believed that civil liberties outrank military necessity, a notion many other judges trumpet only in peacetime. Felix Frankfurter was only one of numerous constitutional scholars who have come to believe that Taney was a Civil War casualty, unfairly maligned and vastly underrated. Putting *Dred Scott* aside, Frankfurter said, "The intellectual power of his opinions and their enduring contributions to a workable adjustment of the theoretical distribution of authority between two governments for a single people, place Taney second only to Marshall in the constitutional history of our country."

Provost-marshals of the Third Army Corps, December, 1863. Provost-marshals in the Union Army policed civilians during the war. Library of Congress, Washington, D.C.

Chief Justice Roger B. Taney near the end of his life. National Archives, Washington, D.C.

President Abraham Lincoln, January 8, 1864. Photograph by Mathew Brady. National Archives, Washington, D.C.

9

THE SECOND AMERICAN REVOLUTION

At the beginning of April 1865, the Justices emerged from their wartime eclipse. The Court was no longer Washington's most invisible monument. The Justices had moved upstairs to the first floor of the Capitol, where the old Senate chamber had been remodeled as an imposing courtroom aglow with splashes of gilt, marble, and velvet. And looming along the high bench, flanked by ten marble columns, were ten Justices—more than ever before, or since.

To those ten men, five of them appointed by Lincoln, the Court's record size was not entirely a source of comfort. It was also a reminder of the Court's weakness, its reliance upon the political branches for everything from the Justices' salaries to their number.

Lincoln's Union government had almost completely restructured the prewar Court of *Dred Scott* notoriety. The old federal judiciary had consisted of nine judicial circuits and nine seats on the Supreme Court. Five of those circuits had encompassed slave states, and five Justices had been Southerners, a distortion in representation of the country's sectional makeup. The Republican Congress had compressed the South into three judicial circuits in 1862, and recognized the new Western states by giving them two new circuits. This plan was not only good for the country, it also enabled Lincoln to appoint new

Justices sensitive to his views.

Lincoln's first appointee was Ohio Republican Noah Swayne, predictably loyal. In 1862 came Justice Samuel F. Miller, a bear-like Iowan of immense physical as well as intellectual strength, who relished life, despised slavery to the point of having personally financed Union troops, and was not only a first-rate lawyer but also the only medical doctor ever to sit on the Supreme Court. Later in 1862 came Justice David Davis, an experienced Illinois judge and close friend of Lincoln's; he had managed the President's campaign in 1860. Davis had substantial political ambitions balanced by a sense of moderation that made him increasingly unhappy with the Administration's use of military courts to try civilians in wartime.

Further changes were inevitable. In 1863, with Chief Justice Taney still presiding, the Court had upheld the legality of the war in *The Prize Cases* by a mere five-to-four vote, and neither Congress nor the President wished to repeat that sort of judicial suspense. Accordingly, Congress had created a tenth judicial circuit encompassing California and Oregon, partly to help Unionize those new states, but also to justify the addition of a tenth Justice. He would presumably provide the Court with a majority of six Justices loyal to the Union and sympathetic to Lincoln's policies.

Lincoln's appointee was Stephen J. Field, a

The new Supreme Court Chamber in the Capitol, 1861–1935 (now the restored old Senate Chamber). Office of the Architect of the Capitol, Washington, D.C.

When the Court moved upstairs to the first floor of the Capitol, the old courtroom became the law library for both Congress and the Court, seen here in this photograph taken c. 1895. Library of Congress, Washington, D.C.

Thomas U. Walter. *Cross-section Plan of the Enlarged Dome of the Capitol.* 1859. Watercolor, 46¹/₂ × 26". Office of the Architect of the Capitol, Washington, D.C.

bright New York lawyer turned California frontiersman. Field had been a gold-rush adventurer, the *alcalde* (mayor) of the small town of Marysville, a distinguished member of the California supreme court, and a crony of Leland Stanford (one of the "Big Four" who controlled the Central Pacific Railroad). Lincoln selected Field partly because he was versed in California's Spanish-bequeathed legal problems. But more importantly, Lincoln had been told that Field was judicially restrained, open-minded about legislative innovations, and clearly a solid vote for Administration policies.

As a member of the Supreme Court, Justice Field turned out to be none of the above. He was an arch-individualist virtually immune to pressure or fear. With his fierce eyes, black beard, and fiery temper, Field had the look of an Old Testament prophet and the self-confidence of one of The Elect. Descended from New England Puritan divines, he had conquered his part of the West with luck, pluck, and gall. At forty-six, Justice Field was no stranger to violence, no friend of the weak, and no disbeliever in predestination. Men who really knew Field, including those who had tangled with him, could have predicted that during his nearly thirty-five-year Supreme Court tenure he would become the most uncompromising apostle of laissez-faire in the judicial history of the United States.

Justice Field epitomized one side of the push-pull forces within the postwar Court. Eager to return to judicial combat, his side wanted to begin immediately placing the Court's imprint on solutions to the country's fundamental problems. According to this view, the Court must act with clarity and courage in order to regain its legitimacy and leadership. But the other side, the Court's cautionary voices, argued that some problems were simply too explosive for the Jus-

122

JUDGE TERRY SLAPS JUSTICE FIELD IN THE FACE AND IS SHOT DEAD BY DEPUTY MARSHAL NEAGLE, AT LATHROP, AUGUST 14, 1889. TERRY SAT AT THE EAST END OF THE FIFTH TABLE. SAME ROW.

Judge Terry slaps Justice Field in the face and is shot dead by Deputy Marshal Neagle, at Lathrop, August 14, 1889. David Smith Terry's notorious feud with Justice Field, which began in California before the Civil War and ended abruptly when Terry attacked Justice Field at a dinner and was shot by a United States marshal, speaks of the violence of the frontier. The New York Public Library. Astor, Lenox and Tilden Foundations

tices to handle, too likely to subject the Court to renewed crippling attacks. If the Court were to undertake them at all, it should only do so long after the fact, when emotions had cooled, post-mortems would be more acceptable, and constitutional blanks could be filled in for future use.

All of this required the Court to find a delicate balance between its majority's views of constitutional imperatives and the political branches' views of wartime necessities. The situation called for a shrewd political straddler. And just then, one of Washington's finest specimens became available. Lincoln made him Chief Justice, thereby positioning Salmon P. Chase on exactly the right fence at the right time.

Tall, handsome, commanding, Salmon Portland Chase looked like everyone's ideal President of the United States. His credentials more than matched his presence. Deeply religious, Chase abhorred slavery and was so generous with his legal skills that in the 1850s he had become famous as "the Attorney General for runaway slaves." By 1864 he had served with distinction as Governor of Ohio, an antislavery stalwart in the

United States Senate, a founder of the Republican Party, and wartime Secretary of the Treasury under Lincoln, who called him "about one and a half times bigger than any man I ever knew."

In mid-October 1864, Roger Taney died after twenty-eight years on the Supreme Court bench, ending the second longest Chief Justiceship in history. Chase immediately applied for the job; nothing would please him more, he said, than to "overrule all the pro-slavery decisions." Lincoln invited him to become the sixth Chief Justice of the United States. Then fifty-six, Chase was confirmed by the Senate on the same day he was appointed (December 6, 1864).

Lincoln had made it quite clear that he expected Chase to uphold the President's war measures, including the Legal Tender Act authorizing the government (through former Treasury Secretary Chase) to issue some 450 million dollars in paper money that had no specie or gold bullion backing. Chief Justice Chase could hardly ignore Lincoln's mandate, but he soon made it equally clear that his primary loyalties were to his conscience, the Court, and the Constitution.

Abraham Lincoln's Second Inauguration, March 4, 1865. President Lincoln is seated to the left of the podium, next to Andrew Johnson. The Supreme Court is seated to the right of the podium. Chief Justice Salmon Portland Chase (in conversation with the man behind him), Justices James Moore Wayne, Samuel Nelson, and Nathan Clifford are in focus in this photograph by Alexander Gardner. The Western Reserve Historical Society, Cleveland

Chief Justice Salmon Portland Chase's appointment to the Supreme Court, December 6, 1864. Collection of the Supreme Court of the United States, Washington, D.C.

The Supreme Court in 1865. From the left: Associate Justices David Davis, Noah Haynes Swayne, Robert Cooper Grier, James Moore Wayne, Chief Justice Salmon Portland Chase, Associate Justices Samuel Nelson, Nathan Clifford, Samuel Freeman Miller, Stephen Johnson Field. Brown Brothers, Sterling, Pennsylvania

By happenstance, Lincoln's efforts to appoint Justices sympathetic to his policies almost providentially provided the Court with four aspiring or potential Presidents (Chase, Miller, Davis, and Field). Such Justices kept their political wits about them. Precisely because Chase himself continued to yearn for the Presidency, he was able to provide the Court with a sense of political realism. His strong-minded brethren, although immune to his control, did the same thing in their own ways.

As the Civil War ended, a Court recovering from *Dred Scott* might have been forgiven for being slow to pick one major constitutional target out of so many possibilities. The war had profoundly changed the national equation. In many ways, the Union forces had wrought a second American Revolution. The Union had indeed been preserved, by force if not by reason. The war confirmed John Marshall's vision: Americans were one people, having delegated their authority to the central government under a Constitution that bound the states irrevocably as

one nation. The United States were indivisible, although not necessarily with liberty and justice for all.

On April 9, 1866, Congress passed a civil-rights act over President Andrew Johnson's veto. The law made blacks American citizens and overruled certain aspects of the harsh Southern laws (Black Codes) controlling former slaves. But equally significant, it was the first major federal law to hurdle a presidential veto in American history. From then on, Congress was in charge of Reconstruction, ready to pressure, indeed bully, a sharply weakened President, and of course keep a watchful eye on the seemingly dormant Supreme Court.

At practically the same moment—on April 3, 1866—the Chase Court produced a decision that not only vindicated Roger Taney's travail in the *Merryman* case, but also cast a constitutional pall over Radical schemes for Reconstruction. In *Ex parte Milligan*, the Court ruled unanimously that Lincoln had violated the Constitution in 1862 when he ordered "disloyal" citizens tried by military courts in places outside the actual war

Chief Justice Salmon Portland Chase. National Archives, Washington, D.C.

Arraigned at Indianapolis for Treason. Indiana Historical Society, Indianapolis

Military Commission That Tried Indiana Conspirators in 1864. Indiana State Library, Indianapolis

President Andrew Johnson. National Archives, Washington, D.C.

Justice David Davis. David Davis Family Papers, Illinois State Historical Library, Springfield

zone—places where the civil courts had remained open.

During the war, many Northerners had been deeply troubled by the fact that civilians had become subject to military justice. The Supreme Court, unable to act effectively on this issue in the *Merryman* episode, had been given a second chance in 1864 when the Justices received an appeal from Clement L. Vallandigham, a former Ohio Congressman and notorious "Copperhead" (a Northerner who sympathized with the South). In 1863 General Ambrose Burnside, the Union commander of Ohio, ordered a crackdown on what he called "express or implied treason," the latter being Burnside's original contribution to American law. When Vallandigham went on a binge of speech-making to denounce Lincoln's policies, Burnside had him arrested and tried by a military commission, which duly found him guilty of aiding and comforting the enemy. He was sentenced to detention for the remainder of the war.

Lincoln promptly had Vallandigham deported to the Confederacy. But the exile managed to appeal to the Supreme Court, alleging that his military trial had been unconstitutional. The Justices denied Vallandigham's appeal on solid ground: at the time, neither Congress nor the Constitution had authorized the Court to review military trials by writ of certiorari, the avenue Vallandigham had chosen for appeal.

But *Ex parte Milligan*, involving a fanatic Indiana Copperhead named Lambdin P. Milligan, came before the Court in the very different climate of 1866. In 1864 Milligan and his fellow fantasizers had concocted a scheme to free Confederate prisoners of war, arm them with weapons seized from Union arsenals, and take over the state governments of Ohio, Indiana, and Illinois.

Indiana was hundreds of miles from the shooting war, so the federal court in Indianapolis was open—but Milligan was tried before a military commission. Found guilty of aiding the enemy and conspiring to incite an insurrection, he was sentenced to death by hanging. Andrew Johnson approved the execution soon after becoming President. He stayed it only to let the Supreme Court hear the case (although he ultimately commuted the sentence to life imprisonment).

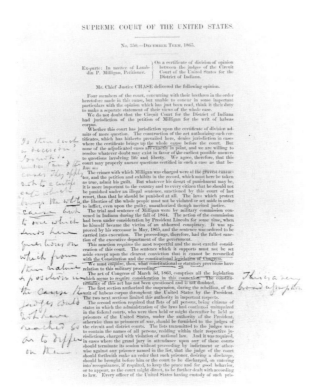

The first page of Chief Justice Chase's concurring opinion in *Ex parte Milligan*, with Justice Davis's marginalia. Justice Davis was deeply upset that the Chief Justice did not share his view of the case. David Davis Family Papers, Illinois State Historical Library

From the Court's perspective, there was an important legal difference between Milligan's case and Vallandigham's. In the interim, Congress had suspended the privilege of the writ of habeas corpus, except under a special circumstance pertaining to Milligan. If a grand jury met and failed to indict a person then in federal custody, he was entitled to habeas corpus release by the federal court with proper jurisdiction over his case.

After the military commission had tried Milligan, the circuit court for Indiana—Supreme Court Justice David Davis presiding—convened a grand jury that discussed Milligan's case and then disbanded without returning an indictment. Milligan therefore petitioned the circuit court for a writ of habeas corpus. He alleged that his military trial had violated practically every one of the Constitution's due-process guarantees, from the right to grand jury indictment to the right of public trial by an impartial jury composed of local citizens.

Justice Davis had protested constantly to his friend Lincoln about the use of military tribunals to punish civilians, and he firmly regarded *Ex*

parte Milligan as "the most important case *ever* brought before the [Supreme] Court." It arrived there because Davis as Circuit Justice made sure it would. He and the local district judge, with whom he had heard Milligan's plea, agreed to disagree on the constitutional validity of military trials (Milligan's actual guilt was never in question). Their split "certified" the issues, as this technique is called, thereby sending the case directly to the Supreme Court, free of all the jurisdictional problems that had impeded Vallandigham's case.

The government's lawyers, headed by Major General Benjamin F. Butler, justified military tribunals as a wartime exigency and constitutionally valid under the President's war powers. But Milligan's team of legal stars, among them Justice Field's eminent brother, David Dudley Field, as well as a future president, Congressman James A. Garfield, called the tribunals "a gross and monstrous usurpation."

The Court ruled that President Lincoln had no constitutional power to order military trials for civilians in areas where civilian courts were still functioning. Accordingly, the military commission in Indiana had no jurisdiction over Milligan—he was a civilian outside the war zone—and he must be set free.

In his eloquent opinion for the Court, Justice Davis clearly limited the government's use of martial law to actual combat areas. "The Constitution of the United States," he wrote, "is a law for rulers and people, equally in war and in peace, and covers with the shield of its protection all classes of men, at all times and under all circumstances. No doctrine, involving more pernicious consequences, was ever invented by the wit of man than that any of its provisions can be suspended during any of the great exigencies of government. . . . Martial law cannot arise from a *threatened* invasion. The necessity must be actual and present; the invasion real, such as effectually closes the courts. . . . Martial law can never exist where the courts are open, and in the proper and unobstructed exercise of their jurisdiction. It is also confined to the locality of actual war."

Despite their unanimity about Lincoln's actions, however, the Justices were sharply divided on the question of whether the Constitution forbids *Congress* as well as the President to authorize military trials for civilians outside war zones. The issue of congressional power was not in fact before the Court. Lincoln had acted unilaterally; Congress had not been involved in the Milligan case. But Justice Davis nonetheless declared in his sweeping opinion that *no one*—not even Congress—could authorize military trials for civilians when the civil courts were still open and functioning.

A minority of four Justices, including Chief Justice Chase, disagreed. While concurring that Milligan must go free because the President's actions were invalid, they contended that Congress, under its delegated war powers, could indeed authorize military trials for civilians. This somewhat undercut Justice Davis's landmark opinion for the Court. Though widely celebrated as a powerful defense of American civil liberties, *Ex parte Milligan* was burdened by the ambiguity that four Justices were by no means ready to stand in the way of military necessity.

The remarkable thing about the *Milligan* decision—at the time—was that a majority of five Justices, including Field, had declared in effect that neither Congress nor the President had the final say on the constitutional limits of military necessity. The Supreme Court, they asserted, must make that judgment.

So the Court had discarded its wartime reticence—and no one was less pleased than the Radical Republicans in Congress who firmly believed that the only way to deal with the still defiant South was to impose military government, including military trials for disobedient civilians.

Although the Court decided *Milligan* in April 1866, it did not release full opinions in the case until mid-December. The Justices had reason to expect harassing fire from Congress. By April 1866, the Court's tenth seat had been vacant for nearly a year, ever since the death of Justice John Catron in May 1865, and President Johnson now tried to fill it by nominating Henry Stanbery, his Attorney General. Instead, Congress abolished the tenth seat—and announced that the next two vacancies after that would not be filled. So the Court, then nine members strong, would eventually shrink to seven members—not one of them to be appointed by Andrew Johnson, if Congress could possibly avoid it.

Overriding President Johnson's objections,

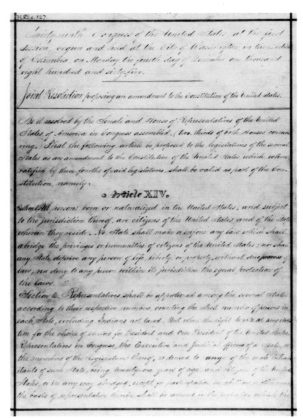

First page of the Joint Resolution which became the Fourteenth Amendment to the Constitution. National Archives, Washington, D.C.

both houses of Congress approved the Fourteenth Amendment in June 1866 and submitted it to the states for ratification. Quickly approved in the North, the proposed Amendment stalled in the South—Congress having asked the former Confederacy for approval rather than having compelled it. As time passed, many non-Southern observers also noted that the proposed Amendment contained within it a profound shift in federal-state relations.

In curbing the white South, the Fourteenth Amendment reduced the power of all states equally, while increasing the central government's power over the states.

The Amendment provided three key steps:

. . . First, it overruled *Dred Scott* and sought to prevent the Court from overturning the 1866 Civil Rights Act, should that law be challenged. Whereas Roger Taney had read the Constitution as ruling out citizenship for blacks, the new Amendment defined American citizenship in a broad way that clearly included blacks. "All persons born or naturalized in the United States, and subject to

Taking the Oath of Allegiance, from John Townsend Trowbridge's *The South: A Tour of its Battle-Fields and Ruined Cities* (Hartford: L. Stebbins, 1866). The New York Public Library. Astor, Lenox and Tilden Foundations

the jurisdiction thereof, are citizens of the United States and of the State where they reside."

. . . Second, the Amendment outlawed the Black Codes and any similar discriminatory legislation. "No State shall make or enforce any law which shall abridge the privileges or immunities of citizens of the United States; nor shall any State deprive any person of life, liberty, or property, without due process of law; nor deny to any person within its jurisdiction the equal protection of the laws."

. . . Third, the Amendment sought to compel the South to enfranchise blacks by penalizing any state that denied the vote to qualified adult male citizens (women were not mentioned). The penalty was to be a proportional slash in the offending state's representation in Congress.

The Fourteenth Amendment had a number of loopholes. It did not explicitly prohibit segregation, for example, and states could still deny black suffrage if they didn't mind having fewer

Congressmen. Yet every Southern state except Tennessee spurned ratification, apparently dooming any chance that the required majority (three-fourths of all state legislatures) could be mustered in favor of the Amendment. As a result, the anti-Southern Radical Republicans in Congress became stronger than ever.

For the Supreme Court, 1867 was a year of trying to avoid the Republicans' monumental quarrels with President Johnson, as well as with the entire South. The tension began in January, when the Court decided a case entitled *Ex parte Garland* by overruling an act of Congress—only the third such decision (after *Marbury* and *Dred Scott*) in the Court's history.

At issue in *Garland* was an 1865 federal law barring lawyers from practicing before the federal courts unless they swore an oath that they had remained loyal Unionists throughout the Civil War. The purpose was to punish former Confederates. But Augustus H. Garland, a distinguished Arkansas lawyer who had practiced before the Supreme Court prior to the war, had no intention of being excluded without a fight. Garland had followed his state out of the Union and served in the Confederate Congress. To salvage his career, he first obtained a full pardon

The Repentant (?) Enemies of the Republic Applying for Pardon to Uncle Sam. A cynical British view of the rush for amnesty after the war, 1865. The New-York Historical Society

from President Johnson for all war-related offenses he might have committed; he then sued for permission to resume his federal practice despite his inability to take the test oath. As he saw it, the federal oath law was a bill of attainder—legislation inflicting punishment without any judicial process. The Constitution (Article I, Section 9) forbids such measures throughout the United States. But even if the law were found to be constitutional, Garland argued, his presidential pardon would free him from complying with it.

Also before the Supreme Court was a companion case (*Cummings* v. *Missouri*) challenging a similar state law that would have barred former Confederates from engaging in *any* profession.

Combined as the *Test Oath Cases*, these two challenges produced an opinion from Justice Field, who ruled both laws unconstitutional under the bill of attainder clause as well as the ex post facto clause. Previous interpretations, as the Court minority noted, had invoked these clauses only against legislation that specifically named the persons to whom it applied. Justice Field had the votes to sustain his view of the federal law as "a

legislative decree of perpetual exclusion" and of Garland's pardon as having permanently immunized him from any kind of punishment for his Civil War role. According to Field, Congress was powerless to touch anyone with executive clemency. "This power of the president is not subject to legislative control."

Field's opinion was widely denounced as "*Dred Scott* Number Three"—*Milligan* having been Number Two—and Congress once again debated various schemes for controlling the Justices, including a proposal that the Court be abolished entirely. Under these circumstances, the Justices had reason to look to their flanks in March 1867, when Congress easily overrode President Johnson's veto and passed the First Reconstruction Act.

That law, dividing the old Confederacy into five military districts under martial law, was aimed at forcing the South to ratify the Fourteenth Amendment.

In April 1867, just before the Reconstruction Act was about to go into effect, the state of Mississippi asked the Court for an injunction to stop President Johnson from enforcing the law. The

TAKING THE OATH
DRAWING and RATIONS

John Rogers. *Taking the Oath and Drawing Rations.* 1865. Bronze. A sentimental view of the Oath. The New-York Historical Society

William H. McCardle. Old Courthouse Museum, Vicksburg, Mississippi

Court unanimously rejected the request. Even Justice Field joined Chief Justice Chase's opinion in *Mississippi* v. *Johnson*, which invoked the "political question" doctrine in holding that, because the President's duties under the new law were political, the Court lacked jurisdiction over his actions. In May the Court rejected a similar request from Georgia, denying jurisdiction on the ground that the suit raised "political questions" and was not justiciable.

In February 1867, Congress had authorized the Supreme Court to review cases in which federal circuit courts had denied writs of habeas corpus. Never before had the Supreme Court been given appellate jurisdiction over this particular category of cases. The new statute applied to prisoners who claimed they were being held in violation of the Constitution or federal laws, and its specific purpose was to protect blacks and federal officials from harassment by white Southerners.

In December 1867, the Court received its first such habeas appeal. The prisoner seeking habeas relief was William H. McCardle, editor of the Vicksburg *Times* and publisher of attacks against freedmen and federal troops. In one of his relentless editorial assaults, for example, McCardle blasted the South's five military commanders as "infamous, cowardly, and abandoned villains . . . who should have their heads shaved, their ears cropped, and their precious persons lodged in a penitentiary."

Major General Edward O.C. Ord, commander of the military district that included Mississippi, ordered the editor arrested and held for military

trial on charges that included inciting insurrection and printing libelous statements. McCardle petitioned the federal circuit court for a writ of habeas corpus, alleging that the Reconstruction Acts were unconstitutional. The court denied the writ, and McCardle's lawyer, Jeremiah S. Black, immediately appealed to the Supreme Court.

In January 1868, perceiving a potential threat to Reconstruction, the House passed a law requiring no fewer than two-thirds of the Justices to support any decision holding federal laws unconstitutional. The Senate refused to go along, so the bill died. The Supreme Court never did rule on the Reconstruction laws, despite their contradiction of the *Milligan* doctrine.

On the second of March, the Court began a full week of hearing arguments on the merits of William McCardle's habeas petition. Although Attorney General Stanbery had refused to argue the government's position—he considered it indefensible—his place was taken by another strong advocate, Senator Lyman Trumbull, while petitioner McCardle was represented by Jeremiah Black and David Dudley Field. Three days after the *McCardle* arguments began, Congress repealed the 1867 law granting the Court appellate jurisdiction over habeas corpus cases; it also forbade the Justices to act on any such pending cases. On March 25, the President vetoed the bill, saying that the precedent it would set would "eventually sweep away every check on arbitrary and unconstitutional legislation." Congress immediately repassed the bill over Johnson's veto.

On March 30, the Court's next opinion day, McCardle's lawyers hovered in the courtroom awaiting some disposition of his case. The McCardle team asked the Court to hear arguments on how the repeal law affected their case. The Court granted this request, then immediately granted another—a request by the government's lawyers to postpone the hearing to allow them to prepare their arguments.

More than a year passed before the Court finally issued a *McCardle* decision on April 12, 1869—a unanimous decision written by Salmon P. Chase. "We are not at liberty to inquire into the motive of the legislature," Chase wrote. "We can only examine into its power under the Constitution, and the power to make exceptions to the

Fortieth Congress of the United States of America;

At the *third* Session,

Begun and held at the city of Washington, on Monday, the *seventh* day of *December*, one thousand eight hundred and *sixty-eight*.

A RESOLUTION

Proposing an amendment to the Constitution of the United States.

Resolved by the Senate and House of Representatives of the United States of America in Congress assembled, (two-thirds of both Houses concurring) That the following article be proposed to the legislatures of the several States as an amendment to the Constitution of the United States, which, when ratified by three-fourths of said legislatures shall be valid as part of the Constitution, namely:

Article XV.

Section 1. The right of citizens of the United States to vote shall not be denied or abridged by the United States or by any State on account of race, color, or previous condition of servitude —

Section 2. The Congress shall have power to enforce this article by appropriate legislation —

Schuyler Colfax
Speaker of the House of Representatives.

B. F. Wade
President of the Senate pro tempore.

Attest:
Edw. McPherson
Clerk of House of Representatives.

Geo. C. Gorham
Secy of Senate U.S.

A Resolution Proposing an amendment to the Constitution of the United States. It was ratified as the Fifteenth Amendment, February 3, 1870. National Archives, Washington, D.C.

---

appellate jurisdiction is given by express words" (Article III, Section 2). The habeas corpus repeal law was therefore valid; the Court's jurisdiction over *McCardle* was invalid. "Without jurisdiction the Court cannot proceed at all in any cause," Chase concluded. "Jurisdiction is power to declare the law, and when it ceases to exist, the only function remaining to the Court is that of announcing the fact and dismissing the cause."

The Fifteenth Amendment was passed and submitted to the states for ratification in February 1869. This Amendment forbids any state, as well as the federal government, to deny American citizens the right to vote "on account of race, color, or previous condition of servitude." (Discrimination by "sex" was omitted.)

When the Amendment was ratified on February 3, 1870, President Grant called it "the most important event that has occurred since the nation came to life."

Four days after the Fifteenth Amendment became part of the Constitution, the Chase Court issued a decision in *Hepburn* v. *Griswold*. At issue in *Hepburn* was the validity of the wartime Legal Tender Acts, a matter involving vast sums of money. Until the Civil War, the United States had no national currency as such, and gold was the preferred medium of exchange. But during the war the Union government had begun to run short of gold to pay its escalating war debts, including its soldiers' salaries. In 1862 and 1863, at the behest of Lincoln's Treasury secretary— Salmon P. Chase—Congress had authorized the printing of 450 million dollars in paper money not backed by specie and popularly called "greenbacks." The first Legal Tender Act declared these United States notes to be legal tender for all debts, public or private, contracted before or after the law was passed.

At issue was the legal tender status of paper money not backed by specie or gold bullion. The Constitution specifically authorizes Congress (Article I, Section 8) "To coin Money, regulate the value thereof, and of foreign Coin . . ." However, since greenbacks were not coin, were worth far less than gold—and constituted money only because Congress said they did—lower courts across the country were soon besieged with the question of whether debtors could legally force their creditors to accept the fiat money. When the issue first reached the Supreme Court in 1863, the Justices claimed they lacked jurisdiction.

Hepburn v. *Griswold* involved a Kentucky creditor who had refused to accept greenbacks for a debt contracted before 1862, when the paper money was first issued. By 1869 the Legal Tender Acts had been found constitutional by fifteen out of sixteen state courts that had handed down decisions on the matter. The government itself defended the legal tender rule for paper money as a "necessary and proper" means of carrying

out its war powers. And all of the country's major borrowers, from land buyers to municipalities to the railroads, had a strong and abiding interest in being free to repay their prewar gold-based debts with depreciated greenbacks. Equally anxious about the Court's ultimate decision in *Hepburn* were all of the country's major lenders, such as banks, which sought repayment in gold.

Hepburn was a total victory for the nation's creditors. Chief Justice Chase spoke for the *Hepburn* majority in holding that creditors could refuse payment in greenbacks for debts contracted before the passage of the first Legal Tender Act.

The *Hepburn* decision lasted only fifteen months, the shortest life of any major Court doctrine prior to the tumultuous New Deal era. On February 7, 1871—the very day Chase read his *Hepburn* opinion—President Ulysses S. Grant nominated two new Justices to bring the Court to its full strength of nine members. Grant's appointees were William Strong, a Philadelphia lawyer who had upheld the legal tender laws while serving as a member of the Pennsylvania supreme court; and Joseph P. Bradley, a prominent New Jersey lawyer whose chief clients were railroads, the industry most worried by the prospect of having to repay its obligations in gold rather than paper. Strong and Bradley were quickly confirmed.

On May 1, 1871, the Court overruled *Hepburn* by another slim majority (five to four), and this time the opinion in what is now called *The Second Legal Tender Case* was written by Justice Strong with a concurrence from Justice Bradley. In rebutting *Hepburn* point-by-point, Strong dismissed Chase's premise that the Court had the final say concerning the manner in which Congress implemented its expressly granted powers. Once the Court determined that Congress had a certain power, Strong held, then Congress was the judge of whether the means used to carry it out were, in the words of Chief Justice Marshall, "appropriate, plainly adapted, really calculated" to achieve whatever was necessary and proper. In ruling that the national government's control of its own currency, especially in wartime, was a matter of "self-preservation"—the Framers' "paramount object"—Strong sanctioned Congress's discretion to issue greenbacks and upheld the validity of the paper currency.

10

THE CONSTITUTION AND WHITE SUPREMACY

In the famous *Slaughterhouse Cases* of 1873, the Supreme Court gave its first interpretation of the Fourteenth Amendment. Yet the dispute at issue had nothing whatever to do with slavery, much less with race. The appellants were white butchers seeking economic justice.

In 1869, Louisiana's carpetbag legislature had granted the new Crescent City Slaughterhouse a twenty-five-year monopoly on the butchering of all livestock in New Orleans and its environs. The lawmakers cited health reasons, professing admirable fastidiousness about the condition of the Mississippi River. The Butchers' Benevolent Association hired a top-notch local lawyer—none other than John A. Campbell, a prewar Supreme Court Justice whose Southern antecedents had overcome his strong anti-secession feelings and impelled him to serve the Confederacy as assistant secretary of war.

Campbell argued that his butchers had a constitutional right to practice their trade free of state meddling. That right was among the "privileges and immunities" cited by the Fourteenth Amendment. Campbell assumed his clients were also covered by the Amendment's guarantees of due process and equal protection. Indeed, he believed that this historic addition to the Constitution now made the entire federal Bill of Rights binding upon the states and applicable to every citizen, not just newly freed slaves. So expansive a

view of federal power, it may be recalled, had been rejected by Chief Justice Marshall in 1833 (*Barron* v. *Baltimore*).

The Justice assigned to write the *Slaughterhouse* decision seemed the ideal target for Campbell's argument. Samuel F. Miller was a big, generous Iowan, the first Justice from west of the Mississippi, and one who evidenced genuine concern for individual liberty. But Miller was worried about the weak condition of the Southern states. He had lately perceived the Union as being more endangered by federal excesses than by state and local injustices.

In his opinion for a five-man majority, Miller held that the butchers' right to do business was neither a privilege nor an immunity protected by the Fourteenth Amendment—nor, for that matter, was it the kind of "property" that the Amendment's due-process guarantee was intended to protect. According to Miller, the Privileges and Immunities Clause was written solely to confer upon freedmen the federal rights of United States citizenship, not the rights of state citizenship. Among the rights of national citizenship, Miller included the right to petition for grievances, and to come and go on the high seas, the privilege of the writ of habeas corpus, and the right of a citizen of the United States to become a citizen of the state where he resides. The list was strikingly short. In contrast, Miller and his four

Extract from the Reconstructed Constitution of the State of Louisiana. With Portraits of the Distinguished Members of the Convention & Assembly. 1868. The New-York Historical Society

The Crescent City Live Stock Landing and Slaughter House Company. Engraving by J. W. Orr. 1873. The Historic New Orleans Collection

brethren defined the rights of state citizenship so broadly that they included every civil right not explicitly within federal jurisdiction.

The Court majority rejected the idea that the Fourteenth Amendment was "intended to bring within the power of Congress the entire domain of civil rights heretofore belonging exclusively to the states." Had the Court upheld the butchers, Miller warned, the result "would constitute this court a perpetual censor upon all legislation of the States on the civil rights of their own citizens, with authority to nullify such as it did not approve . . ."

Hints of the future were apparent in the dissenting opinions in the *Slaughterhouse Cases.* Justice Field, speaking on behalf of himself, as well as Chase, Swayne, and Bradley, expressed their "profound regret" that the majority had seen fit to violate "the right of free labor, one of the most sacred and imprescriptible rights of man." Such natural rights belonged to every citizen of the United States, no matter in which state he happened to live. The states could not infringe upon them. According to Field, the Fourteenth Amendment now unequivocally protected all natural rights against state action.

Justice Bradley's separate dissent focused on the two great waves of the constitutional future—the Fourteenth Amendment's Due Process and Equal Protection Clauses. Bradley argued that a state law excluding a large class of persons (e.g., the butchers) from lawful employment clearly deprived them of both liberty and property without due process of law. It also deprived them of equal protection of the laws, he said.

While visiting New York on May 7, 1873, Salmon P. Chase died suddenly of a paralytic stroke at the age of sixty-four. His colleagues unanimously praised their late Chief's sincerity, decency, and dignity. President Grant spent most of a year trying to find an adequate successor. A national sigh of relief thus greeted Grant's seventh and final choice, Morrison Remick Waite, fifty-eight, a successful if little known railroad lawyer from Ohio.

Waite had no judicial experience and had never practiced before the Supreme Court; his nomination for Chief Justice apparently startled him as much as it did everyone else. But his obvious integrity, a singular trait in Grant's Washington, helped reassure the Senate, which confirmed him unanimously in January 1874.

Waite proved to be a first-rate judicial manager—a blessing at a time when the Court's docket had suddenly begun to double every decade. He was a natural leader and effective peacekeeper on a bench laden with large egos. Best of all, he was completely apolitical. Soon mentioned as a potential President, he instantly disavowed any such ambitions. In a note to his nephew, a Connecticut Congressman, Waite declared, "No man ought to accept this place unless he takes a vow to leave it as honorable as he found it."

The new Chief Justice saw no constitutional reason to disturb the social conventions of the day. In one of his first opinions, *Minor* v. *Happersett* (1875), Waite spoke for a unanimous Court in holding that it was constitutional for states to prevent women from voting.

Under Missouri law, which limited suffrage to males, election officials had refused to register Mrs. Francis Minor, a prominent Saint Louis woman whose lawyer husband then brought suit. The Minors argued that voting was a privilege of United States citizenship protected by the Fourteenth Amendment. Not so, said Waite. "The Constitution of the United States does not confer the right of suffrage upon anyone." Within a year, this phrase was applied to voting rights for blacks as well as women.

In *United States* v. *Reese* (1876), federal authorities had prosecuted white election officials in Kentucky for refusing not only to register a qualified black voter but also to accept his payment of a compulsory head tax. Chief Justice Waite, speaking for an eight-man majority, upheld the election officials. "The Fifteenth Amendment does not confer the right of suffrage upon anyone," Waite ruled. It merely established a new federal right to be free from racial discrimination while the voter was in the actual process of voting. The right to vote itself was a state-regulated right, beyond the reach of federal laws.

United States v. *Cruikshank* (1876), issued the same day as *Reese*, dealt with ninety-six Louisiana whites who had been indicted by federal authorities under an 1871 federal law for conspiracy to intimidate would-be black voters, sixty of whom the whites shot and killed. The Chief Justice held that the whites could not be prosecuted under

Chief Justice Morrison Remick Waite, with his son and grandson. Collection of the Supreme Court of the United States, Washington, D.C.

federal law because the blacks' right to vote was not a federal right.

Waite further ruled that the black victims had not been covered by the Fourteenth Amendment's Equal Protection clause. That guarantee applied only to "state action," he said, and the whites who killed the blacks were *private* individuals acting on their own.

As in *Reese*, Waite held that Congress had exceeded its powers by enacting laws protecting rights outside its jurisdiction.

In the four decades after the Civil War, the Supreme Court issued dozens of decisions on racial issues, but the three that shaped all the others were the *Slaughterhouse Cases* (1873), the *Civil Rights Cases* (1883), and *Plessy* v. *Ferguson* (1896).

The second of this trio arose from a series of lower-court decisions upholding the right of hotel proprietors and the like to exclude whomever they wished, including blacks. As a result, Congress passed the Civil Rights Act of 1875, which made it a federal crime to deny any person "the full and equal enjoyment" of public accommodations, ranging from inns to railroads.

The law inspired great resistance in the South, where major hotels closed their doors in protest. It also inspired the federal government to launch

Advertisement for *Myers Federal Decisions,* with an endorsement by Chief Justice Waite. Collection of the Supreme Court of the United States, Washington, D.C.

theaters in New York and San Francisco that had refused to seat blacks. In each of the first five cases, the court below had ruled in favor of the white defendants. The sixth case was a private suit for recovery of damages against a Southern railroad that had refused to honor a black couple's first-class tickets.

Speaking for an eight-to-one majority on October 15, 1883, Justice Bradley threw out *United States* v. *Hamilton* on a technical point and decided the remaining five *Civil Rights Cases* on the ground that the 1875 Civil Rights Act was unconstitutional.

Bradley's opinion held that Congress in passing the law had exceeded its authority to enforce the Fourteenth Amendment. In his view, the law "proceeds ex directo to declare that certain acts committed by individuals shall be deemed offenses . . . and lays down rules for the conduct of individuals in society towards each other." But the Fourteenth Amendment forbade only state action, Bradley said, not "individual invasion of individual rights." It authorized Congress to pass laws correcting wrongful state laws, but not to assume control over the field covered by those laws. "It does not authorize Congress to create a code of municipal law for the regulation of private rights," Bradley said. Such a notion was "repugnant to the Tenth Amendment" protecting states' rights. In any case, the civil rights protected by the Constitution against state aggression were not so protected against individual aggression. "The wrongful act of an individual unsupported by [state] authority is simply a private wrong, or a crime of that individual . . ."

Having nullified any use of the Fourteenth Amendment to combat acts of private discrimination, Bradley next ruled that Congress had misread the Thirteenth Amendment as authority for outlawing "badges of servitude" derived from racial discrimination. The Thirteenth Amendment abolished only slavery per se, Bradley held. "It would be running the slavery argument into the ground to make it apply to every act of discrimination which a person may see fit to make as to the guest he will entertain, or as to the people he will take into his coach or cab or car, or admit to his concert or theatre, or deal with in other matters of intercourse or business."

In his *Civil Rights Cases* dissent—the only dissent—Justice John Marshall Harlan argued that

suits on behalf of blacks denied service in public places from New York to California. About one hundred such cases were appealed, resulting in an impasse between federal circuits that upheld the 1875 law and others that declared it unconstitutional.

By 1883, the Supreme Court had six well-ripened cases on its docket (*United States* v. *Hamilton, United States* v. *Stanley, United States* v. *Nichols, United States* v. *Singleton, United States* v. *Ryan*, and *Robinson & Wife* v. *Memphis and Charleston Railroad Company*). Combined as the *Civil Rights Cases*, they involved criminal charges against, respectively, a Tennessee train conductor who had barred a black woman from the "ladies" car to which she held a first-class ticket; hotels in Kansas and Missouri that had excluded blacks; and

Answer of

C. O. H. Thomas, A. M., D. D. B.

Pastor ——————— Chapel.

African M. E. Church.

Natchez, Miss. 11/10/ 18 3

Hon. Sir and Bro

All hail! Thanks for your
noble and manly position, so was
so patriotically manifested in your
dissent from the decision recently rendered upon the Civil Rights Bill.
I our 7,000,000 of Negroes bow the
knee in gratitude, and will ever
remember with approving suff cession
your timely and most humane eff.
I make bold back a favor that
is, please remit me a copy or as many copies of your dissent for my own
use, and for judicious distributing
or inform me where, and how they
can be gotten. By so doing you
will confer a lasting favor on

Yours ever

C. O. H. Thomas

Justice Harlan kept scrapbooks of responses, both public and private, to his dissents. These letters refer to his dissent in the *Civil Rights Cases*. The one from H. W. Coffin reads, "For your noble stand the civilized nations of the world will honor you." Harlan Papers, University of Louisville, Kentucky

the Thirteenth Amendment had not only abolished slavery itself, but had also "decreed universal *civil freedom* throughout the United States." To him, excluding blacks from state-licensed public facilities was, in effect, an extension of slavery by other means and unquestionably a violation of the barred person's civil freedom.

Harlan disputed the Court's view of "state action" under the Fourteenth Amendment. That concept did not render the 1875 Act unconstitutional, he said. It did not preclude Congress from outlawing so-called private discrimination in public facilities. The fact was that "railroad corporations, keepers of inns and managers of public amusement are agents of the state because amenable, in respect of their public duties and functions, to public regulation." As state agents, they were obliged to respect the individual rights that Congress had not only sought to protect but was fully empowered to protect. If the Amendments were enforced according to the intent of their drafters, said Harlan, "there cannot be in this republic any class of human beings in practical subjection to another class."

In 1890, the Louisiana legislature had passed "An Act to promote the comfort of passengers" that compelled railroads to "provide equal but separate accommodations for the white and colored races." In a deliberate test case two years

Colonel John Marshall Harlan, 10th Kentucky Volunteer Infantry. Collection of the Supreme Court of the United States, Washington, D.C.

Justice John Marshall Harlan. Collection of the Supreme Court of the United States, Washington, D.C.

later, Homer Adolph Plessy, who described himself as "seven-eighths Caucasian," entered a whites-only car on a train bound from New Orleans thirty miles north to Covington, Louisiana. Plessy was charged with violating the Jim Crow law by not moving to the black coach; he argued that the law was unconstitutional. After losing his case in every state court, he eventually obtained a writ of error putting the matter before the Supreme Court, which issued a decision in May 1896.

By a vote of seven to one, the Justices ruled that the Louisiana law, as applied to Homer Plessy, did not impinge upon the federal Commerce Power because the train involved was local. Nor did the law violate the Thirteenth Amendment: it implied "merely a legal distinction" between the races without destroying their "legal equality." Nor did it violate the Fourteenth Amendment guarantee of legal equality, which "in the nature of things . . . could not have been intended to abolish distinctions based upon color, or to enforce social, as distinguished from political equality, or a commingling of the two races upon terms unsatisfactory to either."

The author of this memorable opinion was Justice Henry Billings Brown, a Massachusetts-born graduate of Harvard Law School.

In his view, *Plessy* was entirely a matter of state police power and the only real issue was whether the segregation law was reasonable. To determine reasonableness, he felt, the Court was "at liberty to act with reference to the established usage, customs, and traditions of the people, and with a view to the promotion of their comfort, and the preservation of the public peace and good order." By that standard, the people in question being white, the statute appeared eminently reasonable.

[We] consider the underlying fallacy of the plaintiff's argument to consist in the assumption that the enforced separation of the two races stamps the colored race with a badge of inferiority. If this be so, it is not by reason of anything found in the act, but solely because the colored race chooses to put that construction upon it. . . . [Legislation] is powerless to eradicate racial instincts or to abolish distinctions based upon physical differences, and the attempt to do so can only result in accentuating the difficulties of the present situation. If the civil and political rights of both races be equal one cannot be inferior to the other civilly or politically. If one race be inferior to the other socially, the [Constitution of the United States] cannot put them upon the same plane.

Justice Harlan's dissent—again the only dissent—had the eloquence of prophecy. "In the eye of the law," he wrote, "there is in this country no superior, dominant ruling class of citizens. There is no caste here. Our constitution is color-blind, and neither knows nor tolerates classes among citizens. . . ." In his view, the Court had betrayed these fundamental American principles by rendering a decision sure to perpetuate distrust, hatred, and violence between the races. *Plessy* v. *Ferguson*, he predicted, would "prove to be quite as pernicious as the decision made [in] the *Dred Scott* case."

According to Harlan, the underlying fallacy of Brown's opinion was that it brushed aside the Louisiana law's clearly unconstitutional purpose:

The arbitrary separation of citizens, on the basis of race, while they are on a public highway, is a badge of servitude wholly inconsistent with the civil freedom and the equality before the law established by the Constitution. . . . [We] boast of the freedom enjoyed by our people above all other peoples. But it is difficult to reconcile the boast with a state of the law which, practically, puts the brand

The New Orleans waterfront in 1890. To the left, with a white sign, is the L & N Railroad Station, where Plessy boarded a train and was arrested. The Historic New Orleans Collection

Ticket for the East Louisiana Railroad Co. The Ferguson whose name appears on the ticket was not the Ferguson who was a party in the case. The Historic New Orleans Collection

of servitude and degradation upon a large class of our fellow citizens—our equals before the law. The thin disguise of "equal" accommodations for passengers in railroad coaches will not mislead anyone, nor atone for the wrong this day done.

In terms of group survival, the worst disability for Southern blacks was being robbed of voting power, and only rarely during those years did the Supreme Court extend a helping hand to the victims. One of the few exceptions was *Ex parte Yarbrough* (1884), which involved Jasper Yarbrough and seven other Georgia Ku Klux Klansmen who had beaten a black man, Berry Saunders, to dissuade him from voting in a congressional election. The attackers were convicted under remnants of the 1870 federal law enforcing the Fifteenth Amendment, and one might have assumed from the harsh precedents of *Reese* and *Cruikshank* that Mr. Saunders would be found devoid of any voting rights that the Justices were bound to respect. But it was not so.

In a dazzling opinion for a unanimous Court, Justice Miller made the distinction that voting in national elections was a *federal* right that Congress was fully entitled to enforce because government must have the power of self-preservation— "the power to protect the elections on which its existence depends from violence and corruption." The idea that federal suffrage, at least, was essential to the national interest and therefore beyond the reach of state control (or bigotry) was a brilliant course correction that future Justices would find invaluable.

Justices David J. Brewer and Henry Billings Brown. Collection of the Supreme Court of the United States, Washington, D.C.

11

THE COURT IN THE GILDED AGE

When Chief Justice Waite began his fourteen-year tenure in 1874, the *Slaughterhouse* decision had freed the states to police business practices. And during the country's headlong economic expansion after the Civil War—a period of relentless materialism that Mark Twain dubbed "The Gilded Age"—there were endless legal clashes between state regulators and private entrepreneurs accused of cheating the public. In defending themselves, businessmen increasingly saw the Fourteenth Amendment as a mighty fortress protecting capitalism from collectivism.

In the 1870s, Midwest states passed tough laws curbing abuses by railroads, such as arbitrary rates and land-grant frauds. The pressure for action came from new farm groups, especially the National Grange of the Patrons of Husbandry. With nearly a million members, "Grangers" controlled the legislatures in several states, such as Illinois and Minnesota, which established railroad commissions empowered to set maximum rates, end discrimination, and enforce their orders.

Railroad officials quickly appealed to federal courts challenging the state "Granger laws" as unconstitutional violations of the Contract Clause, the Commerce Clause, and the Fourteenth Amendment. The chairman of one big railroad declared, "Happily, we have the law on our side."

For several years the Waite Court was far too busy to agree or disagree with the railroads. Flooded with postwar economic disputes, the Justices' docket nearly doubled between 1870 and 1880 to more than twelve hundred pending cases. In 1875 the Court decided 193 cases—considerably more than its yearly output a century later. Congress then made the Justices work even harder by its passage of the 1875 Removal Act, a major change in federal jurisdiction that, for the first time, permitted the transfer of federal-question cases from state courts to federal courts.

Laboring under its workload, the Waite Court took four years to hear and ponder eight "Granger Cases" in which four states defended their regulatory laws as reasonable curbs on unreasonable monopolies. The most significant case, *Munn* v. *Illinois*, involved a Chicago grain elevator operator named Ira Y. Munn, whose success in cheating farmers and merchants had inspired the state of Illinois to subject grain elevators to licensing and inspection. Ira Munn's refusal to comply with the Warehouse Act wound up in the Illinois supreme court, which ruled that the state could regulate all matters involving "the public welfare."

Chief Justice Waite viewed the Granger litigation as "perhaps the most important series of cases in the country's history." Accordingly, Waite assigned himself to speak for the Court in

The Supreme Court of the United States, 1882. Standing, from left: Associate Justices William Burnham Woods, Horace Gray, John Marshall Harlan, Samuel Blatchford. Seated, from left: Associate Justices Joseph P. Bradley, Samuel Freeman Miller, Chief Justice Morrison Remick Waite, Associate Justices Stephen Johnson Field, Stanley Matthews. Photograph by C. M. Bell. Collection of the Supreme Court of the United States, Washington, D.C.

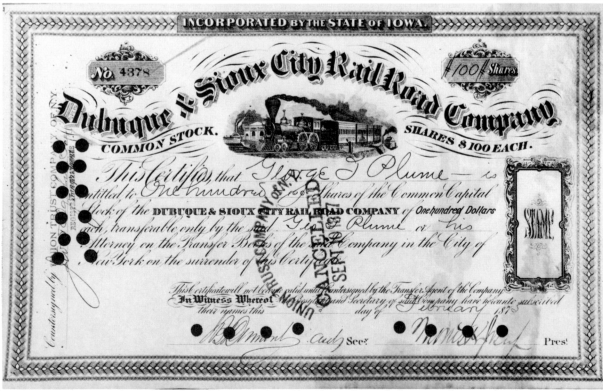

Stock certificate for the Dubuque & Sioux City Rail Road Company, issued in 1875, and cancelled two years later. National Museum of American History, Smithsonian Institution, Washington, D.C.

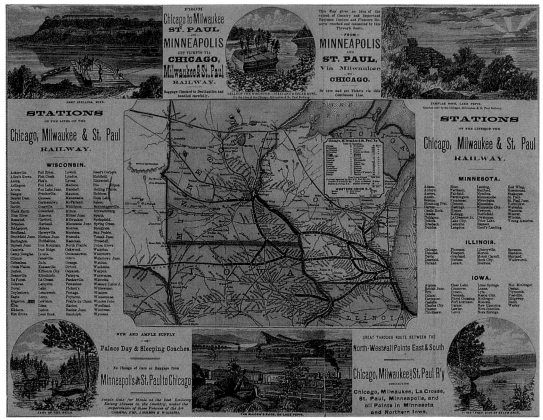

Map of the Chicago, Milwaukee & St. Paul Railroad, published by Rand McNally and Company, 1874, to promote business and immigration. Library of Congress, Washington, D.C.

all eight cases. But he focused on *Munn* for his main opinion because it so clearly posed a key issue—the reach of the Due Process Clause. When, if ever, could government invade the marketplace and tell a private business how much it could charge its customers?

Delivered on March 1, 1877, Waite's opinion in *Munn* v. *Illinois* emphasized the public-use aspect of Chicago grain elevators. Virtually all eastbound grain journeyed through them; the owners collected "toll from all who pass." Citing Britain's Lord Hale, pioneer of the common-law concept of "publick interest," Waite ruled that an owner who "devotes his property to a use in which the public has an interest . . . in effect grants the public an interest in that use, and must submit to be controlled by the public for the common good; to the extent of the interest he has thus created."

Waite found the Illinois Warehouse Act consistent with previous American laws setting maximum charges for private businesses devoted to public use. The act did not deprive grain elevator operators of their property without due process

of law, he ruled. On the contrary, it was a valid exercise of the state's police power, mandated by the people's representatives, and the operators must obey it.

Waite did not entirely dismiss the Fourteenth Amendment argument. He allowed that "under some circumstances" state regulation might go beyond constitutional bounds. But even if lawmakers did go too far, he continued, the Supreme Court was not the best source of redress. "For protection against abuses by legislatures," Waite declared, "the people must resort to the polls, not to the courts."

As to the seven other *Granger Railroad Cases,* Waite ruled that none of the challenged rate regulations affected interstate commerce or impaired contract rights; and he upheld all the state laws in question under the *Munn* public-interest rule.

Only a year after *Munn,* Chief Justice Waite wrote a significant opinion affirming the national commerce power, however unexercised by Congress at the time. Speaking for the Court in *Pensa-*

146

cola Telegraph Company v. *Western Union Company* (1878), Waite held that states could not grant telegraph monopolies in conflict with Congress's commerce and postal powers. The novelty of the commerce in dispute moved Waite to note the Constitution's adaptability. To the Framers, the telegraph was unknown. But the powers of Congress, Waite wrote, "are not confined to the instrumentalities of commerce . . . known or in use when the Constitution was adopted, but they keep pace with the progress of the country."

From 1877 through 1888, the Supreme Court issued at least twenty-one decisions voiding state commerce laws on grounds of federal preemption. And the pace quickened: nine such decisions were handed down in 1887–88 alone.

Probably the most important of these cases was *Wabash Railway Company* v. *Illinois* (1886), which overruled a key part of Waite's opinion in the Granger cases headed by *Munn* v. *Illinois*. Waite had upheld a Wisconsin law setting maximum charges for the intrastate portion of all rail traffic passing through the state. The Court's premise was that railroads were still largely local. But only

ten years after *Munn*, hundreds of small lines were bankrupt, huge lines had taken over, and the nation had an interstate rail system. Over dissents by Waite and Bradley, the *Wabash* majority prohibited states from regulating the rates charged by any railroad linked to an interstate network, even if such regulation affected only trips within the state.

In the late 1870s the Justices consistently refused to review the constitutionality of state action except on procedural grounds. By the early 1880s they were signaling a major concern with the fundamental justice of state action, in terms of substance as well as procedure.

In *Hurtado* v. *California* (1884), the Court followed precedent in holding that the Due Process Clause did not require states to emulate precisely the Bill of Rights in their criminal-law procedures. But Justice Stanley Matthews, speaking for the Court, pointedly declared that "arbitrary power . . . is not law." And he made it clear that the Justices would not tolerate official abuses, such as "the violence of public agents transcend-

View from 12th Street Bridge, Chicago, showing grain elevators, including Munn's, from *Chicago*, 1866, lithograph by Jevne and Almini after Louis Kurz. Chicago Historical Society

ing the limits of lawful authority." State variations in due process were permissible, Matthews held, but the result must safeguard liberty and justice "in furtherance of the general public good."

Three years later, in *Mugler* v. *Kansas* (1887), the Court upheld a state law putting liquor dealers out of business, but Justice Harlan's opinion for the majority went far toward restricting the police power. He limited it to promoting public health, morals, and safety. And Harlan construed the Due Process Clause as a potential curb on state regulations. According to Harlan, the states in applying their police power, must realize that "there are, of necessity, limits beyond which legislation cannot rightfully go."

Justice Harlan's *Mugler* opinion stressed the Court's growing sense that it was now compelled to appraise the substance of challenged laws:

> The courts are not bound by mere forms, nor are they to be misled by mere pretenses. They are at liberty—indeed, are under a solemn duty—to look at the substance of things, whenever they enter upon the inquiry whether the legislature has transcended the limits of its authority. If, therefore, a statute purporting to have been enacted to protect the public health, the public morals, or the public safety, has no real or substantial relation to those objects, or is a palpable invasion of rights secured by the fundamental law, it is the duty of the courts to so adjudge, and thereby give effect to the Constitution.

Three months after the *Mugler* decision, Chief Justice Waite was characteristically helping his sick coachman outdoors in raw weather when he caught a chill and developed a bad cold. Waite was extremely conscientious about his work—he had just finished a mammoth opinion, *The Telephone Cases*, that fills an entire volume in *United States Reports*—and he was equally considerate of his family and his colleagues. Mrs. Waite was

Justice Joseph P. Bradley in his study, c. 1890. Photograph by Elgar Richards. Collection of the Supreme Court of the United States, Washington, D.C.

vacationing in California; the Chief Justice did not want her to read in the newspapers that he was at home, sick in bed. Besides, his overworked Court needed him.

So, Morrison Waite maintained his virtually perfect attendance record and went on appearing in Court as usual. His cold worsened. A touch of pneumonia, the doctor said, nothing serious. But on March 23, 1888, Waite's condition suddenly deteriorated, and by day's end he was dead. He was seventy-one.

Waite was the second of three Ohioans to serve as Chief Justice of the United States. The others were Salmon P. Chase and William Howard Taft. No other state equals that record.

Waite was not an outstanding Chief Justice in the pioneering sense of Marshall or Taney. He was merely indispensable. At the close of the Court's first century, during a confused period in national history, rife with pressures and polemics, Waite managed to enhance both the tribunal's judicial balance and its stability. He achieved

his goal of being the kind of Chief Justice who left the Court "as honorable as he found it."

12

THE THIN JUDICIAL LINE

Invitation to the banquet for the Centennial Celebration of the Organization of the Federal Judiciary, February 4, 1890. On the first page, Chief Justice Melville Fuller faces the first Chief Justice, John Jay. The second page portrays the Associate Justices in 1890. Clockwise from the upper left, they are Associate Justices Samuel Freeman Miller, Stephen Johnson Field, Joseph P. Bradley, John Marshall Harlan, David Josiah Brewer, Lucius Quintus Cincinnatus Lamar, Samuel Blatchford, and Horace Gray. Harlan Papers, University of Louisville Library

President Grover Cleveland sent Melville Weston Fuller's name to the Senate in April 1888. A Maine-born Chicago corporation lawyer, Fuller was the first nominee for Chief Justice who had never held any previous federal office.

Cleveland had met Fuller on a Midwest tour and was favorably impressed by his hard-money position, his considerable charm, and his availability as a fine lawyer and faithful Democrat from Illinois, a state of particular concern to Cleveland as the 1888 presidential election approached. The Senate debated Fuller's nomination for nearly three months, largely because he was the target of a hostile pamphlet entitled, "The War Record of Melville Fuller," which decried the evil of "a copperhead Chief Justice." The copperhead charge did not survive examination, and Fuller was eventually confirmed by a vote of forty-one to twenty.

Of the old Court's luminaries, Miller died in 1890, Bradley in 1892, and Field left the bench in 1897.

But the Court's jurisprudential leadership did not fall upon Chief Justice Fuller. Instead, it shifted to Field's nephew, Justice David J. Brewer, who arrived two years after Fuller; and to Justice Rufus W. Peckham (1896–1909), a former New York State judge and a friend of President Cleveland, the former governor of New York. Justice Peckham cherished the indi-

vidualism of a vanishing America. Gallant, obsolete, or quixotic, depending upon one's perspective, Peckham wrote some of the most conservative opinions in Supreme Court history.

Chief Justice Fuller was further overshadowed by two other new luminaries—his future successor, Justice Edward D. White of Louisiana, a Confederate veteran appointed to the Court in 1894; and Justice Oliver Wendell Holmes, Jr., of Massachusetts, a former Union officer, whose appointment in 1902 began a thirty-year stream of memorable opinions. The Court also included the aging but tireless Justice Harlan, who continued to produce fervent dissents term after term until he died in 1911, a year after Fuller's death.

Yet Melville Fuller did profoundly influence the business of the Court. He was an extraordinarily good manager of men and logistics. Generous, sympathetic, gregarious—many called him "lovable"—Fuller deliberately cultivated personal friendships with every single Justice, whatever the man's views or propensities. He presided over the Justices' private conferences with unusual grace and a saving wit. It was Fuller who originated the now-famous practice of each Justice shaking hands with every other Justice as they begin their conferences, and before they enter the courtroom.

Felix Frankfurter, who argued a number of cases before Fuller, extolled his "great but gentle

Chief Justice Melville Weston Fuller. National Archives, Washington, D.C.

Justice Stephen Johnson Field in his library, on the occasion of his eightieth birthday, 1896. Justice Field's tenure on the Court, thirty-four years, was the longest until 1973, when Justice William Orville Douglas surpassed it. Justice Field retired in 1897, a year after this photograph was taken. Collection of the Supreme Court of the United States, Washington, D.C.

firmness" and his ability to make contentious lawyers feel themselves "in the presence of a Chief whom they could greatly respect."

Fuller's gift for dealing with people was reinforced by his organizational skills. When he became Chief Justice in 1888, the Court was overwhelmed with 1,500 pending cases, and though 400 of them were disposed of that year, nearly 600 were filed the following year. To find a solution to this growing backlog, the Chief Justice turned his charm on the Senate Judiciary Committee, the chairman of which had voted against his confirmation. In due course that gentleman himself asked the Court to draft its own remedy.

The result was the Circuit Court of Appeals Act, passed in March 1891. That law finally ended the circuit-riding duties that had burdened Supreme Court Justices for a century. It established nine new federal circuit courts, defined unequivocally as intermediate appellate courts, with final jurisdiction over certain kinds of federal cases, ranging from admiralty to diversity to most commercial law. The new courts' decisions, however, remained subject to discretionary review by the Supreme Court itself, usually via writs of certiorari. In other words, the Court was now freer to select fewer cases, all of greater importance, a priority underlying nearly all subsequent acts of Congress affecting the Court.

Within nine years, the Court's backlog decreased by more than one-third and the average number of cases decided with full opinions dropped from 250 per year to less than 200. Even so, the Court hardly became a retreat. During Fuller's two decades, the Justices averaged 248 decisions per year and produced a total of 5,465 opinions, exceeding the Court's output under any other Chief Justice.

The Anglo-Venezuelan Arbitration Commission at Paris, *Harper's Weekly,* 1899. Justice David Josiah Brewer, who also served on the Commission, is in the front row to the left; Chief Justice Melville Weston Fuller is second from the right. The New-York Historical Society

Fuller worked harder than anyone else. He was an indefatigable Chancellor of the Smithsonian Institution—one of the Chief Justice's extra duties—as well as a volunteer arbitrator in various international disputes. Fuller was particularly admired for his hard work in arbitrating the boundary between Venezuela and British Guiana, a task that kept him in Paris throughout the sweltering summer of 1899.

In his last years, his wife having died in 1904 and their ten children having moved away, Fuller was greatly buoyed by a faithful Sunday visitor—Justice Holmes. No two men could have been less alike, but Holmes became extremely fond of Fuller, partly because he cherished competence wherever he found it. In 1910 the Chief Justice died suddenly of a heart attack on the Fourth of July at his summer home in Maine; he was seventy-eight. Holmes wrote: "I think the public will not realize what a great man it has lost

. . . I think he was extraordinary. He had the business of the Court at his finger ends, he was perfectly courageous, prompt, decided. He turned off the matters that daily called for action, easily, swiftly, with the least possible friction, with inestimable good humor and with a humor that relieved any tension with a laugh."

Throughout the two decades (1890–1910) that spanned Fuller's tenure, the American ideal of free enterprise was besieged by its friends as well as its enemies. The ideal assumed a self-sufficient people, a land of opportunity in which everyone had an equal chance to go as far as he could, the corollary being that government must not interfere. But the frontier had nearly vanished, the rural poor were flocking to urban factories, immigrants were desperate for work however low the wages, and the logic of industrialism was overcoming the ethos of individualism.

Our Overworked Supreme Court: "It is unequal to the ever increasing labor thrust upon it—Will Congress take prompt measures for the relief of the people?" Joseph Keppler cartoon for *Puck*, January 9, 1885. It took Chief Justice Fuller to press Congress for the necessary relief, which came in 1891. The New-York Historical Society

Young America's Dilemma: "Shall I be wise and great, or rich and powerful." Cartoon by Dalrymple from *Puck*, June 12, 1901. The New-York Historical Society

By 1901 many of the country's major industries were dominated by huge trusts that controlled prices with little or no competition.

For about thirty years, the Justices were thus called upon to define the limits of government intervention in private enterprise.

The Court chose the month of January 1895 to release the first of its three bombshells that year. In *United States* v. *E. C. Knight Company*, by a vote of eight to one (Harlan), the Court forbade the government to employ the Sherman Antitrust Act to break up the Sugar Trust.

Four months later, in May 1895, the Court ruled five to four that the first general income tax law enacted by Congress was unconstitutional, despite the Court's previous 1881 decision (*Springer* v. *United States*) upholding a temporary income tax during the Civil War. One week later, the Justices unanimously denied a writ of habeas corpus to Eugene V. Debs, founder of the American Railway Union, who had been imprisoned for disobeying a federal injunction ordering him and other union leaders to halt the Pullman strike.

According to the lower federal court, the strikers had "restrained" trade and thus violated the Sherman Act. Justice Brewer upheld the lower-court injunction not only on that ground but on the loftier one of national sovereignty. The federal government was empowered to remove all obstructions to interstate commerce and transportation of the mails, he said.

In 1896 the Court interpreted the nine-year-old Interstate Commerce Act to mean that the Interstate Commerce Commission was powerless to fix rail rates (*Cincinnati, New Orleans and Texas Pacific Railway Co.* v. *I.C.C.*). The I.C.C., Justice Harlan observed in his dissent, "has been shorn, by judicial interpretation, of authority to do anything of an effective character."

The I.C.C. remained moribund until 1906 when Congress passed the Hepburn Act, which clearly empowered the commission to fix maximum rail rates.

Thereafter, the Court began to uphold the I.C.C. in decision after decision, notably the famous 1914 *Shreveport Rate Case*, which declared that Congress may regulate *intra*state rail rates whenever they affect interstate rates to the point that one can't be regulated without regulating the other. The Court's "*Shreveport* Doctrine" enabled Congress to go beyond railroads and regulate many other intrastate matters affecting interstate commerce.

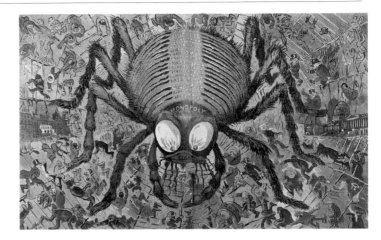

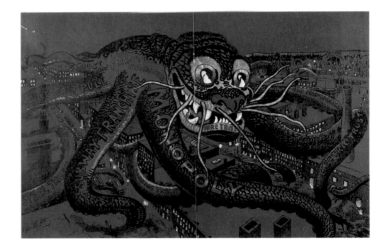

By the turn of the century, public feeling against trusts was running high. In these three cartoons from the shortlived magazine, *The Verdict*, published in 1899 and 1900, the trust is symbolized by a hog, a spider, and an octopus. The latter two were done by artist George B. Luks. New York Public Library. Astor, Lenox and Tilden Foundations

Investors had a different view of trusts. This *Map Showing the Properties of The United States Steel Corporation*, published by White and Kemble in 1903, displays the holdings of the first billion-dollar holding company. Library of Congress, Washington, D.C.

The Framers had placed very few restrictions on the taxing power of Congress. Only two were particularly significant. Article I says clearly that all duties, imposts, and excises must be uniform throughout the country. But it then says that all "direct" federal taxes must be apportioned among the states according to their relative populations. What is a direct tax?

In 1796 the Justices had ruled in *Hylton* v. *United States* that only two kinds of taxes were direct and thus subject to apportionment by population. They were head taxes and land taxes. As a result, other federal taxes were considered indirect and could be apportioned on some basis other than population—by income, for example.

Heeding this logic, the Court ruled in 1881 (*Springer* v. *United States*) that the temporary Civil War income tax—which had expired in 1872—had been an indirect tax and, therefore, constitutional. Thus it remained that only head taxes and land taxes were considered direct levies subject to the apportionment rule.

But in the early 1890s a severe depression cut federal revenues. After much agitation, Congress decided to mobilize its taxing power to replenish the treasury. By modern standards, the resulting federal income tax was a mosquito bite. First imposed in 1895, it consisted of a two-percent levy on personal incomes above $4,000 per year—a formula that exempted ninety-eight percent of the population at that time.

A test case was quickly carpentered in the form of an alleged dispute between one Charles Pollock and a New York bank, the Farmers' Loan and Trust Company. Pollock, a stockholder in the bank, sought to enjoin Farmers' Loan from paying taxes on income derived from land. In his view, such a tax was unconstitutional. It was indistinguishable from a "direct" tax on the land itself, he said. Yet the income tax, contrary to the constitutional rule for direct taxes, had not been apportioned by population. Should the tax be ruled "indirect," Pollock had a fallback position. Because it affected only high incomes, he claimed, the tax was not uniform and hence not constitutional.

Pollock v. *Farmers' Loan & Trust Co.* sailed through the straits of the Court's three-year backlog to reach the Justices in a few weeks.

The Court's decision, handed down on April 8,

Attorney General Olney Addressing the Supreme Court on the Income Tax, from the *New York Herald,* May 12, 1895. Harlan Papers, University of Louisville

1895, involved only eight Justices, owing to the illness of the ninth, Howell E. Jackson. Six of the eight upheld Charles Pollock's claim that an unapportioned tax on the income from land was unconstitutional. But the eight were split evenly on two larger issues: 1) Did the same reasoning apply to a tax on *personal* income? 2) Did the Court's invalidation of one part of the law logically invalidate the whole law?

Pollock's lawyers persuaded the Court to reconsider these issues. More arguments were heard; and on May 20, 1895, a second decision was announced, only six weeks after the first one. This time all nine Justices participated—and down went the entire income tax law.

The vote was five to four, and the fact that Justice Jackson had now joined the minority meant that one of the six majority Justices in the first case had switched his vote to the minority in the second case.

Chief Justice Fuller wrote both *Pollock* opinions. He asserted that taxes on income from both land and personal income were direct taxes and therefore unconstitutional because they were unapportioned. He further ruled that voiding the law's main provisions made it necessary to void the entire law.

The country finally reached a consensus in 1913 and ratified the Sixteenth Amendment, which empowered Congress to levy taxes, without apportionment on income, "from whatever source derived." The Court duly upheld the income tax in 1916, nullifying *Pollock* v. *Farmers' Loan*.

The taxing power had never been limited to raising revenue. Congress had employed it for purposes of regulation as well as for financing ever since the First Congress imposed the first protective tariff in 1789. But the undisputed power to use taxation as a policing tool is one thing; the purpose of the policing is another. And the purpose itself may be invalid. Or so the Court began to hint. The ultimate question, of course, came down to who would have the final say—Congress or the Justices?

If the Justices had the final say, their decisions would presumably rest on constitutional premises, not on personal or political opinions. But such premises evaded strict formulation, as may be seen in a stream of cases that began in 1904 when the Court upheld a stiff federal tax on oleomargarine colored yellow to resemble butter. The yellow product was taxed at ten cents a pound; uncolored oleo was taxed at only a quarter-cent a pound. Clearly aimed at preventing oleo from competing with butter, the tax was challenged in *McCray* v. *United States* as a violation of both state police power and due process. The Court did something unexpected. It not only upheld the position that Congress was empowered to impose the tax, but it also refused to "restrain the exercise of a lawful power on the assumption that a wrongful purpose or motive has caused the power to be exerted."

Reformers were delighted—*McCray* seemed to be a green light for all kinds of government regulation via taxes, without Court interference. But the Justices soon had second thoughts. Now they began to imply that a tax might not be valid if its primary purpose was to alter behavior rather than collect revenues. This became explicit in *Bailey* v. *Drexel Furniture Co.* (1922), the famous decision forbidding Congress to impose a ten-percent tax on the net profits of any company employing children under a certain age.

The Court ruled that this tax, unlike the oleo tax, was primarily a form of social control designed to stop employers from exploiting children. It had thus lost its character as a revenue producer and become "a mere penalty with the characteristics of regulation and punishment." As such it had invaded the power of the states to police their own internal affairs. *Bailey* implied that the Court would now be the final authority for determining Congress's primary motive in imposing a tax. This was tinder that would ignite during the Court's power struggle with the Roosevelt administration in the 1930s.

The potential strain was even greater on another front—the federal government's increasing use of the commerce power to curb monopolies. Nearly every case since *Gibbons* v. *Ogden* had affirmed plenary federal power over interstate commerce, permitting state authority only by federal sufferance. But the upsurge in federal action troubled the Justices, there being so few limits on national control of the economy. They struggled to find some powerful logic for saying "No" while avoiding the weakness of judicial fiat.

The effort got off to a poor start with *United States* v. *E. C. Knight Company* (1895). The case involved the Pennsylvania-based American Sugar Refining Company, which had paid off its competitors and acquired control of ninety-eight percent of the sugar processing business in the United States. The Sugar Trust had raised prices accordingly. The government eventually invoked the Sherman Antitrust Act, charging a conspiracy to restrain trade and monopolize interstate commerce in sugar.

In his *Knight* opinion, Chief Justice Fuller conceded the existence of "a monopoly over the manufacture of sugar," but then simply removed manufacturing from the reach of the antitrust law.

Fuller called manufacturing a local process that affected interstate commerce only "indirectly" and therefore was subject only to state regulation. Interstate commerce did not begin, he said, until goods left one state for another. While in transit, they were subject to the provisions of the Sherman Act, and the shipper was forbidden to plot any "direct" restraint upon their movement; but once they entered another state, they reverted to state-regulated "manufacture," safe from the federal government's interference. So, even though the Sugar Trust's products were sold all over the country, they were immune to the antitrust law, unless the monopolists tried to tinker with transit, which, of course, they had no need to do.

In other words, *Knight* created a distinction between production and commerce, and then narrowly defined interstate commerce as little more than transportation.

Fuller's rationale was the need to preserve state police power. If all manufacturing were subject to national control, he wrote, "comparatively little of business operations and affairs would be left for state control." On the other hand, no single state was capable of regulating the giant manufacturing monopolies that now did business throughout the nation. Justice Harlan, the sole dissenter, pointed out that *Knight* had immunized the trusts from *both* federal and state control. The public, he protested, was left "entirely at the mercy" of monopolies.

Knight had not actually declared the Sherman Act unconstitutional, and the law, although considerably weakened, was still available for use by federal trustbusters.

Within two years, the Court began cautiously modifying *Knight* with five-to-four decisions upholding the Sherman Act against various price-fixing schemes. In one such case, *United States* v. *Trans-Missouri Freight Association* (1897), a combination of eighteen railroads argued in part that the Sherman Act permitted "reasonable" restraints of trade, such as theirs, and forbade only "unreasonable" restraints—whatever those might be. The Court majority rejected this construction, holding that the law barred *all* combinations, good or bad. But Justice White wrote a 10,000-word dissent deploring what he considered the decision's inhibiting effect on business and groping for a "rule of reason" as the proper antitrust standard. White's formulation, much improved, finally prevailed thirteen years later.

Equally interesting in *Trans-Missouri* was Justice Peckham's majority opinion upholding the government. The railroads had claimed that their scheme would actually reduce rates, but Peckham responded that lower rates would, in turn, permit big business to ruin small entrepreneurs. In a passionate defense of early American individualism, Peckham wrote that nothing good would come of turning the independent businessman into an organization man, "a mere servant or agent of a corporation for selling the commodities which he once manufactured or dealt in . . ."

Two years later, Peckham spoke for another narrow majority when the Court first sustained the use of the Sherman Act against an industrial combine (*Addyston Pipe and Steel Company* v. *United States*). The case involved a marketing agreement between six companies that made and sold iron pipe interstate. They pleaded *Knight*'s protective cloak of immunity for manufacturing monopolies. Justice Peckham whisked the cloak away, finding the pipe combine "clearly involved in selling as well as manufacturing."

The next substantial modification of *Knight* was the famous 1904 case of *Northern Securities Company* v. *United States*. The appellant was a holding company designed to monopolize western railroads. It had been created after a ferocious struggle on the New York Stock Exchange for control of the Northern Pacific. The battle had run the railroad's share price up to $1,000, threatened a major panic, and ended in a stalemate among the combatants—J. P. Morgan, James J. Hill, and E. H. Harriman.

The three tycoons had divided the spoils via their holding company, which soon controlled nearly every foot of track west of Chicago. President Theodore Roosevelt ordered his Justice Department to hit Northern Securities with the Sherman Act.

The Supreme Court ordered the Northern Securities Company dissolved. In yet another five-to-four decision, this one written by that frequent dissenter, Justice Harlan, the Court applied the antitrust law to a holding company for the first time. The company had argued that it was beyond the law because it merely controlled its subsidiaries' stock and was not specifically engaged in interstate commerce. Harlan ruled that, by its very nature, the company restrained commerce sufficiently to come under the Sherman Act.

In anguished dissent, Justice White attacked Harlan for effectively approving the regulation of stock ownership, a notion White considered unconstitutional. By contrast, Justice Holmes in his own dissent showed that Congress had *not* done what Harlan assumed and White deplored. It had not made stock-cornering a crime under

Edward H. Harriman was the brilliant railroad man who initiated the struggle that led to the formation of the Northern Securities Co. Brown Brothers, Sterling, Pennsylvania

Chief Justice Edward D. White. Collection of the Supreme Court of the United States, Washington, D.C.

James J. Hill, in the white suit, resisted Harriman's depredations. Brown Brothers, Sterling, Pennsylvania

The industrial trust was devised in 1882 by Samuel C. T. Dodd, the corporation counsel of the Standard Oil Company of Ohio. By the time of *Standard Oil* v. *United States*, the company controlled the world supply of oil and related products. Because it had virtually no competitors in such a wide field of industry, it came to symbolize to many monopoly power in the economy.

Samuel C. T. Dodd. Courtesy of Exxon Corporation

the Sherman Act. The holding company's creators might have been guilty of many things, but the non-crime of which they were being accused was not one of them. This was the dissent in which Holmes coined his memorable aphorism, "Great cases, like hard cases, make bad law." Also memorable was Teddy Roosevelt's crack when he learned that Holmes, whom he had appointed to the Court as a supposed anti-monopolist, had sided with the holding company. "I could carve out of a banana a judge with more backbone than that," fumed the President.

Whatever the merits of its logic, *Northern Securities* affirmed the government's power to curb monopolies; a year later, the Court upheld that power against the "beef trust" in *Swift and Company* v. *United States* (1905), a landmark decision that refitted the Commerce Clause for duty in a modern economy. Swift and other meatpackers had joined in fixing prices in the Chicago stockyards. Swift claimed immunity from the antitrust law on the premise that its livestock were bought and sold locally, keeping them outside the boundaries of interstate commerce. But a unanimous Court, this time speaking crisply through Justice Holmes, laid Swift's reasoning to rest. Although the packers had literally restrained trade in just one state, Holmes noted, they had effectively restrained it in many states, and he

then formulated his "stream of commerce" doctrine:

> When cattle are sent for sale from a place in one State, with the expectation that they will end their transit, after purchase, in another, and when in effect they do so, with only the interruption necessary to find a purchaser at the stock yards, and when this is a typical, constantly recurring course, the current thus existing is a current of commerce among the States, and that purchase of cattle is a part and incident of such commerce.

The stream of commerce doctrine adjusted the Commerce Clause to new business realities, while renewing its original purpose—to foster a national common market free of local restraints. But *Swift* also enhanced the probability of greater federal control, despite Congress's procrastination.

The Court had previously read the Sherman Act to mean that Congress had outlawed *any* combination in restraint of trade. But in May 1911, this literalism was discarded in *Standard Oil* v. *United States*, an opinion that some historians view as the Magna Carta of American corporations. It was written by Melville Fuller's successor, Edward D. White, the first Associate Justice to become Chief Justice.

Edward D. White's Court career (1894–1921) was largely devoted to an area that he, as well as his friend Theodore Roosevelt, considered of prime importance—the need for an antitrust policy that would force monopolists to serve the public interest rather than one that would drive them out of business. Hence White's long campaign for a "rule of reason" to replace the Court's uncompromising view that the Sherman Act had banned all combinations. For White, the end of the rainbow was the 1911 *Standard Oil* case.

At issue was a lower-court order breaking up John D. Rockefeller's oil empire into its component parts. Since these included more than forty large companies and myriad offshoots, the antitrust violation was irrefutable, and all nine Justices upheld the break-up order. But the real question mark was the basis upon which the Oil

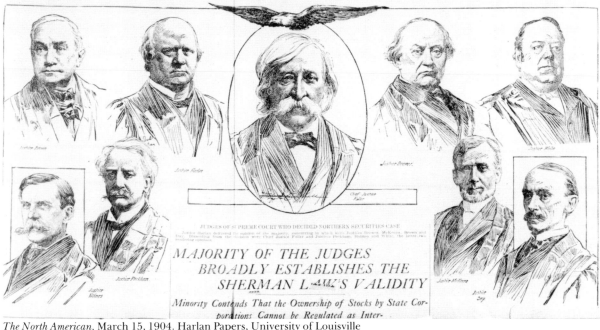

SUPREME COURT DEALS DEATH BLOW TO TRUSTS
IN DISSOLVING THE NORTHERN SECURITIES MERGER

MAJORITY OF THE JUDGES
BROADLY ESTABLISHES THE
SHERMAN LAW'S VALIDITY

Minority Contends That the Ownership of Stocks by State Corporations Cannot be Regulated as Inter-

The North American, March 15, 1904. Harlan Papers, University of Louisville

Trust's appeal would be denied. Even though Edward White had led the Court for only six months, his dominance was already clear. Seven Justices joined their Chief in ruling that Standard Oil was guilty of "unreasonable" restraint of trade—the yardstick White had finally succeeded in grafting onto the Sherman Act. Mere size or the act of combining were no longer deemed per se violations of the antitrust law. Even more significant, the law was now a license for growth—the Court had clearly implied that the Sherman Act *permitted* "reasonable" restraints of trade.

As so often before, Justice Harlan was the sole dissenter in this case. The "rule of reason," declared the Great Dissenter, was nothing less than a blatant attempt to "usurp the functions of Congress by indulging in judicial legislation."

In *Adair* v. *United States* (1908), the Court held that labor relations do not directly affect interstate commerce, a premise enabling the Justices to invalidate a federal law barring the use of "yellow-dog contracts." In short, it was now legal for employers to compel workers to sign written pledges not to join unions as a condition of their employment. According to *Adair*, moreover, the Fifth Amendment protected an employer's "personal liberty" to require such yellow-dog contracts. The opinion was written by the eminent libertarian, Justice Harlan.

A month later, in the well-known Danbury Hatters' case (*Loewe* v. *Lawlor*), the Court agreed, even more strongly than it had in the Eugene Debs case, that the Sherman Act could be conscripted for service against unions. At issue was the American Federation of Labor's effort to organize the workers at a hat factory in Danbury, Connecticut. To pressure the company, the A.F.L. had organized boycotts of stores selling the factory's hats in other states.

All nine Justices agreed that such "secondary boycotts" were illegal restraints of interstate commerce. The Sherman Act reached "any combination whatever," declared Chief Justice Fuller. What's more, he applied the stream of commerce doctrine to unions—so that national unions were now subject to federal antitrust prosecution for

Hat making involved many separate operations, some more hazardous than others, as these photographs of the Mallory Co. factory in Danbury taken c. 1900 show. In the carroting room, rabbit furs were coated with a solution of nitric acid and mercury which caused the fur fibers to felt together.

their activities *inside* states as well as among them.

By 1914, Congress had felt sufficient pressure over the Danbury decision to make a significant concession to labor. The lawmakers amended the Clayton Antitrust Act to exempt unions from antitrust actions. But in 1921, the Court interpreted the Clayton Act to mean that unions could still be enjoined from secondary boycotts; and for another decade the Justices upheld other antitrust crackdowns on unions. Only in 1932 did Congress finally pass the Norris-LaGuardia Act, specifically banning federal court injunctions in labor disputes. The Court upheld that law in 1938. The new ruling simply affirmed the power of Congress to define the jurisdiction of lower federal courts.

Another form of federal expansion arose from the fact that many new social ills spilled across state lines, beyond the police power of individual states. Federal remedies were required. The Constitution grants Congress no explicit authority over public health, morals, or welfare, these being traditional state prerogatives.

Even so, there was one avenue to federal authority—the unquestioned power of Congress to regulate interstate commerce. In a new mood of experimentation, Congress began using the federal commerce power to justify laws dealing with just about any problem that crossed state lines.

The litigants who first challenged this phenomenon found the Court surprisingly unalarmed. At issue in *Champion* v. *Ames* (1903), was whether Congress could attempt to slake the country's gambling fever via a federal law banning use of the mails to send lottery tickets between states. Gambling had always been a state domain. But a narrow majority of five Justices, speaking through Harlan, ruled that "Congress may arbitrarily exclude from commerce among the states any article . . . which it may choose, no matter with what motive."

The result was a new federal police power—a dimension of the Commerce Clause that had previously escaped the Court's scrutiny. Congress promptly applied it to such interstate scourges as food adulteration and "white slavery" or forced prostitution. The Court responded in kind by upholding the 1906 Pure Food and Drug

Until the use of mercury was ended in the 1920s, back shop workers got the "hatter's shakes" from exposure to the mercury. Work was much less arduous in the front shop, and finishers had their own union. Danbury Scott-Fanton Museum and Historical Society, Connecticut

Act, followed by the 1910 Mann Act outlawing the transportation of women across state lines for immoral purposes.

Emboldened by these decisions, Congress saw a new way of dealing with child labor, a social evil that had previously eluded federal law. According to one *Knight* dictum, only the states could regulate production, so that Congress could not directly outlaw the employment of children in factories. But the new federal police power seemingly covered a factory's products as soon as they entered interstate commerce. Accordingly, in 1916, Congress shut that door to all products made or mined by companies employing children under the age of fourteen. Such products could no longer be shipped in interstate commerce.

The child-labor law was quickly challenged by one Roland Dagenhart, father of two stunted boys working in a North Carolina cotton mill. He sued the local United States prosecutor, W.C. Hammer, to enjoin him from enforcing the law and cutting off the father's income from his children's jobs. Dagenhart won in the lower courts, and Hammer appealed to the Supreme Court.

The cotton mill engineered Dagenhart's suit and paid his legal fees.

By the time the Justices heard *Hammer* v. *Dagenhart* in 1918, a narrow majority had developed qualms about the new federal police power. By permitting Congress to ban any undesirable article from interstate commerce, the Court had potentially enabled the lawmakers to control production in general, since most factories necessarily sold their output in more than one state. It was one thing to uphold federal efforts to police interstate commerce and enhance the national economy. But the *Champion* precedent, carried to its logical conclusion fifteen years later, seemed to presage the imminent descent of federal inspectors from Washington upon the local mine or mill. To be sure, these enterprises were by now probably owned or controlled by some interstate corporation. But no matter: the precinct of production was off limits to federal regulators. Otherwise, where would it all end?

Speaking for a five-to-four majority, Justice William R. Day declared the 1916 child labor law unconstitutional.

First, Day said Congress had no "right to for-

Child labor was widespread in nineteenth-century America, although it came to be perceived as a social evil by many after the turn of the century. Here, young girls polish tin sheets at the American Sheet & Tin Plate Co., Pittsburgh in an anonymous photograph of April, 1908.

bid commerce from moving." (Its power was limited to the *means* of movement.) Since the Court had, in fact, already upheld federal bans on the movement of lottery tickets, tainted food, and prostitutes, Day's dictum required an agile distinction, which he duly provided. Certain things *were* bannable, he said, if their movement produced "harmful results," such as poisoning from spoiled food or untested drugs.

This category of contraband items excluded goods produced by child labor. Why? Because they were harmless in themselves; only child labor itself was harmful. And since child labor was an evil *preceding* interstate commerce, whereas its fruits were not evil, Congress's remedy was inappropriate and invalid.

Second, Day dredged up the *Knight* distinction between commerce and production, the latter being supposedly immune to federal control. Accordingly, he ruled the child labor law unconstitutional on two grounds—the new "harmful results" doctrine and the old one that regulation

of production is reserved to the states. "If Congress can thus regulate matters entrusted to local authority," he warned, "the power of the states over local matters may be eliminated, and thus our system of government practically destroyed."

Speaking for the four *Dagenhart* dissenters, Justice Holmes argued that banning child labor products from interstate transportation was a wholly valid exercise of the federal commerce power. "It does not matter whether the evil precedes or follows the transportation," he wrote. "It is enough that in the opinion of Congress the transportation encourages the evil." As to Day's fear for the Republic, Holmes noted that the Court itself had long dismissed all state claims to power over products crossing state lines, even when federal laws affected *intra*state commerce. In fact, the only ground Holmes could find for the majority Justices' ruling was their personal distaste for the child labor law.

Evidence for that supposition was supplied by the Court's subsequent approval of federal bans

Here, boys run a loom at the Bibb Mill No. 1, Macon, Georgia, in Lewis Hine's photograph of c. 1908–12. Division of Archives and Manuscripts, Pennsylvania Historical and Museum Commission, Harrisburg, and National Archives, Washington, D.C.

on interstate transportation of stolen cars and kidnapped persons. As with child labor products, these things were harmless in themselves. Yet the Court held in 1925 that Congress "can certainly" outlaw the use of commerce "as an agency to promote immorality, dishonesty or the spread of any evil or harm to the people of other states" (*Brooks* v. *United States*). To Holmes and others, the Court's distinction between car theft and child labor seemed to be a matter of personal opinion as to what constituted "evil or harm" to society.

Without the social evil issue, those fighting child labor were on shaky constitutional ground. When Congress tried to get around *Hammer* v. *Dagenhart*, by imposing a high tax on child labor products, eight Justices including Holmes ruled the tax invalid (*Bailey* v. *Drexel*). Two years later, in 1924, Congress doggedly passed a constitutional amendment outlawing child labor. But it was still pending ratification by the states in 1938 when Congress passed yet another law forbid-

ding child labor—and this time, with a very different set of Justices, the Court upheld the new law in a 1941 decision (*United States* v. *Darby Lumber Company*), specifically reversing *Hammer* v. *Dagenhart* and adopting Holmes's dissent in the process.

LAW AND THE COURT

. . . . Vanity is the most philosophical of those feelings that we are taught to despise. For vanity recognizes that if a man is a minority of one we lock him up, and therefore longs for an assurance from others that one's work has not been in vain. If a man's ambition is the thirst for power that comes not from office but from within, he never can be sure that . . . he sits on that other bench reserved for the masters of those who know. Then, too, at least until one draws near to 70, one is less likely to hear the trumpets than the rolling fire of the front. I have passed that age, but I still am on the firing line, and it is only in rare moments like this that there comes a pause and for half an hour one feels a trembling hope. They are the rewards of a lifetime's work.

But let me turn to more palpable realities—to that other visible court to which for 10 now accomplished years it has been my opportunity to belong. We are very quiet there, but it is the quiet of a storm center, as we all know. Science has taught the world scepticism, and has made it legitimate to put everything to the test of proof. Many beautiful and noble reverences are impaired, but in these days no one can complain if any institution, system, or belief is called on to justify its continuance in life. Of course we are not excepted and have not escaped. Doubts are expressed that go to our very being. Not only are we told that when Marshall pronounced an act of Congress unconstitutional he usurped a power that the Constitution did not give, but we are told that we are the representatives of a class—a tool of the money power. I get letters, not always anonymous, intimating that we are corrupt. Well, gentlemen, I admit that it makes my heart ache. It is very painful, when one spends all the energies of one's soul in trying to do good work, with no thought but that of solving a problem according to the rules by which one is bound, to know that many see sinister motives and would be glad of evidence that one was consciously bad. But we must take such things philosophically and try to see what we can learn from hatred and distrust, and whether behind them there may not be some germ of inarticulate truth.

The attacks upon the court are merely an expression of the unrest that seems to wonder vaguely whether law and order pay. When the ignorant are taught to doubt they do not know what they safely may believe. And it seems to me that at this time we need education in the obvious more than investigation of the obscure. . . .

. . . As law embodies beliefs that have triumphed in the battle of ideas and then have translated themselves into action; while there still is doubt, while opposite convictions still keep a battle front against each other, the time for law has not come; the notion destined to prevail is not yet entitled to the field. It is a misfortune if a judge reads his conscious or unconscious sympathy with one side or the other prematurely into the law, and forgets that what seem to him to be first principles are believed by half his fellow men to be wrong. I think that we have suffered from this misfortune, in State courts at least, and that this is another and very important truth to be extracted from the popular discontent. When 20 years ago a vague terror went over the earth and the word socialism began to be heard, I thought and still think that fear was translated into doctrines that had no proper place in the Constitution or the common law. Judges are apt to be naif, simple-minded men, and they need something of Mephistopheles. We, too, need education in the obvious—to learn to transcend our own convictions and to

leave room for much that we hold dear to be done away with short of revolution by the orderly change of law.

I have no belief in panaceas and almost none in sudden ruin. I believe with Montesquieu that if the chance of a battle—I may add, the passage of a law—has ruined a State, there was a general cause at work that made the State ready to perish by a single battle or law. Hence I am not much interested one way or the other in the nostrums now so strenuously urged. I do not think the United States would come to an end if we lost our power to declare an act of Congress void. I do think the Union would be imperiled if we could not make that declaration as to the laws of the several States. For one in my place sees how often a local policy prevails with those who are not trained to national views and how often action is taken that embodies what the commerce clause was meant to end. But I am not aware that there is any serious desire to limit the court's power in this regard. For most of the things that properly can be called evils in the present state of the law I think the main remedy, as for the evils of public opinion, is for us to grow more civilized.

If I am right, it will be a slow business for our people to reach rational views, assuming that we are allowed to work peaceably to that end. But as I grow older I grow calm. If I feel what are perhaps an old man's apprehensions, that competition from new races will cut deeper than workingmen's disputes and will test whether we can hang together and can fight; if I fear that we are running through the world's resources at a pace that we cannot keep; I do not lose my hopes. I do not pin my dreams for the future to my country or even to my race. I think it probable that civilization somehow will last as long as I care to look ahead—perhaps

with smaller numbers, but perhaps also bred of greatness and splendor by science. I think it not improbable that man, like the grub that prepares a chamber for the winged thing it never has seen but is to be, that man may have cosmic destinies that he does not understand. And so beyond the vision of battling races and an impoverished earth I catch a dreaming glimpse of peace.

The other day my dream was pictured to my mind. It was evening. I was walking homeward on Pennsylvania Avenue near the Treasury, and as I looked beyond Sherman's statue to the west the sky was aflame with scarlet and crimson from the setting sun. But, like the note of downfall in Wagner's opera, below the sky line there came from little globes the pallid discord of the electric lights. And I thought to myself the Götterdämmerung will end, and from those globes clustered like evil eggs will come the new masters of the sky. It is like the time in which we live. But then I remembered the faith that I partly have expressed, faith in a universe not measured by our fears, a universe that has thought and more than thought inside of it, and as I gazed, after the sunset and above the electric lights there shone the stars.

Justice Oliver Wendell Holmes

Speech at a dinner of the Harvard
Law School Association of New York

February 15, 1913

13

THE END OF LAISSEZ-FAIRE

Poster commemorating the 1869 National Eight Hour Law, which embraced United States government employees. The Supreme Court continued to find hours legislation for all workers unconstitutional until 1917. The Archives of Labor and Urban Affairs, Wayne State University, Detroit

The Court majority could not halt the rising tide of state and federal regulation simply by setting new limits on the federal commerce and taxing powers. Accordingly, these Justices turned again to the Due Process Clause of the Fourteenth Amendment, which could arguably be used to curb big government at *both* the state and federal level.

Due process was not to be an automatic carte blanche for entrepreneurs. By and large the Court stuck to its *Munn*-derived doctrine upholding state police power to regulate business "affected with a public interest." But the number of economic areas included in this category kept dwindling with the years, and the Court was particularly resistant to state laws regulating prices, wages, and hours.

The curb of choice was "substantive due process," which the Court first used to invalidate a state economic regulation in *Chicago, Milwaukee and St. Paul R.R. Co.* v. *Minnesota* (1890). Six Justices felt the Minnesota railroad commission had prevented the company from charging reasonable rates. Accordingly, this majority held that corporations (already deemed "persons") had a constitutional right to due process, which mandated judicial review of rates imposed upon them by states. The Minnesota railroad commission law failed to provide judicial review; it fell. The significance of the case was that *courts* would now have the last word on whether railroad rates were "reasonable."

Two years later, the Court momentarily flinched from the *Chicago* doctrine when it permitted a New York commission to set maximum rates for the state's grain elevators. But that case (*Budd* v. *New York*) is best remembered for Justice Brewer's dissent. Denouncing regulation as "radically unsound," Brewer warned that socialism was just around the corner, and declared, "The paternal theory of government is to me odious."

The odium factor doubtless helped the Justices swing back to *Chicago* in 1897, when a unanimous Court dispelled all confusion as to the locus of final power in rate setting. Neither elected legislatures nor appointed commissions had that power, the Court held in *Smyth* v. *Ames*. Since corporations were entitled to due process, states must set rates high enough to net a fair return for the investors, and the power to enforce this stan-

Joseph Lochner and his wife, Catherine (right), with a friend and two unidentified employees, in the backyard of his bakery. Courtesy Anne Lochner Brady, Clinton, New York

dard lay with judges—the special custodians of due process.

The Court was now clearly focused on the heart of nineteenth-century free enterprise— the right to buy services and sell goods free of state interference and subject to control only by unhampered market forces. In defense of this principle, the Court mobilized a concept derived from the Bradley-Field dissents in *The Slaughterhouse Cases* (1873). Two decades later, those dissents became majority opinion, and in *Allgeyer* v. *Louisiana* (1897), Justice Peckham unveiled "liberty of contract."

The plaintiff, Allgeyer, had challenged a Louisiana law barring that state's citizens from doing business with out-of-state insurance companies. Speaking for a unanimous Court, Justice Peckham had the easy option of declaring the law an undue interference with interstate commerce. Instead, he said Allgeyer had been deprived of liberty without due process of law. Liberty included not only freedom from physical restraint, Peckham declared, but also "the right of the citizen to be free in the enjoyment of all his faculties; to be free to use them in all lawful ways; to live and work where he will; to earn his livelihood by any lawful calling; to pursue any livelihood or avocation; and for that purpose to enter into all contracts which may be proper, necessary and essential to his carrying out to a successful conclusion the purposes above mentioned."

Peckham's opinion had the effect of allowing employers to "contract" with workers as to wages and hours. Peckham's theory of contractual liberty assumed that all contracting parties had equal bargaining power.

Unlike Peckham and his ally, Brewer, seven Justices conceded a state's power to remedy dangerous working conditions; and such was the voting line-up in *Holden* v. *Hardy* (1898), when the

169

Captain Oliver Wendell Holmes, 20th Massachusetts Regiment. Collection of the Supreme Court of the United States, Washington, D.C.

Peckham found the New York law devoid of reasonableness. It did not protect the public: "Clean and wholesome bread does not depend upon whether the baker works but ten hours per day or only sixty hours a week." Nor did bakers need special protection, their trade being "vastly more healthy than . . . others." Peckham found no reason for legislative interference with "the right of labor," and he considered it self-evident that "the limits of the police power have been reached and passed in this case."

If a law fixing bakers' hours were upheld, Peckham wrote, the next step would be laws regulating everybody—bankers, brokers, and even lawyers toiling in offices where "the sun penetrates but for a short time in each day." Such "meddlesome interference with the rights of the individual" posed the specter of the state as a pater familias, subjecting folk to "the mercy of legislative majorities." The "real object" of the New York lawmakers was to subvert "the freedom of master and employee to contract with each other." As Peckham saw it, the Due Process Clause stood firmly in the way.

Not surprisingly, there were four dissenters. In one of his first and pithiest dissents, Justice Holmes wrote:

> I think that the word liberty in the Fourteenth Amendment is perverted when it is held to prevent the natural outcome of a dominant opinion unless it can be said that a rational and fair man necessarily would admit that the statute proposed would infringe fundamental principles as they have been understood by the traditions of our people and our law. It does not need research to show that no such sweeping condemnation can be passed upon the statute before us.

Peckham was hardly alone. The "dominant" *legal* (if not social or economic) opinion of the day generally supported the position he espoused. Between 1897 and 1937, due-process challengers persuaded the court to invalidate some 200 state and federal laws. But the challengers lost many more cases than they won. Between 1897 and 1918 alone, the Court *upheld* 369 state laws as properly enacted under the police power.

Even Thomas Cooley (1828–98), the laissez-

Court upheld a Utah law that limited miners to eight hours' work per day in underground mines. Where health or life were at stake, the Court ruled, liberty of contract must yield to state regulation.

That concession was temporary. At issue in *Lochner* v. *New York* (1905) was a state law limiting bakery employees to a ten-hour work day or a sixty-hour week. New York's highest court had upheld the law as a valid exercise of state police power. But Peckham, speaking for a five-Justice majority, ruled the law unconstitutional.

If a state could limit bakers' hours, it could do the same for all workers, and contractual liberty would be doomed. Peckham was willing to yield to states what he called "the somewhat vaguely termed police powers," but he warned that further Court permissiveness, as in *Holden*, would allow legislators to use health laws and the like as "a mere pretext" for unbridled statism.

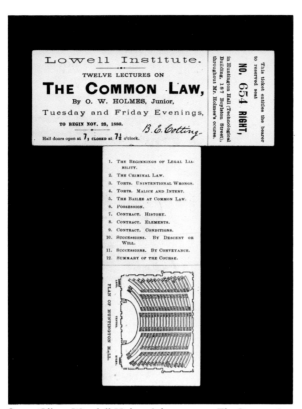

Ticket to Professor Oliver Wendell Holmes's lectures on *The Common Law*. Harvard Law School, Cambridge

Professor Oliver Wendell Holmes, 1888. Harvard Law Art Collection, Cambridge

faire theorist of nineteenth-century American law, had been more yielding than *Lochner* v. *New York*. Years before, Cooley had conceded the need for laws protecting especially weak or vulnerable persons. Judges must not be blind to "distinctions that exist in the nature of things," he had written in 1868. The majesty of law required not only consistency but also compassion, a certain respect for the human condition.

Only three years after *Lochner*, the Court upheld an Oregon law fixing a maximum ten-hour day for women working in laundries. Justice Peckham did not object. In fact, *Muller* v. *Oregon* (1908) was a unanimous decision, written by none other than Peckham's alter ego, Justice Brewer.

Under *Lochner*, state police power ended where the health reason was insufficient to justify the hours limit. But *Muller* was different: the Oregon law was defended by Louis D. Brandeis, the brilliant future Justice, then a highly successful Boston lawyer known as "The People's Attorney" for his devotion to pro bono causes across the country. Brandeis presented the Justices with a carefully organized collection of irrefutable

data from all over the world verifying his claim that long hours could impair a woman's childbearing function, and that Oregon's ten-hour workday for women was therefore a valid health measure. The "Brandeis brief," as lawyers called it, provided the reasonableness standard with an ingredient previously missing—evidence.

In his *Muller* opinion for the Court, Justice Brewer went out of his way to compliment Brandeis in a lengthy footnote. Brewer now conceded that liberty of contract was "not absolute," and women's "disadvantage in the struggle for subsistence" placed the female worker "in a class by herself" entitled to state protection. Brewer had always been judicially sympathetic to women. But Justice Peckham wrote no opinion; his position upholding the Oregon law remains a puzzle.

For a brief period after *Muller* and the deaths of Peckham (1909) and Brewer (1910), the views of Justice Holmes came to the fore. The epitome of courageous skepticism, Holmes had forced himself to defer to legislative wisdom, even when he considered it folly. "The Fourteenth Amendment does not enact Mr. Herbert Spencer's *Social*

Justice Oliver Wendell Holmes's library, in his I Street home, Washington, D.C. His Civil War mementos hang over the fireplace. Harvard Law Art Collection, Cambridge

Statics," he had declared in his *Lochner* dissent. "A constitution is not intended to embody a particular economic theory. . . . It is made for people of fundamentally different views."

Holmes was a scholar of reality. His intense pragmatism had flowered in *The Common Law* (1881), his pioneering analysis of the Anglo-American heritage. The fourth sentence of that classic, published when Holmes was forty, had foreshadowed his judicial philosophy—"The life of the law has not been logic; it has been experience."

Holmes's openness to experience and experiment derived from his Darwinian view that society progresses insofar as it nurtures "the marketplace of ideas." An empiricist, not a reformer, he doubted that what he called "tinkering with the system" would significantly help the helpless. But he had no doubt that judges should not be in the business of second-guessing the vot-

ers. "We, too, need education in the obvious—to learn to transcend our own convictions and to leave room for much that we hold dear to be done away with short of revolution by the orderly change of law."

Justice Pierce Butler once persuaded Holmes to join him in a particular case. With his usual solemnity, Butler intoned: "I am glad we have finally arrived at a *just* decision." Holmes instantly replied, "Hell is paved with *just* intentions." Even more typical of Holmes was his reported comment to a lawyer after an antitrust argument: "Of course I know, and every sensible man knows, that the Sherman Act is damnable nonsense, but if my country wants to go to hell, I am here to help it."

Actually, Holmes had an exquisite sense of limits as well as liberties. He is probably best known for resisting what he deemed the most egregious kind of legislative excess—laws curbing free speech and thought. He considered the First Amendment crucial to republican government. His dissent in *Abrams* v. *United States* (1919) is a masterpiece of English prose that ranks among history's most eloquent statements concerning political freedom.

Holmes's great gift to the Court and the country was his unfailing vote for tough-minded tolerance—a kind of moral compass that pointed unerringly at the Constitution's true north. For over twenty-nine years (1902–32), in more than two thousand opinions, Holmes steered a majestic course between the shoals of statism and laissez-faire, serving under four Chief Justices and five Presidents.

The laissez-faire judges had reversed the tradition that a challenged regulatory statute would be presumed valid until proven otherwise beyond a reasonable doubt, with the burden of proof on the challenger—typically a corporation.

By insisting that America's First Principle was "liberty of contract," they had created a new standard replacing the doctrine of presumed validity. Under this standard, exemplified by *Lochner* v. *New York* (1905), any law restraining business was presumed invalid until proven necessary beyond a reasonable doubt, and the burden of proof was on the law's creators and beneficiaries.

In the *Muller* case, Louis D. Brandeis had opened the Court to the power of facts in assessing social legislation. The Justices seemed increasingly to agree that "reasonableness" was best measured by data rather than dogma. Brandeis was soon to stress that view in the Conference Room itself.

Appointed by President Woodrow Wilson in January 1916, Justice Brandeis encountered a six-month confirmation fight, mainly over his social activism. When he finally became the Court's first Jewish member in June 1916, Brandeis initially took no part in cases such as *Bunting* v. *Oregon* (1916), which challenged that state's law fixing maximum hours—this time, a ten-hour day for *all* industrial workers, male or female.

Voting five to three in *Bunting*, the Court upheld the hours law as a valid health measure, conspicuously ignoring the antithetical precedent of *Lochner* v. *New York*, which Justice Joseph McKenna did not even mention in his opinion for the majority.

The *Bunting* challengers had argued that the ten-hour law was not so much a health measure as an impermissible attempt to regulate *wages*. Indeed, the law required overtime pay—one-and-a-half times regular wages—and it set minimum wages for women and children. But Justice McKenna took the route of presumed validity, ruling that the challengers had failed to sustain their contention that the law was unnecessary for workers' health. In his view, "It is enough for our decision if the legislation under review was passed in the exercise of an admitted power of government." By upholding the entire law, the Court implied approval of the minimum wage provisions as well.

Given the Court's record, *Bunting* was extraordinary. It apparently freed states to regulate hours and wages, without due-process challenge, provided the regulations had some clear link to public health and safety.

Judicial excellence was particularly important to President William Howard Taft, who made six Court appointments during his single four-year term (1908–12). Taft's big catch was Charles Evans Hughes, a prominent liberal Republican lawyer with a national reputation for racket-busting that had made him Governor of New York. Hughes was bright, dignified, organized, and—at forty-eight—one of Taft's potential rivals for the 1912 Republican nomination. Taft removed

Telegram, Justice Oliver Wendell Holmes to Justice Louis Dembitz Brandeis, June 2, 1916. Brandeis Papers, University of Louisville

that danger in May 1910 when Hughes startled his supporters by accepting a Court seat.

Hughes plunged into crafting the kind of positive opinions that made the early White Court a promising model of constitutional adjustment to social change. In this period, the Justices upheld the Pure Food and Drug Act, backed White's antitrust "rule of reason," and joined Hughes's significant opinion in the *Shreveport Case*, which permitted the Interstate Commerce Commission to fix intrastate rail rates where necessary to protect interstate commerce.

The 1917 *Bunting* decision was a patent rejection of *Lochner* (1905), but only a year later, the *Lochner* attitude rebounded in *Hammer* v. *Dagenhart* (1918), striking down the federal ban on child labor products.

In the same term, however, the Court sustained federal power over personal liberty by upholding the World War I draft law. Passed in 1917, the law had required nine-and-a-half million men to register for military service. In the *Selective Draft Cases* (1918), the law's challengers argued that compulsory conscription exceeded federal power and violated the Thirteenth Amendment ban on involuntary servitude. But the Court ruled the law a valid exercise of Congress's specific power to raise armies and of its general authority under the Necessary and Proper Clause.

Wars inflate government power, and most judges have acquiesced—for the duration. The 1917 Espionage Act made it a federal crime to publish or utter any false statement intended to

Charles Evans Hughes, c. 1905–1906, shortly before his first term as Governor of New York. Brown Brothers, Sterling, Pennsylvania

obstruct the armed forces. The 1918 Sedition Act made it a crime to write, publish, or utter anything intended to *criticize* the government. These laws produced about two thousand prosecutions and one thousand convictions.

In 1919 and 1920, World War I having ended, the Court reviewed six major cases that challenged the espionage and sedition laws as violations of the First Amendment's free speech guarantee. At issue was whether free speech was an absolute right; or whether it could be limited, and if so, how and when.

The initial point was easy. The First Amendment presumably followed the common law in protecting honest opinions, whatever their con-

sequences. Conversely, it presumably did not protect lies or incitements or similar expressions deliberately aimed at unlawful results.

The Justices agreed that the First Amendment was not absolute, and Congress could punish speech it deemed seditious. But as to precise limits and proof of intent, the Court split sharply, the majority being content with elastic standards, while the eloquent dissenters (Holmes, Brandeis), insisted upon proof that accused seditionists actually intended to sabotage the war effort.

In its first decision, *Schenck* v. *United States* (1919), the Court unanimously sustained the Espionage Act, ruling that free speech must give way to wartime exigencies. Schenck was a Socialist Party official who had mailed 15,000 leaflets to draftees quoting the Thirteenth Amendment, denouncing the draft as unconstitutional, and urging the recipients to "assert their rights" or else be ground into cannon fodder serving Wall Street interests. Tried for sedition, Schenck argued that he had simply exercised his First Amendment right to speak freely on public issues. There was no evidence that he had in fact corrupted a single draftee; publication alone was deemed sufficient to prove his guilt.

At that stage in the six-case series, Justice Holmes spoke for the unanimous Court. He agreed that the leaflets were entitled to protection—but in peacetime, not wartime. "The character of every act depends upon the circumstances in which it is done," Holmes wrote. He then announced his famous "clear and present danger test" for determining when government may constitutionally restrain speech. As Holmes put it, the First Amendment would not save a man who falsely cried "Fire!" in a crowded theater and caused a panic. Accordingly, the standard was "whether the words are used in such circumstances and are of such a nature as to create a clear and present danger that they will bring about the substantive dangers that Congress has a right to prevent. It is a question of proximity and degree."

Schenck's leaflets created such a danger, Holmes ruled. That Schenck had failed to obstruct the draft was irrelevant; the law applied to failed attempts as well as successes. Schenck's mistake was to publish, in wartime, words admittedly intended to halt conscription. "When a nation is at war," Holmes wrote, "many things that might be said in time of peace are such a hindrance to its effort that their utterance will not be endured so long as men fight and that no Court could regard them as protected by any constitutional right."

A week later, Holmes spoke for the Court in two more unanimous decisions sustaining the Espionage and Sedition Acts. One of the appellants was Eugene V. Debs, the Socialist leader and five-time Presidential candidate who—running his campaign from a jail cell—won nearly a million votes in 1920. Debs had made a relatively innocuous antiwar speech; he was promptly handed a ten-year sentence for obstructing recruitment and inciting mutiny. The evidence

of criminal intent in his case was much shakier than in *Schenck*, and Holmes's opinion was correspondingly weaker. In applying the *Schenck* standard, Holmes did not question what he called the trial jury's "reasonable" finding that Debs was guilty as charged because his speech had "the natural and intended effect" of cooling military ardor, whether or not it actually did so. If Debs "used words tending to obstruct the recruiting service," Holmes wrote, "he meant that they should have that effect."

The Holmes test actually *narrowed* the area of unprotected speech, committing the Court to a broad view of whatever speech remained immune to government restraint. In that sense, *Schenck* was a signal advance for free expression in the United States. However, once Holmes began refining the test, the Court began dividing sharply in free-speech cases.

Eight months after *Schenck*, in November 1919, Holmes and Brandeis dissented in *Abrams* v. *United States*, a case that found seven Justices willing to jail a man for uttering unpopular words with consequences too remote to prove.

Abrams arose from President Wilson's attempt to intervene in the Russian revolution by sending United States troops to Archangel and Vladivostok. Abrams and four other Russian immigrants were New York garment workers and Bolshevik sympathizers opposed to the 1918 expedition, which they denounced in suitably colorful terms in a couple of crude pamphlets, one in English, the other in Yiddish. The authors called the President a cowardly hypocrite secretly allied with German militarists to crush the embryo Soviets. The pamphlets warned munitions workers that their products would now kill Russians as well as Germans, and they called for a general strike to halt arms shipments to counterrevolutionary forces.

The publication of these works was by way of a Manhattan factory window from which they were tossed to the street below. The five tossers were convicted under the Espionage Act of trying to sabotage the war *with Germany*, and they were each sentenced to twenty years in prison.

The majority opinion sustaining these convictions was written by Justice John H. Clarke, a liberal Ohio Democrat appointed by President Wilson largely because of his progressive views. Justice Clarke dismissed the appellants' free-

175

The White Court, 1916 to 1921, after the departure of Justice Hughes. Standing, from left: Associate Justices Louis Dembitz Brandeis, Mahlon Pitney, James Clark McReynolds, John Hessin Clarke. Seated, from left: Associate Justices William Rufus Day, Joseph McKenna, Chief Justice Edward Douglas White, Associate Justices Oliver Wendell Holmes, Willis Van Devanter. Photograph by Clinedinst. Collection of the Supreme Court of the United States, Washington, D.C.

speech claims, citing *Schenck* as precedent, and said the only question was whether the jury had sufficient evidence to find guilt.

As Clarke saw it, "Much evidence was before the jury tending to prove that the defendants were guilty as charged."

Abrams was argued and decided in the fall of 1919—at the height of the Red Scare. By eliminating the need to prove direct obstruction of the war effort—Holmes's "question of proximity and degree"—Clarke's opinion sharply broadened the restraints on civil liberties that *Schenck* had made permissible.

Holmes's dissent was scathing. "Congress certainly cannot forbid all effort to change the mind of the country," he declared, and therefore "it is only the present danger of immediate evil or an intent to bring it about" that warrants restraint. "In this case," Holmes wrote, "sentences of twenty years imprisonment have been imposed for the publishing of two leaflets that I believe the defendants had as much right to publish as the Government has to publish the Constitution of the United States now vainly invoked by them."

Abrams is best remembered for the great Holmes passage in which he articulated a First Amendment philosophy stressing free trade in ideas as the key to liberty. The premise that dialogue corrects democracy's errors suggests that the First Amendment should be construed to

176

Chief Justice William Howard Taft signs his Oath of Office as the tenth Chief Justice of the Supreme Court, July 11, 1921. UPI/Bettmann Archive

favor more speech, not less; and that only in dire circumstances, where the dialogue itself threatens the state, should it be curtailed. Eight years after *Abrams*, Justice Brandeis synthesized these ideas in *Whitney* v. *California* (1927), to which he contributed a memorable concurring opinion joined by Holmes.

At the beginning of 1920, no American alive was more concerned about the Supreme Court— or more anxious to join it—than William Howard Taft, perhaps the most experienced officeholder of his day. Taft had been variously a local prosecutor in his native Ohio, a state trial judge, Solicitor General of the United States, Federal Circuit Court Judge, Governor General of the Philippines, Secretary of War, President of the United States, and Yale professor of constitutional law.

Taft saw judicial review as the linchpin of American liberty. "The greatest advantage of our plan of government over every other," he wrote, "is the character of the judicial power vested in the Supreme Court." That power, admired the world over, enabled a non-elected branch of government to check the impulsiveness of the political branches, and above all, to

combat the potential tyranny of popular majorities.

In May 1921, Edward D. White died at the age of seventy-five, ending his twenty-six years as a Supreme Court Justice, the last ten of them as Chief. The recently elected Republican President, Warren G. Harding, quickly turned to his eager fellow Republican, William Howard Taft. On the same day that Harding sent Taft's name to the Senate—June 30, 1921—the twenty-seventh President was confirmed by a voice vote as the tenth Chief Justice of the United States.

At this point the Supreme Court was badly in need of a dynamic organizer. The Justices were falling behind with an ever growing docket and ever slower handing down of decisions. The Court's once limited jurisdiction had been expanded as Congress increased the number of mandatory appeals. The 1891 law creating federal circuit courts of appeals had made the decisions of those courts final in many areas, ranging from admiralty law to non-capital crimes. But in many others, notably constitutional cases, the Justices were obliged to hear the losing parties, together with federal questions from top state courts and certain direct appeals from federal

177

district courts.

The forceful new Chief immediately launched a campaign to energize the entire federal judiciary. Within a year, Taft persuaded Congress to approve a national governing board composed of senior circuit judges, with himself as chairman. That body, created in 1922, later became the much larger United States Judicial Conference that now supervises all federal courts.

Taft's determination to light a fire under his colleagues ignited sparks of friction, but by the end of the 1922 term the results were impressive. Along with speedier procedures, Taft's prodding had slashed three months from the usual delay between filing and hearing, and the Justices had set an all-time record in disposing of cases.

Taft's masterstroke was the 1925 Judiciary Act, often called "The Judges' Bill" because the Justices wrote it. In response to Taft's intense lobbying, Congress agreed to shift the Court's primary focus from mandatory to discretionary review. This was accomplished by making the decisions of the circuit courts truly final in nearly all the cases they heard. The Supreme Court was obliged to review only those circuit decisions holding a state law invalid under federal laws, treaties, or the Constitution. The Court would still review other kinds of appellate decisions—but only if a minimum of four Justices voted to issue a writ of certiorari. In a few remaining areas, such as antitrust law, the government retained the right to appeal an adverse district court ruling directly to the Supreme Court. The net effect of all this was to give the Justices enormous control over their docket.

The most visible fruit of Taft's lobbying was the Supreme Court building, a dream he first began to promote in 1912, and tirelessly pursued for the next seventeen years, until Congress in 1929 appropriated the sum of $9,740,000 to house the Court permanently in "a building of dignity and importance."

Taft was a man of large vision. His drive for judicial reform is generally seen as the core of his strategy for protecting conservative values. According to Alpheus T. Mason, one of his principal biographers, "Taft believed that judicial reform could reduce the threat to private property by removing a justifiable source of popular unrest. By revising outmoded judicial organization and procedure, the legal profession might counteract the disruptive influence of the wild-eyed reformers. This, indeed, was the link which bound together judicial reform and judicial defense of property."

In the beginning the Chief's prevailing good humor softened his harder edges, and his pleas for unanimity succeeded, reinforced by his technique of reassigning opinions whenever the original writer failed to carry a substantial majority. Brandeis was an indicator of the Chief's determined charm. "Things go happily in the conference room with Taft," he wrote a friend. "The judges go home less tired emotionally and less weary physically than in White's day. . . . It's all very friendly."

This era of good feelings continued for almost four years. But its end might have been predicted six months after Taft's arrival, when he wrote his first major opinion, *Truax* v. *Corrigan* (1921). The appellants were Arizona restaurant owners who had sought to enjoin striking employees from picketing and promoting a boycott of their establishment. Unfortunately for the owners, Arizona had a law barring state courts from issuing injunctions in labor disputes. The only exception was to prevent violence and property damage. Since these strikers were peaceful, the owners lost all the way to the Supreme Court. But there, speaking for a bare majority of five to four, Taft ruled the anti-injunction law unconstitutional. It violated the Fourteenth Amendment by depriving the restaurant owners of their property without due process of law, he said. Moreover, it denied equal protection of the laws by immunizing labor disputes from the remedy of injunctions.

Taft called the employer's right to enjoin strikers "a fundamental principle of liberty and justice, which inheres in the very idea of free government." "The Constitution was intended," Taft declared, "its very purpose was, to prevent experimentation with the fundamental rights of the individual."

The four dissenters tore into Taft's view that the Constitution barred legislative experimentation with a so-called fundamental right. In a detailed opinion with fifty-one footnotes, Brandeis traced widespread dissatisfaction with labor injunctions throughout the English-speaking world. All this persuaded him that "the rights of property and the liberty of the individual must

.... Persecution for the expression of opinions seems to me perfectly logical. If you have no doubt of your premises or your power and want a certain result with all your heart you naturally express your wishes in law and sweep away all opposition. To allow opposition by speech seems to indicate that you think the speech impotent, as when a man says that he has squared the circle, or that you do not care wholeheartedly for the result, or that you doubt either your power or your premises. But when men have realized that time has upset many fighting faiths, they may come to believe even more than they believe the very foundations of their own conduct that the ultimate good desired is better reached by free trade in ideas—that the best test of truth is the power of the thought to get itself accepted in the competition of the market, and that truth is the only ground upon which their wishes safely can be carried out. That at any rate is the theory of our Constitution. It is an experiment, as all life is an experiment. Every year if not every day we have to wager our salvation upon some prophecy based upon imperfect

knowledge. While that experiment is part of our system I think that we should be eternally vigilant against attempts to check the expression of opinions that we loathe and believe to be fraught with death, unless they so imminently threaten immediate interference with the lawful and pressing purposes of the law that an immediate check is required to save the country.... Only the emergency that makes it immediately dangerous to leave the correction of evil counsels to time warrants making any exception to the sweeping command, "Congress shall make no law ... abridging the freedom of speech."

Justice Oliver Wendell Holmes

Dissenting
Abrams v. *United States*

1918

be remolded from time to time, to meet the changing needs of society."

Holmes confined himself largely to his own counter-dictum, "Legislation may begin where an evil begins." To which he added, "There is nothing that I more deprecate than the use of the Fourteenth Amendment beyond the absolute compulsion of its words to prevent the making of social experiments that an important part of the community desires, in the insulated chambers afforded by the several States, even though the experiments may seem futile or even noxious to me and to those whose judgment I most respect."

Bolstered by four Harding appointees, the Taft Court entered the 1920s eager to strike down what the Chief called "ill-digested legislation." Six years after *Bunting* v. *Oregon*, in the famous case of *Adkins* v. *Children's Hospital* (1923), the Justices voted five to three—Brandeis abstaining—to halt legislative interference with free-market wages and prices.

At issue was the constitutionality of a federal board created by Congress to fix minimum wages

for women and children in the District of Columbia. According to the enabling act, the board's purpose was to protect the District's women and children "from conditions detrimental to their health and morals, resulting from wages which are inadequate to maintain decent standards of living."

Two appellants charged the board and the law with violating their liberty of contract, supposedly guaranteed by the Due Process Clause of the Fifth Amendment. In the leading case, the hospital claimed that its women employees were happy to work for less than the board-ordered minimum wage and should be allowed to do so. In the second case, a hotel elevator operator claimed she had lost her $35-per-month job, and could find no other, because the board had decreed a raise the hotel couldn't afford.

Speaking for the Court, Justice George Sutherland acknowledged that contractual liberty was no more absolute than other liberties, all of them being subject to certain restraints. But Sutherland declared, "Freedom of contract is, nevertheless, the general rule and restraint the ex-

OATH OF OFFICE FOR UNITED STATES JUDGES.
(Sections 712 and 1757, Revised Statutes.)

I, William Howard Taft, do solemnly swear that I will administer justice without respect to persons, and do equal right to the poor and to the rich, and that I will faithfully and impartially discharge and perform all the duties incumbent on me as Chief Justice of the United States, according to the best of my abilities and understanding, agreeably to the Constitution and laws of the United States; and that I will support and defend the Constitution of the United States against all enemies, foreign and domestic; that I will bear true faith and allegiance to the same; that I take this obligation freely, without any mental reservation or purpose of evasion; and that I will well and faithfully discharge the duties of the office on which I am about to enter. So HELP ME GOD.

Subscribed and sworn to before me, this 11ª day of July, 1921.

Associate Justice of the Supreme Court of the District of Columbia.

Date of birth

Date of entry on duty

NOTE.—The Act of May 1, 1876 (1st Sup. R. S. 100), provides that the oaths of *Territorial Officers* shall be administered in the Territory in which the office is held.

Oath of Office for United States Judges, signed by Chief Justice William Howard Taft. Collection of the Supreme Court of the United States, Washington, D.C.

STUDY FOR SUPREME COURT

ception." Laws abridging it could be justified only by "exceptional circumstances."

Sutherland, a former Republican Senator from Utah, held that the Nineteenth Amendment (1920), guaranteeing women the right to vote, had so equalized the sexes as to bar all regulation of women's working conditions save in the area of their physical differences with men. Thus, limits on working hours were still permissible as health measures. But not so laws requiring employers to pay minimum wages to women—or to men for that matter, Sutherland implied. Such laws penalized employers for social ills beyond their control, sabotaged the free market, and violated "the individual freedom of action contemplated by the Constitution."

The law in question was "simply and exclusively a price-fixing law, confined to adult women . . . who are legally as capable of contracting for themselves as men." "It cannot be shown," Sutherland held, "that well paid women safeguard their morals more carefully than women who are poorly paid."

Sutherland described the law's effect as "so clearly the product of a naked, arbitrary exercise of power that it cannot be allowed to stand under the Constitution." And he added a shrewd debater's point. Wage laws could be double-edged swords: if labor costs soared, future lawmakers might clamp down. "The power to fix high wages," Sutherland remarked, connotes "the power to fix low wages."

Justice Holmes, whose penetrating dissents tended to be either quizzical or eloquent, filed one of the former. "This statute does not compel anybody to pay anything," he wrote. "It simply forbids employment at rates below those fixed as the minimum requirements of health and right living." Holmes said he was baffled by "the principle on which the power to fix a minimum for the wages of women can be denied by those who admit the power to fix a maximum for their hours of work. . . . I perceive no difference in

Sketch by Cass Gilbert for his Supreme Court building, 1928. Collection of the Supreme Court of the United States, Washington, D.C.

Justices Oliver Wendell Holmes and Louis D. Brandeis, Washington, D.C. 1920s. Collection of the Supreme Court of the United States, Washington, D.C.

the kind or degree of interference with liberty . . . between one case and the other."

But far more unexpected was another *Adkins* dissenter—the Chief Justice. Taft chided Sutherland for judicially vetoing an act of Congress by creating "a distinction [between hours and wages] that is formal rather than real."

Taft, unlike Sutherland, viewed contractual liberty as a discredited doctrine. He believed laissez-faire could be defended more effectively by neutralizing the regulators' own doctrines, such as the principle established in *Munn* v. *Illinois* that due process must yield to state police power when a business was "affected with a public interest." When a privately owned grain elevator was vital to community needs, for example, the state was justified in fixing its prices or wages.

In 1923, the same year as *Adkins*, Chief Justice Taft used this approach to strike down—not sustain—a Kansas law permitting state wage controls in the meat-packing industry. Taft simply ruled that the industry was not *sufficiently* public

to justify state regulation.

Justice Sutherland immediately grasped the power of the not-public-enough doctrine. It freed the Court to second-guess legislatures as to which business regulations were valid or invalid. Sutherland duly wrote three major opinions using the Taft vaccine to immunize various businesses from the virus of regulation.

In *Tyson Bros.* v. *Banton* (1927), for example, New York theater ticket brokers had challenged a state law that set a top broker's fee of fifty cents per seat above the box office price. The lawmakers had responded to public dismay over the exorbitant fees being charged by many brokers, and the law was based on the premise that theaters were as much devoted to public use as, say, banks or streetcars. Speaking for a narrow majority of five Justices, however, Sutherland ruled theaters not-public-enough, and by calling ticket brokers "mere appendages" of theaters, he removed them from regulation.

Justice Edward T. Sanford wrote a crisp dis-

The Taft Court in 1925. Standing, from left: Associate Justices Edward Terry Sanford, George Sutherland, Pierce Butler, Harlan Fiske Stone. Seated, from left: Associate Justices James Clark McReynolds, Oliver Wendell Holmes, Chief Justice William Howard Taft, Associate Justices Willis Van Devanter, Louis Dembritz Brandeis. Photograph by Harris & Ewing. Collection of the Supreme Court of the United States, Washington, D.C.

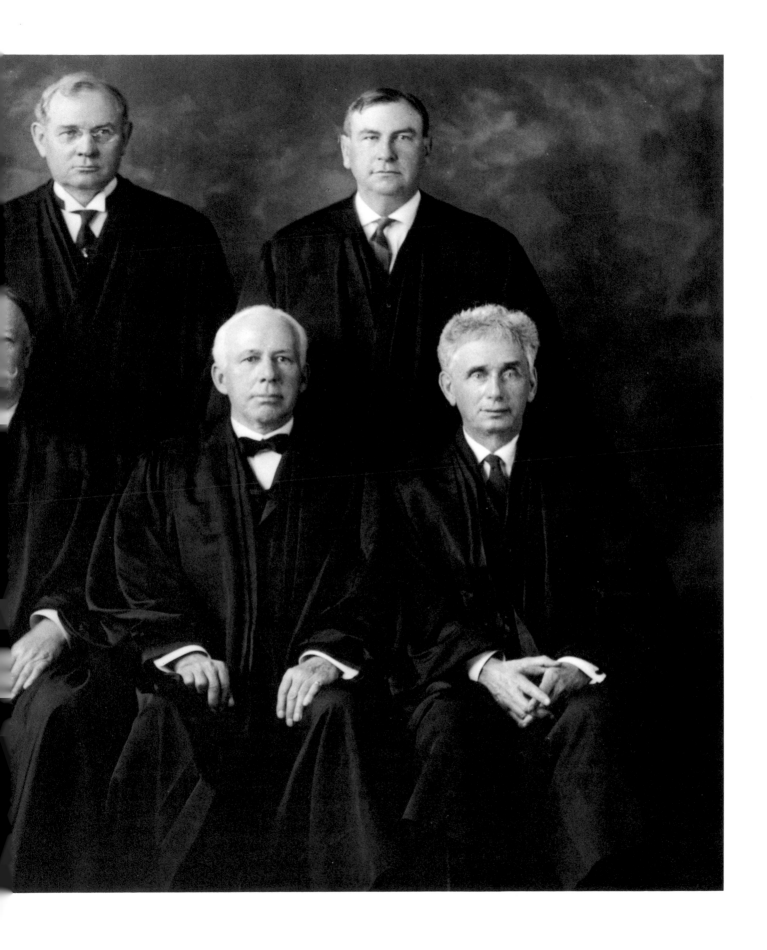

sent supporting the state's right to regulate "brokers who stand in 'the very gateway' between the theaters and the public, depriving the public of access to the theaters for the purchase of desirable seats at the regular prices." Another strong dissenter was a newcomer, Justice Harlan Fiske Stone, the former Attorney General whom President Coolidge had appointed to the Court in 1925 The clearest dissent came from Justice Holmes. In his view, "The legislature may forbid or restrict any business when it has a sufficient force of public opinion behind it. . . . If the people of the State of New York want it [the scalper law], I see nothing in the Constitution of the United States to prevent their will."

Chief Justice Taft, gravely ill, retired on February 3, 1930, and died a month later. He was seventy-two. President Herbert Hoover's choice for his successor was former Justice Charles Evans Hughes, who had left the Supreme Court in 1916 to run unsuccessfully as the Republican nominee for the Presidency against Woodrow Wilson. By 1930, Hughes had also served as Secretary of State under two Presidents and become a major figure in American law.

Hughes was sixty-seven—older than any previous nominee for Chief Justice—and he had specifically requested and received Hoover's assurance that the Senate would confirm him "without a scrap." It was not to be. The former Governor of New York had an impeccable reputation for integrity and statesmanship that roused initial cheers across the country. But he was also one of America's richest corporate lawyers, and it soon became evident that more than a few Senators, notably George Norris, chairman of the Senate Judiciary Committee, wished to employ the confirmation hearings as a forum for their misgivings about the Supreme Court's activism in defense of nineteenth-century business mores.

Norris, a Republican from Nebraska, took a Western Granger's view of the unelected Court as a citadel for Eastern reactionaries, and he saw no reason to put a Tory like Hughes in charge. "No man in public life," declared Norris, "so exemplifies the influence of powerful combinations in the political and financial world as does Mr. Hughes." Norris argued that Hughes would consciously or unconsciously incline the wrong way in judging "contests between organized wealth and the ordinary citizen."

The Senate eventually confirmed Hughes by a vote of fifty-two to twenty-six. He was later joined by two other new appointees, Owen J. Roberts and Benjamin Cardozo, who would play key roles in the Hughes Court's New Deal crisis.

In May 1931, the Court issued its first decision striking down a state law because it violated the First Amendment. At issue in *Stromberg* v. *California* was a statute making it a crime to display a red flag as a symbol of opposition to organized government. Instead of viewing the law as a safeguard, Chief Justice Hughes spoke for a seven-man majority in condemning it as a threat to public security because it curbed free political discussion. Such dialogue was "essential to the security of the Republic," Hughes ruled, "to the end that government may be responsive to the will of the people and that changes may be obtained by lawful means." He called this "a fundamental principle of our constitutional system."

Two weeks later, Hughes spoke for a narrow (five-to-four) majority in declaring another state law unconstitutional on similar grounds. In *Near* v. *Minnesota*, the disputed law enabled prosecutors to silence any "malicious, scandalous and defamatory newspaper, magazine or other periodical." First introduced by a Minnesota legislator to muzzle one critical editor, the law was subsequently invoked against the *Saturday Press*, a weekly devoted to muckraking with an anti-Semitic twist. In nine articles, the paper had described the Minneapolis police chief as being in cahoots with a Jewish gangster who ran the city's bootlegging, gambling, and racketeering operations. The county attorney, whom the paper accused of failing to cope with these illegal activities, was particularly displeased. He used the gag law to force the paper into the legal position of having to cease publication unless it was willing to prove its charges true, sincere, and worthy.

Hughes ruled for the narrow majority that the First Amendment guaranteed the press a qualified "immunity from prior restraints and censorship," and that it was all the more needed at a time when a plague of official corruption "emphasizes the primary need of a vigilant and courageous press, especially in great cities."

These photographs, taken by Cass Gilbert's staff, show the course of construction of the new Supreme Court building. The exterior was almost finished by fall, 1933, but the sculpture on the pediment was not yet carved. The Court held its first session in the new building on October 7, 1935. Collection of the Supreme Court of the United States, Washington, D.C.

February 1, 1932

August 1, 1932

April 3, 1933

November 2, 1933

Construction of the Great Hall, August 1, 1933

Construction of the Courtroom, March 3, 1934

Construction of the Library, February 9, 1935

Benjamin Nathan Cardozo at the time he joined the New York Court of Appeals, c. 1913. Photograph by Harris & Ewing. Collection of the Supreme Court of the United States, Washington, D.C.

Letter from Benjamin Cardozo to Justice Holmes, February 17, 1932: "I know, of course, that I can never fill your place, but it fills me with pride and joy to be told that you are satisfied to have me sit there." Holmes Papers, Harvard Law School Library

Hughes Court, 1932–37. Standing, from left: Associate Justices Owen Josephus Roberts, Pierce Butler, Harlan Fiske Stone, Benjamin Nathan Cardozo. Seated, from left: Associate Justices Louis Dembitz Brandeis, Willis Van Devanter, Chief Justice Charles Evans Hughes, Associate Justices James Clark McReynolds, George Sutherland. Collection of the Supreme Court of the United States, Washington, D.C.

The Court's most unexpected decision of this period was *Powell* v. *Alabama* (1932), a landmark in the development of every American's right to counsel as part of the due process guaranteed by the Fourteenth Amendment. The defendants were the "Scottsboro Boys," nine illiterate young black men aged thirteen to twenty-one, who were accused of raping two young white girls on a freight train passing through Scottsboro, Alabama, a town seething with anti-black emotions. The defendants had no lawyer until the judge drafted a reluctant local attorney on the morning of their trial before an all-white jury. The lawyer did not consult with his clients, much less attempt to prepare a defense. They were convicted and sentenced to death.

Speaking for a seven-man majority, Justice Sutherland described "compelling circumstances" that mandated a new trial. The defendants were "young, ignorant, illiterate, sur-

rounded by hostile sentiment, hauled back and forth under guard of soldiers, charged with an atrocious crime regarded with special horror in the community where they were to be tried."

In this situation, on trial for their lives, the defendants' lack of counsel clearly had left them defenseless. Sutherland noted in his scholarly opinion that in the words of Daniel Webster, American tradition called for "a law which hears before it condemns." And by "hearing," ruled Sutherland, the court now meant that in all capital cases, where the accused was incapable of defending himself, the Sixth and Fourteenth Amendments commanded the trial judge to provide genuinely effective counsel "as a necessary requisite of due process of law."

By 1934 the most important question about the Supreme Court was how the Justices would respond to the New Deal—President Franklin

The Scottsboro Boys with their Attorney Sam Leibowitz. Brown Brothers, Sterling, Pennsylvania

Roosevelt's drastic remedies for the most profound economic collapse in American history.

At first the Court appeared ready to approve extreme measures. In January 1934, by a narrow vote of five to four, the Court upheld a state law empowering courts to postpone mortgage foreclosures. The Minnesota legislature had sought to ease the plight of debt-ridden farmers who were losing their land all over the state. The law was temporary and due to expire in May 1935, but one mortgage holder challenged it on the obvious ground that it violated the Constitution's unequivocal command—no state shall pass any law "impairing the obligation of contracts."

Speaking for a bare majority in *Home Building*

& Loan Association v. *Blaisdell*, Chief Justice Hughes said the Minnesota legislature had acted in the face of widespread hardship and consequent violence, severe enough to make the foreclosure problem a threat to public order. Just as the state was empowered to give temporary relief from the enforcement of contracts in the presence of "physical" disasters, such as floods and earthquakes, so it could respond to public calamities having "economic causes."

Hughes said the moratorium did not impair the obligation of Minnesota debtors to repay their mortgages; it merely delayed the creditors' remedy of foreclosure. "While emergency does not create power," he wrote, "emergency may furnish the occasion for the exercise of power." And the Chief Justice declared, "The policy of protecting contracts against impairment presupposes the maintenance of a government by virtue of which contracts are worthwhile—a government which retains adequate authority to secure the peace and good order of society."

Speaking for the four dissenters—soon to be called "The Four Horsemen"—Justice Sutherland insisted that only actual war could justify any temporary loosening of the constitutional fabric. Economic disaster was not sufficient and never had been. "The present exigency is nothing new," Sutherland reminded his colleagues. Numerous depressions in the past had brought legislative pressure to bypass the impairment clause and "shift the misfortunes of the debtor to the shoulders of the creditor." But experience had repeatedly shown the wisdom of holding the line. "If the provisions of the Constitution be not upheld when they pinch as well as when they comfort," Sutherland declared, "they may as well be abandoned."

Soon after, in March 1934, another five-to-four split between the same Justices produced another decision reassuring to New Deal lawmakers. In *Nebbia* v. *New York*, the majority discarded the old not-public-enough doctrine, which the Taft Court had used to exclude businesses from regulation.

Nebbia arose from the crisis in farm prices. Even in the booming 1920s, American farmers were caught between overproduction and underconsumption, but the Depression had made their situation far worse. In New York, as elsewhere, jobless consumers bought less milk, prices fell, dairy farmers went bankrupt, milk supplies dwindled, and the legislature was forced to act. Prices had to be raised at least enough to cover the farmers' costs. The state lawmakers created a temporary milk control board that pegged the minimum retail price at nine cents per quart. In Rochester, a grocer named Leo Nebbia was convicted of violating the control law by selling milk at less than the fixed minimum, and in due course he appealed to the Supreme Court, which sustained the law mainly on the ground that "the power to promote the general welfare is inherent in government."

Nebbia was written by Justice Roberts, already the crucial fifth "swing" voter between the

Court's two definable four-man groups. Roberts wrote: "The function of courts . . . is to determine in each case whether circumstances vindicate the challenged regulation as a reasonable exertion of governmental authority or condemn it as arbitrary or discriminatory. . . . The phrase 'affected with a public interest' can, in the nature of things, mean no more than that an industry, for adequate reason, is subject to control for the public good. . . . There can be no doubt that upon proper occasion and by appropriate measures the state may regulate a business in any of its aspects.

"The Constitution does not secure to anyone liberty to conduct his business in such fashion as to inflict injury upon the public at large, or upon any substantial group of people. Price control, like any other form of regulation, is unconstitutional only if arbitrary, discriminatory, or demonstrably irrelevant to the policy the legislature is free to adopt, and hence an unnecessary and unwarranted interference with individual liberty."

But the *Nebbia* majority was composed of only five Justices, and if just one of them changed his mind, the four dissenters might well be speaking for the Supreme Court again in the near future. Justice Sutherland, for one, was appalled at the harshness of Leo Nebbia's conviction for selling milk at less than nine cents a quart. Sutherland shared Justice James R. McReynolds's dissent from the majority's "facile disregard of the Constitution as long interpreted and respected."

McReynolds declared: "Plainly, I think, this Court must have regard to the wisdom of the enactment. At least, we must inquire concerning its purpose and decide whether the means proposed have reasonable relation to something within legislative power—whether the end is legitimate, and the means appropriate."

On January 7, 1935, the Court struck down major New Deal legislation for the first time—a section of the National Industrial Recovery Act (NIRA) that empowered the President to bar unregulated "hot oil" from entering interstate commerce. With only Cardozo dissenting, eight Justices held that the disputed section had violated the Separation of Powers by delegating too much legislative power to the President's discretion (*Panama Refining Company* v. *Ryan*).

Justice Owen Josephus Roberts. Collection of the Supreme Court of the United States, Washington, D.C.

Justice James Clark McReynolds. Collection of the Supreme Court of the United States, Washington, D.C.

A month later, on February 18, the Court in effect upheld the President's actions in taking America off the gold standard in order to boost national liquidity. Specifically at issue in the *Gold Clause Cases* was a federal law designed to halt gold hoarding and draw private gold into the Treasury. The law abrogated clauses in private contracts requiring payment in gold. The Court sustained the law under Congress's power to regulate the value of currency.

But New Deal setbacks now accelerated. On May 6, 1935, the Court struck down the year-old Railroad Retirement Act and its new pension system for railroad workers. The law had compelled railroads to contribute to pensions for superannuated employees, but five Justices said this was beyond the scope of Congress's power to regulate interstate commerce. The spokesman in this case (*R. R. Retirement Board* v. *Alton R. R.*) was none other than Justice Roberts. Speaking for the four dissenters, Chief Justice Hughes contended that

Congress was fully empowered to ensure fair treatment for interstate employees, and he criticized the majority for placing "an unwarranted limitation" on the Commerce Clause.

On May 27, 1935, promptly dubbed "Black Monday," the Court issued three *unanimous* decisions flatly rejecting Franklin Roosevelt's concept of presidential power. First, Justice Brandeis spoke for all nine Justices in tossing out a federal mortgage relief program for farmers on the ground that it was unfair to creditors (*Louisville Bank* v. *Radford*). Second, Justice Sutherland sharply limited the President's power to fire high-level federal appointees and specifically barred him from removing members of independent regulatory agencies without the consent of Congress (*Humphrey's Executor* v. *United States*). Third, and most devastating, Chief Justice Hughes spoke for a united Court in ruling the entire NIRA unconstitutional in the historic case of *Schecter Poultry Corp.* v. *United States.*

The Supreme Court in session, February 8, 1935. Clandestine news photograph taken by Erich Salomon. Erich-Salomon-Archiv, Berlinische Galerie, Berlin

From the government's standpoint, *Schecter* was a poor case, chosen only because it was available to test the NIRA's constitutionality. The law required every industry to promulgate its own code of fair business practice, subject to government approval.

Ninety-six percent of the live chickens sold in New York came from other states. The Schecters were Brooklyn middlemen who bought such poultry, slaughtered it, and sold it locally. They were accused of violating the NIRA code for the New York live poultry industry by paying their employees substandard wages, permitting favored customers to reject diseased chickens, and dumping those rejects on the unwary public—a practice so revolting that at one point the city's poultry consumption dropped twenty percent.

Fined and briefly jailed, the Schecters had hired a leading New York lawyer, Frederick W. Wood, who argued that the NIRA code was unconstitutional because Congress had: 1) delegated too much legislative power; and 2) had exceeded its authority to regulate interstate com-

merce. The circuit court had agreed and the government had appealed to the Supreme Court.

"Extraordinary conditions do not create or enlarge constitutional power," declared Chief Justice Hughes. "Congress cannot delegate legislative power to the President to exercise an unfettered discretion to make whatever laws he thinks may be needed or advisable. . . ."

Hughes further ruled that the New York live poultry business was strictly local and hence immune to federal regulation. Because the chickens came to "a permanent rest within the state," he said, they escaped Congress's power over interstate commerce.

According to Hughes, that power covered only intrastate business practices that "directly" affected interstate commerce, and he used Chief Justice Fuller's 1895 rationale of protecting the states against federal encroachment. Hughes wrote: "If the commerce clause were construed to reach all enterprises and transactions which could be said to have an indirect effect upon interstate commerce, the federal authority would embrace practically all the activities of the

192

A.L.A. Schechter, flanked by his attorneys, Joseph Heller (left) and Frederick H. Wood (right), before argument in *Schechter Poultry Corp.* v. *United States*, May 2, 1935. UPI/Bettmann Archive

people and the authority of the state over its domestic concerns would exist only by the sufferance of the federal government."

The *Schecter* ruling was the last big constitutional drama played out in the small former Senate chamber where the Justices had held court for seventy-five years. On October 7, 1935, they convened for the first time in their vast new building on Capitol Hill.

In response to *Schecter*, President Roosevelt replaced parts of the NIRA with separate laws, notably the National Labor Relations Act, known as the Wagner Act, which restored the collective bargaining rights that *Schecter* had erased. The Wagner Act was passed in July 1935, the start of the "Second Hundred Days" that launched the "Second New Deal"—a new round of more carefully drafted laws (such as the Social Security Act of 1935), that have become permanent American institutions.

But the Court majority saw little in these changes. The election year of 1936 was barely a week old when *United States* v. *Butler* struck down

the Agricultural Adjustment Act (AAA).

Farmers stripped of cash had faced the unabated pressure of meeting tax and mortgage payments. The problem was national in scope. The farm economy was then so large that rural devastation threatened the solvency of whole industries and even states.

The solution, if any, supposedly lay in cutting farm output to meet actual demand and avoid the huge surpluses that had undermined agricultural prices.

Accordingly, the New Dealers had created incentives aimed at boosting farm income to the level of the so-called good years 1909 to 1914. In return for not cultivating part of their land, farmers were paid "rent" by the Agricultural Adjustment Administration. The source of this cash was a tax on the processing of farm commodities. The processors added that cost to the prices they charged.

The whole system produced a significant rise in agricultural income. In three years, the prices of corn, wheat, and cotton rose by forty to fifty percent. But then a man named William M. But-

William M. Butler after his victory in *United States* v. *Butler*, January 7, 1936. UPI/Bettmann Archive

ler, receiver for a bankrupt cotton mill, refused to pay the processing tax.

George Wharton Pepper, a Philadelphia lawyer, defended William Butler with a laissez-faire fervor reminiscent of those who implored the 1895 Court to defeat communism by squashing the income tax. "I am standing here today to plead the cause of the America I have loved," Pepper told the Court. "And I pray that not in my time may 'the land of the regimented' be accepted as a worthy substitute for 'the land of the free.' "

At issue in *United States* v. *Butler* was whether Congress had enacted the AAA lawfully under its constitutional power (Article I, Section 8) "to lay and collect Taxes, Duties, Imposts, and Excises, to pay the Debts and provide for the common Defence and general Welfare of the United States." The government contended that this General Welfare Clause empowered Congress to tax and spend for the good of the coun-

try; that the AAA was aimed at the national welfare; and that Congress, not the Court, had the right to determine the best means of promoting that welfare.

Speaking through Justice Roberts, a six-man majority totally dismissed these arguments. Roberts held first that the AAA processing tax was actually not a tax, because it did not support the government. He called it an "expropriation of money from one group for the benefit of another." Such use of the taxing power was impermissible, he said.

Roberts then proceeded to examine the validity of the AAA crop payments under the General Welfare Clause. He accepted Alexander Hamilton's view that the clause gave Congress a power independent of its enumerated powers. But even if Congress could tax and spend for the national welfare, Roberts said, the AAA was invalid because the power to regulate agriculture was not among those "expressly granted" (his words)

194

George Wharton Pepper. Brown Brothers, Sterling, Pennsylvania

to the national government.

In short, agriculture was a state domain protected by the Tenth Amendment. Roberts found the AAA crop payments especially repugnant to the Tenth Amendment because they were so generous that they became coercive—an offer the farmer couldn't refuse. If the AAA were allowed to stand, he said, the central government would soon be "exercising uncontrolled police power in every state of the Union, superseding all local control or regulation of the affairs or concerns of the states."

Roberts insisted that the Court "has only one duty—to lay the article of the Constitution which is invoked beside the statute which is challenged and to decide whether the latter squares with the former. All the Court does, or can do, is to announce its considered judgment upon the question. The only power it has . . . is the power of judgment."

In dissent, joined by Brandeis and Cardozo, Justice Stone decried the majority's narrow view of the spending power as a "tortured construction" of the Constitution. "It is a contradiction in terms," he wrote, "to say that there is power to spend for the national welfare, while rejecting any power to impose conditions reasonably adapted to the attainment of the end which alone would justify the expenditure." Stone found the majority opinion far too subjective. "Courts are concerned only with the power to enact statutes, not with their wisdom," he said. "Courts are not the only agency of government that must be assumed to have capacity to govern."

The divergence within the Court over the boundaries between federal and state power became even sharper in May 1936, when the same six-man majority struck down the 1935 Bituminous Coal Conservation Act.

That law, known as the Guffey Act, had established a national commission empowered to collect a fifteen percent tax from coal mine owners, most of which they got back for complying with a fair-practice code. The law came in two parts. One provided collective bargaining, together with wage and hour standards, for the entire industry; the other fixed national prices for coal. The sponsors of the law clearly stated that its labor and price segments were separable, meaning that if the Court invalidated one, the other could stand on its own.

Justice Sutherland saw it differently. He ruled that the two-part Guffey Act constituted a single plan of regulation. By invalidating one part, he thus killed the entire plan.

Sutherland first attacked the law's apparent weak spot, the labor provisions. He said mining was not commerce but production, an activity reserved for state regulation because (like farming and manufacturing) it did not fall under any of Congress's enumerated powers.

Since mining itself was outside interstate commerce, the only question was whether labor problems in the industry had such a "direct" effect on commerce as to warrant federal regulation. According to Sutherland, coal production was so local that even its most disruptive labor disputes were strictly local problems affecting only local production. "Such effect as they have upon commerce, however extensive it may be," Sutherland declared, "is secondary and indirect."

Having voided the Guffey Act's labor provisions, Sutherland voided its price-fixing provisions on the ground that the latter segment was so dependent on the former that it could not stand on its own.

Sutherland also nullified the Guffey Act on other grounds. He condemned the taxes for being not revenue-raisers, but a means of forcing mine owners to comply with the regulations. And he declared the entire act unconstitutional because it delegated legislative authority to the executive branch, thus violating the Separation of Powers.

In a dissent joined by Brandeis and Stone, Justice Cardozo urged a generous view of the commerce power to fit the circumstances of the time. "The power is as broad as the need that evokes it," he wrote. In rejecting Congress's right to protect the general welfare, Cardozo said, the Court majority had ignored "the indisputable truth that there were ills to be corrected, and the ills had a direct relation to the maintenance of commerce among the states without friction or diversion. An evil existing, and also the power to correct it, the lawmakers were at liberty to use their own discretion in the selection of the means."

Just two weeks later, on June 1, 1936, the Court majority dusted off liberty of contract and used it to nullify state action. In *Morehead* v. *Tipaldo*, Justice Butler spoke for a five-man majority—the Chief Justice dissented—in striking down a minimum-wage law that New York had enacted for women. The state lawmakers thought they had met the objections to such a law raised by Justice Sutherland in his 1923 *Adkins* decision. Hughes, New York's former Governor, thought so, too, and he therefore dissented in *Morehead*. But Justice Butler not only found *Adkins* controlling; he also proclaimed that "the state is without power by any form of legislation to prohibit, change or nullify contracts between employers and adult women workers as to the amount of wages to be paid."

There followed President Roosevelt's landslide reelection in the fall of 1936 and his subsequent "court-packing" plan in February 1937. Aimed at bringing in as many as six new Justices sympathetic to his policies, the plan failed in Congress owing to widespread public doubts about its wisdom, to Chief Justice Hughes's vigorous lobbying against it, and to the Court's own changing views of the economic crisis.

On the morning of March 29, 1937, soon called "White Monday," the Justices signaled an extraordinary turnabout in their resistance to government regulation. In a series of unexpected decisions, the Court upheld state minimum wage laws, federal relief for bankrupt farmers, collective bargaining for railway workers, and a federal tax on gun dealers designed to control firearms.

The key case that day was *West Coast Hotel* v. *Parrish*, a five-to-four decision upholding a Washington state minimum wage law for women that was almost a carbon copy of the New York law struck down in *Morehead* v. *Tipaldo*, another five-to-four decision only ten months old.

The protagonist in the case was Elsie Parrish, a chambermaid who sued the West Coast Hotel to recover the difference between her miniscule

President Franklin Roosevelt addressing the Democratic Victory Dinner, Mayflower Hotel, Washington, March 4, 1937. UPI/Bettmann Archive

pay and the state-fixed minimum wage of $14.50 per week. The state of Washington's highest court upheld Elsie Parrish and the law. The hotel appealed to the Supreme Court alleging deprivation of freedom of contract, guaranteed by the Fourteenth Amendment.

"What is this freedom?" Chief Justice Hughes asked. The Constitution does not mention contractual liberty, he answered. In fact, the liberty protected by the due process clauses of the Fifth and Fourteenth Amendments was something quite different from a license for exploiting others. "The liberty safeguarded," said Hughes, "is liberty in a social organization which requires the protection of the law against the evils which menace the health, safety, morals and welfare of the people . . ."

"The exploitation of a class of workers who are in an unequal position with respect to bargaining power and are thus relatively defenseless against the denial of a living wage is not only detrimental to their health and well being, but casts a direct

Nine Old Men, cartoon reflecting President Roosevelt's view of the Court. *New Masses,* March 9, 1937. Brown Brothers, Sterling, Pennsylvania

burden for their support upon the community. The community is not bound to provide what is in effect a subsidy for unconscionable employers. The community may direct its lawmaking power to correct the abuse which springs from their selfish disregard of the public interest."

Two weeks after White Monday, on April 12,

the same five-man majority (Hughes, Brandeis, Cardozo, Stone, and Roberts) upheld a vital piece of New Deal legislation, the National Labor Relations Act. In a series of five cases led by *NLRB* v. *Jones & Laughlin Steel Corp.,* Chief Justice Hughes conceded that Congress had a broad power to protect interstate commerce from industrial labor warfare.

The 1935 Wagner Labor Relations Act, as it was called, declared that interstate commerce

was directly burdened by strikes and stoppages in industries that forbade workers to organize and bargain collectively. The act set up the National Labor Relations Board (NLRB) to protect workers' rights and prevent employees as well as employers from engaging in certain unfair labor practices.

In the Jones & Laughlin case, the NLRB had ordered the steel company to rehire ten workers who had been fired solely because they were key union members. The company balked, arguing that the Pennsylvania plant in question was immune to NLRB orders because manufacturing and production were outside interstate commerce. Having won in the circuit court, the company had every reason to believe that the Supreme Court would strike down the Wagner Act on the ground that Congress was powerless to regulate so-called local labor relations. The company argued that the act was an unconstitu-

Supreme Court of the United States
Washington, D.C.

March 21, 1937.

My dear Senator Wheeler:

In response to your inquiries, I have the honor to present the following statement with respect to the work of the Supreme Court:

1. The Supreme Court is fully abreast of its work. When we rose on March 15th (for the present recess) we had heard argument in cases in which certiorari had been granted only four weeks before,- February 15th.

During the current Term, which began last October and which we call October Term, 1936, we have heard argument on the merits in 150 cases (180 numbers) and we have 28 cases (30 numbers) awaiting argument. We shall be able to hear all these cases, and such others as may come up for argument, before our adjournment for the Term. There is no congestion of cases upon our calendar.

This gratifying condition has obtained for several years. We have been able for several Terms to adjourn after disposing of all cases which are ready to be heard.

2. The cases on our docket are classified as original and appellate. Our original jurisdiction is defined by the Constitution and embraces cases to which States are parties. There are not many of these. At the present time they number thirteen and are in various stages of progress to submission for determination.

First page of letter from Chief Justice Hughes and Justice Brandeis to Senator Hugh Wheeler, March 21, 1937. Collection of the Supreme Court of the United States, Washington, D.C.

tional denial of every employer's right to hire and fire at will, guaranteed by due process of law.

In his opinion, Chief Justice Hughes disposed of the due process claim by ruling that the act went no further than to protect the "fundamental right" of employees to self-organization and collective bargaining free of coercion by their employers. Hughes said that this right was correlative to the company's right to organize its business and select its officers and agents.

But did the federal commerce power entitle Congress to protect these rights at the local plant level? Hughes noted that the steel plant was part of a huge industrial network involving at least ten states, and even if the plant itself could be deemed a self-contained manufacturer, the "determinative" question was what effect a strike at the plant would have on interstate commerce. "It is idle to say that the effect would be indirect or remote," Hughes wrote. "It is obvious that it would be immediate and might be catastrophic."

In dissent, Justice McReynolds protested that "a more remote and indirect interference with interstate commerce or a more definite invasion of the powers reserved to the states is difficult, if not impossible, to imagine." As he saw it, the Court had given the NLRB "power of control over purely local industry beyond anything heretofore deemed permissible."

Six weeks later, on May 24, the new five-man majority effectively overruled the year-old decision (*United States* v. *Butler*) that had killed the Agricultural Adjustment Act. At issue in *Steward Machine Co.* v. *Davis* was the unemployment compensation part of the 1935 Social Security Act. It required employers to pay a payroll tax, then gave them a tax credit if they contributed to an unemployment insurance system run by the states according to federal specifications. In the AAA case, such a tax had been invalidated because it was deemed coercive and aimed at a social purpose rather than raising revenue.

Speaking for the majority in *Steward Machine*, however, Justice Cardozo held that the power to tax business extended to employment and that the statute reflected federal-state cooperation, not coercion, to solve the common problem of unemployment. "It is too late today," Cardozo wrote, for the argument that "in a crisis so extreme the use of the moneys of the nation to relieve the unemployed and their dependents is a use for any purpose narrower than the promotion of the general welfare."

In a related case that day (*Helvering* v. *Davis*), the Court sustained the Social Security System's old-age benefits. The vote was seven to two with only Butler and McReynolds dissenting. In his majority opinion, Justice Cardozo ruled that the General Welfare Clause does not bar federal spending for a particular group, provided the nation benefits. As to who makes that judgment, he added, "the discretion . . . is not confided to the courts. The discretion belongs to Congress, unless the choice is clearly wrong, a display of arbitrary power, not an exercise of judgment."

Between 1937 and 1943, various deaths and resignations enabled President Roosevelt to make nine Court appointments, including his elevation of Justice Stone in 1941 to replace the retiring Chief Justice Hughes. The Roosevelt Court, as many called it, took a broad view of federal power, especially over interstate commerce.

In *United States* v. *Darby Lumber Company* (1941), the Court unanimously sustained the

Fair Labor Standards Act, a federal law that forbade child labor and also regulated the hours and wages of workers making products shipped in interstate commerce. *Darby* specifically overruled the 1918 decision (*Hammer* v. *Dagenhart*) that had kept child labor beyond federal reach.

Speaking for the Court, Stone called the Tenth Amendment a mere "truism" and irrelevant to the *Darby* decision. "There is nothing in the history of its adoption to suggest that it was more than declaratory of the relationship between the national and state governments as it had been established by the Constitution before the amendment or that its purpose was other than to allay fears that the new national government might seek to exercise powers not granted."

The reconstituted Court soon interpreted the federal commerce power as covering not only manufacturing but anything else within a state that blocked the exercise of the power "in a substantial way."

In *Wickard* v. *Filburn* (1942), "substantial" took on new meaning when the Court found a way to approve regulation of production that was neither interstate nor even commerce.

A farmer named Wickard had been allotted a wheat quota under the 1938 version of the old AAA. When he harvested 269 more bushels than his quota, he was penalized even though he intended the wheat for his personal use, not for sale. The Court unanimously sustained the penalty on the ground that Wickard's personal crop would cause him to buy less wheat that year, presumably reducing the total market demand by 269 bushels.

While thus rebalancing federal-state powers, the Court also issued decisions sharply expanding personal liberties in the United States. In 1937 the Justices held for the first time that the First Amendment right of assembly was on a par with the rights of free speech and free press, all of which were now binding on the states (*DeJonge* v. *Oregon*). A tighter standard resembling the clear and present danger test was imposed on state sedition laws (*Herndon* v. *Lowry*). While rejecting any blanket imposition of the Bill of Rights upon the states, the court ruled that state criminal procedures must protect those rights that embody "the very essence of a scheme of ordered liberty" (*Palko* v. *Connecticut*). Exactly one year later, the Court applied the Equal Protection Clause against school segregation for the first time (*Missouri* v. *Canada*).

The most interesting portent of the Court's future turned up in *United States* v. *Carolene Products Co.* (1938), which involved a federal standard for milk products. Speaking for the majority, Justice Stone said in the body of his opinion that the Court would now generally presume that economic legislation was constitutional, unless a challenger proved otherwise. But to this clear reversal of the old laissez-faire presumption that such laws were invalid, Stone added one of the most famous footnotes in Court history. When it came to laws allegedly violating personal rights, he suggested, the Court might now be disinclined to assume validity and would probably be much tougher than with laws involving property rights.

"There may be narrower scope for operation of the presumption of constitutionality," Stone wrote in his footnote, "when legislation appears on its face to be within a specific prohibition of the Constitution, such as those of the first two amendments . . ."

Stone's rationale was that bad laws should be repealed by the political process, and since that process was healthy only when people could exercise their personal rights, those rights needed extra protection. Stone's *Carolene* comment has since been called "the manifesto in a footnote." It marked the beginning of a new era in Court history, a broader concern for civil liberties than ever before.

14

FREE EXPRESSION IN AN UNFREE WORLD

Angelo Herndon addressing a rally, December 3, 1935. UPI/Bettmann Archive, New York

The changing national mood of the post-1937 period brought before the Court new disputes whose resolution stemmed from interpretations of the Fourteenth Amendment's Due Process, Equal Protection, and Privileges and Immunities Clauses. Increasingly, the Court insisted that a free society's survival depends upon robust public discussion—the kind that engenders a government capable of tolerating dissent, reflecting diverse group interests, and dealing fairly and equitably with all individuals exposed to official power.

The post-1937 Court gave freedom of speech and assembly "a preferred position" in the constitutional scheme because, as Justice Cardozo put it in *Palko* v. *Connecticut*, they comprise "the very essence of a scheme of ordered liberty . . . the matrix, the indispensable condition of nearly every other form of freedom." The Court has declared these preferred or fundamental rights

off limits to intrusion, except where government can sustain the burden of proving some urgent public necessity.

In addition, by "a process of absorption" (Cardozo's phrase), the modern Court has "nationalized" virtually the entire Bill of Rights, which had previously bound only the federal government. Nearly all specific guarantees of the first eight amendments have been ruled part of the Fourteenth Amendment "liberty" that states may not deny without due process of law.

New personal rights, such as privacy, have been extracted largely from the apparently limitless recesses of the Ninth Amendment, which Madison introduced to allay fears that the Bill of Rights might be deemed inclusive, leaving unthought-of rights beyond future claim by the states or the people. In concurring with the majority in *Roe* v. *Wade,* the famous 1973 abortion decision, Justice William O. Douglas

William Z. Foster and Benjamin Gitlow, Presidential and Vice-Presidential candidates of the Communist Workers' Party, at Madison Square Garden, New York, November 4, 1928. UPI/Bettmann Archive, New York

asserted that the Ninth Amendment protects, in his view, nothing less than all "customary, traditional, and time-honored rights, amenities, privileges, and immunities that come within the sweep of 'the Blessings of Liberty' mentioned in the preamble to the Constitution."

One milestone in this evolution was the Court's 1925 decision *(Gitlow* v. *New York)* upholding a New York law that banned speech or publication in favor of overthrowing government by "any unlawful means." The decision proved far more significant than either the state sedition law or its challenger, a far-left New York Socialist named Benjamin Gitlow. He had been convicted under the law for printing and distributing 16,000 copies of a turgid tract, *The Left Wing Manifesto,* that denounced moderate Socialists for being soft on capitalism and urged the proletariat to "organize its own state *for the coercion and suppression of the bourgeoisie"* (emphasis Gitlow's).

The key issue in Gitlow's case was whether he could invoke the First Amendment against a state prosecution. Still in force was John Marshall's 1833 ruling in *Barron* v. *Baltimore* that the entire Bill of Rights (the first ten amendments)

applied only to the federal government and not to the states. Accordingly, Gitlow's lawyers stressed the state-binding Fourteenth Amendment (1868), which had arguably been introduced in part to overcome *Barron.* In forbidding states to deny any person "liberty" without due process of law, the Amendment had undoubtedly been conceived mainly as a guarantee of fair procedure. But the laissez-faire Court of the 1890s had turned the Amendment's "liberty" into a virtual bill of property rights, which were held immune from state impairment, while personal rights were not.

By applying the First Amendment to the states, *Gitlow* v. *New York* obliged the Court to deal with the seemingly boundless question of just when a state could restrict free speech.

In the next state sedition case before the Court — *Whitney* v. *California* (1927)—Justices Brandeis and Holmes joined the majority in sustaining California's criminal syndicalism law. But their concurring opinion, written by Brandeis, sounded more like one of their frequent dissents, and indeed it stands as one of the Court's finest essays in political philosophy.

Those who won our independence believed that the final end of the State was to make men free to develop their faculties; and that in its government the deliberative forces should prevail over the arbitrary. They valued liberty both as an end and as a means. They believed liberty to be the secret of happiness and courage to be the secret of liberty. They believed that freedom to think as you will and to speak as you think are means indispensable to the discovery and spread of political truth; that without free speech and assembly discussion would be futile; that with them, discussion affords ordinarily adequate protection against the dissemination of noxious doctrine; that the greatest menace to freedom is an inert people; that public discussion is a political duty; and that this should be a fundamental principle of the American government. They recognized the risks to which all human institutions are subject. But they knew that order cannot be secured merely through fear of punishment for its infraction; that it is hazardous to discourage thought, hope, and imagination; that fear breeds repression; that repression breeds hate; that hate menaces stable government; that the path of safety lies in the opportunity to discuss freely supposed grievances and proposed remedies; and that the fitting remedy for evil counsels is good ones. Believing in the power of reason as applied through public discussion, they eschewed silence coerced by law—the argument of force in its worst form. Recognizing the occasional tyrannies of governing majorities, they amended the Constitution so that free speech and assembly should be guaranteed.

Fear of serious injury cannot alone justify suppression of free speech and assembly. Men feared witches and burned women. It is the function of speech to free men from the bondage of irrational fears. To justify suppression of free speech there must be reasonable ground to fear that serious evil will result if free speech is practiced. There must be reasonable ground to believe that the evil to be prevented is imminent. There must be reasonable ground to believe that the evil to be prevented is a serious one. Every denunciation of existing law tends in some measure to increase the probability that there will be a violation of it. Condonation of a breach enhances the probability. Expressions of approval add to the probability. Propagation of the criminal state of mind by teaching syndicalism increases it. Advocacy of lawbreaking heightens it still further. But even advocacy of violation, however reprehensible morally, is not a justification for denying free speech where the advocacy falls short of incitement and there is nothing to indicate that the advocacy would be immediately acted on. The wide difference between advocacy and incitement, between preparation and attempt, between assembling and conspiracy, must be borne in mind. In order to support a finding of clear and present danger it must be shown either that immediate serious violence was to be expected or was advocated, or that the past conduct furnished reason to believe that such advocacy was then contemplated.

Those who won our independence by revolution were not cowards. They did not fear political change. They did not exalt order at the cost of liberty. To courageous, self-reliant men, with confidence in the power of free and fearless reasoning applied through the processes of popular government, no danger flowing from speech can be deemed clear and present, unless the incidence of the evil apprehended is so imminent that it may befall before there is opportunity for full discussion. If there be time to expose through discussion the falsehood and fallacies, to avert the evil by the processes of education, the remedy to be applied is more speech, not enforced silence. Only an emergency can justify repression. Such must be the rule if authority is to be reconciled with freedom. Such, in my opinion, is the command of the Constitution. It is therefore always open to Americans to challenge a law abridging free speech and assembly by showing that there was no emergency justifying it.

Justice Louis D. Brandeis

Concurring (with Justice Oliver Wendell Holmes) in *Whitney* v. *California*

1927

It was Chief Justice Hughes who managed—at the very peak of the New Deal uproar—to keep one eye firmly on the First Amendment and to focus on personal guilt rather than guilt by association. In *DeJonge* v. *Oregon* (1937), DeJonge had been convicted of violating Oregon's criminal syndicalism law after he conducted a public meeting called by the Communist Party to protest police brutality during a waterfront strike. Although he had not advocated violence, the state courts read the syndicalism law to mean that it was a crime to attend a meeting sponsored by Communists.

Speaking for the Court, Chief Justice Hughes reversed DeJonge's conviction and extended the First Amendment right of assembly to the states for the first time. In a memorable dictum, Hughes declared that curbing First Amendment rights was the worst way to defend the Republic against subversion; the best way was to expand free political discussion, thus ensuring change by peaceful means. He added:

> Peaceable assembly for lawful discussion cannot be made a crime. The holding of meetings for peaceable political action cannot be proscribed. Those who assist in the conduct of such meetings cannot be branded criminals on that score. The question, if the rights of free speech and peaceable assembly are to be preserved, is not as to the auspices under which the meeting is held but as to its purpose; not as to the relations of the speakers, but whether their utterances transcend the boundaries of the freedom of speech which the Constitution protects. . . .

In a second 1937 decision, *Herndon* v. *Lowry*, the Court voted five to four to employ a test similar to the "clear and present danger" standard. Herndon was a black organizer for the Communist Party who tried to circulate a crude tract exhorting Georgia blacks to rebel against white oppression and create their own government. He was convicted of violating a Georgia law that barred anyone from urging others to join an insurrection. Justice Roberts wrote the majority opinion agreeing with Herndon's lawyers that the prosecution had failed to prove any immediate danger to the state. Roberts invalidated the law, calling it

"merely a dragnet which may enmesh anyone who agitates for a change of government." According to Roberts, "The power of a state to abridge freedom of speech and of assembly is the exception rather than the rule and penalizing even of utterances of a defined character must find its justification in a reasonable apprehension of danger to organized government."

In 1939 the Court affirmed every American's right to communicate ideas in public places *(Haig* v. *C.I.O.)*, and this naturally raised the question of precisely when a state could abridge that right. In *Cantwell* v. *Connecticut* (1940), Jehovah's Witness Jesse Cantwell had been arrested on a New Haven street after playing an anti-Catholic phonograph record and seeking donations from anybody who cared to listen. Two listeners proved to be Catholics, much offended. No violence occurred. But Cantwell had been convicted of soliciting religious contributions without a permit and of inciting others to commit a breach of the peace.

Speaking for the Court, Justice Roberts reversed both convictions and invalidated the breach-of-the-peace ordinance as too vague to meet First Amendment standards. The law covered such a variety of conduct, from sidewalk preaching to outright fighting, Roberts said, that it left officials with too much discretion to punish merely unpopular people. Cantwell had not violated any narrowly drawn law banning his specific conduct; no such law existed. Lacking such a law, Roberts held, the episode posed no "clear and present menace to public peace and order," and Cantwell's free-speech rights far outweighed the benefit of locking him up in order to keep him quiet.

For the first time, the Court directed the states to honor the Amendment's guarantee of free exercise of religion as part of the "fundamental concept of liberty embodied in the Fourteenth Amendment." Accordingly, the Connecticut law requiring Cantwell to secure a soliciting permit was unconstitutional both as prior restraint upon free religious expression and as sheer overkill in light of the state's already existing ways to curb fraud as well as disorder.

The Court's striking unanimity in *Cantwell*—joined even by McReynolds, last of the Four Horsemen—reflected Cardozo's "preferred

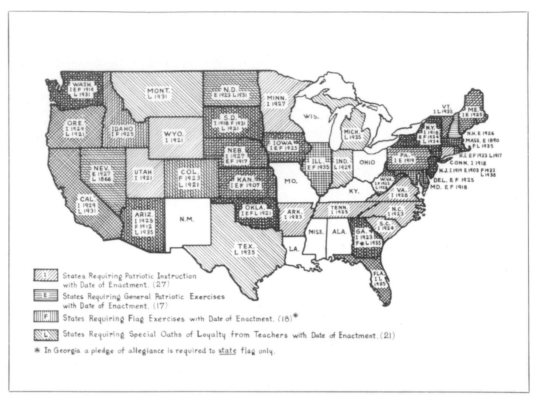

States Requiring Patriotic Instruction with Date of Enactment. (27)

States Requiring General Patriotic Exercises with Date of Enactment. (17)

States Requiring Flag Exercises with Date of Enactment. (18)*

States Requiring Special Oaths of Loyalty from Teachers with Date of Enactment. (21)

* In Georgia a pledge of allegiance is required to state flag only.

"Compulsory Patriotism in the Schools," diagram from *Compulsory Flag Salute in Schools,* published by the Committee on Academic Freedom, American Civil Liberties Union, March, 1936. New York Public Library. Astor, Lenox and Tilden Foundations

position" theory of First Amendment rights (1937) and Stone's famous *Carolene Products* footnote (1938). But World War II rekindled the American zest for public patriotism in a way that tested the Court's special commitment to the First Amendment. At issue in *Minersville School District* v. *Gobitis* (1940) was whether government could force schoolchildren to salute the American flag, when this was contrary to their religious beliefs.

In Minersville, Pennsylvania, the school board had expelled Lillian and William Gobitis, aged twelve and ten, for dissenting from their school's daily Pledge of Allegiance. As Jehovah's Witnesses, the children had been taught not to worship graven images; their parents considered the flag ceremony to be idolatry.

Speaking for an eight-man majority in *Gobitis,* Justice Felix Frankfurter upheld the school board and stressed his familiar deference to legislative authority, reflecting his long disagreement with the judicial activism of the Court's laissez-faire period. Loath to "make us the school board for the country," Frankfurter declared that it was not the Court's business to interfere

with political decisions aimed at encouraging national loyalty, "that unifying sentiment without which there can ultimately be no liberties, civil or religious." In this case, religious liberty must yield to civil duty. According to Frankfurter, the "mere possession of religious convictions which contradict the relevant concerns of a political society does not relieve the citizen from the discharge of political responsibilities."

Justice Stone—the sole dissenter—had previously denounced those 1936 Justices who insisted that "it is the business of courts to sit in judgment on the wisdom of legislative action." In *Gobitis,* Stone took the opposite tack. Consistent with his *Carolene* footnote, he found the Justices obliged to take the offensive against state impairment of First Amendment rights. In this case, he wrote, "the state seeks to coerce these children to express a sentiment which . . . they do not entertain, and which violates their deepest religious convictions." The result clearly denied "the freedom of the individual from compulsion as to what he shall think and what he shall say, at least where the compulsion is to bear false witness to his religion." By its excessive judicial restraint,

206

Walter Gobitis, with his children, William and Lillian, leaving the United States District Court in Philadelphia, February 16, 1938. UPI/Bettmann Archive, New York

Stone warned, the Court had achieved "no more than the surrender of the constitutional protection of the liberty of small minorities to the popular will."

Two years later, in yet another Jehovah's Witnesses case (*Jones* v. *Opelika*), the Court sustained licensing fees for religious peddlers, but three dissenters took the occasion to renounce their own majority votes in *Gobitis*. Justices William O. Douglas, Hugo Black, and Frank Murphy criticized the Court's apparent subordination of religious liberty, and declared that *Gobitis* had been "wrongly decided."

By June 1943, the Court had overruled *Jones* v. *Opelika* and changes in the Court's membership had set the stage for a new look at compulsory flag salutes.

The second flag salute case—*West Virginia State Board of Education* v. *Barnette*—was a total vindication of Stone's dissent in *Gobitis*. In West Virginia, state school officials had taken Frankfurter's *Gobitis* opinion so warmly to heart that failure to venerate the flag every day would not only subject every West Virginia schoolchild to expulsion and delinquency hearings, but would also make

his parents liable to fines and imprisonment.

In his six-to-three opinion for the Court, Justice Robert H. Jackson, the former Attorney General, affirmed every American's right to refuse to participate in state-imposed orthodoxies. Going beyond the appellants' claim to free exercise of religion, Jackson invoked the broadest First Amendment rights of free speech and expression, and he declared that *Gobitis* had erred in ceding those paramount rights to legislative discretion.

"The very purpose of a Bill of Rights," he wrote, "was to withdraw certain subjects from the vicissitudes of political controversy, to place them beyond the reach of majorities and officials and to establish them as legal principles to be applied by the courts."

As to Frankfurter's central rationale—"national unity is the basis of national security"—Jackson drew a distinction between voluntary and involuntary patriotism. The latter would lead first to banning dissent, he said, then to persecuting dissenters. "Compulsory unification achieves only the unanimity of the graveyard." Those who feared dissent failed to grasp that

Chief Justice Harlan Fiske Stone in Chambers. Collection of the Supreme Court of the United States, Washington, D.C.

diversity was the mark of freedom, Jackson said. "But freedom to differ is not limited to things that do not matter much. That would be a mere shadow of freedom. The test of its substance is the right to differ as to things that touch the heart of the existing order.

"If there is any fixed star in our constitutional constellation, it is that no official, high or petty, can prescribe what shall be orthodox in politics, nationalism, religion or other matters of opinion or force citizens to confess by word or act their faith therein. If there are any circumstances which permit an exception, they do not now occur to us."

In dissenting for Justices Roberts, Reed, and himself, Justice Frankfurter insisted that judicial restraint must outweigh personal feeling, a case he chose to make by invoking his own Jewish background.

"One who belongs to the most vilified and persecuted minority in history," Frankfurter wrote, "is not likely to be insensible to the freedoms guaranteed by our Constitution. Were my purely personal attitude relevant I should wholeheartedly associate myself with the generally libertar-

ian views in the Court's opinion, representing as they do the thought and action of a lifetime. But as judges we are neither Jew nor Gentile, neither Catholic nor agnostic. . . . As a member of this Court, I am not justified in writing my private notions of policy into the Constitution, no matter how deeply I may cherish them or how mischievous I may deem their disregard. . . . I cannot bring my mind to believe that the 'liberty' secured by the Due Process Clause gives this Court the authority to deny to the State of West Virginia the attainment of that end which we all recognize as a legitimate end, namely, the promotion of good citizenship, by employment of the means here chosen."

In *Korematsu* v. *United States* (1944), Justice Black spoke for a six-man majority in sustaining the now discredited wartime decision to remove 112,000 persons of Japanese descent from their West Coast homes and relocate them in detention camps. "All legal restrictions which curtail the civil rights of a single racial group are immediately suspect," Black wrote. "Pressing public necessity may sometimes justify the existence of

Justice Robert Hougwout Jackson, United States Chief of Counsel, at Nuremberg, October 4, 1946. On the right is Uri Pokrovski, Assistant Prosecutor for the Soviet Union. UPI/Bettmann Archive, New York

such restrictions; racial antagonism never can."

Having promulgated the Court's first explicit rule against racial discrimination, Black called the mass exclusion a "military imperative" supported by Congress's war powers, rather than a group punishment impermissibly based on race.

A few months later, in *Ex parte Endo*, the Justices ordered the release of Nisei (second-generation) Japanese-American citizens because the military had discovered them to be loyal to the land of their birth, the United States. And some years in the future, Justice Black's "rigid scrutiny" rule would become essential to the Court's historic repudiation of *Plessy* in the 1954 school desegregation case.

According to Harvard Law Professor Laurence H. Tribe, the weakness of judicial review in wartime is a major argument for strong judicial review in peacetime. "If the judiciary does not remind Congress of its constitutional obligations when such reminder is possible," writes Tribe, "it is less than likely that Congress will remember to restrain itself when the courts see no practical alternative to silence."

On the same day in 1942—Monday, June 1— the Court issued two decisions in which the human values at stake in the war against totalitarianism seemed to weigh heavily.

At issue in *Skinner* v. *Oklahoma* was a state law mandating sterilization for "habitual criminals," defined as any Oklahoman convicted twice or more for "felonies involving moral turpitude." A felon was someone convicted of stealing more than twenty dollars, but the law applied only to those tainted by turpitude, meaning behavior that society deemed especially vile.

In *Buck* v. *Bell* (1927), Justice Holmes had upheld Virginia's sterilization of mental hospital inmates, rejecting an equal-protection appeal.

In *Skinner,* Justice Douglas spoke for a unanimous Court in finding a denial of equal protection because the sterilization law applied to some offenders and not to others, though both might have stolen equal amounts. But more important, the law had a class bias: white collar criminals were exempted as non-vile felons. Douglas considered the implications of state power over sterilization. In evil hands, he wrote, that power "can cause races or types which are inimical to the dominant group to wither and disappear."

To prevent any such outcome, the Court for the first time set forth its "fundamental interest" doctrine, meaning that certain matters of personal choice were so fundamental to human personality as to be presumed beyond government reach, except where a compelling state interest could be shown. *Skinner* produced the first of these fundamentals—marriage and procreation, which Douglas called among "the basic civil rights of man." As to sterilization, any law imposing a condition so irreparable on a given class of persons would thenceforth receive the Court's "special scrutiny," a test of alleged discrimination far harsher than mere "reasonableness."

Skinner was significant because it foreshadowed the evolution of a constitutional right of privacy, and also revived "substantive due process." In a new line of decisions under the equal-protection guarantee, the Justices would again examine the *substance* of legislation. According to *Skinner,* the Oklahoma law denied equal protection because of its substance—its deprivation of a man's fundamental right to procreate.

The other key ruling on that first day of June 1942 was *Betts* v. *Brady.* Voting six to three, the Court rejected the seemingly impressive proposition that due process under the Fourteenth Amendment required the states to make sure that every person charged with a crime was defended by a lawyer. In *federal* courts, the right to counsel in capital cases had been guaranteed by the Sixth Amendment as well as federal law ever since 1790, and the Supreme Court had extended the right to *all* federal defendants in 1938 (*Johnson* v. *Zerbst*).

But the Sixth Amendment was still thought to apply only to federal courts. State defendants were "due" only the "process" enigmatically promised by the state-binding Fourteenth Amendment. Yet as far back as 1908 the Court had acknowledged in *Twining* v. *New Jersey* that some guarantees of the federal Bill of Rights (i.e., the first ten amendments) might be so fundamental that a state denying them would be denying due process. And in *Powell* v. *Alabama* (1932), Justice Sutherland had found the right to counsel "of this fundamental character."

Sutherland had ruled that states must provide lawyers for defendants charged with capital crimes, when, as in *Powell,* the accused (the Scottsboro Boys) were indigent or illiterate or otherwise incompetent to represent themselves. Although his landmark opinion did not apply to noncapital cases, Sutherland had vividly described every defendant's need of counsel. "Even the intelligent and educated layman has small and sometimes no skill in the science of law. . . . He requires the guiding hand of counsel at every step in the proceedings against him. Without it, though he be not guilty, he faces the danger of conviction because he does not know how to establish his innocence."

And yet, ten years after *Powell,* here was Justice Roberts insisting for the 1942 Court in *Betts* v. *Brady* that "appointment of counsel is not a fundamental right" for state defendants in noncapital cases.

Of course, any state was free to enact such a right and ignore the Court's distinction between capital and noncapital cases, Roberts said. But in determining whether states had denied due process, the Court itself would avoid specific rules, such as the Sixth Amendment. Instead, it would apply a general standard called "fundamental fairness," which the Justices would discover by appraising "the totality of facts" in each particular case. As Roberts put it, "That which may, in one setting, constitute a denial of fundamental fairness, shocking to the universal sense of justice, may, in other circumstances, and in the light of other considerations, fall short of such denial."

Applying this open-ended standard to the case before them, the *Betts* majority found nothing fundamentally unfair about the plight of a jobless Maryland farmhand named Smith Betts, then serving eight years for robbery, almost certainly because he could not afford a lawyer. Betts's request for appointed counsel had been denied by a judge who then convicted him without a jury and later contended that a lawyer would have done Betts no good. Had the Supreme Court gone beyond the printed record, which omitted exculpatory evidence, the Justices might have questioned the trial judge's contention. The actual "totality of facts" included, for example, a police lineup in which the only suspect on display was Betts, whom the victim identified only after the police dressed and even disguised him to resemble the alleged robber.

Chief Justice Vinson and President Truman, enroute to the Army-Navy Game at Philadelphia, November 27, 1948. Vinson Papers, University of Kentucky

Justice Black, one of three dissenters in *Betts*, became the leading advocate of a way around that decision—the theory that the Fourteenth Amendment was originally designed to impose the Bill of Rights upon the states. If true, the Sixth Amendment would have entitled Smith Betts to a lawyer.

Black promoted this theory with particular vigor in *Adamson* v. *California*, a 1947 self-incrimination case in which the four dissenters (Justices Black, Douglas, Murphy, and Rutledge) came within one vote of transferring the entire Bill of Rights to the states in one swoop. That was the peak of the wholesale incorporation effort. The Court eventually reached the same result on a right-by-right basis.

In his *Adamson* dissent, Justice Black argued that the Court had gone astray in state due process cases because its resistance to any blanket rule had plunged it into subjective judgments about the fairness of each disputed case. The root of this was Justice Cardozo's seminal opinion in *Palko* v. *Connecticut* (1937), which held that the Fourteenth Amendment required states to honor principles of justice "so rooted in the tradi-

tions and conscience of our people as to be ranked as fundamental."

In aid of this evolution, the Court had developed various rules deemed consistent with "a fair trial." But this process was slow, unpredictable, and subject to the vagaries of Court membership. Fairness had proved an elusive concept, and lacking specific standards the Justices had been forced, in Black's view, to "roam at will in the limitless area of their own beliefs as to reasonableness." Black accused the Court of usurping legislative power by creating policy via natural law, which he called "an incongruous excrescence on our Constitution." By ruling that the Fourteenth Amendment incorporated the Bill of Rights, he argued, the Court would provide all Americans with criminal procedures that were fair, equal, consistent, and specific.

The bare majority in *Adamson* was led by Justice Frankfurter. He claimed that the framers of the Fourteenth Amendment had *not* intended to incorporate the Bill of Rights. He insisted that to do so now would lock the states into eighteenth-century procedures, thus subverting not only their freedom to experiment but also the greater

Felix Frankfurter *Hugo L Black* *Fred M Vinson* *Stanley Reed* *Wm O Douglas*
Wiley Rutledge *Frank Murphy* *Robert H Jackson* *Harold H Burton*

The Vinson Court, 1946–49. Standing, from left: Associate Justices Wiley Blount Rutledge, Frank Murphy, Robert Hougwout Jackson, Harold Hitz Burton. Seated, from left: Associate Justices Felix Frankfurter, Hugo Lafayette Black, Chief Justice Frederick Moore Vinson, Associate Justices Stanley Forman Reed, William Orville Douglas. Photograph by Fabian Bachrach. Collection of the Supreme Court of the United States, Washington, D.C.

principle of federalism, which Frankfurter considered the Constitution's paramount value.

By 1967, virtually every provision of the Bill of Rights had been "selectively" absorbed into the Fourteenth Amendment. In the 1963 case of *Gideon* v. *Wainwright,* for example, Justice Black wrote the unanimous opinion that repudiated *Betts* v. *Brady* and established the national rule that every American charged with a serious crime was entitled to a lawyer.

On April 22, 1946, Chief Justice Stone was reading a spirited dissent from the bench when he suffered a stroke. He died later that day. He was seventy-three and had served on the Court for twenty-one years.

Stone was much admired for jurisprudence but not for leadership. During his five-year Chief Justiceship, the Court was prone to divided opinions and public controversy. The possibility that one of the sitting Justices would now become Chief Justice triggered further bickering.

President Harry Truman, an authority on political thermodynamics, nominated his calming friend and strong ally, Treasury Secretary Fred M. Vinson, as Stone's successor. Easily con-

firmed in June 1946, Chief Justice Vinson was a genial New Deal veteran of fifty-six who firmly believed in the benefits of federal power. Truman particularly valued his skills in solving difficult problems and mollifying difficult people.

As it turned out, the Court remained ideologically divided and seldom able to produce unanimous opinions. And ahead lay new constitutional dilemmas arising from the Cold War and the new imperatives of internal security.

Judicial statecraft is sometimes a matter of issuing the most controversial decisions at the least provocative moments. The importance and the difficulties of such timing can be seen in the Court's evolving definition of "fighting words"— language deemed unprotected conduct rather than protected speech.

By 1942 the Court had agreed that states could regulate public speeches, parades, and demonstrations. To help prevent disorder, officials could require permits specifying a parade's time, place, and manner (*Cox* v. *New Hampshire*). There might be a difference between appropriate and inappropriate sites for demonstrations, but that issue would come later, in the 1960s. For now, the

212

Court basically upheld speech regulations that avoided prior restraint and employed the "least restrictive means" to achieve legitimate ends. Catch-all laws were invalid; the rules must be limited to specific offenses and applied impartially.

But still unresolved was the status of public speech that actually incited disorder. At what point did such utterances lose protection? The Court's answer was *Chaplinsky* v. *New Hampshire* (1942), a unanimous decision that the states could simply forget the First Amendment when it came to "fighting words"—words so insulting as to provoke a listener to violence. Justice Murphy's opinion placed fighting words in the same unprotected category as libel and obscenity. They were not protected, he wrote, because "such utterances are no essential part of any exposition of ideas, and are of . . . slight social value as a step to truth."

Chaplinsky himself was yet another Jehovah's Witness. He had predictably started a small riot when he not only blasted Catholicism as "a racket," but also denounced a city marshal as "a damned Fascist" and "God damned racketeer." The Court sustained Chaplinsky's conviction under a New Hampshire law making it a crime to hurl "offensive, derisive, or annoying" words at another person lawfully present in a public place. But the Court sustained the law only because the state court had carefully limited its reach to those epithets virtually guaranteed to cause violence.

One carefully-reasoned opinion on the subject was that of Justice John Marshall Harlan in the famous 1971 case of *Cohen* v. *California*. As a protest against the Vietnam War, Paul R. Cohen had walked silently through the Los Angeles County courthouse wearing a jacket adorned with a terse and scatological statement on conscription. Though all spectators remained as peaceful as Cohen, he was arrested and convicted under a state breach-of-the-peace law forbidding "offensive conduct" that tended to "provoke others to acts of violence . . ."

Justice Harlan reversed the conviction on the ground that Cohen had simply expressed a legitimate political opinion, protected by the First Amendment. He had not violated the state law for the obvious reason that neither he nor his display had provoked any violence. Nobody even complained. So much for "fighting words."

The key issue, Harlan said, was "whether Cali-fornia can excise, as 'offensive conduct,' one particular scurrilous epithet from the public discourse." To uphold the state, Harlan wrote, would give any state "boundless" power to ban the public use of any word officially deemed offensive, despite the social reality, as Harlan put it, that "one man's vulgarity is another man's lyric."

Because the profane is sometimes profound, he ruled, "we cannot indulge the facile assumption that one can forbid particular words without also running a substantial risk of suppressing ideas in the process. Indeed, governments might soon seize upon the censorship of particular words as a convenient guide for banning the expression of unpopular views."

During the first dozen years after the New Deal crisis, the Court sometimes overrode state curbs on free expression with the spirit that marked the *Lochner* Court's approach to business regulation. A narrow majority of Justices, often led by William O. Douglas, pushed the "preferred position" theory of free speech to a point verging on absolutism. In constant dissent, Justice Frankfurter denounced the preferred-theory as "mischievous" because it implied that "every law touching communication is presumptively invalid." Frankfurter, apostle of judicial restraint, kept warning that the Court was again poaching on legislative territory, which it could ill afford.

All this reached a climax during Chief Justice Vinson's first three years, notably in *Terminiello* v. *Chicago* (1949). Terminiello, a defrocked Catholic priest, was a race-baiter with a reputation for excoriating blacks, Jews, and Franklin Roosevelt. While addressing 800 followers inside a private hall, Terminiello attracted 1,000 protesters whom he quickly labeled "Slimy Scum," "New Deal Pinks," and "Murderous Russians." His disciples then cried, "Dirty Kikes" and "Kill the Jews." In turn, the protesters called Terminiello "Hitler," tore clothes off latecomers, heaved rocks through windows, and tried to invade the hall with intent to liquidate "Fascists." The police barely repulsed the mob, then arrested Terminiello. He was convicted of provoking a breach of the peace, indeed a riot.

Yet Justice Douglas, speaking for a five-to-four majority, spurned the obvious question of whether Terminiello had uttered "fighting

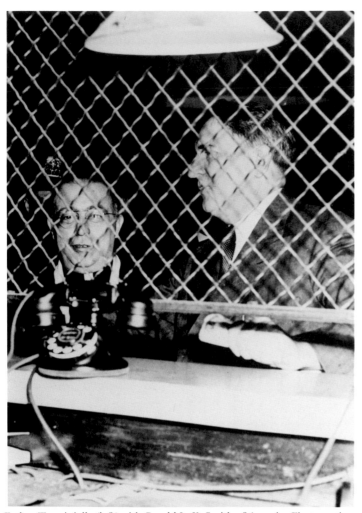

Father Terminiello (left) with Gerald L. K. Smith of America First, posting bond after surrendering to police on charges stemming from a street battle following a meeting, February 25, 1946. UPI/Bettmann Archive, New York

Chief Justice Vinson saw a case of fighting words, not protected speech. Justice Jackson saw protected speech posing a clear and present danger of violence. The police had acted correctly, Jackson insisted, and he added:

"The Court has gone far toward accepting the doctrine that civil liberty means the removal of all restraints from these crowds and that all local attempts to maintain order are impairments of the liberty of the citizen. The choice [for judges] is not between order and liberty. It is between liberty with order and anarchy without either. There is danger that, if the Court does not temper its doctrinaire logic with a little practical wisdom, it will convert the constitutional Bill of Rights into a suicide pact."

The *Terminiello* majority seemed to distrust policemen and it obviously thought the riot reports were exaggerated. Two years later in *Feiner* v. *New York* (1951), the Court accepted the police version of why a Progressive Party organizer named Irvin Feiner had been arrested for disorderly conduct while making a streetcorner speech in Syracuse, New York. The police said about eighty people had gathered as Feiner urged blacks to fight for their rights and assailed President Truman, the American Legion, and the Mayor of Syracuse. When some listeners objected, two policemen arrived, Feiner ignored their request to stop speaking, and he was arrested, supposedly to prevent violence.

Speaking for a six-man majority, Chief Justice Vinson upheld Feiner's conviction for breach of the peace on the ground that Feiner had urged blacks to "rise up in arms," among other provocations, and that the police must be free to act "when as here the speaker passes the bounds of argument or persuasion and undertakes incitement to riot."

Reading the same record, Justice Black found a different situation. In his dissent, Black said, "the police did not even pretend to protect" Feiner from the crowd; he had simply urged blacks to join whites in struggling together "arm in arm," and the only actual fighting words were uttered by one man walking past with "his wife and two small children."

Terminiello and *Feiner* became famous examples of the Court's difficulty in reaching agreement as to whether a danger was "clear and present." Conflicts in factual perception were

words" nullifying his free-speech defense. Instead, Douglas reversed the conviction on the ground that the trial judge had instructed the jury improperly when he defined breach-of-peace, in this case, as speech that "stirs the public to anger, invites dispute, brings about a condition of unrest, or creates a disturbance." According to Douglas, one purpose of free speech is "to invite dispute," and this purpose may best be served when speech "induces a condition of unrest, creates dissatisfaction with conditions as they are, or even stirs people to anger."

All speech is free, Douglas said, "unless shown likely to produce a clear and present danger of a serious substantive evil that arises *far above* public inconvenience, annoyance, or unrest" (emphasis added).

The four dissenters found this decidedly unrealistic, given Terminiello's talent as a firebrand.

doubtless inherent in the very nature of free-speech cases—opinion being so wrought with faith and feeling—but the problem worsened in times of national anxiety, such as the early Cold War. The sharp contrast between *Terminiello* and *Feiner* was linked to that problem, compounded by a significant change in the Court's membership and a new majority's unusual deference to the political branches in free-speech cases.

It is a tribute to the Court's institutional resilience that these decisions were soon followed by others establishing strict procedural safeguards, and with ground-breaking decisions in other areas, notably racial discrimination.

As the Forties ended, Americans awoke to the harsh reality of Communist expansion around the globe from China to Czechoslovakia.

To allay widespread fears of Communist conspiracy, shared by liberals and conservatives alike, President Truman created a Loyalty Review Board to screen all government employees.

At issue in *American Communications Association* v. *Douds* (1950) was a provision of the Taft-Hartley Act that stripped union officials of the protections of federal labor law unless they signed an affidavit swearing, first, they were not members of the Communist Party, and second, that they did not believe in or belong to any group advocating unlawful overthrow of the federal government. Congress thought this test oath would stop Communists from running unions and launching "political strikes" that many considered acts of sabotage.

Chief Justice Vinson spoke for a five-to-one Court (three Justices not participating) that applied a new doctrine—"balancing"—in order to uphold the test oath against a First Amendment challenge. Although mandatory affidavits obviously infringed upon the signers' political rights, Vinson wrote, the actual harm was minor compared with the necessity of halting political strikes. Congress had not attempted to curtail anyone's free speech, he said, and only a handful of union officials had been affected. Accordingly, he upheld the requirement as a valid exercise of Congress's power to regulate interstate commerce. In sum, the government's interest in preventing disruptions of the economy far outweighed the personal rights of a few labor leaders.

Vinson found the clear and present danger test unworkable in this situation. Hence the new balancing test: "When particular conduct is regulated in the interest of public order, and the regulation results in an indirect, conditional, partial abridgement of speech, the duty of the courts is to determine which of these two conflicting interests demands the greater protection under the particular circumstances presented."

The five majority Justices in *Douds* were not in complete agreement. Frankfurter and Jackson upheld only the membership-disclosure part of the disputed affidavits, dissenting from Vinson's approval of belief-disclosure as well. "Under our system," Jackson wrote, "it is time enough for the law to lay hold of the citizen when he acts illegally. . . . I think we must let his mind alone." But Justice Black, the one dissenter, resisted even this compromise. He declared: "The postulate of the First Amendment is that our free institutions can be maintained without proscribing or penalizing political belief, speech, press, assembly, or party affiliation. This is a far bolder philosophy than despotic rulers can afford to follow. It is the heart of the system on which our freedom depends."

Chief Justice Vinson's view that freedom depended on its partial sacrifice was further demonstrated a year later by his majority opinion in *Dennis* v. *United States* (1951).

Dennis tested America's first peacetime federal sedition law since the Sedition Act of 1798. The Smith Act outlawed any organized advocacy of changing the federal government by force or violence. Dormant since it was passed by Congress in 1940, the law had sprung to life with the Cold War. In 1949, after a sensational trial in New York, a federal jury found eleven top leaders of the American Communist Party guilty of violating the Smith Act by conspiring to teach and advocate revolution, and to form groups for that purpose. They were not charged with any overt attempt to overthrow the government—only with conspiring to advocate.

In 1951, by a vote of six to two (Justice Tom C. Clark not participating), the Supreme Court upheld the Smith Act and the eleven convictions. As a result, the government successfully prosecuted more than 125 other Communist Party members.

Dennis required the Court to define the point where public safety justified curbs on political

STEVE NELSON

WILLIAM ALBERTSON

BENJAMIN LOWELL
CAREATHERS, SR.

Mug shots of six district leaders of the Communist Party from Pennsylvania, West Virginia, and Michigan, arrested by the F.B.I. on August 17, 1951. UPI/ Bettmann Archive, New York

association and expression. To this old problem was added a new wrinkle. The Communist defendants were charged with advocating revolution in the *future*, making it difficult to uphold their convictions under the clear and present danger test. Chief Justice Vinson paid lip service to that test in his majority opinion, but he actually used another test devised by Circuit Judge Learned Hand, who had spoken for the United States Court of Appeals in sustaining the convictions before they reached the Supreme Court. Judge Hand's formulation came to be known as the "clear and probable danger" test. "In each case," he held, the courts "must ask whether the gravity of the 'evil,' discounted by its improbability, justifies such invasion of free speech as is necessary to avoid the danger."

Vinson adopted Hand's standard on the ground that potential subversion should be halted long before it became a clear and present danger. Government must be free to nip revolutions in the bud, he wrote, rather than "wait until the *putsch* is about to be executed, the plans have been laid, and the signal is awaited." He found the Communists dangerous not simply because they were guilty of "conspiracy to advocate" future revolution, but because they were so organized, disciplined, and committed to revolution whenever the opportunity arose, that party membership itself constituted an immediate threat to democratic government. "It is the existence of the conspiracy which creates the dan-

ger," Vinson wrote. "If the ingredients of the reaction are present, we cannot bind the government to wait until the catalyst is added."

Vinson spoke for Justices Harold H. Burton, Sherman Minton, and Stanley F. Reed. In concurring opinions, Justices Frankfurter and Jackson expressed some disquiet. But Frankfurter found solace in the Court's having deferred to Congress in resolving the conflict between speech and security; and Jackson mused that government had no visible option in combating "a state within a state, an authoritarian dictatorship within a republic."

In dissent Justices Black and Douglas stressed that the eleven Communists had not been charged with any actual attempt to overthrow government but only with what Black called agreeing "to assemble and talk and publish certain ideas at a later date." Black denounced the Communist prosecution as "a virulent form of prior censorship of speech and press, which I believe the First Amendment forbids." Justice Douglas decried "the vice of treating speech as the equivalent of overt acts of a treasonable or seditious character." The Constitution requires overt acts as proof of treason, he noted, and "not a single seditious act is charged in the indictment." He added: "Free speech—the glory of our system of government—should not be sacrificed on anything less than plain and objective proof of danger that the evil advocated is imminent."

Six years later, the judicial pendulum began a

JAMES HULSE DOLSEN

ANDREW RUDOLPH ONDA

IRVING WEISSMAN

return swing. In *Yates* v. *United States* (1957), with only Justice Clark dissenting, the Court of Earl Warren diluted the *Dennis* impact by redefining the old line between speech and conduct. In reversing the convictions of fourteen people accused of violating the Smith Act, Justice Harlan discarded the clear and present danger test while toughening the clear and probable danger test. He ruled that a card-carrying Communist was not per se a Smith Act violator until he actively fomented revolution.

"The essential distinction," Harlan wrote, "is that those to whom advocacy is addressed must be urged to *do* something now or in the future, rather than merely to *believe* in something." By requiring the government to prove a connection between advocacy and action, *Yates* virtually halted further Smith Act prosecutions.

In 1967 the Court avoided "balancing" when it threw out a sweeping provision of the McCarran Act that banned all Communists, active or inactive, from defense-related jobs. The Court ruled the ban simply too broad, a catch-all that "quite literally establishes guilt by association alone" (*United States* v. *Robel*).

At the height of Cold War tensions, many states passed laws to punish would-be plotters against the *federal* government. The Court examined this phenomenon in *Pennsylvania* v. *Nelson* (1956), which involved that state's prosecution of Steve Nelson, an avowed Communist. Nelson's verbal attacks on the federal government had

earned him a twenty-year sentence and a $10,000 fine for violating Pennsylvania's sedition law. When he appealed this drastic punishment, the state supreme court voided the state law on the ground that the federal Smith Act had superseded it.

The Supreme Court applied this reasoning to all state sedition laws. Without criticizing the profusion or confusion of state restraints on free expression, the Court simply held that the passage of national sedition laws meant that Congress "intended to occupy the field of (federal) sedition" and preempt this aspect of national defense. Accordingly, the Court ruled that state sedition laws could no longer reach alleged plots against the federal government.

In the late 1960s, various states revived their old criminal syndicalism laws in order to hobble what they considered the excesses of antiwar activists and civil rights workers. The Court had last upheld such laws in *Whitney* v. *California,* the 1927 case that produced a memorable Brandeis dissent. Four decades later came *Brandenburg* v. *Ohio* (1969), an unsigned opinion that quietly overruled *Whitney* and provided a strong new version of the clear and present danger test.

Brandenburg was an Ohio Ku Klux Klan leader who had invited news coverage of a cross-burning where he was duly filmed threatening "revengance" against the Justices and others he deemed hostile to white supremacy. Convicted under Ohio's criminal syndicalism act, Branden-

217

John W. Davis, left, attorney for the steel industry, arriving at court with Acting Attorney General Philip B. Perlman, May 13, 1952. Davis was counsel for the defense in the famous school desegregation case of 1954. UPI/ Bettmann Archive, New York

burg appealed to the Court on the ground that his words had failed to produce lawless action. The Court agreed, reversing his conviction with a formulation that synthesized the ideas of Holmes, Brandeis, and Hand.

Called the "incitement test," this approach protects advocacy of the use of force as an abstract doctrine, while outlawing actual incitement to use force. In the Court's words, the so-called *Brandenburg* Rule is "the principle that the constitutional guarantees of free speech and free press do not permit a state to forbid or proscribe advocacy of the use of force or of law violation except where such advocacy is directed to inciting or producing lawless action and is likely to incite or produce such action."

The Court acted boldly in *Youngstown Sheet & Tube Co.* v. *Sawyer,* the great Steel Seizure case of 1952. Alarmed by a threatened strike during the Korean War, President Truman had ordered the Secretary of Commerce to seize and operate the nation's steel mills.

The steel industry sought an injunction against the seizure, arguing that Truman had acted without authority from either Congress or the Constitution, the only legitimate sources of Presidential power. In response, the President's lawyers invoked the familiar theory that the Constitution gives the President "inherent power" to act in the national interest, even when he lacks specific authority from Congress. The dispute involved not only one of the nation's most powerful industries, but also a major collision between the political branches of the national government, compounded by the pressures of war.

By a vote of six to three, the Court ruled President Truman's seizure order unconstitutional on the ground that he had infringed Congress's sole authority to make laws, thus violating the Separation of Powers. The Framers, Justice Black wrote for the Court, "entrusted the lawmaking power to Congress alone in both good and bad times." The Court's strong rejection of "inherent" Presidential power was underscored by Justice Jackson's concurring opinion. "Emergency powers are consistent with free government only when their control is lodged elsewhere than in the Executive who exercises them," Jackson wrote. "This is the safeguard that would be nullified by our adoption of the 'inherent powers' formula."

The Court was cautious about another political

question, the widespread malapportionment of voting districts that grossly distorted election results in many parts of the country.

In *Colegrove* v. *Green* (1946), a political scientist named Kenneth W. Colegrove presented the Court with the fact that the Illinois legislature had refused to reapportion the state's Congressional districts since 1901. The largest district had nine times the population of the smallest, or one-ninth of its voting power. In Illinois, the disparity between districts ran as high as 800,000 people.

The Court refused to act. Speaking through Frankfurter, who represented four Justices out of only seven then sitting, the Court declined to enter the "political thicket" of reapportionment. "It is hostile to a democratic system to involve the judiciary in the politics of the people," Frankfurter declared. The dissenters insisted that federal courts were obliged to remedy denial of federal rights, in this case the right to vote equally for Congressmen, guaranteed by Article I of the Constitution. But Frankfurter carried the day.

The malapportionment case was not typical. In related fields, the Court accepted cases it deemed suitable for judicial settlement and issued decisions that strengthened political democracy in America. For one thing, it struck down a number of racial barriers.

Until 1941, for example, the Court had tolerated the fiction that party primaries were not elections, thus permitting Southern states to bar Negroes from voting in Democratic primaries, which were, in fact, the South's general elections. In 1941 the Court held in *United States* v. *Classic* that primary elections for Congress were subject to federal regulation. Three years later the Court applied to state party primaries the Fifteenth Amendment's mandate that no citizen shall be denied the right to vote "on account of race, color, or previous condition of servitude." When these party primaries are integral to electing public officials, the Court ruled in *Smith* v. *Allwright* (1944), any exclusion of Negroes from voting in primaries is "state action" forbidden by the Fifteenth Amendment and the Equal Protection Clause of the Fourteenth.

In 1946 the Court repudiated its 1890 ruling that states could lawfully segregate black passengers on interstate carriers. In *Morgan* v. *Virginia,*

the Court struck down such state laws as burdens on interstate commerce, holding that the constant change in seating while carriers moved between segregated and unsegregated states required uniform national rules.

Chief Justice Vinson wrote the 1948 decision *(Shelley* v. *Kraemer)* outlawing judicial enforcement of racial covenants in housing as state action forbidden by the Fourteenth Amendment. "Private" racial discrimination remained immune to regulation, as it had since the *Civil Rights Cases* of 1883. But profound changes lay ahead.

In early 1948, the Court issued a unanimous *per curiam* ruling that a state law school must either admit qualified blacks or provide equal training within the state *(Sipuel* v. *Board of Regents of the University of Oklahoma).*

On June 5, 1950, Chief Justice Vinson read a unanimous decision that required for the first time that states live up to *Plessy* v. *Ferguson* (1896) and actually make "separate" mean "equal." In *Sweatt* v. *Painter,* all nine Justices ruled that the University of Texas Law School could not bar a qualified black applicant by shunting him into a newly created "black" school that was obviously inferior to the "white" school he wished to attend because it was the best in Texas. Although Vinson stopped short of any reexamination of *Plessy,* his opinion in *Sweatt* did provide the Court's first order that a white school must admit a black student because the alternative black school was inferior.

On the very same day, Vinson read a second unanimous decision, *McLaurin* v. *Oklahoma State Regents for Higher Education,* that took the whole issue one subtle step further. Going beyond *Sweatt,* the Court outlawed segregation within a biracial setting. Once a state university had admitted a black student, Vinson ruled, it must permit him equal access to *all* its facilities— library, lunchroom, classrooms, etc. He could not be restricted or confined to "black" seats or tables, separate from unrestricted whites.

15

JUDGES AS REFORMERS: THE WARREN COURT

By ordering all-white graduate schools to provide equal facilities for blacks in 1950, the Vinson Court began to crack racial barriers in universities. But the National Association for the Advancement of Colored People (NAACP) was far more concerned about the larger problem of segregated primary and secondary schools. The great question was whether the Supreme Court would stand by the *Plessy* separate-but-equal rule, or examine the NAACP proposition that separate public schools were, per se, unequal and unconstitutional. Supporters of that proposition were heartened in June 1953 when the Court ordered reargument of a key NAACP case from Kansas, and the Justices invited the Eisenhower Administration to submit an amicus curiae brief. Some Court watchers read these signs to mean that *Plessy* v. *Ferguson* was rapidly becoming mutable.

The NAACP had launched five federal suits attacking school segregation in widely ranging places—not only Southern states (Virginia, South Carolina), but also Kansas, Delaware, and Washington, D.C. The plaintiffs were black schoolchildren seeking admission to white schools on the ground that black schools were inferior. Four suits charged that *Plessy* violated the Fourteenth Amendment's Equal Protection Clause because segregation stamped black children themselves as inferior.

Because the Fourteenth Amendment applied only to the states, the federal government was presumably free to practice discrimination, as in the federal District of Columbia's segregated schools. The NAACP's fifth suit (*Bolling* v. *Sharp*) thus attacked racial discrimination in the federal capital on the novel ground that equal protection of the laws was implicit in the "due process" required by the Fifth Amendment, which applied to the federal government. *Bolling* would eventually make constitutional history.

In the suit destined to stand for the rest—*Brown* v. *Board of Education of Topeka*—the target was a Kansas law that permitted Topeka to segregate its primary schools, forcing a black child named Linda Brown to walk twenty blocks through a railroad yard to an all-black school rather than attend her neighborhood school, which was all-white. When Linda's father sued the Topeka school on her behalf, a three-judge federal court was sufficiently impressed by the NAACP's expert witnesses to conclude as "fact" that black children were demoralized by the stigma of segregation itself. "Segregation with the sanction of law," the judges found, "has a tendency to retard the educational and mental development of Negro children." Even so, the court upheld the constitutionality of Topeka's dual school systems on the ground that they were physically comparable and that *Plessy* was still the

Chief Justice Earl Warren. Photograph by Peter Ehrenhaft. Collection of the Supreme Court of the United States, Washington, D.C.

law of the land—until the Supreme Court itself ruled otherwise.

In December 1952 the Supreme Court heard all five cases argued by a team of NAACP lawyers headed by Thurgood Marshall, the future Justice, then forty-four. Their main adversary, representing South Carolina, was that elegant octogenarian, John W. Davis, former Solicitor General, former Ambassador to Britain, and 1924 Democratic nominee for President of the United States. Many considered the tall, silver-haired Davis the finest corporation lawyer of his era. Head of a great Wall Street law firm he had earned millions during the Depression combating New Deal regulators on behalf of clients ranging from Eastman Kodak to Western Union. He had appeared before the Supreme Court at least 135 times, and had just won his greatest legal victory—besting President Truman in the 1952 Steel Seizure Case.

Davis was a strongly conservative West Virginian and he had happily responded to South Carolina Governor (and former Associate Justice) Jimmy Byrnes's plea to defend his state's segregation laws in *Briggs* v. *Elliott,* one of the NAACP's five cases. In his crisp presentation to the Justices, Davis argued with great force that *Plessy* had been rightly decided because the Fourteenth Amendment had never been intended to forbid states to separate black and white chil-

dren, only to forbid unequal treatment.

The Justices remained silent for six months, until June 1953, when they postponed a decision and instead ordered the lawyers to reargue the issues in December 1953. This time the Court wanted answers to three key questions:

1. Was there any historical evidence that the framers had actually aimed the Fourteenth Amendment at segregated public schools?
2. If not, was the Court actually empowered to abolish segregation?
3. If so, how should the Justices carry out this extraordinary task?

Those questions suggested that a Court majority was ready to discard *Plessy*'s separate-but-equal rule, but only if the NAACP lawyers could supply a convincing historical argument for doing so. This proved difficult. As it turned out, when Congress wrote the Fourteenth Amendment, the South was virtually devoid of public schools for either race, and the issue at that time was not segregation but whether the newly freed slaves were to receive *any* education, a burden hard-pressed whites strongly resisted.

When the Amendment was ratified in 1868, racially segregated schools were common in most of the North except in New England, where, as

221

The NAACP Legal Defense Fund attorneys in the school segregation cases. From left to right: Louis L. Redding, Robert L. Carter, Oliver H. Hill, Thurgood Marshall, Spottswood W. Robinson, III, Jack Greenberg, James M. Nabrit, Jr., and George E. C. Hayes. Photograph courtesy NAACP Legal Defense Fund, New York

Ben Shahn. *Frankfurter and Black.* 1963. Ink and wash drawing, 20½ × 26″. Private collection

Southerners liked to note, the separate-but-equal doctrine was first devised in the famous 1850 school case of *Roberts* v. *City of Boston*. The same Congress that passed the Amendment also permitted segregated schools in the District of Columbia. Nor did the states that adopted the Amendment generally construe the new constitutional right of "equal protection" to mean that segregated schools must be abandoned. Of thirty-seven states then comprising the Union, only five so interpreted the new right, and three of those soon resegregated their schools. When *Plessy* v. *Ferguson* upheld the separate-but-equal doctrine in 1896, laws sanctioning racially segregated schools were already on the books not only throughout the South, but in a total of nearly thirty states, ranging from New York to Kansas to California.

In tracing what the Fourteenth Amendment *was* meant to achieve, the NAACP lawyers were initially discouraged by the legislative history of its precursor, the Civil Rights Act of 1866. The intent of that law was expected to illuminate the intent of the Amendment. Unfortunately, the House had apparently refused to approve the act until it had been shorn of sweeping language ("There shall be no discrimination in civil rights . . .") that would have erased segregation laws in every state. Moreover, the member who urged this key dilution was none other than Ohio Republican John A. Bingham, one of the lead-

ing House Radicals and the principal drafter of the Fourteenth Amendment itself. What had Bingham been up to?

Further research indicated that Bingham was not so much retreating as acknowledging that Congress alone should not attack discrimination without the authority of a state-approved constitutional amendment, which he subsequently proposed. The Fourteenth Amendment was apparently intended to put the whole subject beyond political reach, immune to expediency. Vague yet commanding, it was worded in such a way as to avoid immediate controversy over specifics while allowing future enforcers to carry out the framers' broad purpose. And what, precisely, was that purpose? According to Senator Poland of Vermont, for example, the goal was to "uproot and destroy" every discriminatory law that "violates the spirit of the Declaration of Independence." Thaddeus Stevens, the chief House Radical, was typically explicit. The Amendment empowered Congress to crack down on "any state" with invidious laws, he said, adding that "no distinctions would be tolerated in this purified Republic, but what arose from merit and conduct."

Although it was thus impossible to claim that the framers were concerned about segregated schools, at a time when few black children were even attending school, it was equally impossible to deny that the Fourteenth Amendment left future generations free to deal with any aspect of racial discrimination, whether by Congressional action or judicial review. When President Dwight D. Eisenhower's Justice Department entered the Brown case as an amicus curiae endorsing desegregation, as President Truman's had done in 1952, Attorney General Herbert Brownell's brief offered a summary of the Amendment's legislative record. It was "not conclusive" regarding the framers' position on schools, Brownell said, but there was ample evidence that the Amendment "established the broad constitutional principle of full and complete equality of all persons under the law and that it forbade all distinctions based on race or color." Brownell urged the Court to outlaw school segregation but to give the South a one-year breather in order to calm the inevitable reaction.

In any decision of such historical importance, the Court makes a special effort to achieve unanimity. But for the Justices facing the school cases, the summer of 1953 was no season for consensus. Already divided personally as well as philosophically, the Vinson Court had split further over the painful case of Ethel and Julius Rosenberg, the first American civilians executed for espionage in peacetime.

Convicted of passing atomic secrets to the Russians, the Rosenbergs had appealed to the Court six times, all in the nine months comprising the October 1952 term. Only three Justices (Black, Frankfurter, and Burton) had considered the issues serious enough to warrant a hearing. Justice Douglas, the famous libertarian, reportedly voted against the Rosenbergs on five separate occasions. When the term ended on Monday, June 15, 1953, the case appeared finally closed. The Justices began scattering for the summer. The Rosenbergs, scheduled for electrocution on Friday night, began the last week of their lives at New York's Sing Sing Prison.

At that point, Justice Douglas made a sudden move that stunned both the country and his colleagues. On Wednesday, June 17, acting alone, Douglas invoked his power under the Court's rules to grant the Rosenbergs a stay of execution, pending the other Justices' review of a last-minute point that troubled Douglas.

Lawyers for the Rosenbergs had reached Douglas with a claim that their clients had been wrongly convicted under the 1917 Espionage Act, which they said had been superseded by the 1946 Atomic Energy Act. They argued that the Rosenbergs should have been tried under the 1946 act, which provided that convicted spies could be sentenced to death only upon a jury's recommendation. No such thing had occurred in the Rosenberg case.

While the press clamored and various Congressmen called for Douglas's impeachment, Douglas headed West by car under the impression that his stay would freeze the case until the fall term, when the full Court could hear arguments. Instead, somewhere in Pennsylvania, Douglas learned from his car radio that Chief Justice Vinson had recalled all Justices for a special session—only the second in Court history. Vinson wanted the matter resolved immediately.

Back in Washington, during the angry conferences that ensued, four Justices voted to keep the stay in force, partly on the ground that the Chief Justice had failed to poll the entire Court before convening a special session. But five other Justices voted to vacate the stay, at which point Burton switched his vote, making it six to three.

On Friday, June 19, the Justices entered the courtroom, where Vinson delivered a brief unsigned opinion. "We think the question is not substantial," he read. "Accordingly, we vacate the stay."

After that corrosive experience, the Justices seemed even more distant from the collegial spirit that might spur unanimity in the school cases. It appeared highly unlikely that all nine Justices would vote to overrule *Plessy*. Kentucky-born Justice Stanley Reed, for one, had serious misgivings about the NAACP case. In a letter that summer, he wrote, "'Segregation' as now presented does not mean 'discrimination' to me."

At three o'clock on the morning of September 8, 1953, while asleep in his Washington apartment, Chief Justice Fred M. Vinson suffered a heart attack and died at the age of sixty-three. Within three weeks, President Eisenhower had named his successor, Governor Earl Warren of California, the first of Eisenhower's five Court appointees.

Warren had a modest background. Raised near Bakersfield, California, where his father repaired railroad cars (and later was murdered

Attorney General Herbert Brownell, Jr., who filed a brief on behalf of plaintiffs in the school desegregation cases, prepares a petition for an injunction against Orval Faubus to force the Governor of Arkansas to disperse the National Guard in Little Rock and desegregate Central High School, September 11, 1957. UPI/Bettmann Archive, New York

in a crime that remains unsolved), Warren began working early in life as everything from iceman to mechanic's helper. He put himself through college and law school at Berkeley, served in World War I as an Army bayonet instructor, then became a $150-a-month assistant prosecutor for Alameda County. By 1925 he was the thirty-four-year-old district attorney of Alameda, the state's third largest county, encompassing the cities of Oakland, Berkeley, and Alameda.

Reelected three times, Warren next ran for state attorney general in 1938; he was the nominee and winning candidate of three parties (Republican, Democratic, and Progressive). Earning a reputation as a hard-line, law-and-order man, in 1942 he became the Republican nominee for Governor. He overwhelmed the favored Democrat and was reelected twice. In 1946 Californians were so fond of their Governor that both major parties endorsed his reelection; in 1950 he defeated Democrat James Roosevelt, F.D.R.'s son, by a margin of nearly two to one. Not surprisingly, Warren's admirers dreamed of the Presidency in 1952.

With Congress in recess, Warren was given an interim appointment only five days before the Court's new term began on October 5, 1953. The governor terminated his political career on a Wednesday and left Sacramento in time to preside as Chief Justice on Monday morning.

When the three-day *Brown* reargument began on December 7th, Justice Frankfurter bombarded Thurgood Marshall with questions. His redoubtable opponent, John W. Davis, escaped any serious probing of his proposition that "equal protection" permitted separate-but-equal schools, whereas desegregation would have a devastating impact on the whites of any predominantly black school district. Davis cited South Carolina's Clarendon County, which had 2,800 black students and only 300 whites:

If [desegregation] is done on the mathematical basis, with 30 children as a maximum . . . you would have twenty-seven Negro children and three whites in one school room. Would that make the children any happier? Would they learn any more quickly? Would their lives be more serene?

Children of that age are not the most considerate animals in the world, as we all know. Would the terrible psychological disaster being wrought, according to some of these witnesses, to the colored child be removed if he had three white children sitting somewhere in the same school room?

Would white children be prevented from getting a distorted idea of racial relations if they sat with twenty-seven Negro children? I have posed that question because it is the very one that cannot be denied.

At the end, his eyes glistening with tears, Davis beseeched the Justices to presume the good intentions of his clients and not attempt to act "as a glorified board of education for the state of South Carolina or any other state." South Carolina had done its best to equalize its separate schools, he declared. "It is convinced that the happiness, the progress and the welfare of these children is best promoted in segregated schools. . . . Here is equal education, not promised, not prophesied, but present. Shall it be thrown away on some fancied question of racial prestige?"

The next day, Thurgood Marshall confronted the Davis argument with his own easy style:

. . . . I got the feeling on hearing the discussion yesterday that when you put a white child in a school with a whole lot of colored children, the child would fall apart or something. Everybody knows that is not true.

Those same kids in Virginia and South Carolina—and I have seen them do it—they play in the streets together, they play on their farms together, they go down the road together, they separate to go to school, they come out of school and play ball together. They have to be separated in school.

There is some magic to it. You can have them voting together, you can have them not restricted because of law in the houses they live in. You can have them going to the same State university and the same college, but if they go to elementary and high school, the world will fall apart. . . .

"They can't take race out of this case," Marshall declared and the only way for the Justices to uphold segregation today was "to find that for some reason Negroes are inferior to all other human beings."

School segregation was sheer racism, Marshall concluded. It reflected "an inherent determination that the people who were formerly kept in slavery, regardless of anything else, shall be kept as near that stage as possible, and now is the time, we submit, that this Court should make it clear that that is not what our Constitution stands for."

John W. Davis had implored the Justices not to use mere "sociological" reasoning to outlaw a school system that had "stood for three quarters of a century." That approach, he insisted, was "not within the judicial power."

But even more troubling for the NAACP case was Davis's sally at the other limits of judicial power. The Supreme Court might declare school segregation unconstitutional, but then what? Must the Court actually desegregate Southern schools? How? Government lawyers told the Justices that federal district courts should oversee the process "according to criteria presented and set out by this Court." Jackson kept pressing: "What criteria do you propose?" The lower courts would just have to work it out case-by-case, he was told. Jackson remarked: "I foresee a generation of litigation."

In the end, all nine Justices voted to overrule *Plessy*.

When Chief Justice Warren read his landmark opinion to a hushed courtroom on May 17, 1954, his listeners were struck by the document's brevity, simplicity, and remarkable directness. Only thirteen paragraphs long, *Brown* v. *Board of Education* traversed all the prickly issues of legislative intent that had vexed lawyers on both sides. It took for granted that the South was striving to equalize its separate schools in "tangible" terms. For that very reason, Warren said, the Court must examine the intangibles of the matter and look at the "effect of segregation itself on public education."

Warren found that, in modern America, public education had become "perhaps the most important function" of state and local government, mainly because schooling was essential to every child's development as a citizen trained for adulthood in a complex society. "In these days," Warren wrote, "it is doubtful that any child can reasonably be expected to succeed in life if he is denied the opportunity of an education."

Since the state must provide equal schooling wherever it chose to provide schools, the ques-

The Warren Court that decided *Brown* v. *Board of Education of Topeka*, 1953–55. Standing, from left: Associate Justices Tom Campbell Clark, Robert Hougwout Jackson, Harold Hitz Burton, Sherman Minton. Seated, from left: Associate Justices Felix Frankfurter, Hugo Lafayette Black, Chief Justice Earl Warren, Associate Justices Stanley Forman Reed, William Orville Douglas. Photograph by Ackad, Washington, D.C. Collection of the Supreme Court of the United States, Washington, D.C.

tion was whether racial segregation alone—all physical facilities being equal—deprived minority group children of equal educational opportunities. Said Warren: "We believe that it does."

He added: "To separate [young children] from others of similar age and qualifications solely because of their race generates a feeling of inferiority as to their status in the community that may affect their hearts and minds in a way unlikely ever to be undone."

According to Warren, this finding was "amply supported by modern authorities," and in his famous Footnote 11, he cited seven sociological studies on the demoralizing effects of involuntary segregation. Critics later attacked the footnote as too weak to support such a profound Court decision. But it was simply Warren's way of refuting *Plessy's* logic. He then quietly arrived at one

of the great turning points in American history:

> We conclude that in the field of public education the doctrine of "separate but equal" has no place. Separate educational facilities are inherently unequal. Therefore, we hold that the plaintiffs and others similarly situated for whom the actions have been brought are, by reason of the segregation complained of, deprived of the equal protection of the laws guaranteed by the Fourteenth Amendment.

Since called *Brown I,* the 1954 decision postponed a specific remedy for school segregation until the litigants in all five cases reargued the matter a year later. The result, *Brown II,* was announced by Chief Justice Warren on May 31, 1955. Supervised by local federal courts, he said, school boards had the primary responsibility for

the standards certainly of those who at the start are in the phrase of George

Orwell, "more equal". ~~Integration~~ could *also* lower the standards of those now

under discrimination. It would indeed make a mockery of the Constitutional

process in vindicating a claim to equal treatment to achieve "integrated" but

lower educational standards. *Surely we can take as a starting-point* ~~I assume that it is a fair assumption~~ that in en-

forcing the Fourteenth Amendment the Court is, broadly speaking, promoting

a process of social betterment and not of social deterioration. ~~A Court being~~ *Not being a*

fallible and finite, ~~cannot~~ in a day change a deplorable situation into the

ideal. It does its duty if it ~~gets~~ effectively *deeply state policy the laws* under way the righting of a

wrong ~~and~~ when the wrong is a rooted *an constitutional measures* does its duty if

it ~~structures steps~~ *policy so as to uproot it "with all deliberate speed"* that reverse the direction of the *(Va.-Gir)*

So far as fashioning a decree is concerned, the problem before the *West Virginia 222 U.S. 17, 20*

Court is ~~not~~ a fact-finding problem. Only on the basis of facts not now

known will it be possible to judge how ills inherent in segregation of Negro

children can be terminated without substantially diminishing the *quality* ~~level of~~

~~school~~ education for all children. The Court does not know that a simple

scrambling of the two school systems may not work. It is entitled to suspect

that this is so, ~~but~~ it is surely entitled to suspect that spreading the

adjustment over time may *will more effectively accomplish its desired end because* ~~be more beneficial to the total situation~~. When the

facts are found - no matter by whom - there are bound to be differences of

opinion concerning the judgment to be based on them. This is almost certain,

and hence future litigation is almost certain. The Court should take fore-

thought in restricting so far as may be both the area and the occasions for

such litigations.

5. Plainly, therefore, an initial decree is bound to confine itself to

general terms, ~~that is~~ *namely* that the inequality of benefits which any segregated

school system begets for Negro children ~~be corrected as soon as possible~~ *cannot stand and should be eliminated*

as soon as this can be done with due regard to ~~consistently with~~ the requirement that school systems be not disrupted

One page of a typed draft with corrections from Justice Felix Frankfurter's memorandum to Chief Justice Earl Warren regarding the Court's decree for carrying out its decision in the segregation cases, January 15, 1954. Justice Frankfurter suggested the formula for compliance that was ultimately adopted by the Court: ". . . the Court does its duty if it decrees measures that reverse the direction of the unconstitutional policy so as to uproot it 'with all deliberate speed.'(*Virginia* v. *West Virginia* 222 US. 17, 20)." Frankfurter Papers, Harvard Law School Library, Cambridge, Massachusetts

desegregating schools "with all deliberate speed"—a principle from equity law that permitted necessary delays but prohibited footdragging and placed the burden of proof squarely on school authorities.

On June 17, 1957, the Warren Court announced two decisions tempering security actions by the federal government. Critics promptly called the double-bill "Red Monday." Many were troubled by Justice Harlan's moderating opinion in *Yates* v. *United States*, which restricted Smith Act prosecutions to advocacy of subversive action, not just talk. Even more dismaying to some was Chief Justice Warren's opinion in *Watkins* v. *United States*, which reversed the contempt conviction of a union official who had answered the House Un-American Activities Committee's questions about his own links to the Communist Party, but had refused to implicate others.

"There is no congressional power to expose for the sake of exposure," Warren declared. *Watkins* held that congressional investigations must be limited to a clear legislative purpose within the scope of each committee's jurisdiction.

Two years later, a new and seemingly more cautious majority of five Justices retreated from *Watkins* in the case of *Barenblatt* v. *United States* (1959). Speaking through Justice Harlan over Warren's dissent, the Court now applied a balancing test to congressional investigators, holding that a Vassar College instructor could be prosecuted for having refused to answer the House Un-American Activities Committee's questions about his alleged Communist links. According to Harlan, the government's interest in self-preservation could, as here, outweigh a witness's First Amendment rights.

Justice Black's lengthy dissent argued that *Barenblatt* licensed congressional headline hunters to abuse the legislative function by turning hearings into trials of unpopular citizens. The real issue, Black insisted, was "whether we as a people will try fearfully and futilely to preserve democracy by adopting totalitarian methods, or

Justice Black. Photograph by Barrett Gallagher for *Fortune* Magazine. Collection of the Supreme Court of the United States, Washington, D.C.

whether in accordance with our traditions and our Constitution we will have the confidence and the courage to be free."

In *Jencks* v. *United States* (1957), a union president had been charged with falsifying his non-Communist oath under the Taft-Hartley Act. Clinton Jencks was convicted of perjury mainly on the testimony of FBI-paid informants. The government had not shown his lawyers the pre-trial reports filed by those informants. As a result, the defense argued it could not adequately cross-examine the key witnesses against Jencks. By a vote of five to three, the Court reversed his conviction and ruled that such pre-trial reports must thenceforth be shown to defendants in federal trials, or else the government must drop the case.

Justice Tom Clark's dissent asserted that *Jencks* would produce a "Roman holiday" enabling criminals to "rummage" through secret files. Unless Congress immediately nullified the deci-sion, he declared, "those intelligence agencies of our government engaged in law enforcement might as well close up shop."

Attorney General Brownell quickly proposed legislation that would reverse the Jencks deci-sion. Within weeks, the full Senate approved a supposed *Jencks*-killer by a voice vote; the House version sailed past a mere seventeen dissenters. Yet the ultimate bill, signed into law by President Eisenhower, did not reverse *Jencks* but simply restricted pre-trial discovery to relevant prosecu-tion documents without upsetting the basic *Jencks* rule.

In June 1957, the Court released other deci-sions that fanned the political flames. In *Roth* v. *United States*, for example, the Court affirmed that obscene material was not protected by the First Amendment and took its first cut at the tedi-ous chore of trying to define what is or isn't obscene. *Roth* displeased critics of all hues, but worse, it generated simple-minded ridicule that

228

tended to undermine the Court on more serious fronts. Obscenity soon proved to be among the most thankless subjects the Justices had ever confronted.

On the same day it announced *Roth*, the Court released a due-process ruling that provoked a much fiercer storm. *Mallory* v. *United States* (1957) dealt with federal police and the age-old problem of coerced confessions, this time in a rape case from the nation's increasingly black capital city, where the mounting crime rate had worsened racial tensions.

In *Mallory*, Justice Frankfurter spoke for a unanimous Court in reaffirming the federal rule (not then binding on the states) that an arrested person must be taken promptly before a magistrate who decides whether the police have sufficient evidence to charge him. Designed to "avoid all the evil implications of secret interrogation," Frankfurter wrote, the rule codified the constitutional guarantees against arbitrary arrest and self-incrimination. Most important, it flatly barred the use of confessions elicited during unlawful detentions.

Mallory specifically nullified the death sentence imposed on a young Washington black of limited intelligence, who had confessed to rape after being questioned, without notice of his rights, for more than eighteen hours between his arrest and arraignment. Upholding what he had earlier called "civilized standards of procedure and evidence," Frankfurter condemned "unwarranted detention" as an invitation to impatient police to force suspects to confess to crimes they might or might not have committed. The judicial purpose of determining the truth about a crime was hardly served when a man "confessed" simply to end mental or physical pain.

But the anti-Court forces persisted. On August 23, 1958, the legally prestigious Conference of Chief Justices of the states professed its "greatest concern" over what the state judges perceived as the Supreme Court's quarter-century tendency to expand federal power and "adopt the role of policy maker without proper judicial restraint."

Undaunted by such comments, many of them linked to Southern resistance to *Brown*, the Court met in rare special session on August 28, 1958, setting the stage for a landmark assertion of federal judicial power. In *Cooper* v. *Aaron*, the full Court defended the constitutional scheme as uncompromisingly as Chief Justice Marshall had in *Marbury* v. *Madison*.

Cooper arose in Little Rock, Arkansas, where Governor Orval Faubus and other segregationists had pressured the school board so mercilessly that it finally sought and received the local federal court's permission to withdraw the black students at Central High School and postpone further desegregation for two and a half years. An appeals court reversed that decision. On September 12, a day after hearing arguments on the matter, the Supreme Court issued an unsigned *per curiam* order affirming the reversal; a week later came a formal opinion sharply censuring Faubus and the Arkansas legislature for sabotaging desegregation.

Although the school board had acted in good faith, the Court said, "the constitutional rights of [black] respondents are not to be sacrificed or yielded to the violence and disorder which have followed upon the actions of the Governor and the Legislature." Those gentlemen were reminded that the Fourteenth Amendment specifically forbids state officials to deny any person equal protection of the laws. Said the Court: "No state legislator or executive or judicial officer can war against the Constitution without violating his undertaking to support it."

As to the validity of its ruling that the Fourteenth Amendment outlawed school segregation, the Court declared:

> . . . . The basic decision in *Brown* was unanimously reached by this Court only after the case had been briefed and twice argued and the issues had been given the most serious consideration. Since the first *Brown* opinion three new Justices have come to the Court. They are at one with the Justices still on the Court who participated in that basic decision as to its correctness, and that decision is now unanimously reaffirmed. The principles announced in that decision and the obedience of the States to them . . . are indispensable for the protection of the freedoms guaranteed by our fundamental charter for all of us. Our Constitutional ideal of equal justice under law is thus made a living truth.

Each of the nine Justices signed *Cooper* v.

The Warren Court in 1962. Standing, from left: Associate Justices Potter Stewart, John Marshall Harlan, William Joseph Brennan, Jr., Byron Raymond White. Seated, from left: Associate Justices William Orville Douglas, Hugo Lafayette Black, Chief Justice Earl Warren, Associate Justices Felix Frankfurter, Tom Campbell Clark. Photograph Harris and Ewing. Collection of the Supreme Court of the United States, Washington, D.C.

Aaron, an unprecedented gesture stressing their unanimous condemnation of official violence in Arkansas.

B*rown* shaped the judicial history of the 1960s. Going beyond public schools, the Justices outlawed de jure segregation in all sorts of public facilities, including beaches, courts, buses, jails, parks, and swimming pools. Even privately owned lunch counters were found guilty of state-enforced discrimination, as in *Peterson* v. *City of Greenville* (1963).

Such decrees merely suggested the Court's potential as an instrument of social and political change by its reading of the Constitution. The Warren Court appeared willing to uproot large areas of the legal status quo previously considered immutable.

Until 1964, for example, the First Amendment did not protect libel. In all but a handful of states, as in English common law, the publication of false and defamatory statements of fact invariably entitled the alleged victim to a damage award, whether he was a private person or a pub-

lic figure. For the press, the only sure defense was error-free truth, a burden of proof that perhaps instilled journalistic timidity and encouraged self-censorship.

In *New York Times Co.* v. *Sullivan* (1964), the Court fundamentally changed the law of libel as it affected public officials. At issue was an advertisement entitled "Heed Their Rising Voices" that four black clergymen had placed in the nation's leading newspaper on March 29, 1960. Aimed at soliciting funds for Southern civil rights workers, the text recited various acts of official violence in Montgomery, Alabama, and though it did not mention that city's police commissioner, L. B. Sullivan, he professed himself defamed, by association. Having also spotted six factual errors Sullivan sued for damages under Alabama libel law and won a $500,000 verdict. His victory spurred other white Alabamians to sue the *Times* for alleged damages totaling $5,600,000.

Four years later, speaking for a unanimous Court, Justice William J. Brennan, Jr., threw out the verdict against the *Times* and with it nearly two centuries of legal precedents and presumptions. "We consider this case," Brennan wrote, "against the background of a profound national commitment to the principle that debate on public issues should be uninhibited, robust, and wide-open, and that it may well include vehement, caustic, and sometimes unpleasantly sharp attacks on government and public officials."

Given that principle, Brennan said, the press needed more leeway to perform effectively for the common good. Accordingly, *Times* v. *Sullivan* held that the First Amendment "prohibits a public official from recovering damages for a defamatory falsehood relating to his official conduct unless he proves that the statement was made with 'actual malice'—that is, with knowledge that it was false or with reckless disregard for whether it was false or not."

In *Dombrowski* v. *Pfister* (1965), the Court sustained another race-related challenge to an old doctrine that had previously seemed as indestructible as the supposed lawlessness of libel.

Until then, federal judges had deferred to federalism by rarely exercising their power to enjoin allegedly unconstitutional state laws or proceedings. Called "abstention," this rule was enshrined in federal law going back to 1793, so that federal courts generally stayed out of local criminal-law matters, leaving state courts to go as far as they could in resolving any constitutional issues.

In 1963 Louisiana police went after the Southern Conference Educational Fund by arresting the civil-rights group's leaders, including executive director Joseph A. Dombrowski, and charging them with violating state laws against Communist subversion and propaganda. The charges were dropped, but the police kept threatening further prosecution.

Dombrowski refused either to flee or tolerate intimidation. He sought an immediate federal injunction against the harassment, and because of the abstention doctrine, he lost.

The Court disagreed. By a vote of six to two, they held that Dombrowski's First Amendment rights were being violated by state laws and actions that produced "a chilling effect on free expression." Sustaining the federal injunction, Justice Brennan ruled that abstention was not necessary when state laws were "justifiably attacked on their face as abridging free expression or as applied for the purpose of discouraging protected activities."

The biggest *Brown* fallout affecting federal courts was the enormous complexity of not only enforcing desegregation, but of defining precisely what it meant and how far federal judges must go to achieve it. The Court faced the implications of the legendary remark attributed to Andrew Jackson: "John Marshall has made his decision; now let him enforce it."

While guaranteeing "equal protection of the laws," the Fourteenth Amendment had never required states to treat everybody alike. They could always classify people according to homogeneous groups (doctors, farmers, etc.) for purposes of licensing or regulation. But the *Brown* decision and others virtually outlawed all racial classifications. According to *McLaughlin* v. *Florida* (1964), for example, racial groupings were now deemed "in most circumstances irrelevant to any constitutionally acceptable purpose."

While the nation continued to struggle with the stubborn realities of desegregation, the Supreme Court unexpectedly plunged into yet another area of constitutional controversy that teemed with "what-next" questions.

Malapportionment: an ugly word for an ugly blight upon the democratic process. In state after state, the most populous areas had become the political supplicants of the least populous areas. If one-fifth of all Floridians lived in Dade County (Miami), and the state legislature had 133 members, democratic arithmetic would suggest that roughly twenty-seven (one-fifth) of those legislators represented Miami. But not so: only four did. Or consider Los Angeles County, which in 1960 contained thirty-eight percent of California's entire population but was entitled to elect only one of California's forty state senators.

In *Gomillion* v. *Lightfoot* (1960), Justice Frankfurter spoke for all nine Justices in outlawing racial gerrymandering. Gerrymandering, an old technique of drawing election district boundaries to favor the political party in power, was being used to minimize or exclude black voting strength. At issue in *Gomillion* was an Alabama law recarving the city limits of Tuskegee from a square to a twenty-eight-sided figure that banished virtually every black voter from the rolls.

C.C. Gomillion, a professor at Tuskegee Institute, argued for himself and other blacks that such unequal protection of the laws could hardly

not "justiciable" (fit for judicial settlement); it was a political matter to be resolved politically.

In 1962 the city-dwelling voters of Tennessee nudged the Supreme Court a giant step forward into the political thicket. In *Baker* v. *Carr*, the Justices pondered not the merits of the case, but whether federal courts should hear it in the first place. Six Justices held that apportionment was *not* a "political question" which would foreclose the Court's attention. Speaking through Justice Brennan, they reasoned that a case involving fundamental fairness, arising under the Equal Protection Clause and brought by litigants with standing to sue, presented a "justiciable controversy" for the federal courts to decide, not a political question for them to avoid. Said Brennan: "The mere fact that the suit seeks protection of a political right does not mean it presents a political question."

Frankfurter's dissent, his last major opinion, decried the majority's "massive repudiation of the experience of our whole past in asserting destructively novel judicial power." He insisted judges were incapable of "accommodating the incommensurable factors of policy" that reapportionment would require. Frankfurter concluded that, "there is not under our Constitution a judicial remedy for every political mischief, for every undesirable exercise of legislative power."

Within two years of *Baker* v. *Carr*'s green light, reapportionment suits were underway in forty-one states. In 1963, the Court outlawed Georgia's "county unit" system of electing state officials on the ground that it violated the Fourteenth Amendment, favoring rural voters at the expense of city dwellers (*Gray* v. *Sanders*). With only Harlan dissenting, eight Justices invoked the Equal Protection Clause in holding that all votes in a statewide election must carry equal weight.

Gray was the case in which the Court, speaking through Justice Douglas, asserted that once the geographical unit for political representation was chosen, all voters within that unit must have an equal vote, whatever their race, sex, income, etc. From the Declaration of Independence to the Nineteenth Amendment, Douglas asserted, "the [American] conception of political equality . . . can mean only one thing—one person, one vote."

Justice Harlan protested that the one person/

Justice Frankfurter. Collection of the Supreme Court of the United States, Washington, D.C.

coexist with the Fourteenth Amendment.

Justice Frankfurter rejected that logic, as he had previously done in *Colegrove* v. *Green*, a 1946 case in which he had emphatically warned the Court to shun the "political thicket" of reapportionment. Accordingly, Frankfurter now demonstrated his skill in making distinctions.

In *Colegrove*, he recalled, the appellants had basically complained only about state "legislative inertia," which the Fourteenth Amendment (in his view) did not require federal courts to redress. In *Gomillion*, however, the gerrymander resulted from "affirmative legislative action" denying a federally protected right. Ergo, Alabama had violated the Fifteenth Amendment granting suffrage for black citizens. According to Frankfurter, malapportionment itself remained immune to the Equal Protection Clause. It was

one vote principle "flies in the face of history," having never been universally accepted in either Britain or America. He insisted, as he had in *Baker,* that nothing in the Constitution prevented any state from choosing any rational apportionment system it thought "best suited to the interests, temper, and customs of its people."

A year later, in *Wesberry* v. *Sanders* (1964), the Court held by a six-to-three decision that equality must be the standard for states in redrawing their congressional districts. *Wesberry* was based not on the Fourteenth Amendment's equality clause, but on Article I's command (Section 2) that members of the House of Representatives shall be "chosen . . . by the People of the several States." In these words, the court majority discerned an "equal representation" standard (one man, one vote) that Justice Harlan decried as "manufactured out of whole cloth."

Four months later, on June 15, 1964, Harlan was again the sole dissenter as Chief Justice Warren spoke for the Court in *Reynolds* v. *Sims,* the landmark ruling that both houses of bicameral state legislatures must be elected from districts with "substantially equal" populations. *Reynolds* specifically remedied the Alabama legislature's failure to reapportion itself for the past sixty years. But it simultaneously resolved five other cases affecting reapportionment in Colorado, Delaware, New York, Maryland, and Virginia. In time, *Reynolds* reshaped the legislatures of all fifty states.

"Legislators represent people, not trees or acres," Warren wrote. "Legislators are elected by voters, not farms or cities or economic interests. As long as ours is a representative form of government, and our legislatures are those instruments of government elected directly by and directly representative of the people, the right to elect legislators in a free and unimpaired fashion is a bedrock of our political system. . . ."

". . . . The fact that an individual lives here or there is not a legitimate reason for overweighting or diluting the efficacy of his vote. The complexions of societies and civilizations change, often with amazing rapidity. A nation once primarily rural in character becomes predominantly urban. Representation schemes once fair and equitable become archaic and outdated. But the basic principle of representative government remains, and must remain, unchanged—the weight of a citizen's vote cannot be made to depend on where he lives. Population is, of necessity, the starting point for consideration and the controlling criterion for judgment in legislative apportionment controversies. A citizen, qualified voter, is not more nor less so because he lives in the city or on the farm. This is the clear and strong command of our Constitution's Equal Protection Clause. This is an essential part of the concept of a government of laws and not men. . . ."

Justice Harlan disagreed.

In his solitary dissent, Harlan dismissed the majority's entire constitutional premise. Citing extensive historical sources, he declared, "The Equal Protection Clause was never intended to inhibit the states in choosing any democratic method they pleased for the apportionment of their legislatures." Such methods were traditionally responsive to each area's particular interests, he said. They enabled legislatures to fairly represent farmers, ethnic groups, sparsely settled counties, etc. Such was republican government. By outlawing all of this, Harlan said, the Court had impermissibly amended the Constitution and effectively placed the very heart of state politics "under the pervasive overlordship of the federal judiciary."

Calling such intervention "profoundly ill advised" as well as unconstitutional, Harlan warned that judges were unequipped to function as governors. "The cold truth [is] that cases of this type are not amenable to judicial standards." Harlan further asserted that the reapportionment decisions would sap the vitality of the political system and "cut deeply into the fabric of our federalism."

Harlan said the rulings encouraged "a current mistaken view of the Constitution and the constitutional function of this Court. This view, in a nutshell, is that every major social ill in this country can find its cure in some constitutional 'principle,' and that this Court should 'take the lead' in promoting reform when other branches of government fail to act. The Constitution is not a panacea for every blot upon the public welfare, nor should this Court, ordained as a judicial body, be thought of as a haven for reform movements."

In 1969 the Court dealt again with congressional districts, ordering the states to draw their boundaries "as nearly as practicable" to conform with strictly equal units of population. In that decision (*Kirkpatrick* v. *Preisler*), the Court split six to three, Byron R. White and Potter Stewart having joined Harlan in dissent because of their concern about the judiciary's deepening involvement in what White called "the abrasive task of drawing district lines." Said Harlan: "Strait indeed is the path of the righteous legislator. Slide rule in hand, he must avoid all thought of county lines, local traditions, politics, history, and economics, so as to achieve the magic formula: one man, one vote."

In point of fact, the nation's congressional districts were soon making significant progress toward population equality. Of 435 House members elected in 1972, for example, 385 represented districts whose populations varied less than one percent from their state's average congressional district population.

Even so, Justice Harlan was prescient in asserting that "the rule of absolute equality is perfectly compatible with 'gerrymandering' of the worst sort." Thanks to computers, the party in power can draw boundaries favorable to itself without violating the rules of population equality.

The Supreme Court has been more flexible in state legislative apportionment cases. In a series of 1973 decisions, notably *Mahan* v. *Howell*, the Court's new conservative majority held that neither the Fourteenth Amendment nor *Reynolds* v. *Sims* required mathematical exactness in state legislative boundaries. The Court permitted deviations from population equality of ten percent or less. Larger variances were held to create prima facie cases of discrimination, requiring state justification. This could be achieved when a disputed apportionment plan was shown to advance a "rational state policy," such as respecting political subdivisions, or preserving minority-group voting strength.

Mahan held that a sixteen percent deviation from population equality "may well approach tolerable limits." But ten years later the Court ruled in *Brown* v. *Thomson* (1983) that a deviation of eighty-nine percent was permissible. In *Brown*, Wyoming had allocated one of its sixty-four state representatives to its least populated county in order to preserve the county's boundaries and avoid combining it with another county. The Court approved this purpose.

In the aftermath of John F. Kennedy's assassination, Congress responded to Lyndon Johnson's pleas and passed the Civil Rights Act of 1964, the Voting Rights Act of 1965, and the Fair Housing Act of 1968. The Warren Court reinforced Congress, promptly declaring the new laws constitutional.

In *Heart of Atlanta Motel* v. *United States* (1964), all nine Justices upheld provisions of the 1964 law barring racial discrimination in privately owned public accommodations, such as hotels and restaurants, that had any link to interstate commerce. The law had been challenged by a motel owner in downtown Atlanta who refused to receive blacks. He said Congress had overstepped its commerce power and also violated what he considered his Fifth Amendment right to choose his own customers. But the Court, speaking through Justice Clark, anchored the law firmly in the commerce power, holding that discrimination against black travelers was not only morally wrong but commercially harmful, a burden on interstate business. As to the owner's property rights, Clark noted that the Court had long ago "rejected the claim that the prohibition of racial discrimination in public accommodations interferes with personal liberties."

The 1965 Voting Rights Act suspended literacy tests in all areas where less than half the potential voters were registered. This rule was quickly challenged as a violation of every state's right to regulate its own elections. But in *South Carolina* v. *Katzenbach* (1966), with only Justice Black dissenting in part, the Court upheld the law as a valid exercise of Congress's power to enforce the Fifteenth Amendment, which banned racial discrimination in voting. Speaking for the Court, Chief Justice Warren dismissed fears that ignorance would now invade the voting booth. He said Congress had simply concluded that "states and political subdivisions which had been allowing white illiterates to vote for years could not sincerely complain about 'dilution' of their electorates through the registration of Negro illiterates."

At issue in *Loving* v. *Virginia* (1967), was the determination of two Virginians, one black and one white, to marry one another despite Virginia's antimiscegenation law. When they reached the Supreme Court, the *Loving* couple won by a unanimous decision which held that all state laws banning racial intermarriage violated the Equal Protection Clause. "Under our Constitution," wrote chief Justice Warren, "the freedom to marry or not to marry a person of another race resides with the individual and cannot be infringed by the State."

Soon after Congress passed the 1968 Fair Housing Act, the first federal law banning any form of discrimination (not just racial) in housing, the Court indirectly reinforced it in a decision written by Justice Potter Stewart. Called *Jones* v. *Alfred H. Mayer Co.*, the case arose from the refusal of a St. Louis developer to sell a suburban house to Joseph Lee Jones solely because he was black. With the federal open-housing law not yet in force, Jones had sued Mayer under the 1866 Civil Rights Act, now on the federal books as Sections 1981 and 1982 of the U.S. Code, Title 42. Jones cited Section 1982, which reads: "All citizens of the United States shall have the same right in every State . . . as is enjoyed by white citizens thereof to inherit, purchase, lease, sell, hold and convey real and personal property."

Jones lost in the lower courts: they insisted that Section 1982 barred only prejudicial state action, not *private* racial discrimination.

In his 1968 *Jones* opinion, Justice Stewart spoke for a seven-man majority. In Stewart's view, the legislative history of the 1866 act clearly showed the drafters' intent to erase all racial discrimination, private as well as public, with respect to certain key rights. Cited in the 1866 law, they were every citizen's right "to make and enforce contracts, to sue, be parties, and give evidence, to inherit, purchase, lease, sell, hold, and convey real and personal property . . . any law, statute, ordinance, regulation, or custom, to the contrary notwithstanding." By including "custom," Stewart held, Congress plainly meant to secure the enumerated rights "from any source whatever, whether governmental or private."

Stewart ruled the 1866 law a valid enforcement of the Thirteenth Amendment, which fully empowered Congress to define and eradicate "the badges and incidents of slavery," such as racial discrimination that "herds men into ghettos and makes their ability to buy property turn on the color of their skin." At the very least, Stewart wrote, "the freedom that Congress is empowered to secure under the Thirteenth Amendment includes the freedom to buy whatever a white man can buy, the right to live wherever a white man can live. If Congress cannot say that being a free man means at least this much, then the Thirteenth Amendment made a promise the Nation cannot keep."

Eight years after *Jones* v. *Mayer*, the Court had occasion to construe that portion of the 1866 act banning discrimination that infringes upon every citizen's right to "make and enforce contracts." At issue in *Runyon* v. *McCrary* (1976) was whether a private school open to all white students could exclude other children simply because they were black. Speaking for the Court again, Justice Stewart held that such exclusion would be valid only if the private school were truly private (like a club) and closed to the general public. In this case, the 1866 law entitled the black applicants to sign a school contract, because that right was open to any white applicant.

When Congress passed the 1964 Civil Rights Act, invoking its long neglected power to enforce the Civil War Amendments, the Supreme Court broke a long silence on the subject of Southern public schools.

In its first major school decision since 1954, the Court rebuked a Virginia county for defying a desegregation order by closing its public schools and using public funds to operate private schools for whites, leaving black children without schools. Speaking for the Court in *Griffin* v. *County School Board of Prince Edward County* (1964), Justice Black denounced the county's delaying tactics and declared, "There has been entirely too much deliberation and not enough speed." A 1965 decision involving Richmond, Virginia, was even more emphatic. In an unsigned opinion, the Court warned, "Delays in desegregating public school systems are no longer tolerable."

In May 1968 the Justices unanimously shifted from a position of simply forbidding racial segregation to one of requiring actual integration. This inevitable step arose from an impasse in Virginia's rural New Kent County. Although black and white families were interspersed throughout New Kent County, its two schools had always been segregated—one black, one white. Ordered to desegregate, the school board had adopted a "freedom of choice" plan, allowing every child to attend whichever school he wished. After three years, no white child had chosen the black school and only fifteen percent of the black children had enrolled in the white school.

Speaking for the Court in *Green* v. *County School Board of New Kent County* (1968), Justice Brennan ruled that freedom of choice obviously reinforced dual school systems. The Court limited the county's freedom of choice to a new system "without a 'white school' and a 'Negro school,' but just schools." Said Brennan: "The burden on a school board today is to come forward with a plan that promises realistically to work, and promises realistically to work *now*."

Despite Brennan's urgent tone in *Green*, the Court refrained from specifying any ideal integration plan. The Justices hoped that it was necessary only to state the objective, leaving school boards free to carry it out by whatever methods were best suited to each community's particular needs.

In the first six decades of the Fourteenth Amendment's history, majority Justices perceived "due process" mainly in terms of protecting property rather than life or liberty. In *Hurtado* v. *California* (1884), for example, the Court sustained a state murder conviction even though the defendant had never been indicted. The Justices held that the Due Process Clause did not require states to honor the Fifth Amendment, which bans capital charges "unless on a presentment or indictment of a grand jury."

In *Twining* v. *New Jersey* (1908), the Justices agreed with New Jersey's supreme court that a trial judge had not violated a defendant's rights by stressing to the jury that he had failed to testify in his own behalf, implying that his silence was an admission of guilt. The Court held that the Fourteenth Amendment had not granted state defendants the Fifth Amendment privilege against being compelled to be a witness against oneself, or any other provisions of the Bill of Rights. "If the people of New Jersey are not content with the law as declared in repeated decisions of their courts," wrote Justice William Moody, "the remedy is in their own hands."

In *Moore* v. *Dempsey* (1923), however, an Arkansas mob had invaded a courtroom where five black men were on trial for murder. Within fifty minutes, the entire trial was over and the jury had voted for death. The mob was in charge; acquittal would have ignited a lynching. This travesty was duly upheld by Arkansas's supreme court—but not by the United States Supreme Court, where Justice Holmes sternly declared that state due process included the Sixth Amendment right to a fair trial.

All this took years. The Court's next use of the Due Process Clause to void a state conviction did not occur until 1932. In *Powell* v. *Alabama,* the Justices forbade Alabama to execute the "Scottsboro Boys" because the five illiterate young blacks, accused of raping two white girls, had been denied effective counsel. Reading part of the Sixth Amendment into the Fourteenth, the Justices ruled that in state capital crime cases, due process included the right to counsel, just as it did for federal defendants. A second Scottsboro Case three years later held that Alabama's exclusion of blacks from jury duty had denied the defendant's due-process right to trial by a fairly chosen jury.

In 1936 the Justices ordered state courts to exclude confessions extorted by torture. In *Brown* v. *Mississippi*, sheriff's deputies aided by a mob had strung up, whipped, and nearly strangled five black suspects until they gasped out "voluntary" confessions. The Justices unanimously condemned this "revolting" procedure as a denial of due process of law. *Brown* was the first of the Court's thirty-six major confession decisions over the next twenty-five years.

In *Palko* v. *Connecticut* (1937), Justice Cardozo devised the "fundamental fairness" standard. Tried twice for the same murder, Palko had naturally invoked the Fifth Amendment guarantee against double jeopardy. But the Fifth Amendment didn't apply to state defendants, Cardozo said. What did apply was the Fourteenth Amendment's Due Process Clause. And when did state action violate due process? Cardozo announced a new test: Had Palko's obvious double jeopardy constituted "a hardship so acute and shocking that our polity will not endure it?" Had it violated "those fundamental principles of liberty and justice which lie at the base of all our civil and political institutions?" For Palko, a man sentenced first to life and then to death, Cardozo ruled, "the answer must surely be 'no.'"

To insure the voluntariness of confessions, the Court spent almost twenty years seeking a more objective due-process standard than "fundamental fairness." In 1943, the Justices tried a new approach in federal criminal procedure that Frankfurter, for one, hoped the states would emulate. In *McNabb* v. *United States,* the murder of a federal revenue agent had led to the arrest of several suspects, who were questioned steadily for three days in the absence of any defense counsel, as a result of which they confessed. Only then were they taken before a magistrate and charged with the crime.

Speaking for the Court, Frankfurter ruled their confessions inadmissible not on the Fifth Amendment ground that they were coerced, but because the interrogators had violated a federal statute requiring prompt arraignment. As supervisor of federal courts, Frankfurter said, the Supreme Court was obliged to uphold "civilized standards of procedure and evidence." He then declared that the purpose of the arraignment law was to stamp out "those reprehensible practices known as the 'third degree.'" In federal criminal cases, *McNabb* held, any confession obtained during prolonged detention in violation of the statute was automatically inadmissible, even if it was voluntary.

Fourteen years passed. In *Mallory* v. *United States* (1957), Frankfurter reaffirmed for a unanimous Court that any confession obtained during "unwarranted detention" (extent not specified) between a federal suspect's arrest and his arraignment was ipso facto useless as evidence against him. But the *McNabb-Mallory* Rule was limited to federal cases and did not work well in practice. Moreover, it did nothing to solve the problem of coerced confessions at the state level.

To govern state confession cases, the Court eventually turned to the famous Exclusionary Rule, which the Court had established years before to make federal agents obey the Fourth Amendment ban on "unreasonable" searches.

That rule was rooted in *Boyd* v. *United States* (1886), the Court's first major interpretation of the Fourth Amendment. Boyd had been a glass manufacturer accused of cheating on a federal contract. At his trial, the judge ordered him to produce his private records, which were then used to convict him. In reversing his conviction, Justice Joseph Bradley observed that "the Fourth and Fifth Amendments run almost into each other," meaning that unreasonable searches were, among other things, those violating the privilege against self-incrimination.

In *Weeks* v. *United States* (1914), reversing a conviction based on a warrantless arrest and search, Justice William R. Day decried "the tendency of those who execute the criminal laws of the country to obtain convictions by means of unlawful seizures and enforced confessions." State courts should repudiate such practices, he said. Federal courts absolutely must. Accordingly, the Exclusionary Rule obliged federal trial judges to exclude any evidence, however incriminating, that a defendant could show had been seized in violation of his federally protected right to be secure from unreasonable searches and seizures. In practice, the rule meant that federal agents normally did their best to avoid warrantless searches and instead used valid judge-signed warrants that would protect their evidence in court.

By 1949 only about a third of the states had adopted the Exclusionary Rule on their own initiative. In *Wolf* v. *Colorado,* Justice Frankfurter tried to warn all states to follow suit. The appellant, Dr. Julius A. Wolf, had been convicted by a Colorado court of conspiracy to commit abortion on the basis of a diary the police had seized from his office without a search warrant. Frankfurter's opinion began with an announcement that the moment had finally arrived for the Court to impose the Fourth Amendment upon the states. The values it protected, notably "the security of one's privacy against intrusion by the police," were so basic to "the concept of ordered liberty" that they were now to be considered part of the Due Process Clause of the state-binding Fourteenth Amendment.

Paradoxically, Frankfurter added that the Exclusionary Rule itself was *not* binding on the states. That was because the rule had been established by judges, not commanded by the Constitution.

Over the next dozen years, *Wolf* produced mixed results. In *Rochin* v. *California* (1952), Antonio Rochin had been convicted for possessing narcotics. Three deputy sheriffs had broken into his bedroom without a warrant. He gulped down three capsules. They rushed him to a hospital and forced him to vomit up the evidence that jailed him. Justice Frankfurter wrote the Court's unanimous opinion reversing Rochin's conviction owing to police "conduct that shocks the conscience." In *Irvine* v. *California* (1954), Patrick Irvine had been convicted for bookmaking through illegal evidence derived from warrantless bugging. Four Justices thought *Wolf* required them to sustain the conviction; four others thought *Rochin* mandated reversal. Tom Clark, the ninth Justice, broke the tie and voted for upholding the conviction.

Speaking for the Court in *Irvine*, Justice Jackson hinted that hold-out states should adopt the federal rule soon, or the tolerant *Wolf* decision might be overruled. That is exactly what happened in 1961. The hold-out state of Ohio, provided the opportunity in the case of Dollree Mapp, an outraged black woman whose Cleveland home had been invaded by seven policemen allegedly tracking a bombing suspect.

When the officers first appeared at her door, Mapp phoned a lawyer and took his advice to keep the door locked unless her visitors produced a search warrant. The police broke the lock and rushed in waving a "warrant." When Mapp grabbed this piece of paper, they snatched it back, twisted her arm, and locked her in handcuffs because she had been "belligerent" in trying to see the so-called warrant. The police then rifled the entire two-story house from attic to basement, where by chance they found a suitcase containing a former boarder's memorabilia— "four little pamphlets, a couple of photographs and a little pencil doodle."

Dollree Mapp was promptly charged with what Ohio considered the crime of possessing these items, described as "certain lewd and lascivious books, pictures, and photographs." Mapp appealed to the Ohio supreme court. She lost: the court ruled that the evidence was admissible even though "unlawfully seized during an unlawful search of defendant's home." The reason the police conduct didn't matter, the state judges explained, was that *Wolf* said it didn't.

In appealing next to the Supreme Court of the United States, Dollree Mapp enabled the Justices to consider a far larger question. Was *Mapp* v. *Ohio* the right case to extend the Exclusionary Rule to the States?

Four Justices including Clark, voted "yes." Four voted "no." Hugo Black, the ninth and senior Justice, voted "yes."

With Black's fifth vote, the narrowly divided Court issued a landmark opinion written by Jus-

tice Clark that brought all American law enforcers, state as well as federal, under the clear Exclusionary Rule. Those in favor particularly applauded Clark's reminder in *Mapp*: "Nothing can destroy a government more quickly than its failure to observe its own laws, or worse, its disregard of the character of its own existence."

The Court now began a rapid expansion, right by right, of nearly all the Bill of Rights safeguards to the states. To the First Amendment (in 1952) and the Fourth (in 1949), the Court added the Eighth's ban on "cruel and unusual punishment" in 1962 (*Robinson* v. *California*), and the Sixth's right to "the assistance of counsel" in 1963 (*Gideon* v. *Wainwright*). By 1969 every significant provision of the first Eight Amendments had been applied to all state as well as federal actions.

The famous 1963 Gideon case involved a penniless Florida drifter arrested for breaking into a poolroom and pilfering some cash and cigarettes. Clarence Gideon had pleaded not guilty and requested a court-appointed lawyer. The trial judge refused, noting that only in capital crimes cases were indigents then entitled to that right (*Powell* v. *Alabama*). Sentenced to five years in a Florida prison, Gideon had mailed a handwritten petition to the Supreme Court seeking his release.

By requiring states to honor the Sixth Amendment right to counsel, *Gideon* v. *Wainwright* set an objective standard. All indigents now received counsel in felony cases; those denied lawyers would be absolved, period. A similar rule thus became feasible for confession cases. With *Gideon* added to *Mapp*, even suspects not yet formally accused might be entitled to lawyers, and if so, then a confession extracted in the absence of a lawyer might be nullified by the Exclusionary Rule.

In May 1964, *Massiah* v. *United States* moved the right of counsel back to the pretrial stage of indictment. A month later, *Malloy* v. *Hogan* made the Fifth Amendment privilege against self-incrimination binding on states, thereby overruling the *Twining* and *Adamson* decisions of 1908 and 1947, which had said the privilege was *not* part of the Due Process Clause.

A week later, the Court held in *Escobedo* v. *Illinois* that because criminal prosecutions actually began with police questioning, so must the right

Card used by police in San Francisco to alert arrested persons of their rights as required by the Court in *Miranda* v. *Arizona*. UPI/Bettmann Archive, New York

In forma pauperis petition filed by Clarence Earl Gideon. National Archives, Washington, D.C.

to counsel. To bar legal aid at that point, wrote Justice Arthur J. Goldberg for the five-man majority, "would make the trial no more than an appeal from the interrogation."

Illinois law guaranteed a suspect's right to counsel. But although a young Chicago murder suspect named Danny Escobedo had a lawyer, the police had barred him throughout the long interrogation. At trial, Escobedo recanted his statement, but the judge ruled it voluntary and handed him a twenty-year sentence.

In voiding Escobedo's confession, Justice Goldberg reasoned that the Sixth Amendment right to counsel, amplified by *Gideon,* would be meaningless, if suspects were furnished lawyers only *after* the police induced them to make incriminating statements.

"We hold only," Goldberg wrote, "that when the process shifts from investigatory to accusatory—when its focus is on the accused and its purpose is to elicit a confession—our adversary system begins to operate, and under the circumstances here, the accused must be permitted to consult his lawyer . . ."

"A system of law enforcement which comes to depend on the confession, will in the long run, be less reliable than a system which depends on extrinsic evidence independently secured through skillful investigation. If the exercise of constitutional rights will thwart a system of law enforcement, then there is something very wrong with that system."

As it turned out, *Escobedo* raised more questions than it answered, thus generating a flurry of conflicting appellate court decisions that required swift clarification. Accordingly, the Supreme Court sifted 170 more confession cases and accepted four that embodied the key issues at stake. Headed by *Miranda* v. *Arizona,* the cases posed three major questions left unresolved by *Escobedo.* Did a suspect's new right to counsel include a right to be *warned* that he could have a lawyer? Were indigent suspects entitled to *appointed* counsel? When and how could a suspect *waive* these rights?

In none of the four cases before the Supreme Court was there evidence of blatant coercion, physical or mental, nor did the appellants claim that their confessions were inadmissible in the traditional due process sense. What they all had in common was that they had talked while in police custody, without access to legal help and in three cases without knowledge of their rights. Although they had been interrogated for periods ranging from two hours to five days, the issue was no longer whether specific pressures had so overcome a specific person's will that his confession must be deemed involuntary. The question now before the Court was a more fundamental one. Should incommunicado police questioning by itself be considered so inherently coercive that *any* suspect's answers were per se involuntary and hence inadmissible?

Chief Justice Warren announced the Court's five-to-four *Miranda* decision on June 13, 1966:

> . . . the prosecution may not use statements, whether exculpatory or inculpatory, stemming from custodial interrogation of the defendant unless it demonstrates the use of procedural safeguards effective to secure the privilege against self-incrimination. By custodial interrogation, we mean questioning by law enforcement officers after a person has been taken into custody or otherwise deprived of his freedom of action in any significant way. . . . Prior to any questioning, the person must be warned that he has a right to remain silent, that any statement he does make may be used as evidence against him, and that he has a right to the presence of an attorney, either retained or appointed. The defendant may waive effectuation of these rights, provided the waiver is made voluntarily, knowingly and intelligently. If, however, he indicates in any manner and at any stage of the process, that he wishes to consult with an attorney before speaking there can be no questioning. Likewise, if the individual is alone and indicates in any manner that he does not wish to be interrogated, the police may not question him. . . .

Escobedo had moved the Sixth Amendment right to counsel from the courtroom to the "critical" state of police questioning. *Miranda*, with greater clarity, had armored the suspect with the Fifth Amendment privilege against self-incrimination. Now the suspect need only tell the police at any moment that he wished to remain silent, and all interrogation must cease. Once he invoked his Fifth Amendment privilege, Warren ruled, any further statement extracted from the suspect "cannot be other than the product of compulsion, subtle or otherwise."

The *Miranda* decision initially disturbed many Americans concerned about rising crime.

Attacks on the Warren Court during the 1960s were also fueled by the Justices' rulings on religious exercises in tax-supported public schools.

The First Amendment is explicit: "Congress shall make no law respecting an establishment of religion . . ." At issue in *Engel* v. *Vitale* (1962) was whether this Establishment Clause forbade the New York State Board of Regents to recommend daily readings of a nondenominational prayer in the state's public schools. To be repeated by students voluntarily, the brief prayer read: "Almighty God, we acknowledge our dependence upon Thee, and we beg Thy blessings upon us, our parents, our teachers and our country."

The parents of ten students in Hyde Park, New York sued to halt the prayer readings, arguing that their children were being forced to participate in "official religion" that violated the Establishment Clause and their own religious beliefs. Voting six to one, the Justices agreed, ruling that even a supposedly voluntary prayer brought "indirect coercive pressure upon religious minorities to conform to the prevailing officially approved religion . . ."

A year later in *School District of Abington Township* v. *Schemp* (1963), the Court struck down a Pennsylvania law requiring all public school children to participate in the daily reading of at least ten verses of the Bible, followed by recitation of the Lord's Prayer and the pledge to the flag. By a vote of eight to one, the Court ruled in *Schemp* (the Schemps were Unitarian parents) that public schools were constitutionally free to encourage children to study the Bible for its historical and literary merits, but they were forbidden to require its use in devotional exercises. That would coerce nonbelievers to conform to officially approved beliefs, violating the "position of neutrality" that the Constitution requires states to maintain toward religion.

In 1965 the Warren Court established a new constitutional right to privacy. At issue in *Griswold* v. *Connecticut* was that state's statute making it a crime for anyone, including married couples, to use any birth control device. Another statute forbade even doctors to give advice in violation of the anti-contraceptive law. In a seven-to-two decision voiding the law, *Griswold* produced six different opinions. Justice Douglas

Justice Abe Fortas, at hearings into his nomination to succeed Chief Justice Earl Warren, July 17, 1968. UPI/Bettmann Archive, New York

spoke for the majority.

As Douglas saw it, the First, Third, Fourth, Fifth and Ninth Amendments have "penumbras, formed by emanations from those guarantees that help give them life and substance." What all these radiations added up to, said Douglas, was "a zone of privacy" that walled off the marital bedroom from state interference.

Finding no such guarantee in his own copy of the Constitution, Justice Black filed a strong dissent lamenting *Griswold*'s flirtation with "natural justice" and insisting that judges were powerless to determine constitutionally on the basis of whether they personally considered laws wise or unwise. "The power to make such decisions," Black wrote, "is of course that of a legislative body."

In three 1967–68 decisions, the Warren Court placed new limits on the Fourth Amendment, reflecting the majority's willingness to give the police some constitutional reinforcement, even at the price of modifying the individual's guarantee against unreasonable searches.

The Court discarded the "mere evidence" rule that previously limited search warrants to the actual spoils and tools of crime, thus barring police from rummaging through personal effects until they found incriminating evidence. Mainly because that rule had proved confusing, the Court held in *Warden* v. *Hayden* that police searchers could now seize *any* incriminating evidence, provided they had probable cause to do so, ordinarily backed by a judge-signed warrant. Still left open, however, was whether *Hayden* permitted the seizure of one's private papers, such as diaries and letters containing the writer's protected thoughts.

In its second 1967 decision, *McCray* v. *Illinois*, the Court held that it was not unreasonable for police to search people in the street on the strength of alleged tips from informers who needn't be identified. And in *Terry* v. *Ohio* (1968), the Court authorized police to "stop and frisk" anybody suspected of carrying any dangerous weapon. Eight Justices thus ruled for the first time in American history that mere suspicion—not probable cause—was sufficient to justify searches and seizures.

Before *Terry*, the Exclusionary Rule had arguably impaired both the fairness and efficiency of big-city police. It neither prevented illegal street searches nor permitted the conviction of people found carrying weapons. As Chief Justice Warren conceded in his *Terry* opinion, "The Exclusionary Rule has its limitations . . . as a tool of judicial control."

In June 1968, Earl Warren announced his retirement after fifteen years as Chief Justice. President Johnson's nominee to succeed him—Associate Justice Abe Fortas—encountered such Senate opposition that he withdrew in October. Accordingly, Chief Justice Warren continued in office for eleven months after his announced retirement, a lame-duck incumbency notable for new Court decisions strengthening the rights of accused persons.

During this period, the Court required federal agents seeking search warrants to prove that alleged informers' tips came from real informers (*Spinelli* v. *United States*). It also gave federal defendants the right to examine the fruits of illegal bugging by government agents, even in espionage cases (*Alderman* v. *United States*). In state cases, the Court sharply narrowed the area that police could search without a warrant incident to arrest (*Chimel* v. *California*). And the Justices extended *Miranda* to the very first moment of custody. Now the suspect must be warned about his rights whenever and wherever the police began asking questions, even if he was in his own house (*Orozco* v. *Texas*).

On the evening of May 21, 1969, President Richard Nixon appeared on national television with his entire Cabinet to introduce his nominee for Chief Justice—Warren Earl Burger, sixty-one, a veteran of thirteen years as a judge on the United States Court of Appeals for the District of Columbia.

Soon confirmed by a Senate vote of seventy-four to three, the fifteenth Chief Justice was sworn in by his predecessor on June 23 in a courtroom ceremony attended by President Nixon. Among the fascinations of the event was the Warren Court's final bit of business—three decisions including *Benton* v. *Maryland*, which held that states must now honor the Fifth Amendment guarantee against double jeopardy. By thus overruling *Palko* v. *Connecticut* (1937), the Court completed the historic process whereby the Fourteenth Amendment had "incorporated" all pertinent safeguards of personal liberty set forth in the national Bill of Rights.

Chief Justice Earl Warren leaves the Court as a private citizen after administering the oath of office to Chief Justice Warren E. Burger, June 23, 1969. UPI/Bettmann Archive, New York

16

RESTRAINT REVISITED: THE BURGER COURT

Before selecting Warren Burger, President Nixon had considered a handful of other potential Chief Justices, including his own Attorney General John Mitchell, the future Watergate casualty, and Justice Potter Stewart, the Court's much respected centrist. Stewart had asked the President to rule him out on the ground, partly derived from Harlan Stone's experience, that no sitting Justice should take over the Center Chair.

Warren E. Burger fit the bill. An energetic Minnesotan from a hardworking family of Austrian-Swiss-German descent, he had worked his way through seven years of night studies at the University of Minnesota and the St. Paul College of Law to a magna cum laude degree. He then joined a prestigious St. Paul law firm and became active in local civic affairs and liberal Republican politics. Burger had served for three years as Assistant Attorney General for civil litigation in the Eisenhower Justice Department. In 1956 President Eisenhower had launched his judicial career by appointing him to the United States Court of Appeals in Washington, D.C., a particularly influential tribunal sometimes called "the little Supreme Court."

As a circuit judge he had pressed for improvement in court management, saying "great ideals are not self-executing." A seasoned jurist with a gift for administration, he had emerged among federal appellate judges as a vocal pragmatist with decisive views about criminal law.

Burger's pre-judicial experience, unlike Earl Warren's, was largely in private practice. But he had spent much of his early career in public and civic affairs, notably working with Whitney Young, then head of St. Paul's Urban League.

Burger organized and was president of St. Paul's first Council on Human Relations, where his attention was caught by the misdemeanor conviction of a young black for indecent exposure. Normally, this called for a fine or suspended sentence, but the young man was sentenced to an unprecedented one-year jail term.

Burger organized a defense team including two young labor lawyers and took the case to the Minnesota supreme court. The conviction was reversed and the case dismissed. Because the accused was a leader of the Young Communist League at the University of Minnesota, the case attracted widespread public attention, confirming Burger's reputation as an unconventional advocate.

As a leader of the Council on Human Relations, Burger co-chaired a special committee to find homes and jobs for Japanese-Americans forcibly displaced from their homes in California after the outbreak of World War II. Later, as

The Burger Court, 1969–70. Standing, from left: Associate Justices Thurgood Marshall, Potter Stewart, Byron Raymond White. Seated, from left: Associate Justices John Marshall Harlan, Hugo Lafayette Black, Chief Justice Warren E. Burger, Associate Justices William Orville Douglas, William Joseph Brennan, Jr. (The Court had only eight Justices during this year due to a vacancy left by the resignation of Justice Fortas in May 1969, which was not filled until the appointment of Harry A. Blackmun to the Bench in June 1970.) Photograph by the *National Geographic.* Collection of the Supreme Court of the United States, Washington, D.C.

Assistant Attorney General, he administered a program to make reparations to them.

In May 1970, Burger was joined on the Court by another Nixon appointee whom he had known since childhood. The Chief's fellow Minnesotan was Harry A. Blackmun, sixty-one, a member of the United States Court of Appeals for the Eighth Circuit, to which President Eisenhower had appointed him in 1957.

As of 1984, the Supreme Court's Burger era could be divided into three periods roughly corresponding to the Nixon Presidency (1969 to 1974), the Ford and Carter years (1974 to 1980), and the first Reagan Administration beginning in 1981.

During the Nixon period, the Court began to narrow some Warren-era rulings, yet no landmark was overturned. During its second phase, the Court resisted type-casting.

During its third phase, beginning in 1981, the Burger Court, soon with the first woman Justice, Sandra Day O'Connor, increasingly applied procedural brakes that diverted more litigants to state courts or to the political process.

On February 23, 1971, with only Douglas dissenting, the Court held in *Younger* v. *Harris* that federal judges should normally abstain from enjoining on-going state criminal proceedings unless the prosecution was shown to be acting in bad faith and threatening irreparable harm to the person seeking the injunction. Speaking for the Court in *Younger,* Justice Black attributed the decision to "a proper respect for state functions."

Beginning with *Younger* in February, the Justices produced a year-long harvest of key decisions. Highlights:

V I N T A G E   1 9 7 1

February 24: The Court reexamined the *Miranda* doctrine, erasing the widespread impression that the 1966 decision had barred *any* use of statements that police obtained from a suspect before advising him of his rights to silence and counsel. In *Harris* v. *New York,* the Court through Chief Justice Burger affirmed that uncounseled statements not usable as evidence per se against the defendant would be admissible to impeach the defendant if he chose to take the witness stand at his trial. Then his uncounseled statements to the police could be used to contradict his courtroom testimony, even if the police had refused his request for a lawyer. According to Burger, "The shield provided by *Miranda* cannot be perverted into a license to use perjury by way of a defense, free from the risk of confrontation with prior inconsistent statements."

Chief Justice Warren E. Burger. Photograph by Dennis Brack. Collection of the Supreme Court of the United States, Washington, D.C.

March 8: For the first time, the Justices upheld Congress's right to bar job discrimination based on race. Speaking for a unanimous Court in *Griggs* v. *Duke Power Co.,* Chief Justice Burger ruled that the 1964 Civil Rights Act forbade employers to use IQ tests or require high school diplomas as conditions for employment or promotion that effectively excluded minority groups. In this case, five times as many blacks as whites had failed the test. Unless employers showed that such tests were directly related to job performance, *Griggs* held, any "disproportionate impact" on minority members would be considered discrimination violating the statute, regardless of the employer's intent.

In later years, the Burger Court drew a sharp distinction between statutory cases such as *Griggs,* where the measure of unlawful discrimination was unmistakable impact, and constitutional cases in which the Justices required something far more difficult—proof of actual intent to discriminate.

April 20: The Burger Court's first major ruling on de jure school segregation, and its last unanimous one, provided judges with the first post-*Brown* guidelines for prodding laggard school boards into creating unitary systems. In *Swann* v. *Charlotte-Mecklenburg Board of Education*, written by Chief Justice Burger, the Court approved a number of specific integrating methods, including the limited use of racial ratios, gerrymandered school districts, paired schools, and busing that did not harm the children's health or education. "The objective is to dismantle the dual system," Burger wrote. Addressing the challenge to busing, he pointed out that bus transportation had been an integral part of the system for years, "perhaps the single most important factor in the transition from the one-room schoolhouse to the consolidated school."

June 14: In *Graham* v. *Richardson*, the Court unanimously gave alienage the same "suspect" status as race in equal-protection cases.

June 21: Six Justices held that federal agents may be individually liable for damages when they violate constitutional rights. In *Bivens* v. *Six Unknown Agents of the Federal Narcotics Bureau*, the agents had broken into Bivens's home, searched it, and arrested him, all without a warrant or justification. In violating his rights, the Court said, the invaders committed a "constitutional tort" that entitled the victim to bring suit directly in a federal court without an authorizing statute.

Chief Justice Burger dissented, objecting that the Court's damage remedy for police misconduct was not only unauthorized by either Congress or the Constitution, but was also unworkable, since juries would more likely side with police officers than with their alleged victims. Burger used his dissent to sharply criticize another remedy, the Exclusionary Rule or what he termed the "suppression doctrine," calling it "conceptually sterile and practically ineffective." As a substitute, he argued for a suit against the officer and the "master," or government.

June 21: In *Coolidge* v. *New Hampshire*, five Justices refused to relax Fourth Amendment restrictions on police searches. Edward Coolidge had been suspected of brutally murdering a teenage girl. After his arrest, the police towed his car from his driveway to headquarters and vacuumed it at leisure in search of microscopic evidence, which eventually sealed his conviction. Unfortunately, their search warrant had proved defective, and the key issue was whether they had needed one in the first place. The Court said they did. Accordingly, Coolidge was entitled to a new trial without vacuumed evidence, which was held inadmissible under the Exclusionary Rule. Justice Stewart spoke for the majority, Justice White for the dissenters.

Justice Stewart's opinion noted that the police may search a person without a warrant "incident to arrest," providing they have probable cause to make the arrest. But that rule did not apply to a parked car under police control with its owner in jail, since there was no danger of losing potential evidence and ample time to secure a valid warrant.

Stewart reaffirmed the rule that "searches conducted outside the judicial process, without prior approval by judge or magistrate, are per se unreasonable under the Fourth Amendment— subject only to a few specifically established and well-delineated exceptions." The *Coolidge* majority held firm to the principle that "the police must obtain a warrant when they intend to seize an object outside the scope of a valid search incident to an arrest."

June 28: At issue in *Lemon* v. *Kurtzman* were "parochiaid" laws in Rhode Island and Pennsylvania authorizing state payment of salaries to parochial school teachers of secular subjects.

Writing for a unanimous Court, Chief Justice Burger established a three-part test for determining whether such aid violates the First Amendment's Establishment Clause. State aid is permissible, Burger said, when its purpose is secular, its primary effect neither advances nor inhibits religion, and it does not foster "an excessive government entanglement with religion."

The laws at issue in *Lemon* failed the third part of the test. To ensure the religious neutrality of state-paid religious teachers, wrote Burger, would require constant state surveillance, resulting in excessive government entanglement with religion.

June 30: The Supreme Court's most famous case of prior restraint under the First Amendment arose in mid-June 1971 when the *New York Times* and the *Washington Post* began publishing antiwar activist Daniel Ellsberg's purloined excerpts of the forty-seven volume "Pentagon Papers," a classified official history of American involvement in Vietnam. The Justice Department, alleging grave harm to national security, sought injunctions against the newspapers to prevent further publication. After whirlwind proceedings in the lower courts, the case reached the Justices on June 24 in the form of a *Times* appeal from a government victory in one court and a government appeal from a *Post* victory in another court.

Only four days after hearing arguments, the Court issued an unsigned opinion declaring that any request for prior restraint of the press bears a "heavy presumption against its constitutional validity." Voting six to three, the Court held that in this instance the government had failed to justify sufficient need to suppress the Pentagon Papers. But three dissenters, including the Chief Justice, decried the haste of the decision after the *Times* had had four months to study the "stolen" papers. Given more time, Burger argued, the trial courts might have "flushed" good reasons for restraint. In the event, all nine Justices wrote separate opinions covering a range of First Amendment positions so broad that the two newspapers could be variously considered immune to any prior restraint; subject to censorship in an emergency; guilty of not reporting to the government their receipt of "stolen property"; or liable to criminal penalties *after* publishing secret documents.

The chief of the presses checks the first edition of *The Washington Post* off the presses after the Court's decision regarding publication of the Pentagon Papers, June 30, 1971. Papers all over the country resumed the series immediately following the decision. UPI/Bettmann Archive, New York

November 22: Most state laws are presumed valid under the Equal Protection Clause unless shown to be arbitrary or devoid of any rational purpose. Such "lower-tier" review seldom overturns a challenged law. But when a law classifies people by race or by national origin, the Court invokes a higher equal-protection standard and subjects it to "upper-tier" review. The law is inherently "suspect" and presumed guilty of unlawful discrimination unless proven "necessary to a compelling state interest."

In *Reed* v. *Reed,* an Idaho couple named Sally and Cecil Reed had adopted a minor child, and then separated. When the child died without a will, both Reeds sought to administer its estate. The probate court appointed Cecil Reed: under Idaho law, men were favored over women as estate administrators. Sally Reed appealed to the Supreme Court.

For the first time in Court history, the Justices struck down a state law because it discriminated against women. Speaking for a unanimous Court, Chief Justice Burger held that sex classifications were now "subject to scrutiny" and considered valid only if they bore "a fair and

substantial relation to the object of the legislation." The Idaho law failed that test. It was supposed to minimize disputes in probate cases; instead, it discriminated against women, which Burger said could not be done.

The Supreme Court's vintage year of 1971 rushed to a climax in September when, six days apart, Justices Black and Harlan retired because of rapidly failing health. Black, eighty-five, had suffered a stroke; he died eight days after retiring. Harlan, seventy-two, died shortly after Christmas. In his thirty-four years on the bench, Hugo Black had become one of the Court's dozen or so all-time giants. John M. Harlan's sixteen years had stamped him as a superb craftsman. Each renowned in his own way, the two strong Justices would be difficult to replace.

On October 21, President Nixon nominated two accomplished lawyers to succeed Black and Harlan. Within eight weeks, both nominees had been confirmed.

Black's successor was Lewis Franklin Powell, Jr., a distinguished private lawyer and Virginia Democrat.

Harlan's successor, William Hubbs Rehnquist,

was the Assistant Attorney General in charge of the Office of Legal Counsel giving opinions to the Executive Branch.

At forty-seven, Justice Rehnquist was the Court's youngest member. His appointment was Nixon's fourth in his first term.

Justices Powell and Rehnquist took their seats in January 1972.

DEATH AND TAXES

In *United States* v. *United States District Court (1972)*, with Rehnquist not participating, six Justices speaking through Powell rejected the Nixon Justice Department's assertion that the President had inherent power to wiretap Americans without judicial approval whenever the government claimed that "national security" was at stake.

"The price of lawful dissent must not be a dread of subjection to an unchecked surveillance power," Powell wrote. "Nor must the fear of unauthorized official eavesdropping deter vigorous citizen dissent and discussion of government action in private conversation. . . . We cannot accept the government's argument that internal security matters are too subtle and complex for judicial evaluation. . . . If the threat is too subtle or complex for our senior law enforcement officers to convey its significance to a court, one may question whether there is probable cause for surveillance."

The Court's most arresting 1972 decision was *Furman* v. *Georgia,* which nullified all existing death penalty laws in the United States. In a ruling opposed by all four Nixon appointees, five Justices held that such laws were so devoid of standards that judges and juries were ordering executions for personal rather than legal reasons. The result was arbitrary, capricious, unjust, and therefore unconstitutional. "The imposition and carrying out of the death penalty in these cases," the Court ruled, "constitutes cruel and unusual punishment under the Eighth and Fourteenth Amendments." *Furman* did not abolish the death penalty itself—only the way it was being administered.

In *Furman,* the issues split the Court to the point that all nine Justices wrote separate opinions. Brennan's focus on human worth led him to denounce the death penalty as "degrading to human dignity," even if rigid standards governed it. In his view, execution was per se unconstitutional. Marshall, too, called execution impermissible because it was "excessive" and hence "morally unacceptable." Stewart and White condemned not the penalty itself but its capricious administration. "These death sentences are cruel and unusual in the same way that being struck by lightning is cruel and unusual," wrote Stewart. Those doomed to die might or might not be the most culpable: they were simply "a capriciously selected random handful" of all those convicted of rapes and murders, and in Stewart's view the Constitution could not tolerate a penalty "so wantonly and so freakishly imposed."

Speaking for the four dissenters, Chief Justice Burger criticized the Court for undue activism in erasing all death laws from the books. Noting that the Constitution takes capital punishment for granted, he argued that its form and future should be determined by legislators, not judges, in accordance with the Constitution. And he stressed that Justices Stewart and White had, in fact, paved the way for the states to pass new death penalty laws imposing constitutional standards for judges and juries to follow. Within four years, thirty-five states had passed new death penalty laws.

At issue in *Roe* v. *Wade* was the validity of a Texas law that made abortion a serious crime except when it was essential to save a woman's life. Under the law, a woman could be imprisoned for aborting an unwanted pregnancy, even if she did it herself. A licensed physician who performed the operation with the mother's consent faced a five-year prison sentence, and if she died, the charge was murder. Similar laws were standard in most states.

Jane Roe, the pseudonymous petitioner, alleged that she was single and pregnant and wished to be aborted by a good doctor in her native Dallas. Joined by Dr. James H. Hallford, a licensed physician, Roe asked a federal court to enjoin the local district attorney from enforcing the anti-abortion law. The court declared the law unconstitutional but abstained from granting injunctive relief, and the case duly reached the Supreme Court.

On January 22, 1973, with only Rehnquist and

White dissenting, Justice Blackmun spoke for the Court in declaring that the Constitution protects a right of personal privacy, which encompasses every woman's qualified right to terminate an unwanted pregnancy.

Citing a long line of decisions, ranging from *Boyd* v. *United States* (1886) to *Griswold* v. *Connecticut* (1965), Blackmun said the Court had "recognized that a right of personal privacy, or a guarantee of certain areas or zones of privacy, does exist under the Constitution. . . . These decisions make it clear that only personal rights that can be deemed 'fundamental' or 'implicit' in the concept of 'ordered liberty' are included in this guarantee of personal privacy. They also make it clear that the right has some extension to activities relating to marriage, procreation, contraception, family relationships, and child rearing and education."

By this reasoning, Blackmun continued, the right of personal privacy was not only broad enough to encompass abortion but also so "fundamental," and thus entitled to "strict" protection, that it could be infringed only by a "compelling state interest" spelled out in narrowly drawn legislation.

Roe v. *Wade* identified two such valid state interests—safeguarding the woman's health and protecting potential life—and Blackmun held that these interests became stronger as the pregnancy advanced. During the first trimester, he said, neither interest was sufficiently compelling to justify any state interference with abortion. In the second trimester, the state interest in the woman's health warranted strict abortion rules. In the third trimester, the state's interest in the fetus's survival permitted a ban on all abortions except where necessary to protect the woman's health or life. Rehnquist called *Roe* a piece of "judicial legislation."

But in March 1973, two months after *Roe,* the Burger Court epitomized judicial restraint in *San Antonio School District* v. *Rodriguez.*

For generations, the nation's public schools had been financed mainly by taxing real property within each school district. As a result, wealthy suburban districts could spend far more on their public schools than could lower-income areas. In Texas, for example, the *Rodriguez* case arose from a budgetary spread of $594 per pupil in the richest district to $356 in the poorest. A federal court ruled the entire Texas system unconstitutional.

On appeal, the Supreme Court reversed the lower court's *Rodriguez* decision, reinstated the Texas property-tax system, and rejected the plaintiffs' assumption that the Equal Protection Clause could help correct one of the country's obvious inequalities.

Speaking for a bare majority of five, Justice Powell dismissed the dissenters' contention that disparities created by the property-tax system constituted official discrimination, outlawed by the Fourteenth Amendment. Powell said there was nothing unconstitutional about a wealth classification, as long as it did not deprive specific groups or individuals of some public benefit. The Texas system did not actually bar any children from public schooling, he continued, and though it created disparities between districts, "the Equal Protection Clause does not require equality of precisely equal advantages."

In Powell's view, nothing in the Constitution either specifies or implies that education is a federally protected right. No matter how vital education might be to a child's future, Powell wrote, "It is not the province of this Court to create substantive constitutional rights in the name of guaranteeing equal protection of the laws."

Accordingly, the *Rodriguez* majority did not apply strict scrutiny to the Texas system. All the Court needed was the lower-tier "rationality" approach, which presumes that a challenged state law is valid unless proven to be blatantly irrational, arbitrary, or capricious. "The constitutional standard under the Equal Protection Clause," Powell asserted, "is whether the challenged state action rationally furthers a legitimate state purpose or interest. We hold that the Texas plan abundantly satisfies this standard."

QUALIFYING RULES

In *Keyes* v. *School District* (1973), the Court sought a standard for determining when lawful *de facto* segregation becomes unlawful *de jure* segregation. When does school segregation lose its innocence as the mere effect of housing patterns and become the impermissible equivalent of official discrimination?

In its first Northern *de facto* case, the Court

ruled seven to one that because the Denver school board had deliberately made certain schools predominantly white, it was potentially liable for causing the *de facto* segregation of other schools that were heavily black and Chicano. In short, official discrimination in one part of a school system was now presumed to affect the whole system. But the test was not to be a simple matter of impact, of apparent cause and presumed effect. The school board would be compelled to desegregate the black schools only if it failed to prove its innocence. "We emphasize that the differential factor between *de jure* segregation and so-called *de facto* segregation," Justice Brennan wrote for the *Keyes* majority, "is *purpose* or *intent* to segregate."

Justice Powell agreed with the result, but criticized the majority's new standard of "segregative intent" as far too elusive for courts to determine.

Powell urged the Court to discard the *de jure/de facto* distinction, together with the intent test, and instead use an effect test for all school segregation cases. Under his proposal, a showing of substantial segregation would establish a prima facie case of official discrimination, requiring the school board to prove that it was nonetheless running an integrated system.

Justice Powell later wrote *United States* v. *Calandra* (1974), a six-to-three decision that sharply qualified the Exclusionary Rule. The issue was whether the rule permitted a federal grand jury witness to refuse to answer questions based on illegally seized evidence. The Court held that the witness must answer. The Exclusionary Rule was not a Fourth Amendment protection but merely a "judicially created remedy" for deterring police misconduct.

By focusing on deterrence as the Exclusionary Rule's sole purpose, Justice Powell devised a cost-benefit analysis as to when unlawful evidence should and should not be suppressed in order to promote deterrence. In *Calandra*, he held that excluding tainted evidence from a grand jury was not an effective way to deter police misconduct, and the price was too high to justify the exclusion. The "potential injury" to the grand jury's work outweighed the "potential benefits" in policing the police.

In June 1974, the Court took an equally strict view of taxpayers suing the federal government. In *United States* v. *Richardson,* a taxpayer sought to challenge the secrecy of the CIA's budget. He alleged that Congress was neglecting its duty under the Statement and Account Clause (Article I, Section 9), which says, ". . . a regular Statement and Account of the Receipts and Expenditures of all public Money shall be published from time to time."

The Supreme Court has always been leery of federal taxpayer suits. Thus in 1923 *(Frothingham* v. *Mellon),* the Court ruled that federal taxpayers lacked standing to challenge federal spending programs because they were not directly injured by them. The decision barred federal taxpayers from using federal courts as "a forum in which to air . . . generalized grievances about the conduct of government or the allocation of power within the federal system."

In 1968 *(Flast* v. *Cohen),* the Warren Court modified *Frothingham,* ruling that a federal taxpayer might have the requisite standing if he attacked spending or taxing programs rather than regulatory policies, and if the alleged misspending violated a constitutional restriction on Congress's financial powers. Chief Justice Warren's opinion for the Court firmly retained the rule that a party has standing to seek relief only if he has a personal stake in the outcome of the controversy.

In *Richardson,* six years later, Chief Justice Burger spoke for a narrow (five-to-four) majority, holding that a taxpayer lacked standing to challenge the CIA's budgetary secrecy as a violation of the Statement and Account Clause. Burger's opinion held that *Flast* did not apply in this case. The taxpayer was not attacking federal spending itself but only the secrecy in which part of it was conducted. The secrecy was regulatory policy, which *Flast* did not cover. Moreover, the taxpayer had not demonstrated that the secrecy injured him personally in any concrete way, hence he had no standing to sue.

Justice Powell's concurrence went further: he dissected the *Flast* test of standing and found it so wanting in principled content as to be on its way to collapse. When that happened, he said, the Court should return to pre-*Flast* stringency and fully restore the old rule—"in the absence of a statutory grant of the right of review, a plaintiff must allege some particularized injury that sets him apart from the man on the street."

In Powell's view, this was not a matter of

begrudging the citizen's access to federal courts—it was political wisdom. Easier standing rules produced greater judicial power, which Powell considered undesirable. "It seems to me inescapable," he wrote in *Richardson,* "that allowing unrestrained taxpayer or citizen standing would significantly alter the allocation of power at the national level, with a shift away from a democratic form of government."

CHIEF IN DEED

Chief Justice Burger's work during this period stamped him as the most innovative head of the federal court system since Chief Justice Taft. Burger either initiated or helped to launch everything from the nation's first training center for professional court administrators to the first systematic cooperation between federal and state judges; from the now widespread use of six-person juries in federal civil cases to the "individual calendar" system that speeds up federal trials by assigning and focusing responsibility for each case to a single judge from beginning to end.

At the Supreme Court level, the Chief Justice spoke out frequently about the problems of the Court's ever rising caseload, and his solutions were multiform. Burger persuaded his colleagues to curtail the tedious practice of reading their complex opinions aloud from the bench; oral arguments were quickened by cutting the presentation time allotted to each case from two hours to one; and the Court was swept into the modern world of copying machines, computers, and word processors. He changed the shape of the high bench from a straight line to one with two shallow angles, improving acoustics and making it easier for the Justices to see and hear each other during oral argument. He turned the cavernous empty marble halls of the ground floor into a museum-like setting for periodic historical exhibits, while on its walls were hung formerly unseen oil portraits of the long succession of Justices.

In his quest for judical efficiency, Burger also set up the 1971 Study Group on The Caseload of the Supreme Court, headed by Harvard Law Professor Paul A. Freund. Although the Freund Commission's proposals have not yet emerged from controversy to consensus, they have been at the heart of the caseload debate ever since Chief Justice Burger started to publicize the problem

soon after he began to occupy the Center Chair.

Given his high-energy focus on the federal judicial system, plus such extra-judicial duties as being a Regent of the Smithsonian Institution, as well as serving on the boards of both The National Gallery of Art and the Hirshhorn Museum, it might have been understandable if Burger had assigned himself relatively few or easy opinions . But this was not so . He consistently issued more opinions per term than the average of his eight colleagues.

In June 1973, the Chief Justice managed to produce the first legal definition of obscenity to command a Court majority since the *Roth* case in 1957. To be sure, the majority in *Miller* v. *California* numbered only five Justices, but that was a triumph compared with, say, the memorable day in 1966 when the Justices' collective vexations in three obscenity cases had produced fourteen separate opinions.

In *Miller,* Burger held that states do not violate the First Amendment when they enact narrowly drawn laws regulating obscene material. The decision made local prosecution much easier by specifically rejecting a national standard as well as a 1964 test under which material was deemed obscene only if it was "utterly without redeeming social value." In *Miller,* which Burger said was aimed only at hard-core pornography, the Court devised a new three-part test. Material was now obscene and unprotected if: 1) the average person (i.e., a juror), applying contemporary local standards, found that it appealed to prurient interest; *and* if 2) it depicted certain sexual acts, specified in the law, in a patently offensive way; *and* if 3) the material, taken as a whole, lacked "serious literary, artistic, political, or scientific value."

In July 1974, Chief Justice Burger spoke for a five-to-four majority that modified the Court's views of Northern school segregation. At issue in *Milliken* v. *Bradley* was a federal district judge's plan for desegregating the public schools of Detroit, where seventy percent of the city's 290,000 pupils were black, thirty percent were white, and virtually all of them attended schools effectively restricted to one race or the other. Myriad official actions had caused this pattern to develop, the district judge found, requiring him to remedy what seemed to him a clear denial of Fourteenth Amendment rights. But white flight to the suburbs had made it impossible to integrate the city schools without drafting white children from elsewhere, namely the suburbs. So the judge had devised a "metropolitan" plan expanding the desegregation area to include not only Detroit but also fifty-three additional school districts, with a total of 750,000 pupils in three counties. Approved by the circuit court, the multi-district remedy called for extensive busing to achieve a per-school racial mixture reflecting that of the entire fifty-four districts.

Chief Justice Burger, stressing "local autonomy" as central to American public schools, held that district boundaries were presumed inviolable and desegregation remedies must be limited to the legal jurisdiction of a *de jure* offense. *Inter*district solutions were allowed only when one district's segregation produced "a significant segregative effect" on another district. Since Detroit's segregation had not, on the record, caused the other fifty-three districts to practice segregation, Burger held, the area-wide busing plan was "wholly impermissible." Any new plan must be limited to *intra*district relief: the courts need only protect "the constitutional right of the Negro respondents residing in Detroit . . . to attend a unitary system in that district."

In short, the Supreme Court did not require racial integration per se, but only remedies designed "to restore the victims of discriminatory conduct to the position they would have occupied in the absence of such conduct." The Court's acceptance of segregated schools in Detroit rested on the *Milliken* majority's conclusion that the condition was not caused by state action.

In mid-1973 the Senate Committee investigating the Watergate scandal discovered that President Nixon had taped his executive conversations since 1971. Special Prosecutor Archibald Cox subpoenaed the tapes of nine specific conversations for presentation to a federal grand jury, which needed all possible evidence before deciding whether or not to indict certain Presidential aides for obstructing justice by covering up White House involvement in the Watergate break-in.

The President's lawyers claimed absolute executive privilege to withhold the tapes, regardless of any court order. They invoked every President's need for utter confidentiality while discus-

Subpoena Duces Tecum, July 26, 1973, commanding Richard Nixon to bring tapes of nine conversations to the Grand Jury investigating the Watergate break-in. National Archives, Washington, D.C.

sing secrets of state in the privacy of the Oval Office. The President must be protected from disclosures that could wreck vital decisions and policies, even lead to war. The President was "answerable to the nation but not to the courts."

Federal District Judge John J. Sirica failed to "perceive any reason for suspending the power of the courts to get evidence and rule on questions of privilege in criminal matters simply because it is the President of the United States who holds the evidence." Judge Sirica ordered the President to furnish him with the tapes so that the judge could hear them in private and decide whether the grand jury should also hear them. An appeals court upheld Sirica's order, whereupon the President submitted the designated tapes.

On April 18 Judge Sirica issued another subpoena, this one for the tapes of sixty-four more White House conversations.

The President released edited transcripts of some of the tapes requested, but not the tapes themselves. Resisting the new subpoena, his lawyers restated his position concerning presidential immunity to court orders, and Nixon himself asserted that further tape revelations "would be

White House attorney James St. Clair arguing before the Supreme Court in the case of *United States* v. *Richard M. Nixon*, July 8, 1974. On the bench can be seen Chief Justice Warren Burger, Justices William Brennan, Byron White, Henry Blackmun, and the empty chair of Justice William Rehnquist, who disqualified himself from hearing the case. UPI/Bettmann Archive, New York

contrary to the public interest." Judge Sirica once again rejected the President's absolute privilege claim, and the case rapidly ascended to the Supreme Court.

On July 24 the eight participating Justices unanimously sustained Judge Sirica's order that Nixon must comply with the subpoena. The President was thereby told to deliver all tapes for Sirica's *in camera* examination, so that the judge could remove irrelevancies and forward all admissible evidence to the prosecutor.

Speaking for the Court, Chief Justice Burger dismissed the theory that no court may review a President's claim of privilege. Echoing John Marshall in *Marbury* v. *Madison*, Burger declared, "We therefore reaffirm that it is 'emphatically the province and duty' of this court 'to say what the law is' with respect to the claim of privilege in this case." Further echoing Marshall, Burger's opinion for a unanimous Court took note that in 1807, Marshall, sitting as a trial judge—as Justices did in those days—ordered President Jefferson to produce military reports on Aaron Burr's activities when Burr was being tried for treason at Jefferson's insistence.

"The President's need for complete candor and objectivity from advisers calls for great deference from the courts," Burger observed. "However, when the privilege depends solely on the broad undifferentiated claim of public interest in the confidentiality of such conversations, a confrontation with other values arises. Absent a claim of need to protect military, diplomatic or sensitive national security secrets, we find it difficult to accept the argument that even the very important interest in confidentiality of Presidential communications is significantly diminished by production of such material for *in camera* inspection. . . ."

While stressing "a presumptive privilege for Presidential communication," Burger found that in this case the privilege was outweighed by the imperatives of criminal justice. "The very integrity of the judicial system and public confidence in the system depend on full disclosure of all the facts, within the framework of the rules of evidence," he wrote. Here, the tapes were essential for determining the truth. Said Burger:

"When the ground for asserting privilege as to subpoenaed materials for use in a criminal trial is

Justice William Orville Douglas. March 27, 1950. This photograph was taken on Justice Douglas's first day back in Court after having broken twenty-three ribs in a fall from his horse the previous September. Photograph Harris & Ewing. Collection of the Supreme Court of the United States, Washington, D.C.

based only on the generalized interest in confidentiality, it cannot prevail over the fundamental demands of due process of law in the fair administration of criminal justice. The generalized assertion of privilege must yield to the demonstrated specific need for evidence in a pending criminal trial."

STANDING FIRM

In 1973 William O. Douglas surpassed Stephen J. Field's record (thirty-four years) as the longest serving Justice in history. Douglas, then chairman of the new Securities and Exchange Commission, was forty when he joined the Court in 1939—the youngest person to become a Justice in the twentieth century. He eventually served for thirty-six-and-one-half years.

In his resignation letter to President Ford on November 12, 1975, Douglas explained, "I have been bothered with incessant and demanding pain which depletes my energy to the point that I have been unable to shoulder my full share of the burden."

To make his first and only Court appointment, President Ford nominated John Paul Stevens of the United States Court of Appeals for the Seventh Circuit. Judge Stevens, fifty-five, had been a top-flight antitrust lawyer in Chicago. Confirmed by a unanimous Senate vote, Stevens joined the Court just before Christmas 1975. In his first full term, skipping the junior Justice's customary reticence, he wrote forty-four separate (concurring or dissenting) opinions, far more than any other Justice.

The Supreme Court has always practiced restraint in determining a plaintiff's "standing" to challenge the constitutionality of government action. In such public-law cases—as opposed to private disputes—the challenger's distance from the action has often been the weak link in the chain of causality required for standing in a federal court.

During the Nixon Administration, the Court barred a suit against Pentagon officials responsible for keeping antiwar dissenters under Army surveillance that allegedly "chilled" their admittedly lawful activities. In *Laird* v. *Tatum* (1972), the Court ruled five to four that the plaintiffs lacked standing because they had not personally suffered "injury in fact," meaning a present or imminent threat of irreparable harm from unlawful government action that a federal court could actually stop. If the *Laird* plaintiffs were allowed to sue, wrote the Chief Justice, the federal courts would become "virtually continuing monitors of the wisdom and soundness of Executive action," a task for Congressmen, not judges.

In 1972 the Court approved environmental injury as a basis for standing *(Sierra Club* v. *Morton)*. In 1973 the Justices ruled five to three that while environmental plaintiffs must show personal injury to acquire standing, the injury needn't be large *(United States* v. *Students Challenging Regulatory Agency Procedures) (SCRAP)*. The plaintiffs in that case were Washington D.C. law students challenging a federally-approved railroad rate hike. They said higher shipping rates would boost the cost of recyclable containers, thus increasing the use of cheaper nonrecyclable plastics, which in turn would proliferate litter— the injury they were attacking. Justice Stewart's majority opinion held that "perceptible harm" was sufficient for environmental challengers. And though the law students eventually lost their case on the merits, they did establish that federal agencies may be sued regardless of the *amount* of individual harm at stake.

The Supreme Court has always been highly sensitive to its delicate role in a government of separated powers. Ever since Congress passed the Anti-Injunction Act in 1973, it has been a bedrock Court rule in every era that federal judges shall not enjoin ongoing state court proceedings unless Congress approves such writs or they become necessary to safeguard the integrity of the Court's decisions. (The Court may, of course, order state officials to stop enforcing unconstitutional state laws.)

The Burger Court's wariness of federal injunctions, shared by nearly all Justices and underscored by renewed stress on federalism, was signaled in the important 1971 case of *Younger* v. *Harris*. With only Douglas dissenting, eight Justices spoke through Hugo Black in holding that federal courts may enjoin ongoing state criminal proceedings *only* when there is a showing of bad faith by the prosecution or a threat of irreparable

harm to the petitioner. Under *Younger*, federal judges were admonished to resume strict abstention from state criminal matters until all state remedies had been exhausted.

In January 1976, Justice Rehnquist built on *Younger* in a case that involved not a state court proceeding but a dispute between a Northern police force and the city's black population. At issue in *Rizzo* v. *Goode* was the validity of a federal injunction requiring Philadelphia's mayor and police commissioner to set up formal procedures for dealing with an onslaught of citizen complaints concerning police brutality.

The federal order had resulted from a damage suit brought under the 1871 Civil Rights Act, now known as "Section 1983" of the United States Code. Section 1983 suits (unlike *Younger*) did not require federal abstention. The federal district court had found a pattern of pervasive police misconduct; the circuit court had upheld the injunction, and the proposed relief was presumably workable, since a departmental complaint system had been suggested by the Philadelphia police themselves.

Even so, the Supreme Court vacated the injunction. According to Rehnquist, the lower courts had overlooked "the well-established rule that the Government had traditionally been granted the widest latitude in 'the dispatch of its own internal affairs'. . ." He held that the mayor and police commissioner were immune to Section 1983 damage suits—only individual police officers could be sued. The lower courts, Rehnquist held, were guilty of "unwarranted federal judicial intrusion into the discretionary authority" of Philadelphia's city leaders.

In March 1976, Rehnquist spoke for another five-to-three majority in *Paul* v. *Davis*, which further curbed the scope of Section 1983 relief. Edward Davis, a newspaper photographer, had been falsely charged with shoplifting in Louisville, Kentucky. Although the charge was dismissed, the police circulated his name and picture on a flier publicizing "active" shoplifters. Davis sued in federal court, alleging that the police chief had damaged his reputation under color of law. The circuit court upheld him on the ground, among others, that reputation was an aspect of liberty and property safeguarded against arbitrary state action by the Due Process Clause of the Fourteenth Amendment.

Not so, ruled Justice Rehnquist. The Constitution did not protect one's reputation alone, only one's "reputation-plus," meaning that Davis had to lose not only his good name but also his job or equivalent "property" before he had grounds for a federal suit. To be sure, Davis could sue for defamation in a state court, Rehnquist said. But a federal civil rights damage suit was precluded, there being no constitutional right at stake. As Rehnquist put it, "We hold that the interest in reputation asserted in his case is neither 'liberty' nor 'property' . . ."

Paul v. *Davis* mainly reflected the majority's concern that upholding Davis would have opened the federal courts to all manner of suits alleging wrongs by state officials, whereas the same wrongs (or at least defamation) could presumably be resolved by state courts.

In June 1976, Justice Rehnquist achieved a milestone reflecting the country's growing disenchantment with federal bureaucracy and his own concern with state sovereignty. What Rehnquist produced in a five-to-four decision entitled *National League of Cities* v. *Usery* was the first Court curb on Congress's use of the commerce power to regulate state activities in more than forty years.

For two decades, the Court had upheld federal laws affecting everything from civil rights to labor relations to the environment, under the ever wider umbrella of Congress's authority to regulate interstate commerce. Among those laws was the 1938 Fair Labor Standards Act, which originally required only private employers to pay the federal minimum wage. As government swelled, the law was gradually extended to public employees.

At issue in *National League of Cities* was another expansion of the federal minimum wage law, this one to cover some 3.4 million other public employees, including firemen and policemen. Justice Rehnquist argued that the resulting financial burden on the states was an impermissible burden on their sovereignty. Four other Justices agreed, holding that while the commerce power reached every aspect of private business, Congress had gone too far when its wage policies affected the "States as States."

According to Rehnquist, the Court had "repeatedly recognized that there are attributes of sovereignty attaching to every state government which may not be impaired by Congress." They included every state's right to pay wages of its choice. That choice heavily influenced the states' "delivery of those governmental services which their citizens require."

The federal law would effectively usurp the state's "integral governmental functions. . . . If Congress may withdraw from the States the authority to make . . . fundamental employment decisions affecting services . . . we think there would be little left of the States' separate and independent existence."

Nine years later, Rehnquist's opinion in *National League of Cities* was overruled as "impracticable and doctrinally barren" by another five-to-four decision in *Garcia* v. *San Antonio Metropolitan Transit Authority* (1985). In vigorous dissents, however, the minority Justices insisted that *Garcia* was not the Court's last word on the proper relationship between Congress's commerce power and state sovereignty.

Justice Potter Stewart avoided retiring when he became sixty-five in January 1980 because he thought it best not to create a vacancy in a presidential election year. He planned to go the next year, though, no matter who won the presidency, and so he did, on July 3, 1981. Stewart had served for nearly twenty-three years. With customary succinctness, he declared, "It's better to go too soon than to stay too long."

Thus in August 1981, President Ronald Reagan sent his first Court nomination to the Senate. His choice for the Court's 102nd member and first woman Justice was Sandra Day O'Connor, a fifty-one-year-old Arizonan who had served three years as the state senate's first woman majority leader, five years as a state trial judge, and two years as a member of the middle-level Arizona Court of Appeals. The President called her "a person for all seasons."

None of the current Justices had ever held a state elective office; only Brennan had been a state court judge. O'Connor would be unique in bringing a state-level perspective to the Court's deliberations. Justice O'Connor was confirmed on September 19, 1981. The vote: unanimous.

In the long run, the views of individual Justices are merely parts of a nine-part whole, the Court consensus, the net of what all the Justices collectively say the Constitution is. By June 1984, the Burger Court's fifteenth year, one could add up its bottom-line rulings on key parts of the Constitution and arrive at a reasonably accurate sense of how these particular Justices had affected American law in their particular time. A partial summary follows:

FIRST AMENDMENT

Free Speech. Discarding precedents to the contrary, the Court held in 1975 that commercial speech—advertising—was protected when it conveyed important information *(Bigelow v. Virginia)*. Further rulings in 1976 and 1977 held that states could no longer ban "tasteless" advertising, even for contraceptives *(Carey v. Population Services)* because the public's right to know required the free flow of all forms of non-fraudulent commercial speech. One result: Lawyers were now free to advertise.

Censorship. In 1976 the Court held, in an opinion by Chief Justice Burger, that judicial "gag" orders barring press coverage of sensational trials constituted prior restraint and were impermissible unless there was no other way to protect the defendant's right to a fair trial *(Nebraska Press Association v. Stuart)*. But the Court was not sympathetic to what many viewed as press claims to special privilege and what the press viewed as journalistic tools, vital to its role as the public's surrogate. Thus in 1972 *(Branzburg v. Hayes)*, the Court saw nothing sacred about the confidentiality of a reporter's unpublished notes or knowledge. Voting five to four, the Court ruled that reporters could be held in contempt for refusing to reveal their sources to a grand jury investigating a crime. The majority said that a reporter was like any other citizen in being obliged to tell whatever he knew about a crime.

Writing for the Court six years later, Justice White held that neither the First nor the Fourth Amendment barred police from searching newspaper offices and files in quest of criminal evidence. According to *Zurcher* v. *The Stanford Daily* (1978), the police were not required to subpoena the information and then wait for the newspaper to produce it. All they needed was a warrant to search the premises.

Libel. At first, the *Times* v. *Sullivan* decision of 1964 seemed to immunize the press from libel suits by just about anybody in the public eye. Not only public officials but also "public figures," such as famous football coaches, were required to prove "actual malice"—intentional publication of libelous falsehoods—before they could recover for damages. But in *Gertz* v. *Robert Welch, Inc.* (1974), the Court held that private citizens thrust into the news involuntarily were exempt from proving actual malice because, for one thing, they lacked a public figure's resources to redress libel.

Church and State. Ever since Chief Justice Burger announced it in 1971 *(Lemon v. Kurtzman)*, the Court had used a three-part test for construing the First Amendment ban on government conduct "establishing" religion. A challenged law or action could satisfy the Establishment Clause only if: 1) it reflected a clearly secular purpose; 2) it neither advanced nor inhibited religion; and 3) it avoided excessive government entanglement in religion.

In a 1983 opinion *(Mueller v. Allen)* written by Justice Rehnquist, the Court upheld a Minnesota law that allowed parents of children in *all* schools, private or public, to deduct a wide variety of school expenses (tuition, textbooks, transportation, etc.) from their state income taxes. Applying the *Lemon* test, Rehnquist said the Minnesota plan was secular because it bolstered all education, nonreligious because it benefited all parents, and nonentangling because the state was only peripherally involved.

A year later, the Court ruled that the *Lemon* test did not prohibit a tax-financed Nativity scene—the Christmas season creche that Pawtucket, Rhode Island, had erected in front of City Hall for the past forty years.

Two lower courts had enjoined the display as a case of government impermissibly favoring one religion over others that found it offensive, as did some nonbelievers. But in *Lynch* v. *Donnelly* (1984), five Justices overruled the lower courts. Writing for the majority, Chief Justice Burger declared that in celebrating a national holiday, combining religiosity and retailing, the creche served "legitimate secular purposes," and for the Court to forbid it would be "a stilted over-reaction contrary to our history and our holdings."

In a freedom of religion case in 1972 that did

not involve the *Lemon* test, the Court ruled that the right to free exercise of religion outweighed part of Wisconsin's compulsory education law. Three Amish families had refused to send their children to high school after they had completed the eighth grade, asserting that modern secondary education was contrary to their religion; the fathers of the children were convicted of violating the law and fined. The Court reversed the conviction in an opinion by Chief Justice Burger (*Yoder* v. *Yoder*), who said the Amish were entitled to the protection of the First Amendment and, after their children had completed elementary school, could follow their centuries-old tradition of learning at home.

FOURTH AMENDMENT

Reasonable Search and Seizure. The Fourth Amendment was designed to protect Americans from "unreasonable" searches and seizures. What was "reasonable"? The Warrant Clause answered: When the police obtained a judge-signed warrant, based on probable cause and specifying the items or persons to be seized, they had fully complied with the Framers' intent—to prevent arbitrary invasions of privacy and lawless detentions, as in a police state.

Over the years, however, the need for broader police discretion had produced exceptions to the warrant rule. Warrants were not required to search a moving vehicle or a lawfully arrested person, for example. Such warrantless actions were considered reasonable. But even they required probable cause: the police might or might not have a warrant to detain someone and search his person or property, but if they acted without probable cause, they had crossed the "unreasonable" line and violated the Fourth Amendment. By definition, searches and seizures were reasonable *only* if based on probable cause.

In 1968 the Warren Court made a significant exception to these rules. Under *Terry* v. *Ohio*, the police were authorized to briefly stop and frisk a person for weapons whenever they had "reason to believe" someone was armed and dangerous. *Terry* acknowledged the reality of street life and police work. It held that in this one specific situation, probable cause was an unrealistic—indeed,

unreasonable—standard to impose on a police officer forced to act swiftly to protect himself and others. Agreeing that an officer's safety outweighed a suspect's privacy, eight Justices approved a lower standard ("reasonable suspicion") that justified a pat-down search for weapons—but only weapons.

The Burger Court was called upon to heed the vast influx of drugs ravaging the nation. Building on "*Terry*-type investigative stops," the Court gradually enlarged the category of situations in which law enforcement needs outweighed individual privacy. Many such cases involved airports, drug smugglers, and armed motorists. In lieu of probable cause, the Court held, the police were increasingly free to seize evidence whenever they had "an articulable suspicion that a person had committed or is about to commit a crime."

Justice O'Connor wrote for the Court in a 1983 drug case, *Michigan* v. *Long*, that posed an interesting question of federalism. The police had stopped Long for drunken driving, noticed a hunting knife in his car, and then found marijuana. Did their alleged *Terry* search for weapons justify Long's conviction for possession of marijuana?

No, said the Michigan supreme court, basing its reversal on both the Fourth Amendment and the Michigan state constitution. Yes, said the United States Supreme Court.

Historically, the Supreme Court did not review state court interpretations of state laws and constitutions, unless they infringed federal rights. But state courts handle the overwhelming majority of criminal cases in America, and in recent years the nationalization of the Bill of Rights had drawn state courts into interpreting federal law on a vast scale. As a result, more and more state cases reaching the Supreme Court rested on federal as well as state law. If either law was sufficient alone to decide a case, which law prevailed?

"Respect for the independence of state courts," Justice O'Connor asserted in *Long,* required a new approach to state court decisions blending state and federal law. "In the absence of a plain statement that the decision below rested on an adequate and independent state ground," O'Connor held, the Supreme Court would take jurisdiction and apply federal law.

The four *Long* dissenters accused the majority of ill-disguised judicial activism. Justice Stevens wrote: "I am thoroughly baffled by the Court's suggestion that it must stretch its jurisdiction and reverse the judgment of the Michigan Supreme Court in order to show 'respect for the independence of state courts.'"

Exclusionary Rule. Court dicta going back to 1914 had viewed the Exclusionary Rule as so essential in righting Fourth Amendment wrongs that it was considered integral to the Constitution. Not so, Justice Powell contended in *United States* v. *Calandra* (1974). Made by judges, he noted, the rule could be unmade by judges. Aimed solely at deterring police misconduct, he said, it was subject to "cost benefit" analysis as to that purpose and that purpose alone.

In *Stone* v. *Powell* (1976) Justice Powell held that federal courts needn't enforce the Exclusionary Rule by granting habeas corpus writs to state prisoners seeking federal help in excluding the allegedly illegal evidence that had convicted them. According to Powell, this use of the rule cost too much in federal energy and state resentment to justify its minor effect on police conduct.

In *Illinois* v. *Gates* (1983), yet another drug case, the Court further curbed the Exclusionary Rule by softening the probable-cause standard for arrest and search warrants. For two decades, the Court had required police seeking judicial warrants to show that "anonymous" tips came from real informants. The idea was to prevent fictional probable cause.

In *Gates*, Justice Rehnquist said it was time to change the "overly technical" probable-cause rules and go back to the "totality of circumstances" approach. When police applied for warrants from then on, Rehnquist held, they needn't identify anonymous tipsters. The issuing judge was required only to "make a practical, common-sense decision whether, given all the circumstances set forth in the affidavit before him, there is a fair probability that contraband or evidence of a crime will be found in a particular place."

In *United States* v. *Leon* (1984), still another drug case, the Court held that a defective search warrant was now effective when the police honestly thought it was. This "good faith exception" to the Exclusionary Rule arose when a cocaine dealer challenged the warrant used to search his premises in Burbank, California. The police had dutifully supplied the issuing judge with what they thought was probable cause, namely an informant's tip. They had then seized ample evidence to send the dealer to prison. But at the later suppression hearing, it turned out that the tipster was unreliable and his information was five months old. Out went the warrant for lack of probable cause; out went the prosecutor's case for lack of admissible evidence; out walked the guilty dealer, a free man.

With all parties agreed that probable cause was absent and not to be debated, the Supreme Court reviewed *Leon* simply to consider the Reagan Justice Department's advocacy of a good-faith exception to the Exclusionary Rule. Relying heavily on cost-benefit analysis, Justice White wrote for a six-to-three majority that "penalizing the officer for the magistrate's error, rather than his own, cannot logically contribute to the deterrence of Fourth Amendment violations."

In a *Leon* situation, when police had an "objectively reasonable belief" in the validity of a search warrant, White held, a later finding to the contrary no longer justified "the extreme sanction of exclusion."

The three dissenters protested that *Leon* would degrade the Fourth Amendment by assuring the police that defective warrants no longer mattered.

FIFTH AMENDMENT

Miranda Rule. Saved by *stare decisis* and a relative paucity of proof that it was foiling police or freeing criminals, the Warren Court's 1966 antidote to coerced confessions—*Miranda* v. *Arizona*—had survived at least ten Burger Court rulings by 1984. None of these decisions had fundamentally changed the *Miranda* rule that before questioning anyone in their custody, the police must warn him of his Fifth Amendment right to silence and his Sixth Amendment right to counsel.

Ten years later, speaking for the Court in *New York* v. *Quarles* (1984), Justice Rehnquist announced a change of potentially great significance.

In *Quarles*, four New York City policemen had chased a suspected and reportedly armed rapist into a big supermarket late at night. The place was empty, no customers in sight. Guns drawn, the police quickly found, subdued, and searched the man. Finding an empty shoulder holster, they handcuffed him and asked, "Where's the gun?" He said, "Over there." Only after retrieving his pistol had the police warned Benjamin Quarles about his rights, which he then waived, admitting the gun was his. Not prosecuted for rape, he was charged with and convicted of illegally possessing a weapon.

On this record, the New York Court of Appeals suppressed the evidence on the ground that the police—not in danger and fully in control—should have taken a moment to recite the *Miranda* warnings before they retrieved the gun. On the same record, the Supreme Court reversed the state court.

Concerned about potential danger, the Supreme Court held that *Miranda* must now be modified by a "public safety exception" permitting the police to ask questions first and give warnings later whenever they confronted "situations presenting danger to the public safety."

Quarles troubled Justice O'Connor, who dissented in part from the Rehnquist opinion. "In my view," she wrote, "a 'public safety exception' unnecessarily blurs the edges of the clear line heretofore established and makes *Miranda*'s requirements much more difficult to understand. . . . The end result will be a finespun new doctrine on public safety exigencies . . . complete with the hairsplitting distinctions that currently plague our Fourth Amendment jurisprudence."

EIGHTH AMENDMENT

Capital Punishment. The Eighth Amendment ban on "cruel and unusual punishment" doubtless reflects the Framers' abhorrence of torture, but otherwise casts its interpreters adrift upon a sea of public qualms. Since at least the thirteenth century, there has been common-law authority for the proposition that punishment should fit the crime, and the Eighth Amendment has generally been read to ban penalties deemed barbaric or disproportionate. Still, judicial views as to whether a specific crime deserves a specific penalty must inevitably derive in large part from a contemporary moral consensus, which may vary dramatically according to time, place, and communal fears. This is especially true of the

ultimate penalty for the ultimate crime, execution for murder.

In a much-quoted 1958 opinion *(Trop v. Dulles)*, Chief Justice Warren said the Eighth Amendment mandated "civilized" methods of punishment consistent with "the dignity of man." He concluded, "The Amendment must draw its meaning from the evolving standards of decency that mark the progress of a maturing society."

It was the Burger Court that struck down all state death penalty laws in 1972 *(Furman v. Georgia)*, a startling five-to-four decision that effectively, if not intentionally, brought capital punishment before the bar of American moral opinion. *Furman* did not abolish the penalty, only its capricious administration, so that states were now free to either pass better laws or discard execution, as they saw fit.

By 1976, Congress and thirty-five states had passed new death penalty laws aimed at meeting *Furman*'s clearest critique—a previous lack of statutory standards so egregious that judges and juries were, as Justice Stewart had put it, selecting the condemned "wantonly and freakishly."

Ten states had responded by simply making death mandatory for anybody convicted of first-degree murder. In those states, objectivity meant that jurors could no longer even consider mitigating circumstances. But in twenty-five other states, new laws provided for individual differences by giving jurors and judges specific criteria that presumably limited execution to the "worst" killers.

In July 1976, a five-Justice majority rejected the mandatory death sentence for murder as repugnant to "the respect for humanity underlying the Eighth Amendment." In three other decisions on the same day, seven Justices declared that the Amendment did not forbid execution, "an extreme sanction suitable to the most extreme of crimes," and upheld the "guided discretion" approach to sentencing as a sufficient check on the arbitrariness Justice Stewart had decried in *Furman*. Noting that the Framers had accepted "the existence of capital punishment," Stewart spoke for the Court in the day's leading decision, *Gregg v. Georgia*.

That case involved one Troy Gregg, a vicious highwayman who had hitched a ride with two unsuspecting Georgia motorists, shot and robbed them, left their bodies in a ditch, and sped off in their car. Under Georgia's new law, the jury had first found Gregg guilty of murder, then decided separately whether he deserved a life sentence or a death sentence. The law required the jurors to consider both mitigating and aggravating circumstances, and they could not impose death without stating in writing that they had found at least one of ten aggravating circumstances which were spelled out in the statute. Moreover, Georgia's supreme court automatically reviewed each death sentence for arbitrariness or disproportion.

The Supreme Court's approval of such two-stage laws in *Gregg* v. *Georgia* hardly erased capital punishment from its docket. *Gregg* was only the beginning of a long series of refining decisions. Over the next six years, the Court banned mandatory execution for police killers *(Roberts* v. *Louisiana)*, outlawed death sentences for rape *(Coker* v. *Georgia)*, and ruled death excessive for the crime of felony-murder, provided the defendant had not himself participated in the killing *(Enmund* v. *Florida)*. Still, the appeals kept coming. Sharply criticizing defense lawyers for "calculated efforts to frustrate valid judgments," Chief Justice Burger declared, "At some point there must be finality."

Proportionate Punishment. Speaking through Justice Powell in 1983, the Court ruled for the first time in history that a prison sentence could violate the Eighth Amendment if it was so disproportionate to the crime that it constituted cruel and unusual punishment. Significantly, the Court had previously applied that analysis only to death sentences for less-than-murder crimes, such as rape.

In *Solem* v. *Helm*, the appellant was an alcoholic who had spent almost half his thirty-six years in South Dakota jails for offenses ranging from drunk driving to third-degree burglary. Legally, these added up to six felony convictions, and under South Dakota's unforgiving repeater law (matched only in Nevada), a judge could sentence a *three*-time felon to life imprisonment without parole, no matter how minor his fourth offense.

Thus, when Jerry Helm pleaded guilty to writing a rubber $100 check, a judge had immediately pronounced him "beyond rehabilitation" and sentenced him to permanent imprisonment.

But Helm eventually persuaded five Justices

that his life sentence, the harshest South Dakota meted out for *any* crime, violated the "principle of proportionality" going back to the Magna Carta and implicit in the Eighth Amendment. "We hold," Justice Powell wrote in *Solem* v. *Helm*, "that a criminal sentence must be proportionate to the crime for which the defendant has been convicted."

Chief Justice Burger dissented, contending that proportionality applied only to capital cases; that the majority "trespasses gravely on the authority of the states" to fix prison sentences; that Powell's opinion was "bankrupt of realistic guiding principles," and that *Helm* was "nothing more than a bald substitution of individual subjective morals for those of the legislature." As for Jerry Helm himself, the Chief Justice wrote, "Surely seven felony convictions warrant the conclusion that respondent is incorrigible."

Whatever *Helm*'s precedential effect on death-sentence appeals, if any, the Chief Justice prevailed a year later when the Court said the Constitution did not require judicial examination of whether a defendant's death sentence was disproportionate to lesser sentences meted out for the same crime in the same state *(Pulley* v. *Harris)*. The Court thus removed one more obstacle to swifter executions. Thirty-eight states now authorize capital punishment, albeit with far greater protections for the guilty defendant than ever before.

F O U R T E E N T H
A M E N D M E N T

Racial Discrimination. Three decades after *Brown* v. *Board of Education*, the Burger Court was still dealing with thorny, often complex issues of discrimination and desegregation.

In the curious case of *Bob Jones University* v. *United States* (1983), the Internal Revenue Service had revoked a private educational institution's tax exemption on the ground that it discriminated against blacks. The institution, a fundamentalist Christian school in South Carolina, argued that it was merely obeying the Bible. The IRS said Bob Jones's bigotry violated a "national policy to discourage racial discrimination in education," thus rendering it legally a noncharitable institution that had to pay taxes. Having been billed for more than half a million dollars in back taxes, the school had reason to resist the revocation, which it said violated its First Amendment right to practice its brand of religion free of government meddling.

Voting eight to one, the Supreme Court firmly upheld the IRS's right to revoke tax breaks for segregationist private schools. With only Rehnquist dissenting (on other grounds), Chief Justice Burger, writing for the Court, held that in this instance a compelling secular interest must outweigh asserted religious beliefs. With special emphasis, Burger declared: "An unbroken line of cases following *Brown* v. *Board of Education* establishes beyond doubt this Court's view that racial discrimination in education violates a most fundamental national policy . . ."

The end of legal segregation in America had raised a new equal protection problem. A challenged law might appear quite neutral on its face yet produce racial discrimination. Did such laws deserve the Court's "strict scrutiny"—and probable veto?

In *Washington* v. *Davis* (1976), a seven-to-two majority significantly augmented the proof required from plaintiffs to trigger strict scrutiny in any suit charging officials with unconstitutional discrimination.

The case involved two black men who wanted to become policemen in Washington, D.C. They had taken a verbal aptitude test given to all police candidates. Rejected for low test scores, they discovered that black applicants had failed the test four times more often than whites. Citing Chief Justice Burger's opinion for a unanimous Court in *Griggs* v. *Duke Power Co.* (1971), they argued that the test was invalid because it was not directly related to job performance and had a disproportionate impact on blacks, who were markedly underrepresented on the police force, compared with the city's predominantly black population.

The Court ruled against them. It held that impact alone did not establish that a challenged law was sufficiently "invidious" to trigger strict scrutiny. In addition to impact, Justice White wrote, the plaintiff must prove official intent—"a racially discriminatory purpose." In this case, White found no such intent and ruled the test "facially neutral," thereby obviating any need to look much beyond its stated purpose. The verbal test was deemed a rational way for the police force to achieve a valid goal, namely "upgrading the communicative abilities of its employees."

From then on, the Court required a showing of intent to discriminate before it found official actions in violation of the Equal Protection Clause.

But what if a classification *favored* a minority at the expense of the majority? "Affirmative action" programs did just that. To compensate for past discrimination and help bring the disadvantaged into the economic mainstream, such programs favored blacks over whites, or women over men.

Suppose that certain majority members— whites disfavored by affirmative action—complained that *they* had been denied equal protection? After all, the Constitution was "color-blind" and supposedly mandated impartiality toward whites as well as blacks. Did so-called "benign" racial discrimination justify the standard of strict scrutiny?

When the Court considered an affirmative action program in 1978 *(University of California Regents* v. *Bakke)*, the Justices could only agree to disagree on precisely how vigorously such programs should be scrutinized.

In that famous case, the University of California's Davis Medical School had set out to produce more minority-group physicians by reserving sixteen places for minority students in each of its one hundred-place classes. Alan Bakke, a white engineer, sought admission to the medical school but was rejected twice. Since his qualifications surpassed those of some students admitted under the preference system, he sued for equal protection all the way to the Supreme Court, which upheld his complaint—but not on constitutional grounds.

This oddity emerged from an impasse between two four-Justice blocs. The first group took the restrained view that *Bakke* needn't be a constitutional case. Since the university received federal aid, they upheld Alan Bakke under a federal statute (Title VI of the 1964 Civil Rights Act) that clearly barred racial discrimination in any federally aided program. By contrast, the other four Justices took the constitutional plunge, ruling for the university on the ground that the Equal Protection Clause did not forbid governmental racial quotas designed to benefit a minority rather than demean it.

The impasse was broken by Justice Powell, who stood alone in agreeing with *both* blocs and whose solo opinion therefore became controlling, even though nobody else supported it. Powell's fifth vote upheld each bloc's contention by a vote of five to four. So the *Bakke* decision said, first, that the federal law compelled the medical school to accept Alan Bakke, and second, that the university was entitled to take race into account in its admission policies. But Powell added his own third point, which overshadowed the others.

In his view, affirmative action was constitutional only if "necessary to promote a substantial state interest." The only such interest he approved was remedying past discrimination, which he insisted must be clearly proved in order to justify even a benign divergence from the color-blind-Constitution concept. In *Bakke*, he concluded, the medical school had failed to prove sufficient injury to necessitate its remedy.

Affirmative action seemed to be left in constitutional limbo. But the Court traditionally avoids constitutional rulings if it can decide a case on other grounds, and so it did in subsequent decisions on the issue. In 1979, for example, the federal law banning racial discrimination in employment was ruled no barrier to affirmative action by private industry *(United Steelworkers* v. *Weber)*. According to the majority, Congress did not intend the anti-discrimination law to forbid private voluntary efforts to remedy discrimination.

In 1984, on the other hand, the Court dealt a blow to affirmative action programs in *Firefighters Union Local 1784* v. *Stotts*. Memphis had hired Carl Stotts and other black firefighters under the terms of a 1980 consent decree aimed at the fact that blacks comprised only four percent of the city's fire department, compared with thirty-five percent of the city's labor force. During the 1981 recession, Memphis prepared to lay off some firefighters, using its last-hired, first-fired seniority system. But with blacks still at less than twelve percent of the fire department, the federal court enforcing the 1980 decree ordered the city to give top priority to preserving its racial hiring gains.

As a result, three black firefighters kept their jobs, while three whites with more seniority lost theirs (for a month). The firefighters union sued the blacks, arguing that seniority was a trust immunized from affirmative action by the 1964 Civil Rights Act.

Voting six to three, the Court upheld the contention that lower courts had no authority to protect the jobs of recently hired black employees at the expense of whites with greater seniority. The three dissenters protested that the case was moot, the layoff having ended well before any court actually heard the merits. Justice Blackmun deplored the decision as "an improper exercise of judicial power."

Sex Discrimination. The Court developed a "middle-tier" test devised by Justice Brennan in sex discrimination cases. Brennan had originally argued that gender-based classifications were inherently suspect, like those based on race and alienage. In *Frontiero* v. *Richardson* (1973), a woman Air Force officer had sought certain benefits for her civilian husband as a military dependent. She was turned down: the law bestowed greater family benefits on military men than on military women. In effect, a soldier's wife was a legitimate dependent but a soldier's husband was not. With only Rehnquist dissenting, eight Justices erased this inequity from the books.

But only three of them agreed with Brennan, who wrote a plurality opinion announcing the Court's decision. He argued that strict scrutiny should be applied to laws "invidiously relegating the entire class of females to inferior legal status," regardless of their individual abilities. Only a compelling governmental interest, absent in *Frontiero*, justified such laws, he said. But other Justices demurred, saying the rationality standard would have produced the same *Frontiero* result, so that Brennan's theory lacked the fifth vote that would have made it constitutional doctrine.

Then came *Craig* v. *Boren* (1976), challenging an Oklahoma law that banned the sale of 3.2 percent beer to women under the age of 18 and men under the age of 21. Why this age disparity? Surely everybody knew that young men became drunken drivers far more often than young women, Oklahoma responded. And surely everybody supported the law's worthy goal of curbing drunk driving in order to save lives.

The law was accused of harboring sexual stereotypes. To overcome constitutional challenge, Justice Brennan wrote for a seven-man majority, "classifications by gender must serve important governmental objectives and must be substantially related to achievement of those objectives."

By that standard, the Oklahoma law served an important goal (safe driving), but could not stand because it used a gender distinction the Court found more invidious than invaluable in achieving the goal. In Brennan's words, the state simply hadn't proved that "sex represents a legitimate, accurate proxy for the regulation of drinking and driving."

Craig's perspective had major consequences. Gender-based laws appeared untenable and indeed invalid, unless they actually solved some urgent problem in a way acceptable to both sexes.

Accordingly, the Burger Court produced significant precedents in sex discrimination cases. It ruled that husbands and wives must co-manage community property, that spouses were equally eligible to administer a relative's estate, and that a man was no less entitled to alimony than a woman. It abolished male-female disparities in the benefits wage-earners received from Social Security, military, and welfare programs. It insisted that daughters of divorced couples were entitled to the same support as sons, and that widowers must receive the same child-care aid as widows did.

Second, the *Craig* test provided a flexibility in Equal Protection jurisprudence that made a difference in how the Court resolved other forms of alleged discrimination. At issue in *Plyler* v. *Doe* (1982), for example, was a Texas law preventing the children of illegal aliens from attending public schools. Strict scrutiny did not apply: *illegal* aliens were not a "suspect" class, nor was education a "fundamental right." But *Craig*'s "intermediate scrutiny" enabled five Justices to strike down the law.

Education was not a fundamental right, the *Plyler* majority reiterated. But its social essentiality made it more than "merely some governmental benefit." Any official denial of access to schooling required heightened review, especially when, as here, the denial "imposes a lifetime hardship on a discrete class of children not accountable for their status." Such discrimination was permissible only if it promoted a "substantial goal of the State." But the only purpose served by the law, Justice Brennan held, was "the creation and perpetuation of a subclass of illiterates within our boundaries, surely adding to . . . unemployment, welfare, and crime."

The Court's first woman member consistently expressed strong views opposing gender-based discrimination. But when six Justices, including Burger, strongly reaffirmed the Court's ten-year-old abortion decision in 1983 *(Akron* v. *Akron Center for Reproductive Health)*, Justice O'Connor wrote a forceful dissent that questioned the Court's rationale for a measure of free choice in the decision whether to abort a pregnancy.

Citing *Roe* v. *Wade* (1973), which permitted limited state regulation only after the first trimester, the Court's *Akron* decision struck down various local restrictions in twenty-two states. The immediate case involved a "model" ordinance in Akron, Ohio, that made it a crime to have an abortion outside a hospital after the first trimester. Among sixteen other provisions, the law required a twenty-four-hour waiting period for the woman to ponder a mandatory warning from her doctor that abortion could be dangerous and that the fetus "is a human life from the moment of conception."

Speaking for the Court, Justice Powell voided all these obstacles to free-choice, noting especially that the hospital-only rule forced women to spend twice as much for a procedure that could now be done for half the cost in a doctor's office. Key to this ruling were medical advances over the ten years since *Roe* that had made outpatient abortions the preferred treatment up to the eighteenth week of pregnancy.

In dissent, Justice O'Connor noted *Akron*'s finding that "the safety of second-trimester abortions had increased dramatically"—and added the striking corollary that "fetal viability in the first trimester . . . may be possible in the not too distant future." She thus pronounced the entire *Roe* formulation "on a collision course with itself." As medical risks decreased, she said, "the point at which the State may regulate for reasons of maternal health is moved further forward to actual childbirth. As medical science becomes better able to provide for the separate existence of the fetus, the point of viability is moved further back toward conception."

In O'Connor's opinion, the state's interests in regulating maternal health and fetal viability were no longer divisible by trimesters. In her view, "these interests are present *throughout* pregnancy"—a conclusion that would obviously give the state preemptive control over the woman's constitutional right to choose abortion.

SEPARATION OF POWERS

In June 1983, Chief Justice Burger announced a seven-to-two decision striking down the "legislative veto," an expedient used by Congress to keep the President and his myriad agencies in check for the past fifty years. In more than 200 laws, Congress had delegated authority to the President while retaining the power to veto the way in which the Executive Branch executed those laws.

In an otherwise obscure immigration case, *Immigration and Naturalization Service* v. *Chadha*, the Court had finally ended years of debate over the legislative veto and outlawed it as a usurpation of power by Congress. Given its vast potential impact upon the balance of power between Congress and the President, Chief Justice Burger's sweeping opinion in *Chadha* was the Court's most significant constitutional ruling since *United States* v. *Nixon* (1974), nine years earlier.

Of all American contributions to political liberty, those curbing undue concentrations of power are indispensable. To foil despotic legislators, the Constitution divided Congress into two contrasting houses and empowered them to legislate, but only if both houses approved new bills and submitted them to the President. A bill became law only if the President signed it. If he disapproved it, Congress could override his veto, but only if it mustered a two-thirds vote in both houses.

Congress had produced more than 350 veto clauses over the years, and those still on the books gave the lawmakers a post-enactment grip on everything from consumer regulations to Social Security and foreign arms sales.

Jagdish Chadha, an Indian born in Kenya and carrying a British passport, had earned a college

The Burger Court, 1981–86. Standing, from left: Associate Justices John Paul Stevens, Louis Franklin Powell, Jr., William Hubbs Rehnquist, Sandra Day O'Connor. Seated, from left: Associate Justices Thurgood Marshall, William Joseph Brennan, Jr., Chief Justice Warren E. Burger, Associate Justices Byron Raymond White, Harry A. Blackmun. Photograph by the *National Geographic*. Collection of the Supreme Court of the United States, Washington, D.C.

degree in Ohio. When Kenya later refused to take him back and Britain barred him for a year, he tried to become an American citizen, only to be ordered out of the country. When the Immigration Service eventually relented, permitting him to remain as a hardship case, Chadha's euphoria was quickly dashed by a House subcommittee overseeing immigration laws. Reviewing a list of 340 aliens seeking permanent resident status, the subcommittee decided his was not a hardship case and vetoed the Immigration Service's decision by striking Chadha from the list.

Nine years later, Chadha was still fighting back with the help of a public-law firm that appealed his plight to the courts. Indeed, he had achieved much success and in some ways his case was arguably moot. By the time it finally reached the Supreme Court, he had married an American, thus avoiding deportation, and was well on the way to gaining citizenship.

But Chadha's case was now destined for constitutional history. The legislative veto exercised by Congress against Jagdish Chadha had become the death knell of a practice that Chief Justice Burger found totally out of step with "the Framers' decision that the legislative power of the federal government be exercised in accord with a single, finely wrought and exhaustively considered procedure."

In his opinion for the Court, Chief Justice Burger held that Congress's decision to deport Chadha was a legislative act, subject to all the constitutional rules of enacting legislation, namely "bicameral passage followed by presentment to the President." Instead, the subcommittee's "one-house veto" in Chadha's case had unlawfully overruled Executive branch officers without the concurrence of the Senate or the President, in a decision the Executive had been authorized to make, save for the one-house veto clause, which Burger now declared unconstitutional. To maintain the separation of powers, designed to prevent "improvident exercise of power," Burger wrote, "the carefully defined limits on the power of each Branch must not be eroded."

In a lone dissenting opinion, which he read aloud from the bench—a rare step—Justice White defended the legislative veto as a practical application of the Framers' intentions to the reality of "the modern administrative state." White called the veto "a central means by which Congress secures the accountability of executive and independent agencies." Instead of preserving this tool for keeping the people's representatives on top of the unelected bureaucracy, he said, the Court had wrongly taken a "destructive" step that "strikes down in one fell swoop provisions in more laws enacted by Congress than the Court had cumulatively invalidated in its history."

Whatever the effects, the Supreme Court had ensured that they would be achieved by the book, according to the Framers' specifications. "With all the obvious flaws of delay, untidiness, and potential for abuse" those specifications may impose on twentieth-century government, Chief Justice Burger wrote, "we have not yet found a better way to preserve freedom than by making the exercise of power subject to the carefully crafted restraints spelled out in the Constitution."

Epilogue
IMAGINE AMERICA WITHOUT THE SUPREME COURT . . .

Begin with a great American riddle: If a country's basic values are freedom and equality, which takes precedence? How can they be made to co-exist?

A society wedded to the ideals of both freedom and equality is bound to struggle with conflicting imperatives.

For nearly two hundred years, the Supreme Court has held these dual claims in delicate balance. It has generally deferred to liberty, while striving to curb abuses of natural inequality and prevent the strong from exploiting the weak. The entire thrust of the Constitution, with its ingenious system of checks and balances, is against undue concentrations of power. This sacred command has been the Court's guiding principle. One astonishing result is that the Court has actually made liberty and equality apparently compatible.

Slowly but surely, the United States has extended national liberties to *all* its inhabitants, making the Republic freer as it ages—an outcome exactly opposite to that of most revolutions. The Supreme Court cannot take sole credit for this probably unique phenomenon—yet the keeper of the Constitution is, by definition, the keeper of the national conscience, and the Court's contribution is so substantial as to be incalculable.

The truism that freedom should never be taken for granted has never been truer. Freedom is more often lost than stolen. "Safety from external danger is the most powerful director of national conduct," Hamilton wrote two centuries ago. "Even the ardent love of liberty will, after a time, give way to its dictates. The violent destruction of life and property incident to war, the continual effort and alarm attendant on a state of continual danger, will compel nations the most attached to liberty to resort for repose and security to institutions which have a tendency to destroy their civil and political rights. To be more safe, they at length become willing to run the risk of being less free."

In other countries, the curbs on liberty that national emergencies allegedly require have a way of outlasting the emergencies by years or decades. Thus far, the United States has upheld a very different tradition. With certain exceptions, America has demobilized such measures when the crisis truly ended. In this regard, the Supreme Court has played a starring role. While conceding that judicial power is no match for wartime claims of military necessity, the Court has never failed to lead the way to a post-emergency restoration of constitutional guarantees. It has always acted *as if* all guarantees were fully in force, even if temporarily out of order. The Court has thus achieved a moral authority unique among secular bodies.

But that authority is no more final than it is automatic. In America, the final word is spoken by the nation's political majority—not by the President, the Congress, the Court, or even the Constitution, which the people can always amend. In short, the Court must ultimately join Presidents, Senators, and Representatives in the test of majority approval. The Court's power is directly proportional to its perceived legitimacy in the eyes of the voters. When the Justices articulate the tenets of a just society, the Court's legitimacy—and power—are assured.

As the Court enters its third century, its constitutional role appears no less essential to national survival. In the end, though, that role is largely *up to us*. The Court can appeal to our best instincts as a nation; it can prove its impartiality, retaining its majesty and mystery and proper distance from any political faction. With its institutional survival techniques and self-renewing tradition of dissent, it can avoid doctrinal extremes and sustain the rule of law with both finality and flexibility. But ultimately the Justices can inspire their countrymen only to the degree that we share in the promises the Court keeps.

THE CONSTITUTION OF
THE UNITED STATES OF AMERICA

The Constitution

OF THE
UNITED STATES
OF AMERICA

We the People *of the United States, in Order to form a more perfect Union, establish Justice, insure domestic Tranquility, provide for the common defence, promote the general Welfare, and secure the Blessings of Liberty to ourselves and our Posterity, do ordain and establish this Constitution for the United States of America.*

ARTICLE I.

SECTION 1. All legislative Powers herein granted shall be vested in a Congress of the United States, which shall consist of a Senate and House of Representatives.

SECTION 2. The House of Representatives shall be composed of Members chosen every second Year by the People of the several States, and the Electors in each State shall have the Qualifications requisite for Electors of the most numerous Branch of the State Legislature.

No Person shall be a Representative who shall not have attained to the Age of twenty-five Years, and been seven Years a Citizen of the United States, and who shall not, when elected, be an Inhabitant of that State in which he shall be chosen.

[Representatives and direct Taxes shall be apportioned among the several States which may be included within this Union, according to their respective Numbers, which shall be

[NOTE: The Constitution and all amendments are presented in their original form. Items which have since been amended or superseded, as identified in the footnotes, are bracketed.]

determined by adding to the whole Number of free Persons, including those bound to Service for a Term of Years, and excluding Indians not taxed, three fifths of all other Persons.]* The actual Enumeration shall be made within three Years after the first Meeting of the Congress of the United States, and within every subsequent Term of ten Years, in such Manner as they shall by Law direct. The Number of Representatives shall not exceed one for every thirty Thousand,** but each State shall have at Least one Representative; and until such enumeration shall be made, the State of New Hampshire shall be entitled to chuse three, Massachusetts eight, Rhode-Island and Providence Plantations one, Connecticut five, New-York six, New Jersey four, Pennsylvania eight, Delaware one, Maryland six, Virginia ten, North Carolina five, South Carolina five, and Georgia three.

When vacancies happen in the Representation from any State, the Executive Authority thereof shall issue Writs of Election to fill such Vacancies.

The House of Representatives shall chuse their Speaker and other Officers; and shall have the sole Power of Impeachment.

SECTION 3. The Senate of the United States shall be composed of two Senators from each State, [chosen by the Legislature thereof,]*** for six Years; and each Senator shall have one Vote.

Immediately after they shall be assembled in Consequence of the first Election, they shall be divided as equally as may be into three Classes. The Seats of the Senators of the first Class shall be vacated at the Expiration of the second Year, of the

*Changed by section 2 of the fourteenth amendment.
**Ratio in 1965 was one to over 410,000.
***Changed by section 1 of the seventeenth amendment.

second Class at the Expiration of the fourth Year, and of the third Class at the Expiration of the sixth Year, so that one-third may be chosen every second Year; [and if Vacancies happen by Resignation, or otherwise, during the Recess of the Legislature of any State, the Executive thereof may make temporary Appointments until the next Meeting of the Legislature, which shall then fill such Vacancies.]*

No Person shall be a Senator who shall not have attained to the Age of thirty Years, and been nine Years a Citizen of the United States, and who shall not, when elected, be an Inhabitant of that State for which he shall be chosen.

The Vice President of the United States shall be President of the Senate, but shall have no Vote, unless they be equally divided.

The Senate shall chuse their other Officers, and also a President pro tempore, in the absence of the Vice President, or when he shall exercise the Office of President of the United States.

The Senate shall have the sole Power to try all Impeachments. When sitting for that Purpose, they shall be on Oath or Affirmation. When the President of the United States is tried, the Chief Justice shall preside: And no Person shall be convicted without the Concurrence of two thirds of the Members present.

Judgment in Cases of Impeachment shall not extend further than to removal from Office, and disqualification to hold and enjoy any Office of honor, Trust or Profit under the United States: but the Party convicted shall nevertheless be liable and subject to Indictment, Trial, Judgment and Punishment, according to Law.

SECTION 4. The Times, Places and Manner of holding Elec-
*Changed by clause 2 of the seventeenth amendment.

tions for Senators and Representatives, shall be prescribed in each State by the Legislature thereof; but the Congress may at any time by Law make or alter such Regulations, except as to the Place of Chusing Senators.

The Congress shall assemble at least once in every Year, and such Meeting shall [be on the first Monday in December,]** unless they shall by Law appoint a different Day.

SECTION 5. Each House shall be the Judge of the Elections, Returns and Qualifications of its own Members, and a Majority of each shall constitute a Quorum to do Business; but a smaller number may adjourn from day to day, and may be authorized to compel the Attendance of absent Members, in such Manner, and under such Penalties as each House may provide.

Each House may determine the Rules of its Proceedings, punish its Members for disorderly Behavior, and, with the Concurrence of two thirds, expel a Member.

Each House shall keep a Journal of its Proceedings, and from time to time publish the same, excepting such Parts as may in their Judgment require Secrecy; and the Yeas and Nays of the Members of either House on any question shall, at the Desire of one fifth of those Present, be entered on the Journal.

Neither House, during the Session of Congress, shall, without the Consent of the other, adjourn for more than three days, nor to any other Place than that in which the two Houses shall be sitting.

SECTION 6. The Senators and Representatives shall receive a Compensation for their Services, to be ascertained by Law, and paid out of the Treasury of the United States. They shall in all Cases, except Treason, Felony and Breach of the Peace,

**Changed by section 2 of the twentieth amendment.

be privileged from Arrest during their Attendance at the Session of their respective Houses, and in going to and returning from the same; and for any Speech or Debate in either House, they shall not be questioned in any other Place.

No Senator or Representative shall, during the Time for which he was elected, be appointed to any civil Office under the Authority of the United States, which shall have been created, or the Emoluments whereof shall have been encreased during such time; and no Person holding any Office under the United States, shall be a Member of either House during his Continuance in Office.

SECTION 7. All Bills for raising Revenue shall originate in the House of Representatives; but the Senate may propose or concur with Amendments as on other Bills.

Every Bill which shall have passed the House of Representatives and the Senate, shall, before it become a Law, be presented to the President of the United States; If he approve he shall sign it, but if not he shall return it, with his Objections to that House in which it shall have originated, who shall enter the Objections at large on their Journal, and proceed to reconsider it. If after such Reconsideration two thirds of that House shall agree to pass the Bill, it shall be sent, together with the Objections, to the other House, by which it shall likewise be reconsidered, and if approved by two thirds of that House, it shall become a Law. But in all Cases the Votes of both Houses shall be determined by Yeas and Nays, and the Names of the Persons voting for and against the Bill shall be entered on the Journal of each House respectively. If any Bill shall not be returned by the President within ten Days (Sundays excepted) after it shall have been presented to him, the Same shall be a Law, in like Manner as if he had signed it, unless the Congress by their Adjournment prevent its

Return, in which Case it shall not be a Law.

Every Order, Resolution, or Vote to which the Concurrence of the Senate and House of Representatives may be necessary (except on a question of Adjournment) shall be presented to the President of the United States; and before the Same shall take Effect, shall be approved by him, or being disapproved by him, shall be repassed by two thirds of the Senate and House of Representatives, according to the Rules and Limitations prescribed in the Case of a Bill.

SECTION 8. The Congress shall have Power To lay and collect Taxes, Duties, Imposts and Excises, to pay the Debts and provide for the common Defense and general Welfare of the United States; but all Duties, Imposts and Excises shall be uniform throughout the United States;

To borrow money on the credit of the United States;

To regulate Commerce with foreign Nations, and among the several States, and with the Indian Tribes;

To establish an uniform Rule of Naturalization, and uniform Laws on the subject of Bankruptcies throughout the United States;

To coin Money, regulate the Value thereof, and of foreign Coin, and fix the Standard of Weights and Measures;

To provide for the Punishment of counterfeiting the Securities and current Coin of the United States;

To establish Post Offices and post Roads;

To promote the Progress of Science and useful Arts, by securing for limited Times to Authors and Inventors the exclusive Right to their respective Writings and Discoveries;

To constitute Tribunals inferior to the supreme Court;

To define and punish Piracies and Felonies committed on the high Seas, and Offenses against the Law of Nations;

To declare War, grant Letters of Marque and Reprisal, and

make Rules concerning Captures on Land and Water;

To raise and support Armies, but no Appropriation of Money to that Use shall be for a longer Term than two Years;

To provide and maintain a Navy;

To make Rules for the Government and Regulation of the land and naval Forces;

To provide for calling forth the Militia to execute the Laws of the Union, suppress Insurrections and repel Invasions;

To provide for organizing, arming, and disciplining the Militia, and for governing such Part of them as may be employed in the Service of the United States, reserving to the States respectively, the Appointment of the Officers, and the Authority of training the Militia according to the discipline prescribed by Congress;

To exercise exclusive Legislation in all Cases whatsoever, over such District (not exceeding ten Miles square) as may, by Cession of particular States, and the acceptance of Congress, become the Seat of the Government of the United States, and to exercise like Authority over all Places purchased by the Consent of the Legislature of the State in which the Same shall be, for the Erection of Forts, Magazines, Arsenals, dock-Yards, and other needful Buildings;—And

To make all Laws which shall be necessary and proper for carrying into Execution the foregoing Powers, and all other Powers vested by this Constitution in the Government of the United States, or in any Department or Officer thereof.

SECTION 9. The Migration or Importation of such Persons as any of the States now existing shall think proper to admit, shall not be prohibited by the Congress prior to the Year one thousand eight hundred and eight, but a tax or duty may be imposed on such Importation, not exceeding ten dollars for each Person.

The privilege of the Writ of Habeas Corpus shall not be suspended, unless when in Cases of Rebellion or Invasion the public Safety may require it.

No Bill of Attainder or ex post facto Law shall be passed.

No capitation, or other direct, Tax shall be laid, unless in Proportion to the Census or Enumeration herein before directed to be taken.*

No Tax or Duty shall be laid on Articles exported from any State.

No Preference shall be given by any Regulation of Commerce or Revenue to the Ports of one State over those of another: nor shall Vessels bound to, or from, one State, be obliged to enter, clear, or pay Duties in another.

No Money shall be drawn from the Treasury, but in Consequence of Appropriations made by Law; and a regular Statement and Account of the Receipts and Expenditures of all public Money shall be published from time to time.

No Title of Nobility shall be granted by the United States: And no Person holding any Office of Profit or Trust under them, shall, without the Consent of the Congress, accept of any present, Emolument, Office, or Title, of any kind whatever, from any King, Prince, or foreign State.

SECTION 10. No State shall enter into any Treaty, Alliance, or Confederation; grant Letters of Marque and Reprisal; coin Money; emit Bills of Credit; make any Thing but gold and silver Coin a Tender in Payment of Debts; pass any Bill of Attainder, ex post facto Law, or Law impairing the Obligation of Contracts, or grant any Title of Nobility.

No State shall, without the Consent of the Congress, lay any Imposts or Duties on Imports or Exports, except what may be absolutely necessary for executing its inspection Laws: and

*But see the sixteenth amendment.

ber of Votes shall be the President, if such Number be a Majority of the whole Number of Electors appointed; and if there be more than one who have such Majority, and have an equal Number of Votes, then the House of Representatives shall immediately chuse by Ballot one of them for President; and if no Person have a Majority, then from the five highest on the List the said House shall in like Manner chuse the President. But in chusing the President, the Votes shall be taken by States, the Representation from each State having one Vote; a quorum for this Purpose shall consist of a Member or Members from two thirds of the States, and a Majority of all the States shall be necessary to a Choice. In every Case, after the Choice of the President, the Person having the greatest Number of Votes of the Electors shall be the Vice President. But if there should remain two or more who have equal Votes, the Senate shall chuse from them by Ballot the Vice-President.]*

The Congress may determine the Time of chusing the Electors, and the Day on which they shall give their Votes; which Day shall be the same throughout the United States.

No person except a natural born Citizen, or a Citizen of the United States, at the time of the Adoption of this Constitution, shall be eligible to the Office of President; neither shall any Person be eligible to that Office who shall not have attained to the Age of thirty-five Years, and been fourteen Years a Resident within the United States.

**[In Case of the Removal of the President from Office, or of his Death, Resignation, or Inability to discharge the Powers and Duties of the said Office, the same shall devolve on the Vice President, and the Congress may by Law, provide for the

*Superseded by the twelfth amendment.

**This clause has been affected by the twenty-fifth amendment.

the net Produce of all Duties and Imposts, laid by any State on Imports or Exports, shall be for the Use of the Treasury of the United States; and all such Laws shall be subject to the Revision and Control of the Congress.

No State shall, without the Consent of Congress, lay any duty of Tonnage, keep Troops, or Ships of War in time of Peace, enter into any Agreement or Compact with another State, or with a foreign Power, or engage in War, unless actually invaded, or in such imminent Danger as will not admit of delay.

ARTICLE II.

SECTION 1. The executive Power shall be vested in a President of the United States of America. He shall hold his Office during the Term of four Years, and, together with the Vice-President, chosen for the same Term, be elected, as follows.

Each State shall appoint, in such Manner as the Legislature thereof may direct, a Number of Electors, equal to the whole Number of Senators and Representatives to which the State may be entitled in the Congress: but no Senator or Representative, or Person holding an Office of Trust or Profit under the United States, shall be appointed an Elector.

[The Electors shall meet in their respective States, and vote by Ballot for two persons, of whom one at least shall not be an Inhabitant of the same State with themselves. And they shall make a List of all the Persons voted for, and of the Number of Votes for each; which List they shall sign and certify, and transmit sealed to the Seat of the Government of the United States, directed to the President of the Senate. The President of the Senate shall, in the Presence of the Senate and House of Representatives, open all the Certificates, and the Votes shall then be counted. The Person having the greatest Num-

Case of Removal, Death, Resignation or Inability, both of the President and Vice President, declaring what Officer shall then act as President, and such Officer shall act accordingly, until the Disability be removed, or a President shall be elected.]

The President shall, at stated Times, receive for his Services, a Compensation, which shall neither be encreased nor diminished during the Period for which he shall have been elected, and he shall not receive within that Period any other Emolument from the United States, or any of them.

Before he enter on the Execution of his Office, he shall take the following Oath or Affirmation:—"I do solemnly swear (or affirm) that I will faithfully execute the Office of President of the United States, and will to the best of my Ability, preserve, protect and defend the Constitution of the United States."

SECTION 2. The President shall be Commander in Chief of the Army and Navy of the United States, and of the Militia of the several States, when called into the actual Service of the United States; he may require the Opinion in writing, of the principal Officer in each of the executive Departments, upon any subject relating to the Duties of their respective Offices, and he shall have Power to Grant Reprieves and Pardons for Offenses against the United States, except in Cases of Impeachment.

He shall have Power, by and with the Advice and Consent of the Senate, to make Treaties, provided two-thirds of the Senators present concur; and he shall nominate, and by and with the Advice and Consent of the Senate, shall appoint Ambassadors, other public Ministers and Consuls, Judges of the supreme Court, and all other Officers of the United States, whose Appointments are not herein otherwise provided for, and which shall be established by Law: but the Congress may by Law vest the Appointment of such inferior Officers, as they think proper, in the President alone, in the Courts of Law, or in the Heads of Departments.

The President shall have Power to fill up all Vacancies that may happen during the Recess of the Senate, by granting Commissions which shall expire at the End of their next Session.

SECTION 3. He shall from time to time give to the Congress Information of the State of the Union, and recommend to their Consideration such Measures as he shall judge necessary and expedient; he may, on extraordinary Occasions, convene both Houses, or either of them, and in Case of Disagreement between them, with Respect to the Time of Adjournment, he may adjourn them to such Time as he shall think proper; he shall receive Ambassadors and other public Ministers; he shall take Care that the Laws be faithfully executed, and shall Commission all the Officers of the United States.

SECTION 4. The President, Vice President and all civil Officers of the United States, shall be removed from Office on Impeachment for, and Conviction of, Treason, Bribery, or other high Crimes and Misdemeanors.

ARTICLE III.

SECTION 1. The judicial Power of the United States, shall be vested in one supreme Court, and in such inferior Courts as the Congress may from time to time ordain and establish. The Judges, both of the supreme and inferior Courts, shall hold their Offices during good Behaviour, and shall, at stated Times, receive for their Services, a Compensation, which shall not be diminished during their Continuance in Office.

SECTION 2. The judicial Power shall extend to all Cases, in Law and Equity, arising under this Constitution, the Laws of the United States, and Treaties made, or which shall be made, under their Authority;—to all Cases affecting Ambassadors, other public Ministers and Consuls;—to all Cases of admiralty and maritime Jurisdiction;—to Controversies to which the United States shall be a Party;—to Controversies between two or more States;—between a State and Citizens of another State;—between Citizens of different States;—between Citizens of the same State claiming Lands under Grants of different States, and between a State, or the Citizens thereof, and foreign States, Citizens or Subjects.

In all Cases affecting Ambassadors, other public Ministers and Consuls, and those in which a State shall be Party, the supreme Court shall have original Jurisdiction. In all the other Cases before mentioned, the supreme Court shall have appellate Jurisdiction, both as to Law and Fact, with such Exceptions, and under such Regulations as the Congress shall make.

The trial of all Crimes, except in Cases of Impeachment, shall be by Jury; and such Trial shall be held in the State where the said Crimes shall have been committed; but when not committed within any State, the Trial shall be at such Place or Places as the Congress may by Law have directed.

SECTION 3. Treason against the United States, shall consist only in levying War against them, or in adhering to their Enemies, giving them Aid and Comfort. No Person shall be convicted of Treason unless on the Testimony of two Witnesses to the same overt Act, or on Confession in open Court.

The Congress shall have Power to declare the Punishment of Treason, but no Attainder of Treason shall work Corruption of Blood, or Forfeiture except during the Life of the Person attainted.

ARTICLE IV.

SECTION 1. Full Faith and Credit shall be given in each State to the public Acts, Records, and judicial Proceedings of every other State. And the Congress may by general Laws prescribe the Manner in which such Acts, Records and Proceedings shall be proved, and the Effect thereof.

SECTION 2. The Citizens of each State shall be entitled to all Privileges and Immunities of Citizens in the several States.

A Person charged in any State with Treason, Felony, or other Crime, who shall flee from Justice, and be found in another State, shall on demand of the executive Authority of the State from which he fled, be delivered up, to be removed to the State having Jurisdiction of the Crime.

[No Person held to Service or Labour in one State, under the Laws thereof, escaping into another, shall, in Consequence of any Law or Regulation therein, be discharged from such Service or Labour, but shall be delivered up on Claim of the Party to whom such Service or Labour may be due.]*

SECTION 3. New States may be admitted by the Congress into this Union; but no new State shall be formed or erected within the Jurisdiction of any other State; nor any State be formed by the Junction of two or more States, or parts of States, without the Consent of the Legislatures of the States concerned as well as of the Congress.

The Congress shall have Power to dispose of and make all needful Rules and Regulations respecting the Territory or other Property belonging to the United States; and nothing in this Constitution shall be so construed as to Prejudice any Claims of the United States, or of any particular State.

SECTION 4. The United States shall guarantee to every State

*Superseded by the thirteenth amendment.

in this Union a Republican Form of Government, and shall protect each of them against Invasion; and on Application of the Legislature, or of the Executive (when the Legislature cannot be convened) against domestic Violence.

ARTICLE V.

The Congress, whenever two-thirds of both Houses shall deem it necessary, shall propose Amendments to this Constitution, or, on the Application of the Legislatures of two-thirds of the several States, shall call a Convention for proposing Amendments, which, in either Case, shall be valid to all Intents and Purposes, as part of this Constitution, when ratified by the Legislatures of three-fourths of the several States, or by Conventions in three-fourths thereof, as the one or the other Mode of Ratification may be proposed by the Congress: Provided that no Amendment which may be made prior to the Year One thousand eight hundred and eight shall in any Manner affect the first and fourth Clauses in the Ninth Section of the first Article; and that no State, without its Consent, shall be deprived of its equal Suffrage in the Senate.

ARTICLE VI.

All Debts contracted and Engagements entered into, before the Adoption of this Constitution, shall be as valid against the United States under this Constitution, as under the Confederation.

This Constitution, and the Laws of the United States which shall be made in Pursuance thereof; and all Treaties made, or which shall be made, under the Authority of the United

States, shall be the supreme Law of the Land; and the Judges in every State shall be bound thereby, any Thing in the Constitution or Laws of any State to the Contrary notwithstanding.

The Senators and Representatives before mentioned, and the Members of the several State Legislatures, and all executive and judicial Officers, both of the United States and of the several States, shall be bound by Oath or Affirmation, to support this Constitution; but no religious Test shall ever be required as a Qualification to any Office or public Trust under the United States.

ARTICLE VII.

The Ratification of the Conventions of nine States shall be sufficient for the Establishment of this Constitution between the States so ratifying the Same.

Done in Convention by the Unanimous Consent of the States present the Seventeenth Day of September in the Year of our Lord one thousand seven hundred and Eighty seven and of the Independence of the United States of America the Twelfth.

In Witness whereof We have hereunto subscribed our Names.

Go *WASHINGTON*
Presidt and deputy from Virginia

17

New Hampshire.

John Langdon
Nicholas Gilman

Massachusetts.

Nathaniel Gorham
Rufus King

New Jersey.

Wil: Livingston
David Brearley.
Wm Paterson.
Jona: Dayton

Pennsylvania.

B Franklin
Robt. Morris
Thos. FitzSimons
James Wilson
Thomas Mifflin
Geo. Clymer
Jared Ingersoll
Gouv Morris

Connecticut.

Wm Saml Johnson
Roger Sherman

New York.

Alexander Hamilton

Maryland.

James McHenry
Danl Carrol
Dan: of St Thos Jenifer

Virginia.

John Blair
James Madison Jr.

North Carolina.

Wm Blount
Hu Williamson
Richd Dobbs Spaight.

18

South Carolina.

Delaware.

Geo: Read
John Dickinson
Jaco: Broom
Gunning Bedford jun
Richard Bassett

J. Rutledge
Charles Pinckney
Charles Cotesworth
   Pinckney
Pierce Butler

Georgia.

William Few
Abr Baldwin

Attest:

WILLIAM JACKSON, *Secretary.*

Articles in Addition To, and Amendment Of, the Constitution of the United States of America, Proposed by Congress, and Ratified by the Legislatures of the Several States, Pursuant to the Fifth Article of the Original Constitution.*

(The first 10 Amendments were ratified December 15, 1791, and form what is known as the "Bill of Rights")

AMENDMENT I

Congress shall make no law respecting an establishment of religion, or prohibiting the free exercise thereof; or abridging the freedom of speech, or of the press; or the right of the people peaceably to assemble, and to petition the Government for a redress of grievances.

*Amendment XXI was not ratified by state legislatures, but by state conventions summoned by Congress.

19

AMENDMENT II

A well regulated Militia, being necessary to the security of a free State, the right of the people to keep and bear Arms, shall not be infringed.

AMENDMENT III

No Soldier shall, in time of peace be quartered in any house, without the consent of the Owner, nor in time of war, but in a manner to be prescribed by law.

AMENDMENT IV

The right of the people to be secure in their persons, houses, papers, and effects, against unreasonable searches and seizures, shall not be violated, and no Warrants shall issue, but upon probable cause, supported by Oath or affirmation, and particularly describing the place to be searched, and the persons or things to be seized.

AMENDMENT V

No person shall be held to answer for a capital, or otherwise infamous crime, unless on a presentment or indictment of a Grand Jury, except in cases arising in the land or naval forces, or in the Militia, when in actual service in time of War or public danger; nor shall any person be subject for the same offence to be twice put in jeopardy of life or limb; nor shall be compelled in any criminal case to be a witness against himself, nor be deprived of life, liberty, or property, without due process of law; nor shall private property be taken for public use, without just compensation.

20

AMENDMENT VI

In all criminal prosecutions, the accused shall enjoy the right to a speedy and public trial, by an impartial jury of the State and district wherein the crime shall have been committed, which district shall have been previously ascertained by law, and to be informed of the nature and cause of the accusation; to be confronted with the witnesses against him; to have compulsory process for obtaining witnesses in his favor, and to have the Assistance of Counsel for his defence.

AMENDMENT VII

In suits at common law, where the value in controversy shall exceed twenty dollars, the right of trial by jury shall be preserved, and no fact tried by a jury, shall be otherwise reexamined in any Court of the United States, than according to the rules of the common law.

AMENDMENT VIII

Excessive bail shall not be required, nor excessive fines imposed, nor cruel and unusual punishments inflicted.

AMENDMENT IX

The enumeration in the Constitution, of certain rights, shall not be construed to deny or disparage others retained by the people.

all the certificates and the votes shall then be counted;—The person having the greatest number of votes for President, shall be the President, if such number be a majority of the whole number of Electors appointed; and if no person have such majority, then from the persons having the highest numbers not exceeding three on the list of those voted for as President, the House of Representatives shall choose immediately, by ballot, the President, But in choosing the President, the votes shall be taken by states, the representation from each state having one vote; a quorum for this purpose shall consist of a member or members from two-thirds of the states, and a majority of all the states shall be necessary to a choice. [And if the House of Representatives shall not choose a President whenever the right of choice shall devolve upon them, before the fourth day of March next following, then the Vice-President shall act as President, as in the case of the death or other constitutional disability of the President.—]* The person having the greatest number of votes as Vice-President, shall be the Vice-President, if such number be a majority of the whole number of Electors appointed, and if no person have a majority, then from the two highest numbers on the list, the Senate shall choose the Vice-President; a quorum for the purpose shall consist of two-thirds of the whole number of Senators, and a majority of the whole number shall be necessary to a choice. But no person constitutionally ineligible to the office of President shall be eligible to that of Vice-President of the United States.

*Superseded by section 3 of the twentieth amendment.

AMENDMENT X

The powers not delegated to the United States by the Constitution, nor prohibited by it to the States, are reserved to the States respectively, or to the people.

AMENDMENT XI
(Ratified February 7, 1795)

The Judicial power of the United States shall not be construed to extend to any suit in law or equity, commenced or prosecuted against one of the United States by Citizens of another State, or by Citizens or Subjects of any Foreign State.

AMENDMENT XII
(Ratified June 15, 1804)

The Electors shall meet in their respective states and vote by ballot for President and Vice-President, one of whom, at least, shall not be an inhabitant of the same state with themselves; they shall name in their ballots the person voted for as President, and in distinct ballots the person voted for as Vice-President, and they shall make distinct lists of all persons voted for as President, and of all persons voted for as Vice-President, and of the number of votes for each, which lists they shall sign and certify, and transmit sealed to the seat of the government of the United States, directed to the President of the Senate;—The President of the Senate shall, in presence of the Senate and House of Representatives, open

AMENDMENT XIII
(Ratified December 6, 1865)

SECTION 1. Neither slavery nor involuntary servitude, except as a punishment for crime whereof the party shall have been duly convicted, shall exist within the United States, or any place subject to their jurisdiction.

SECTION 2. Congress shall have power to enforce this article by appropriate legislation.

AMENDMENT XIV
(Ratified July 9, 1868)

SECTION 1. All persons born or naturalized in the United States, and subject to the jurisdiction thereof, are citizens of the United States and of the State wherein they reside. No State shall make or enforce any law which shall abridge the privileges or immunities of citizens of the United States; nor shall any State deprive any person of life, liberty, or property, without due process of law; nor deny to any person within its jurisdiction the equal protection of the laws.

SECTION 2. Representatives shall be apportioned among the several States according to their respective numbers, counting the whole number of persons in each State, excluding Indians not taxed. But when the right to vote at any election for the choice of electors for President and Vice-President of the United States, Representatives in Congress, the Executive and Judicial officers of a State, or the members of the Legislature thereof, is denied to any of the

21

male inhabitants of such State, being twenty-one years of age,* and citizens of the United States, or in any way abridged, except for participation in rebellion, or other crime, the basis of representation therein shall be reduced in the proportion which the number of such male citizens shall bear to the whole number of male citizens twenty-one years of age in such State.

Section 3. No person shall be a Senator or Representative in Congress, or elector of President and Vice-President, or hold any office, civil or military, under the United States, or under any State, who, having previously taken an oath, as a member of Congress, or as an officer of the United States, or as a member of any State legislature, or as an executive or judicial officer of any State, to support the Constitution of the United States, shall have engaged in insurrection or rebellion against the same, or given aid or comfort to the enemies thereof. But Congress may by a vote of two-thirds of each House, remove such disability.

Section 4. The validity of the public debt of the United States, authorized by law, including debts incurred for payment of pensions and bounties for services in suppressing insurrection or rebellion, shall not be questioned. But neither the United States nor any State shall assume or pay any debt or obligation incurred in aid of insurrection or rebellion against the United States, or any claim for the loss or emancipation of any slave; but all such debts, obligations and claims shall be held illegal and void.

Section 5. The Congress shall have power to enforce, by appropriate legislation, the provisions of this article.

*Changed by section 1 of the twenty-sixth amendment.

AMENDMENT XV
(Ratified February 3, 1870)

Section 1. The right of citizens of the United States to vote shall not be denied or abridged by the United States or by any State on account of race, color, or previous condition of servitude.—

Section 2. The Congress shall have power to enforce this article by appropriate legislation.

AMENDMENT XVI
(Ratified February 3, 1913)

The Congress shall have power to lay and collect taxes on incomes, from whatever source derived, without apportionment among the several States, and without regard to any census or enumeration.

AMENDMENT XVII
(Ratified April 8, 1913)

The Senate of the United States shall be composed of two Senators from each State, elected by the people thereof, for six years; and each Senator shall have one vote. The electors in each State shall have the qualifications requisite for electors of the most numerous branch of the State legislatures.

When vacancies happen in the representation of any State in the Senate, the executive authority of such State shall issue writs of election to fill such vacancies: *Provided,* That the legis-

lature of any State may empower the executive thereof to make temporary appointments until the people fill the vacancies by election as the legislature may direct.

This amendment shall not be so construed as to affect the election or term of any Senator chosen before it becomes valid as part of the Constitution.

AMENDMENT XVIII
(Ratified January 16, 1919)

[Section 1. After one year from the ratification of this article the manufacture, sale, or transportation of intoxicating liquors within, the importation thereof into, or the exportation thereof from the United States and all territory subject to the jurisdiction thereof for beverage purposes is hereby prohibited.

[Section 2. The Congress and the several States shall have concurrent power to enforce this article by appropriate legislation.

[Section 3. This article shall be inoperative unless it shall have been ratified as an amendment to the Constitution by the legislatures of the several States as provided in the Constitution, within seven years from the date of the submission hereof to the States by the Congress.]*

AMENDMENT XIX
(Ratified August 18, 1920)

The right of citizens of the United States to vote shall not be denied or abridged by the United States or by any State on account of sex.

*Repealed by section 1 of the twenty-first amendment.

Congress shall have power to enforce this article by appropriate legislation.

AMENDMENT XX
(Ratified January 23, 1933)

Section 1. The terms of the President and Vice President shall end at noon on the 20th day of January, and the terms of Senators and Representatives at noon on the 3d day of January, of the years in which such terms would have ended if this article had not been ratified; and the terms of their successors shall then begin.

Section 2. The Congress shall assemble at least once in every year, and such meeting shall begin at noon on the 3d day of January, unless they shall by law appoint a different day.

Section 3. If, at the time fixed for the beginning of the term of the President, the President elect shall have died, the Vice President shall become President. If a President shall not have been chosen before the time fixed for the beginning of his term, or if the President elect shall have failed to qualify, then the Vice President elect shall act as President until a President shall have qualified; and the Congress may by law provide for the case wherein neither a President elect nor a Vice President elect shall have qualified, declaring who shall then act as President, or the manner in which one who is to act shall be selected, and such person shall act accordingly until a President or Vice President shall have qualified.

Section 4. The Congress may by law provide for the case of the death of any of the persons from whom the House of Representatives may choose a President whenever the right of choice shall have devolved upon them, and for the case of the death of any of the persons from whom the Senate may choose a Vice President whenever the right of choice shall have devolved upon them.

SECTION 5. Sections 1 and 2 shall take effect on the 15th day of October following the ratification of this article.

SECTION 6. This article shall be inoperative unless it shall have been ratified as an amendment to the Constitution by the legislatures of three-fourths of the several States within seven years from the date of its submission.

AMENDMENT XXI
(Ratified December 5, 1933)

SECTION 1. The eighteenth article of amendment to the Constitution of the United States is hereby repealed.

SECTION 2. The transportation or importation into any State, Territory, or possession of the United States for delivery or use therein of intoxicating liquors, in violation of the laws thereof, is hereby prohibited.

SECTION 3. This article shall be inoperative unless it shall have been ratified as an amendment to the Constitution by conventions in the several States, as provided in the Constitution, within seven years from the date of the submission hereof to the States by the Congress.

AMENDMENT XXII
(Ratified February 27, 1951)

SECTION 1. No person shall be elected to the office of the President more than twice, and no person who has held the office of President, or acted as President, for more than two years of a term to which some other person was elected President shall be elected to the office of the President more than once. But this Article shall not apply to any person holding the office of President when this Article was proposed by the Congress, and shall not prevent any person who may be holding the office of President, or acting as President, during the term within which this Article becomes operative from holding the office of President or acting as President during the remainder of such term.

SECTION 2. This article shall be inoperative unless it shall have been ratified as an amendment to the Constitution by the legislatures of three-fourths of the several States within seven years from the date of its submission to the States by the Congress.

AMENDMENT XXIII
(Ratified March 29, 1961)

SECTION 1. The District constituting the seat of Government of the United States shall appoint in such manner as the Congress may direct:

A number of electors of President and Vice President equal to the whole number of Senators and Representatives in Congress to which the District would be entitled if it were a State,

but in no event more than the least populous State; they shall be in addition to those appointed by the States, but they shall be considered, for the purposes of the election of President and Vice President, to be electors appointed by a State; and they shall meet in the District and perform such duties as provided by the twelfth article of amendment.

SECTION 2. The Congress shall have power to enforce this article by appropriate legislation.

AMENDMENT XXIV
(Ratified January 23, 1964)

SECTION 1. The right of citizens in the United States to vote in any primary or other election for President or Vice President, for electors for President or Vice President, or for Senator or Representative in Congress, shall not be denied or abridged by the United States or any State by reason of failure to pay any poll tax or other tax.

SECTION 2. The Congress shall have power to enforce this article by appropriate legislation.

AMENDMENT XXV
(Ratified February 10, 1967)

SECTION 1. In case of the removal of the President from office or of his death or resignation, the Vice President shall become President.

SECTION 2. Whenever there is a vacancy in the office of the Vice President, the President shall nominate a Vice President who shall take office upon confirmation by a majority vote of both Houses of Congress.

SECTION 3. Whenever the President transmits to the President pro tempore of the Senate and the Speaker of the House of Representatives his written declaration that he is unable to discharge the powers and duties of his office, and until he transmits to them a written declaration to the contrary, such powers and duties shall be discharged by the Vice President as Acting President.

SECTION 4. Whenever the Vice President and a majority of either the principal officers of the executive departments or of such other body as Congress may by law provide, transmit to the President pro tempore of the Senate and the Speaker of the House of Representatives their written declaration that the President is unable to discharge the powers and duties of his office, the Vice President shall immediately assume the powers and duties of the office as Acting President.

Thereafter, when the President transmits to the President pro tempore of the Senate and the Speaker of the House of Representatives his written declaration that no inability exists, he shall resume the powers and duties of his office unless the Vice President and a majority of either the principal officers of the executive department or of such other body as Congress may by law provide, transmit within four days to the President pro tempore of the Senate and the Speaker of the House of Representatives their written declaration that the President is unable to discharge the powers and duties of his office. Thereupon Congress shall decide the issue, assembling within forty-eight hours for that purpose if not in session. If the Congress, within twenty-one days after receipt of the latter written declaration, or, if Congress is not in session, within twenty-one days after Congress is required to assemble, determines by two-thirds vote of both Houses that the President is unable to discharge the powers and duties of his office, the Vice President shall continue to discharge the same as Acting President; otherwise, the President shall resume the powers and duties of his office.

AMENDMENT XXVI
(Ratified July 1, 1971)

SECTION 1. The right of citizens of the United States, who are eighteen years of age or older, to vote shall not be denied or abridged by the United States or by any State on account of age.

SECTION 2. The Congress shall have power to enforce this article by appropriate legislation.

33

BIBLIOGRAPHY

Baker, Gordon E. *The Reapportionment Revolution*. New York: Random House, 1966.

Baum, Lawrence. *The Supreme Court*. Washington, D.C.: Congressional Quarterly Press, 1981.

Berger, Raoul. *Congress vs. The Supreme Court*. Cambridge: Harvard University Press, 1969.

Beveridge, Albert J. *The Life of John Marshall*. 4 vols. Cambridge: Houghton Mifflin Co., The Riverside Press, 1919.

Bickel, Alexander M. *The Least Dangerous Branch*. Indianapolis: Bobbs-Merrill Co., 1962.

Bork, Robert H. "Neutral Principles and Some First Amendment Problems." 47 *Indiana Law Journal* 1 (1971).

Brant, Irving. *The Bill of Rights: Its Original Meaning*. Indianapolis: Bobbs-Merrill Co., 1965.

Brogan, D.W. *Politics in America*. New York: Harper & Brothers, 1954.

Cardozo, Benjamin. *The Nature of the Judicial Process*. New Haven: Yale University Press, 1921.

Carr, Robert K. *The Supreme Court and Judicial Review*. New York: Farrar & Rinehart, 1942.

Commager, Henry Steele, ed. *Documents of American History*. 9th ed. New York: Appleton-Century-Crofts, 1973.

Congressional Quarterly. *Guide to the U.S. Supreme Court*. Washington, D.C.: Congressional Quarterly Inc., 1979.

Congressional Quarterly. *Watergate: Chronology of a Crisis*. Washington, D.C.: Congressional Quarterly, 1975.

Cooley, Thomas M. *A Treatise on the Constitutional Limitations Which Rest Upon the Legislative Power of the States of the American Union*. 8th ed. 2 vols. Boston: Little, Brown & Co., 1927.

Corwin, Edward S., ed. *The Constitution of the United States of America: Analysis and Interpretation*. Washington, D.C.: Library of Congress, Legislative Reference Service. Government Printing Office,1953 (with annual additions).

— *The Constitution and What It Means Today*. 12 ed. Princeton: Princeton University Press, 1958; Atheneum paperback, 1967.

— "The Higher Law Background of Constitutional Law." 42 *Harvard Law Review* 149, 365 (1928).

Cox, Archibald. *The Role of the Supreme Court in American Government*. New York: Oxford University Press, 1976.

Craven, Avery. *Reconstruction: The Ending of the Civil War*. New York: Holt, Rinehart and Winston, Inc., 1969.

Dahl, Robert A. "Decision-Making in a Democracy: The Supreme Court as a National Policy-Maker." 6 *Journal of Public Law* 279 (1958).

Danelski, David. *A Supreme Court Justice Is Appointed*. New York: Random House, 1965.

Emerson, Thomas I. *The System of Freedom of Expression*. New York: Random House, Vintage Books, 1970.

Farrand, Max. *The Records of the Federal Convention of 1787*. 4 vols. New Haven: Yale University Press, 1911, 1937.

Frank, John P. *Marble Palace: The Supreme Court in American Life*. New York: Alfred Knopf, 1958.

Freund, Paul A. *The Supreme Court of the United States: Its Business, Purposes, and Performance*. Cleveland and New York: World Publishing Company, Meridian Books, 1961.

Friedman, Leon; and Israel, Fred L., eds. *The Justices of the United States Supreme Court, 1789–1978, Their Lives and Major Opinions*. 5 vols. New York and London: Chelsea House Publishers in association with R.R. Bowker Company, 1969, 1978.

Friendly, Henry J. "The Bill of Rights as a Code of Criminal Procedure." 53 *California Law Review* 929 (1965).

Garraty, John A. *The American Nation: A History of the United States*. 2 vols. 3rd ed. New York: Harper & Row, 1975.

— *Quarrels That Have Shaped The Constitution*. New York: Harper & Row, 1964; Harper Torchbooks, 1975.

Gellhorn, Walter. *American Rights*. New York: Macmillan Co., 1960.

Graham, Fred P. *The Due Process Revolution: The Warren Court's Impact on Criminal Law*. Rochelle Park, New Jersey: Hayden Book Company, Inc., 1979.

Hamilton, Alexander; Madison, James; and Jay, John. *The Federalist Papers*. Introduction and commentary by Garry Wills. Bantam Books, Bantam Classics, 1982.

Hand, Learned. *The Bill of Rights*. Introduction by Charles E. Wyzanski, Jr. New York: Atheneum, 1964.

Harrell, Mary Ann; and Anderson, Burnett. *Equal Justice Under Law: The Supreme Court in American Life*. Washington, D.C.: The Supreme Court Historical Society with the cooperation of the National Geographic Society, 1982.

Henkin, Louis. *Foreign Affairs and the Constitution*. New York: W.W. Norton & Co., Inc., The Norton Library, 1975.

Hofstadter, Richard, ed. *Great Issues in American History*. 2 vols. New York: Random House, Vintage Books, 1969.

Holmes, Oliver Wendell. *The Common Law*. Boston: Little, Brown, 1881.

— *Collected Legal Papers*. New York: Harcourt Brace, 1920.

Hughes, Charles Evans. *The Supreme Court of the United States: Its Foundations, Methods and Achievements, an Interpretation*. New York: Columbia University Press, 1928.

Jackson, Robert H. *The Struggle for Judicial Supremacy: A Study of a Crisis in American Power Politics*. New York: Random House, Vintage Books, 1941.

Kamisar, Yale; LaFave, Wayne R.; and Israel, Jerrold H. *Modern Criminal Procedure: Cases, Comments and Questions.* St. Paul: West Publishing Co., 1980.

Kelly, Alfred H.; and Harbison, Winfred A. *The American Constitution: Its Origins and Development.* 5th ed. New York: W.W. Norton & Co., 1976.

Kluger, Richard. *Simple Justice: The History of Brown v. Board of Education and Black America's Struggle for Equality.* New York: Alfred A. Knopf, 1976; Vintage Books, 1977.

Kurland, Philip B., ed. *Felix Frankfurter on The Supreme Court: Extrajudicial Essays on The Court and The Constitution.* Cambridge: The Belknap Press of Harvard University Press, 1970.

Lerner, Max. *The Mind and Faith of Justice Holmes.* Boston: Little, Brown & Co., 1943.

Lewis, Anthony. *Gideon's Trumpet.* New York: Random House, 1964; Vintage Books, 1966.

Lockhart, William B.; Kamisar, Yale; and Choper, Jesse H. *Constitutional Law: Cases, Comments, Questions.* St. Paul: West Publishing Co., 1980.

McCloskey, Robert G. *The American Supreme Court.* Chicago History of American Civilization Series. Chicago: University of Chicago Press, 1960.

Magrath, C. Peter. *Morrison R. Waite: The Triumph of Character.* New York: Macmillan Co., 1963.

Mason, Alpheus T. *The Supreme Court from Taft to Burger.* Baton Rouge: Louisiana State University Press, 1980.

— *Brandeis: A Free Man's Life.* New York: Viking Press, 1946.

— *Harlan Fiske Stone: Pillar of the Law.* New York: Viking Press, 1956.

Meiklejohn, Alexander. *Political Freedom: The Constitutional Powers of the People.* New York: Harper & Brothers, 1960.

Miller, Arthur Selwyn. *The Supreme Court and American Capitalism.* The Supreme Court in American Life series. New York: The Free Press, 1968.

Morris, Richard B. *The Framing of the Federal Constitution.* National Park Service Handbook 103. Washington, D.C.: Government Printing Office, 1979.

Murphy, Paul L. *The Constitution in Crisis Times, 1918–1969.* New York: Harper & Row, Harper Torchbooks, 1972.

Myrdal, Gunnar. *An American Dilemma.* New York: Harper & Row, 1944; McGraw-Hill paperback, 1964.

Pfeffer, Leo. *This Honorable Court: A History of the United States Supreme Court.* Boston: Beacon Press, 1965.

Pollak, Louis H., ed. *The Constitution and the Supreme Court: A Documentary History.* 2 vols. Cleveland and New York: The World Publishing Company, 1966.

Pritchett, C. Herman. *The American Constitution.* 3rd ed. New York: McGraw-Hill Book Co., 1977.

Provine, Doris Marie. *Case Selection in the United States Supreme Court.* Chicago: University of Chicago Press, 1980.

Pusey, Merlo F. *Charles Evans Hughes.* 2 vols. New York: Macmillan Publishing Co., 1951.

Rossiter, Clinton. *Alexander Hamilton and the Constitution.* New York: Harcourt Brace, 1964.

Simon, James F. *In His Own Image: The Supreme Court in Richard Nixon's America.* New York: David McKay Co., 1973.

— *Independent Journey: The Life of William O. Douglas.* New York: Harper & Row, 1980.

Stern, Robert L.; and Gressman, Eugene. *Supreme Court Practice.* Washington, D.C.: Bureau of National Affairs, 1978.

Supreme Court. *United States Reports.* 468 volumes, 1875–1984. Washington, D.C.: Government Printing Office.

Supreme Court. *Rules of the Supreme Court of the United States.* rev. 1980. Washington, D.C.: Clerk, Supreme Court.

Swindler, William F. *Court and Constitution in the Twentieth Century. 1889-1968.* 2 vols. Indianapolis: Bobbs-Merrill Co., 1970.

Swisher, Carl Brent. *American Constitutional Development.* 2nd ed. Cambridge: Houghton Mifflin Co., The Riverside Press, 1954.

Tocqueville, Alexis de. *Democracy in America.* J.P. Mayer, ed. New York: Doubleday & Company, Inc., Anchor Books, 1969.

Tribe, Laurence H. *American Constitutional Law.* Mineola, New York: The Foundation Press, 1978.

Warren, Charles. *The Supreme Court in United States History.* 2 vols., rev. ed. Boston: Little, Brown & Co., 1926.

Washington, George; and 39 co-signers. *The Constitution of the United States of America.* Washington, D.C.: Government Printing Office, 1976.

Wechsler, Herbert. "Toward Neutral Principles of Constitutional Law." 73 *Harvard Law Review* 31 (1959).

Westin, Alan F. *The Supreme Court: Views from Inside.* New York: W.W. Norton & Co., 1961.

Wilkinson, J. Harvie, III. *Serving Justice: A Supreme Court Clerk's View.* New York: Charterhouse, 1974.

Williams, Jerre S. *Constitutional Analysis.* St. Paul: West Publishing Company, 1979.

Woodward, C. Vann. *The Strange Career of Jim Crow.* 2nd rev. ed. New York: Oxford University Press, 1966.

Wright, Charles Alan. *Handbook of the Law of Federal Courts.* 2nd. ed. St. Paul: West Publishing Company, 1970.

One hundred and two Justices have served on the Supreme Court since its birth in 1790. The rows of pictures running horizontally present the jurists, with terms of service, in the order of taking the oath. Asterisks indicate the Chief Justices. John Rutledge was named Chief Justice by a recess appointment in 1795 and served briefly, but the Senate rejected him when it reconvened. In 1981, Sandra Day O'Connor became the first woman to serve on the Supreme Court. In 1986, upon the retirement of Chief Justice Warren E. Burger, Associate Justice William H. Rehnquist was nominated to succeed him as Chief Justice, and Judge Antonin Scalia of the United States Court of Appeals for the District of Columbia was nominated to fill the vacant seat on the Court.

JAMES WILSON
1789-98

JOHN JAY*
1789-95

WILLIAM CUSHING
1790-1810

JOHN BLAIR
1790-96

SAMUEL CHASE
1796-1811

OLIVER ELLSWORTH*
1796-1800

BUSHROD WASHINGTON
1799-1829

ALFRED MOORE
1800-04

JOHN MARSHALL*
1801-35

SMITH THOMPSON
1823-43

ROBERT TRIMBLE
1826-28

JOHN MCLEAN
1830-61

HENRY BALDWIN
1830-44

JOHN MCKINLEY
1838-52

PETER VIVIAN DANIEL
1842-60

SAMUEL NELSON
1845-72

LEVI WOODBURY
1845-51

ROBERT C. GRIER
1846-70

DAVID DAVIS
1862-77

STEPHEN J. FIELD
1863-97

SALMON P. CHASE*
1864-73

WILLIAM STRONG
1870-80

WILLIAM B. WOODS
1881-87

STANLEY MATTHEWS
1881-89

JOHN RUTLEDGE*
1790-91; 1795

JAMES IREDELL
1790-99

THOMAS JOHNSON
1792-93

WILLIAM PATERSON
1793-1806

WILLIAM JOHNSON
1804-34

HENRY B. LIVINGSTON
1807-23

THOMAS TODD
1807-26

GABRIEL DUVALL
1811-35

JOSEPH STORY
1812-45

JAMES MOORE WAYNE
1835-67

ROGER B. TANEY*
1836-64

PHILIP P. BARBOUR
1836-41

JOHN CATRON
1837-65

BENJAMIN R. CURTIS
1851-57

JOHN A. CAMPBELL
1853-61

NATHAN CLIFFORD
1858-81

NOAH HAYNES SWAYNE
1862-81

SAMUEL F. MILLER
1862-90

JOSEPH P. BRADLEY
1870-92

WARD HUNT
1873-82

MORRISON R. WAITE*
1874-88

JOHN M. HARLAN
1877-1911

HORACE GRAY
1882-1902

SAMUEL BLATCHFORD
1882-93

LUCIUS Q. C. LAMAR
1883-93

MELVILLE W. FULLER*
1888-1910

DAVID J. BREWER
1890-1910

HENRY B. BROWN
1891-1906

JOSEPH MCKENNA
1898-1925

OLIVER W. HOLMES
1902-32

WILLIAM RUFUS DAY
1903-22

WILLIAM H. MOODY
1906-10

HORACE H. LURTON
1910-14

LOUIS D. BRANDEIS
1916-39

JOHN H. CLARKE
1916-22

WILLIAM H. TAFT*
1921-30

GEORGE SUTHERLAND
1922-38

BENJAMIN N. CARDOZO
1932-38

HUGO L. BLACK
1937-71

STANLEY F. REED
1938-57

FELIX FRANKFURTER
1939-62

WILLIAM O. DOUGLAS
1939-75

FREDERICK M. VINSON*
1946-53

TOM C. CLARK
1949-67

SHERMAN MINTON
1949-56

EARL WARREN*
1953-69

BYRON R. WHITE
1962-

ARTHUR J. GOLDBERG
1962-65

ABE FORTAS
1965-69

THURGOOD MARSHALL
1967-

WARREN E. BURGER*
1969-86

GEORGE SHIRAS, JR.
1892-1903

HOWELL E. JACKSON
1893-95

EDWARD D. WHITE*
1894-1921

RUFUS W. PECKHAM
1896-1909

CHARLES E. HUGHES*
1910-16; 1930-41

WILLIS VAN DEVANTER
1911-37

JOSEPH R. LAMAR
1911-16

MAHLON PITNEY
1912-22

JAMES C. MCREYNOLDS
1914-41

PIERCE BUTLER
1923-39

EDWARD T. SANFORD
1923-30

HARLAN FISKE STONE*
1925-46

OWEN J. ROBERTS
1930-45

FRANK MURPHY
1940-49

JAMES F. BYRNES
1941-42

ROBERT H. JACKSON
1941-54

WILEY B. RUTLEDGE
1943-49

HAROLD H. BURTON
1945-58

JOHN M. HARLAN
1955-71

WILLIAM J. BRENNAN, JR.
1956-

CHARLES E. WHITTAKER
1957-62

POTTER STEWART
1958-81

HARRY A. BLACKMUN
1970-

LEWIS F. POWELL, JR.
1972-

WILLIAM H. REHNQUIST
1972-

JOHN PAUL STEVENS
1975-

SANDRA DAY O'CONNOR
1981-

Congress OF THE

begun and held at the

Wednesday the fourth of March, one

THE Conventions of a number of the Sta

or abuse of its powers, that further declaratory and restrictive clauses should be added: And as ex

RESOLVED by the Senate and

concurring, that the following Articles be proposed to the Legislatures of the several States as amen

said Legislatures, to be valid to all intents and purposes, as part of the said Constitution; vi

ARTICLES in addition to, and Am

of the several States, pursuant to the fifth Article of the original Constitution.

Article the first. .... After the first enumeration required by the first Article of the Constitution, there

which, the proportion shall be so regulated by Congress, that there shall be

until the number of Representatives shall amount to two hundred, after whi

nor more than one Representative for every fifty thousand persons.

Article the second .... No law, varying the compensation for the services of the Senators and Represent

Article the third ...... Congress shall make no law respecting an establishment of religion, or prohibiting

assemble, and to petition the Government for a redress of grievances.

Article the fourth ... A well regulated militia, being necessary to the security of a free State, the

Article the fifth .... No Soldier shall, in time of peace be quartered in any house, without the conse

Article the sixth ...... The right of the people to be secure in their persons, houses, papers, and effec